LORD HAMPTON

of Westwood, Droitwich
HIS LATER YEARS
1868-1880

A Biography

by

Andrew Harris

First Published 2015
Copyright the author

Set in Sabon
Body text 10.5pt on 13.5pt

ISBN no. 978-0-9544193-6-3

Typesetting and design by the author
Printed by Orphans Press Ltd, Leominster

Cover image 'Worcester Sunset'
Kindly supplied by Worcester artist David Birtwhistle

CONTENTS

Introduction	. . . .	4
Chapter 1	The 1868 Election	6
Chapter 2	The Year 1869	26
Chapter 3	1870 – Education, Education, Education	41
Chapter 4	The Years 1871 and 1872	62
Chapter 5	The Contagious Diseases Acts	90
Chapter 6	1873 and the Droitwich Brine Baths	100
Chapter 7	The 1874 Election	112
Chapter 8	The Restoration of Worcester Cathedral	127
Chapter 9	The Cathedral Restored	152
Chapter 10	The Year 1875	175
Chapter 11	1876 – First Civil Service Commissioner	203
Chapter 12	The Years 1877 and 1878	231
Chapter 13	His Last Year	258
Chapter 14	Lord Hampton in Retrospect	285
Index	. . . .	292
Index of Illustrations		298

Introduction

This book is the third and last volume of my three volume biography of Sir John Somerset Pakington, after 1874 the first Lord Hampton. It will seem very generous to devote such a large amount of space to someone who was, at best, a senior Tory politician who served three short terms in the cabinet, and indeed it is. But I have chosen to do it this way partly because of the wealth of material available, and partly because it seems to me that the issues Sir John had to deal with, both at Westminster and back home in Worcestershire, make interesting reading when many of them are still facing us in the 21st century. It is also the case that Sir John was involved in very many activities, both in London and in Worcestershire, and to cover these properly often needs a certain amount of background explanation. I also feel that illustrations enhance the reading experience, and these have expanded the space necessary considerably.

I was originally inspired to undertake this work as Sir John left many diaries covering all periods of his life, although many are now missing, and none have been transcribed before. Those for 1875, 1876, 1878, 1879 and 1880 survive for the period covered by this volume, 1868 to 1880. But there is a wealth of other material available, much of it now accessible on the internet. Hansard is available in this way, and is much easier to access than the original closely printed volumes, and both The Times and Berrow's Worcester Journal (in the text called Berrow's), which are part of the British Library's nineteenth century newspaper collection, are not only available on line, but also searchable. I have also been able to make use of the Parliamentary Papers website in which you can search this vast collection of papers, although for some reason this has very restricted access. I have also made extensive use of the Oxford Dictionary of National Biography.

The Pakington family were an important land-owning family, both in Worcestershire and in Buckinghamshire, going back to Elizabethan times, and their archives form a large collection that was donated to the Worcestershire Record Office in the 1970s, where it is called the Hampton collection. Access is made easier by the fact that the whole collection is now on microfilm, and in the few instances where I have needed to access the original documents I am grateful to the present Lord Hampton for giving me the necessary permission.

There are, of course, very many books covering politics and politicians in the mid-nineteenth century, but I found Angus Hawkins' biography of Lord Derby, 'The Forgotten Prime Minister', Robert Blake's biography of Disraeli, and J R Vincent's edition of the journals of Lord Stanley 1849-69 a valuable help.

This volume covers the last thirteen years of his life, from when he won the first contested election to represent Droitwich, through his later defeat, and appointment as First Civil Service Commissioner, a post he still held when he died. What stands out from his diaries and which will be clear from this book is the tremendous energy he continued to have, right up to his last days. Prior to 1868 he had already suffered the sadness of loosing two wives, and it is clear that his third wife Augusta, whom he calls Madre, suffered frequent bouts of ill-health, and more often than not did not accompany him to his constant social functions, a role that was frequently filled by one of his many nieces. In the period covered in this volume his personal life was increasingly troubled by his elder son's poor health and eventual descent into mental illness, and the early death of his daughter-in-law. Despite this he seems to have retained a cheerful and positive attitude to life, and he frequently refers in his diaries to how grateful he was for his continuing good health.

In the biography I have tended to recount events without too much comment, but at the end of this volume I have attempted a summary of a man who exhibited some contradictory traits of character, and, unusually, seems to have become more liberal as his age advanced.

His greatest campaign, for which he is now best remembered, was to improve the educational standards of the poor, although in the end his own efforts to establish a national education system, described in volume 2, were unsuccessful. William Forster's 1870 act is described in this volume, and, unlike those who opposed the bill, he recognised the importance of the new scheme, and felt he would help it best by supporting it in principle, even though he disagreed with some aspects ot it.

I would particularly like to thank local historian David Everett who proof read my manuscript and made many helpful suggestions both as to content and to style, also Dr Sue Sutton for doing research for me at The National Archives and John Weedy for responding promptly to my many requests for illustrations from the Illustrated London News. David Morrison, the cathedral librarian, was also particularly helpful in allowing me access to the restoration archives, and helping with some of the illustrations.

Chapter 1
The 1868 Election

Sir John Pakington had first been elected as Tory MP for Droitwich in 1837 when he was 38. That had been his fourth attempt, having been defeated in 1832 standing for East Worcestershire, and in 1833 and again in 1835 standing for West Worcestershire. But in 1837 he had not been opposed in Droitwich, and in all subsequent elections up to and including 1866 when he was elected for the eleventh time he continued to be unopposed. Not all these elections had been general elections – Sir John had served in three different ministries under Lord Derby in 1852, 1858 and 1866-7, and under the rules of the time anyone appointed to a government office had to stand for re-election. Although in 1868 he had served 31 years in parliament, he was by no means the longest serving MP. The longest continuously serving member and therefore father of the House before the 1868 election was Thomas Peers Williams who had been MP for Great Marlow since 1826, and a further fifteen members had been first elected before 1837, although, unlike Sir John and Thomas Williams, most had represented more than one constituency, and very few would never have been opposed.

Sir John, as we shall now call him, had served as a cabinet minister in all three of Lord Derby's governments – colonial secretary in 1852, first lord of the Admiralty in 1858, and first lord then minister for war in 1866 to 1868. Now being 69 years old, one might have thought that Sir John would have

Sir John Pakington.

been tempted to retire to his country estate at Westwood Park outside Droitwich. But his election at Droitwich as a widely respected political figure had become something of a habit, and Sir John was still serving as minister for war as the 1868 election approached, and probably did not want to give up his office and the attaching salary when there was still hope of retaining it after the election, provided the Conservatives did well enough.

Before 1832 the borough of Droitwich had been a pocket borough in the gift of the Foley family, and its twenty or so electors returned two MPs, but the Great Reform Act of 1832 very much enlarged the constituency and reduced its representation to a single member. The farming community in the parishes around the constituency probably mostly voted Tory, but the town of Droitwich, where the salt industry had since ancient times been very important, would have contained many who had more liberal tendencies, and Sir John had been wary for some time of a Liberal coming forward against him. He would not have welcomed

Westwood Park, near Droitwich, a photo of 1906. There was a nunnery on the site until the dissolution, when the property was bought by lawyer Sir John Pakington, whose principal seat was at Hampton Lovett. His great nephew Sir John 'Lusty' Pakington built the main part of the present house around 1600, and the four angled extensions were added later in the century. His son, another Sir John, became the first of a line of eight baronets. Sir John Somerset Pakington lived there from the death in 1830 of his uncle, the 8th and last baronet, till he died in 1880.

the occasion on Tuesday 11th August when H D Acland, vice-president of the Reform League, came to address a meeting in Droitwich. Berrow's Worcester Journal, no friend of the League, reported that it was badly attended and that Acland described Droitwich as a 'rotten borough' in the hands of Sir John and the Foleys. Acland did not wish to say anything about Sir John as a gentleman, but denounced him as a member of parliament: "thirty three years is long enough for Sir John to play the fool in the House of Commons". He then referred to the possibility of a Liberal standing against him, and said that he could see the prospect of success if "a man of the right sort" contested the borough.

The 1868 election was held as a result of the Tories' Second Great Reform Act of 1867, which introduced household suffrage in the boroughs, very much widening the franchise, and the election of November 1868 was based on the new electoral register. The enlarged Droitwich constituency's boundaries now included part of Hanbury. The largest landowner in Hanbury was Harry Foley Vernon, who in 1868 was still the Liberal MP for East Worcestershire, and from an early stage Sir John was concerned that some of Vernon's tenants might be persuaded to vote for a Liberal candidate by their landlord's influence.

Harry Vernon himself had decided not to seek re-election in 1868. He had always been on the conservative wing of the Liberal party, and in a crucial vote

Hanbury Hall, the seat of Harry (later Sir Harry) Vernon. It was built in about 1706 by Harry's ancestor and noted chancery lawyer Thomas Vernon.

The 1868 Election

on the 1867 Reform Bill had joined a number of his colleagues in voting against their leader, William Gladstone, ensuring that the Tories won that particular division. This had caused some criticism among his more liberal constituents, and Vernon probably thought he was better out of these controversies, so he could look after his substantial estates and young family. Early in 1868 he had written to his fellow East Worcestershire MP Charles Lyttelton:

> It is not my present intention to offer myself as a candidate at the next general election – this is still confidential – my reasons are that my opinions on certain matters are not entirely in unison with those of the majority of the Liberal electors of the division – consequently I should not have their unanimous support, without which it is more than probable that I should not be elected and the Conservatives would regain the seat.

But if Harry Vernon had hoped that his decision not to stand in the 1868 election would allow him to revert to a quiet life, he was mistaken. One of the principal people who were brought into the constituency under the boundary changes was John Corbett, 'the salt king', who had made his fortune extracting salt at Stoke Works. Corbett was very much a Liberal 'free-trader', and had, it seems, already

(Left) Harry Vernon of Hanbury Hall. His family had lived in Hanbury since 1557 when his ancestor Rev. Richard Vernon arrived as the curate. (Right) John Corbett, 'The Salt King'. Born into a family of boat owners, he had overcome the difficulties in extracting brine at Stoke Works, and built a successful business. In 1868 he lived at Stoke Grange in Stoke Prior, and in the 1870s built the well-known Chateau Impney near Droitwich.

expressed an interest in politics, but two years before, when rumours that he was to oppose Sir John surfaced, he issued a statement saying that 'Whilst I have no wish to oppose the right honourable baronet, I would be willing to stand if he were elevated to the peerage'.

However, it seems that, despite this public denial, things were happening behind the scenes, for on 19th May 1868 Henry Bearcroft, Harry Vernon's local friend and agent, wrote asking him to come to dinner to meet Mr Corbett as he was a 'very important card in our present position in Droitwich'. From this it may be assumed that the possibility of Corbett standing at the next election was already being discussed. Probably aware of this possibility Sir John wrote to Corbett on 17th June as follows:

> I hope you will not consider this letter premature, but as you are the principal person who will be newly added to the constituency of Droitwich under the Boundary Act, I wish to pay you the respect of, as soon as possible, expressing my hope that you may not be unwilling to give me your support. I am aware that your political views are not identical, and that you have entertained some idea of becoming yourself a candidate for the borough. But if I remember right, you made a kind and friendly reservation in my favour, and it is therefore not impossible that you may be inclined to act with those gentlemen who have for many years been good enough to regard my representation of Droitwich on personal rather than political grounds. Indeed, I am disposed in your case to go a step further, and to say that, as I have on several recent occasions been proposed by a Conservative and seconded by a Liberal, it would gratify me very much if you would permit me to look to you as my seconder at the ensuing election.

Corbett, who was evidently already thinking of announcing his candidacy but not yet quite decided, gave a guarded reply:

> I believe that a large number of electors of the borough of Droitwich, irrespective of political creed, have long supported and are willing to support you, from respect to you personally, from your great administrative abilities, and from the eminent positions you have held and continue to hold in the service of the country. I am flattered by your asking me to second your nomination, and, one of my reasons for declining the honour is I do not think I should be serving you by doing so. In regard to the forthcoming election, although I am to some extent committed to the Liberal party and have been pressed by them to come forward under present circumstances, it is not my intention to oppose you, and further, I should not view with indifference any one else opposing you.

Only two days later the Worcester Chronicle had picked up the rumours about the goings-on in Droitwich, and wrote that, with its franchise increased three-fold, it was rumoured that the Liberals were going to oppose Pakington. Sir

The 1868 Election

John, anxious to gather as much support as possible and to do what he could to prevent any one else standing, tried to enlist the help of Harry Vernon, and on 12th August wrote:

> My Dear Vernon, I fear I must not ask you for support at the coming election, but there are several of my Droitwich constituents, as you know, who, though never professing Conservative politics, have either supported me, or discouraged & prevented opposition – And I must wish, as you have now retired from Parl't and are therefore more free from party obligations, that you should let me include you, as a neighbour, at least in the latter section – I hope, in any case, that when my regular canvass begins, you will not object to my calling on your tenants, & that I may find them free to support me…

This letter seems to encapsulate the hope that Harry Vernon would use his influence to prevent a Liberal candidate coming forward, and Harry, still not sure that Corbett was going to stand, sent another very guarded reply:

> My dear Sir John, I cannot of course object to yr calling upon any of my tenants who may be voters for the Borough of Droitwich – But at the same time I cannot but express a hope that you will find that their political opinions coincide with my own. In answer to that part of yr letter in which you refer to myself, I must frankly say that I should be very sorry to see any opposition attempted against yr return for the Borough of Droitwich & I assure you that at the present time I should be most unwilling to originate or encourage any such attempt – But at the same time I must beg you to allow me to consider myself entirely free & unpledged to you in this matter, supposing that circumstances were to arise which should make me feel compelled to act contrary to my wishes.

By the end of August Corbett was allowing pressure to build for him to stand, and Harry Vernon was asked to add his name to a petition, already with 500 signatures, but he gave his usual guarded, even equivocal, reply dated 24th August:

> I should feel bound to support Mr Corbett if he were to stand for Droitwich (supposing that his political opinions were what I believe them to be), but at the same time I hope he may not be persuaded to come forward as I feel that any attempt to unseat Sir John will prove unsuccessful.

But when in early September Corbett finally decided to stand, he felt his first duty was to write explaining his decision to Sir John. He repeated the respect he felt for Sir John (but not to his party), and said he had done everything in his power to prevent a contested election. But it was evident that the Liberal party were determined to fight the seat, and Corbett felt his own honour would be compromised if he refused to stand and let 'a stranger' occupy the ground. Evidently feeling that he could be accused of going back on his earlier statement that he would not oppose Sir John, he concluded:

LORD HAMPTON – HIS LATER YEARS

> I regret much to be placed in this position towards you. I have done all I could to avoid it and it must be apparent to you that I have thereby materially injured my own position by coming forward at comparatively so late a period.

The following day John Corbett also wrote confirming his decision to Harry Vernon, ending 'I hardly need tell you that I attach great importance to the value of your support, which, if you can accord to me, I shall esteem a particular favour – I will take an early opportunity of paying my respects to you'. Vernon, hoping to be allowed to distance himself from the actual campaigning, immediately replied:

> I am sorry that the peace of the borough is to be disturbed, but I can easily believe that you have felt yourself compelled by circumstance to come forward as a candidate. Possessing as you do political opinions so nearly allied to those which I myself entertain I readily promise you my vote & though I must beg of you to allow me to decline any active part in this contest, I shall nevertheless be glad to give you that support which any influence I may have in the borough may enable me to render you.

At the same time, Harry Vernon received a letter from a neighbour, Theodore Galton of Hadzor Hall. Galton was also a Liberal, and urged Vernon to add his name to the committee supporting Corbett. 'The other side have a grand array of

It was a common election ploy to suggest your opponent was a Catholic, which might put some voters off. Theodore Galton's grandfather, Samuel Galton jun., had been a Birmingham Quaker, but his father had reverted to the established church, and Theodore had become a Catholic in about 1862. Whether Sir John Pakington knew about this poster is not known, but as it was accurate he probably would not have objected to it, even though he usually preached religious tolerance.

ELECTORS LOOK OUT!

THESE ARE
FACTS.

THEODORE GALTON, chief supporter of Mr CORBETT, is a Red-hot Roman Catholic. He left his Mother Church to support POPERY.

The wife of his Candidate is also a Roman Catholic, and brings up her Children in the same Faith.

ELECTORS, What must be Mr. CORBETT'S opinions on Religious Matters under such influence?

Don't pull down the Oak to plant a Mushroom!!!

The 1868 Election

names including (with only two or three exceptions) all the gentry and clergy of the neighbourhood.' Liberal support was obviously rather lacking, and if Harry Vernon did not come out openly in support it might seem the Liberal cause was not well supported. Harry replied that he could not refuse his name on Corbett's committee, but still said he regretted the contest.

On the same day Harry Vernon also received a letter from Sir John:

> As Mr Corbett has announced to me his intention to stand for Droitwich, I am sure you will excuse my writing to you to say it will be a great advantage to me if you will kindly inform me what course you intend to take – I regret extremely that I cannot expect your support – But the circumstances of this election are so peculiar in several respects, that I cannot help hoping you may not exert your influence against me – You were good enough to say you would not object to my canvassing your tenants, but if you would kindly intimate to them that you desire them to vote as they wish, I should do so with a much better prospect of securing favourable answers...

Sir John, of course, had no need to ask Harry Vernon's permission to canvass his tenants, but the relationship between a landlord and the way his tenants exercised their franchise was a delicate one, and Sir John no doubt wanted to be polite. In 1868 there was still no secret ballot, and votes were cast by polling, in which a voter openly told the returning officer for whom he wished to vote.

Harry Vernon would certainly have regarded himself as an upholder of Liberal principles, albeit only moderate ones, and in replying to Sir John tried to make it clear that he did not intend to try and influence his tenants in favour of the newly announced Liberal candidate:

> My dear Sir John, In reply to yr letter conveyed to me yesterday by Mr Bearcroft I have no objection to letting you know (as you say it would be of advantage to you) what course I shall take in the event of Mr Corbett placing himself in opposition to you. I have – in accordance with the sentiments I expressed in my letter to you on this subject – held aloof from encouraging & in fact have discouraged as far as I could any attempt to contest the borough – But now that a contest seems inevitable I feel that I cannot withhold my support from any respectable candidate professing Liberal principles – as regards my tenants you will find them perfectly free to exercise their own independent judgement in this matter. I am obliged to you for allowing me to see a copy of Mr Corbett's letter to you. I feel sure that he has come forward as yr opponent with considerable reluctance, but believing as I do that there was more than one ready to do so, if he declined, I do not see how he could have acted otherwise.

This reference to Corbett's letter was to that written on 2nd July in which he appeared to rule out standing against Sir John, and which Sir John was now using to try and discredit him.

LORD HAMPTON – HIS LATER YEARS

Sir John replied thanking Harry Vernon for 'the liberal concession it conveyed which has been very important to me'. But Harry felt he may have gone too far, and felt the need to back-track slightly on what Sir John may have thought he meant, and replied:

> Your letter of this morning conveying yr thanks for the liberal concessions I have made in yr favour, confirms me in believing that my last letter to you led you to think that it was a matter of perfect indifference to me how my tenants voted... My fear that this might be the case was first aroused on Wednesday night by hearing that this impression had been left on the minds of many of them after having been honoured by yr canvass on Tuesday & Wednesday. Now as this was not what I meant to imply in either of my letters to you on this subject I felt compelled yesterday morning to emerge from the retirement in which I had hoped to remain during this contest and to visit several of them in company with Mr Corbett to endeavour to dispel this false impression. I merely mention this because I am most unwilling that you should think yourself more indebted to me than you really are...

Perhaps Harry Vernon might have been better advised not to write this letter, as it was immediately seized on by Sir John, who replied as follows:

> My dear Vernon, On my return from London last night, I read with surprise your note of yesterday – I can only infer from it that you must have forgotten the following very clear words in your letter to me of 12th inst – "as regards my tenants you will find them perfectly free to exercise their own independent judgement in this matter"... There were expressions as to your wish to discourage any contest, which made it probable, and led me to believe, that you would be content to give your own vote against me, without putting pressure on your tenants – I am however now informed that you have expressed dissatisfaction at my having used, when canvassing, that sentence only – With my view, as above stated, of your whole letter, I can see no objection to my so using the only part of the letter which applied to the persons to whom I spoke – But I now propose, to prevent any misunderstanding, to send a copy of the whole letter to each of your tenants...

Harry Vernon clearly felt that Sir John was using his statement that he did not welcome a contest in Droitwich to get his tenants to support Sir John, whereas Harry, as a Liberal, had clearly intended to support Corbett if, welcome or not, he decided to stand. So, somewhat tartly, he fired off a quick reply to Sir John:

> I have a perfect recollection of both my letters to you, that of 24th Aug & that of 12th Sept. What I complain of is that while I had promised to support Mr Corbett with my name and influence, a portion of one of my letters to you was being made use of as a means for obtaining the support of some of my tenants – whereas had the whole correspondence between us been read to them they would have seen what my feelings & intentions in the matter were & the result

of yr canvass would have been different and in this opinion I am confirmed in as much as upon my reading both these letters to several of them, they at once assured me that had they known the contents before they would not have promised their votes – Their promises having been therefore obtained under an erroneous impression… With respect to yr proposal to send my tenants copies of my letter (though I have considered our correspondence as a friendly & private matter) I can have no possible objection to your doing so.

But that, unfortunately for Harry Vernon, was not the end of the matter, as on 24th September a report appeared in the Birmingham Gazette as follows:

A story has reached us which we hope may turn out to be untrue. Before Mr Corbett had consented to stand for Droitwich, it is said Mr H F Vernon, the late MP for East Worcestershire, had written to Sir John Pakington, saying that he should use no influence whatever with his tenants, and that, so far as he was concerned, they would be free to vote for whomever they pleased. Accordingly, Mr Vernon's tenants were canvassed, and many of them promised to vote for Sir John. In the meantime, however, Mr Corbett, the Liberal candidate, issued his address, and a short time ago – so our informant says – Mr Vernon or his agents went round among the tenantry and told them that they must vote for Corbett or they would have to leave their farms.

Although two days later the Gazette retracted that part of its report saying that Vernon had threatened eviction, some of the mud was bound to stick. On 30th September the Worcester Chronicle, a supporter of the Liberal party, repeated the allegations, but said that the fault had lain with Pakington for using a part of Harry Vernon's letter to imply that he wanted them to vote Conservative. All that Corbett had done during his canvass was to explain that it was not the case that Vernon wanted them to vote for Sir John at all, simply that he had not welcomed the contest, but now there was one, his tenants were free to vote as they pleased, and their landlord remained a supporter of the Liberal party and their

Another poster from the 1868 election – Westwood Park is in the background.

candidate, John Corbett. Finally, the Chronicle attacked Sir John for regretting that there was a contest, saying he ought to be grateful for the Liberal party for having allowed him to stand unopposed for so long.

In early September Harry Vernon and his family set out on an autumn trip to Scotland, staying first at Silloth on the Solway Firth, then travelling east to Mellerstain, the seat of the Earl of Haddington, his father-in-law. While in Silloth he received a long letter from Rev. Henry Douglas, Rector of Hanbury and his wife's brother-in-law, picking up on the rumours about the alleged coercion of tenants. It is rather a strange letter, as the writer, who admits to not being of the same political views as Vernon (i.e. he was a Conservative), seems to have been very alarmed by the allegations, perhaps even to the extent of believing them, and urges Vernon to issue a statement denying them. Perhaps Douglas had been listening too closely to propaganda from his fellow Conservatives rather than finding out the truth from his parishioners, and, in the rather rambling letter, he lectures Vernon on the wrongs of coercion.

Any reply to this letter has not survived, but Harry Vernon must have taken it seriously, as he immediately drafted a statement for approval and publication by his agent Henry Bearcroft to the Vernon tenantry. In it he had said he had a "wish that those with whom I may have any influence should take the same course [i.e. vote Liberal]". Bearcroft said that this might be immediately seized on by his enemies as being "indirect coercion" and suggested toning this down a little. As finally issued the statement was as follows:

> My attention has been drawn to a paragraph in the Birmingham Gazette of Saturday publishing a copy of a letter which I lately wrote to Sir John Pakington, and implying that my conduct with regard to the coming election at Droitwich had not been characterised by 'good faith' and suggesting that I am not 'innocent' of using intimidation to influence the votes of my tenants.
>
> Had these remarks concerned myself alone I would not have thought them worthy of notice, but as they also convey the implication that my tenants are not free and independent of their political rights, I feel bound in justice to you to remove, as far as I can, my grounds for such insinuations, and to let you know what my intentions and feelings with regard to this contest really are.
>
> I believe that the political principles which Mr Corbett is prepared to uphold are more likely to uphold the welfare of this country than the political principals which the government of which Sir John Pakington is such a distinguished member. I shall, therefore give Mr Corbett my support...
>
> I believe that some have promised their votes to Sir John Pakington under the erroneous impression that it was my wish that they should do so or, at all events, under the impression that I was indifferent as to which side they supported.

> Whatever my own opinion may be with regard to pledges so given, I nevertheless think that those who have given them under such misapprehension are themselves the proper judges as to how far they conscientiously consider them to be binding.
>
> I am informed that Sir John has sent you a copy of my letter of Sept 12th; I have therefore thought it advisable to send a copy of the whole correspondence which has passed between Sir John and myself to Mr Henry Bearcroft, and I have requested him to show it to you if you have any wish to see it. I have nothing to retract from what I have said in any of my letters to Sir John. I am sure that any Candidate who seeks your support in this contest will find you free and independent either to give or to withhold it, as you think right; and I wish you to feel that, as far as I am concerned, you have nothing to fear whichever side your political convictions may lead you to take.

Whether any of his tenants contacted Henry Bearcroft in order to read the correspondence referred to is not known, but many must have thought that a great deal of fuss was being made, and knew their landlord well enough to know their tenancy was not at risk however they voted, as long as they paid the rent!

One might have thought this would be the end of the matter, but the Sir John was not prepared to let the matter drop. On 27th October he wrote again to Harry Vernon, quoting his Silloth statement, and saying he was therefore

> surprised by hearing in my committee room yesterday morning that several tenants of yours who are bound by promise to vote for me have been deterred from doing so by the interference of your agent Mr Henry Bearcroft, since you wrote the above words. The names most prominently mentioned to me were Elijah Pinfield, John Price and Will'm Hodges. In consequence of this information I rode to Dodderhill Common yesterday. I saw the three men and found that my information was exactly correct – Mr Henry Bearcroft called upon them last Tuesday – he saw Pinfield and Hodges that day & canvassed them for Mr Corbett – they both told him that they had promised me – but he pressed them nevertheless to vote with their landlord – & the result was, in the words of one of them "well, if I cannot vote as I wish I will not vote at all." The other intimated that he was afraid to vote for me, but would certainly not vote the other way. Mr Henry Bearcroft did not succeed in seeing Price till Wednesday, when a similar conversation took place, but with different result – Price seems to be a man of somewhat superior station, & of firmer nerve – for all three expressed most honourable feelings – and he said that having promised me he should fulfil his promise, notwithstanding Mr Henry Bearcroft's solicitations, who renewed the subject with him at an accidental meeting yesterday morning. I am thus deprived by the interference of your agent of the votes of two of your tenants whose "political convictions lead them to take my side" – I consider it due to you as well as myself, I submit these facts for your consideration.

One can perhaps excuse Harry Vernon for being more than a little annoyed by the continuation of the controversy by Sir John – after all, Vernon had retired from active politics to avoid just this sort of nastiness, and while he had clearly offered his support to Corbett, he had no incentive to indulge in any sort of strong arm tactics with his tenants. So his reply was short and to the point:

> I have enquired into the matter referred to in your letter of the 27th, and as Mr Henry Bearcroft assures me that in canvassing on behalf of Mr Corbett – in the particular instances, & in every other instance – he has used none but the most legitimate means of persuasion, I hope that you will excuse my taking any further notice of the matter.

Berrow's was a supporter of Sir John, and gave continuous support. Typical was what it wrote on 19th September:

> "To elect Mr Corbett and turn out Sir John would be like pulling down an oak to plant a mushroom" was the remark of a new elector during a canvas at Droitwich this week. With all due respect to the great salt manufacturer, we fully endorse the sentiment. Sir John is an oak in strength and character. The roots of his family tree fill the soil of the locality. The fame of his house is part of the history of Droitwich. He has had long experience of public life: he has proved himself a statesman in times when ability and honesty are put to the test; and Droitwich is proud of its association with Cabinets and with history through its member. Droitwich, through Sir John Pakington, has made itself felt in great debates, in important public doings, in national undertakings. Sir John has become a local living institution in himself, carrying the weight of his character for straightforward, outspoken manliness into local works and county business; and now in the hey-day of his success, at the height of his honours, the people of Droitwich are called upon to supplant him, and set up another in his stead. They are called upon, as that new elector says, to pull down the oak; and what do they propose to set in its place? – "a mushroom"… We repeat the Droitwich man's remark in no disrespectful sense. Mr Corbett is, we believe, a worthy man; but politically, in comparison with Sir John Pakington, he is a mushroom. His experience has been of the earth, earthy, of the salt, salty… he has lived, as it were, on the ground the mushroom life; whilst the oak has been towering up in the forest, spreading wide its arms amongst giants, rearing its head in the storm, and learning wisdom of the political winds.

Berrow's attacked the other Worcester newspaper, the Chronicle, for supporting Corbett; that newspaper had said that, as Corbett had done so much good for Droitwich through his successful salt business, he should be sent to Westminster; but that logic is faulty, opined Berrow's, as 'we cannot discover in this why Droitwich should turn out its representative statesman and elect a gentleman whose knowledge of salt making and whose success therein are his chief personal attributes'.

The 1868 Election

Sir John issued his election address at the beginning of September. It was longer than usual, mainly because he had something to say about the main issue of the election: the Irish Church. As was described in the previous volume, when still in opposition the previous year, Gladstone had promoted resolutions in parliament favouring disestablishment, and despite fierce opposition from prime minister Disraeli, the resolutions had been passed, the Liberal party being united on this issue. A Liberal victory in the general election would see disestablishment carried through, so the Conservatives hoped that if they could win the election the Irish church could be saved. Sir John himself always seemed to have had somewhat ambivalent views on disestablishment; he had not spoken in the debates of the previous year, and in a letter to Lord Derby had indicated that he thought something of the sort was inevitable.

But the Tories hoped that the public generally would not support this apparent attack on the Protestant church, so Sir John made the point strongly in his election address:

> Its effect would be to reduce the Protestant Church in Ireland to the position of a sect, plundered, depressed, and deprived of the support she now derives from her existing organisation and from the authority of the Crown; while the Roman Catholic church in that country, strong in her long-established hierarchy, and submissive to laws and government prescribed by the sovereign Pontiff, would be placed, free from the competition of any rival on a vantage ground such as she has never yet enjoyed under the Protestant Crown of these Kingdoms. I cannot believe that such a policy will find favour with the British people… I am the more free to declare these views because I have always been willing to relieve my Roman Catholic fellow-subjects from injustice, or oppression, or civil inequality. I regard charity and toleration for the religious beliefs of others as a high Christian duty, in proof of my sincerity I may refer to many passages in my public life.

Sir John had often expressed these latter views, but his record is a little patchy. He had supported the grant to the Maynooth Catholic training college, although he later once said he would have voted differently if he had known how aggressive, as he saw it, the Catholics were to become in the 1850s. He once opposed allowing Roman Catholic priests into prisons, although he later supported the opposite view; and earlier he had opposed the admission of Jews to parliament, although again he later changed his mind. He had also earlier supported the view that further reform of the Irish churches was necessary, and we can perhaps excuse his outspoken words in the 1868 address, as well as some of his earlier illiberalities, as being 'politics' rather than his own opinion. Indeed, later in the address he did write that he did not defend the ecclesiastical condition of Ireland as it now exists, 'and if this great subject had been approached in a calm spirit of honest reform instead for scarcely disguised party objects we might have arrived at a satisfactory modification of existing defects'.

Sir John also referred to education in his address. Since the early 1850s he had conducted a campaign to introduce a national scheme of elementary education, and had introduced two unsuccessful bills, and sat on a royal commission and a select committee on the subject. But the distribution of the government grant towards education was still controlled by a privy council committee, and only went to schools that were already successful, leaving many small rural schools inadequate, and a large army of children in the new large industrial towns with hardly any education at all. The new parliament will, he wrote in his address:

> feel the necessity for liberal and vigorous action on the subject of National Education. The settlement of this question has been rendered more than ever necessary by the recent extension of the franchise… My own views on the subject, often expressed to you, have undergone no change, and I hope and believe they are mainly in accordance with your opinions.

John Corbett's address did not appear in the papers till a week after Sir John's, on 19th September. He began by rather lamely excusing himself for coming forward contrary to his earlier statements, and expressed respect for Sir John, but not his party, and promised general support for Gladstone. His only specific point was that he supported moves to reform local taxation by giving local ratepayers a say in county expenditure. Bills had been brought forward on a number of occasions to form county financial boards and take control away from the magistrates in quarter session – Sir John, as a past chairman of quarter sessions, had understandably led the campaign against these proposals, and it was to be some time before elected county councils were eventually established.

While the election campaign was in progress, Worcestershire was honoured by the visit of a distinguished soldier. In the winter and spring of 1867-68 the army had mounted an expedition to Abyssinia to rescue some British subjects held prisoner by the erratic King Theodore. The expedition, led by Sir Robert Napier, was well organised and successful in its objective, and Napier, now Lord Napier of Magdala, had become something of a national hero. Although he had been secretary for war at the time, Sir John did not control the expedition as its mainly Indian army came under the India office, but Sir John knew Napier well, and at the end of September entertained him at Westwood. Berrow's sent a special reporter, and he wrote a colourful and not altogether flattering description of what Droitwich was like at that time. The streets were 'ankle deep in black mud', and when the correspondent walked to the station

> a walk through the streets of the little town did not promote feelings of very great cheerfulness. Droitwich generally does not seem to be mindful of the injunction to 'shake off dull sloth, and rise early'; for even at half past nine

on Wednesday the day seemed scarcely to have begun… From the salt works belched forth such billows of steam that, passing the narrow entrances which lead to the factories, one could not but think of regions much too hot to dwell in. The steam enveloped both the works and the hundreds of 'hands' there toiling amongst oceans of salt – nothing but a bare footed child or man now and then crossing the streets being seen to remind the passer-by of the stream of humanity which was flowing within…

Nevertheless the inhabitants of Droitwich had gone to some lengths to welcome Lord Napier – the approaches to the stations were decorated with banners with letters of 'salt', and foliage, and the Droitwich Volunteer Rifle Corps and a detachment of the Hanbury troop of the Worcestershire Yeomanry Cavalry were drawn up outside the station. The mayor and other local notables were present, and just before the train arrived at 11.00 Sir John arrived to greet Napier, which was done to the strains of 'See the Conquering Hero comes' played by the rifle corps band.

After a welcoming speech by the mayor, and Lord Napier's reply, the party proceeded to Westwood escorted by the Yeomanry. Soon afterwards the party left for Worcester, where there was to be a grand lunch in the Guildhall. The entry to the city was crowded with sightseers, and most of the premises were decorated with flags and bunting. When the meal was concluded toasts were proposed, and Sir John replied on behalf of the army, navy and local forces. In addition to Lord Napier there were two other distinguished guests in the visiting party: Hon. Reverdy Johnson, the United States Ambassador, and M. de Katte, the Prussian Ambassador. The next toast was to Reverdy Johnson, who replied emphasising the importance of peace between nations. Johnson, then 73, had been a barrister and had become well known defending some notorious defendants, including Mary Surratt, accused of aiding and abetting the assassination of President Lincoln. She was found guilty and executed. Johnson had also been a senator, and soon after his arrival in England negotiated the Johnson-Clarendon Treaty for the settlement of disputes arising out of the Civil War.

He was well briefed on the history of Worcester, referring to its glove manufacture, its porcelain, and its hops. And he talked of its cathedral, of which he said:

> I have been told, and I can readily believe it, that within its walls sin stands rebuked and men's thoughts are instinctively turned towards heaven. There, no man will ever dream of war! There, he will listen to the voice of God, which proclaims 'Peace on earth, goodwill to man'. And wretched will be the fate of that statesman who shall at any time, from the madness of human ambition, undertake to change or to modify that ordinance of Heaven.

LORD HAMPTON – HIS LATER YEARS

Johnson even remembered that King John had been buried at Worcester – "he gave England Magna Carta, the birth-right of Englishmen". Finally the mayor proposed the health of Lord Napier, who in his reply paid tribute to the 'great assistance' during the Abyssinian expedition that he had received from the war department under Sir John Pakington. Before returning to Westwood, the party visited the cathedral, watched by large crowds trying to get a glimpse of their hero.

Sir John had returned to Westwood early in August, but was kept busy with his papers and the need to return to London from time to time – this made Corbett's intervention even more annoying to him. On 29th September he addressed a meeting of his supporters in the George Hotel in Droitwich, and spent some time accusing Corbett of bad faith, and pointing out that had he refused to stand, it would have been unlikely that the Liberals could find anyone else with a chance of winning. Nevertheless, he said his canvass showed that he was well in the lead, even though he had come across cases where voters, who had given their promise to him, had, "under inducements or threats", been persuaded to change their allegiance. Had he not, he asked, attended every parliamentary session from beginning to end, and whenever a question that might affect the prosperity of Droitwich arose, done his best for the town? He gave the example of getting a resolution passed in 1853 that the monopoly of salt production in India by the East India Company should end, and although it was true that this took some time to happen, exports of salt from England to India had risen from about 50,000 tons in 1851 to five times that amount at the present time.

Sir John then turned to more general political matters, and referred to recent speeches by Gladstone attacking the government's extravagant expenditure and in particular that part of it controlled by Sir John's war department. In some detail he justified the expenditure, and said that in one breath Gladstone said it was too high, and in another that some of the increase was justified. Finally, of course, Sir John attacked the proposal to disestablish the Irish church: "I do not believe that the British public is as yet prepared to give such an immense advantage to the Roman Catholic church as would be the result of that plan, or to strike such a blow at our Protestant interests as must be the inevitable result".

Then on 13th November, a week before nomination day, Sir John again addressed a public meeting, this time in a marquee erected in a field near the hustings, along the Worcester Road. He again referred to the Irish question, and said that disestablishment was one thing, but even worse was the 'plundering' of the church's endowments – Gladstone had not yet said what he would do with this windfall. He attacked The O'Donoghue, the nationalist MP for Tralee, and said:

> It would not be for the honour, it would not be for the prosperity or happiness of this great Kingdom that Ireland should be separated from England, and we cannot and we will not consent to it. Let us govern the Irish as justly as we can; let them have no reasonable grounds for complaint; let us adjust the land question so far to meet their wishes as we can; but do not let us mislead the Irish people, or allow them for a single moment to suppose we can possibly consent to separation from England.

Nomination day was 16th November, and for the first time in twelve elections over 31 years two men came forward. A large crowd was expected, and sensibly it had been arranged for a barrier to be put between the supporters of the two candidates. What, Berrow's asked, should be said

> of the tag-rag which honoured Mr Corbett with their votes and interest? A howling, yelling, blaspheming, vote-as-you're-told, mob, men, women and children vied with each other in making the greatest disturbance, and uttering the vilest calumnies upon their opponents… in particular were the women aggressors. Who denominated women 'the weaker sex'? Whomsoever it was could not have had the experience of a contested election at Droitwich in his mind's eye.

So the whole affair was very noisy, and at the beginning the crowd heard 'not a syllable'. Edward Bearcroft from Mere Hall proposed Sir John, but as he could not make himself heard, chose to address his remarks to the reporters instead. When Sir John spoke he several times threatened to stop unless he could make himself heard, but persisted, and before finishing he said he had been handed a paper by a blacksmith from Hanbury, George Jenkins, with ten policy questions on it. Sir John tried to answer them all, but mostly with the answer that he couldn't make any promises and it would depend on the circumstances. One question was whether he would vote for the (secret) ballot? He answered:

> I hate the ballot. I hate the ballot on principle ("you have it in the clubs", someone heckled) because I hold that every Englishman ought to discharge his political duties openly and honestly before the public. But I have seen a good deal during this very Droitwich election which tells me very plainly that the day may come when, whether we like the ballot or not, the protection of the independence of electors in the exercise of their rights may require its adoption.

Conservative policy was to oppose the ballot, but in his answer Sir John suggested it would probably come, indicating again that he was on the liberal wing of his party.

The poll took place the following day. By the Reform Act of 1867 the constituency had more than doubled in size and now contained about 1,500 voters. Many of the new voters would have lived in Stoke Works, where John Corbett had his large salt works, and, whatever Sir John said about the results of his canvas, he must have been apprehensive of the result. But he need not have worried – he received 790 votes against 603 for Corbett, indicating a turnout of over ninety per cent. In the address he published thanking the electors for returning him yet again to parliament, he could not resist the temptation to have yet another dig at his opponent:

> I have been elected after an arduous contest, in which I had to contend with serious disadvantages. Two additions have been made to the area of the borough by the Boundary Commissioners – both populous – both unfavourable to my interest; and for many weeks, during which I was under the belief that no contest would take place, an extensive canvass against me was carried on, under the form of obtaining a requisition to Mr Corbett.

So the tradition of Pakington family MPs in Worcestershire, dating back to Sir John's ancestor and namesake in 1640, was continued. Berrow's opined: 'His return to the seat he has filled with distinction has saved the borough from disgrace, and will be welcomed with rejoicing by the entire Kingdom'.

The Conservatives also did quite well locally, with a Tory being elected after a long gap in both Worcester City (where the Liberal vote was spilt between three candidates) and East Worcestershire, and West Worcestershire remained a Conservative stronghold. But nationally they did not do well, and the Liberals doubled their majority to about 110 seats. The prime minister, Benjamin Disraeli, was used to governing without an overall majority in the Commons, indeed the Liberals had had a theoretical majority ever since the Conservatives split over the Corn Laws in 1846, but he quickly realised that the government could not survive against such a large majority, and the government resigned.

THE DREAM!

Of a would-be M. P. on the night following the DROITWICH ELECTION, 1868.

"BY THE SON OF A OLD SALT"

I had a dream the other night,
I dreamt that I could see
My name – the usual E.S.Q.
Succeeded by M.P.

That I had vanquished great Sir John,
Had left him in the lurch,
By gulling Wych folks, by attacks
Against the Irish church.

My seat secure, my prestige raised,
A full-blown M.P. made!
I dreamt that Stoke New Wych became
And drove a roaring trade.

That 'Clay and Newman' went to dust,
That Bradley crumbled down,
That traffic stopped:– that grass grew in
The streets of the old town.

In Parliament I dreamt I sat,
With Gladstone on my right,
while on my left:– a rising star
I'd Brummagem so *Bright*.

I thought they spoke so friendly,
Familiar and free;
And said "We're glad to see you here;
How are you, *Salty C?*"

Straight to the House of Lords I went,
So quick is fancy's flight,
Dreams made me Minister of War!
Oh what a goody height!

An invite from the Queen I got,
Who made me Sec. of State
And even promised me her crown
If I would only wait.

But the day must dawn, and darkness fly,
Still slumbering hours must pass;
And dreams, tho' pleasing, have an end,
Like that of mine – Alas!

Broad daylight broke the enchantment soon,
The postman came, and then,
With great dismay, I read the words
SIR JOHN'S RETURNED AGAIN

An amusing ditty that appeared in the press during the 1868 election.

Chapter 2
The year 1869

Released from the duties of office after the change of government, Sir John remained in Worcestershire until parliament opened on 16th February. He was able to attend the Hunt Club ball on 20th January, and Berrow's reported that the gay ladies' dresses and the gentlemen's scarlet made for a colourful scene. Sir John opened the dancing with the Duchess d'Aumale – the Duc d'Aumale was an exiled son of King Louis-Phillipe of France, whose main residence was in London. But he also had a 4,000 acre estate nearby at Wood Norton near Evesham, and Sir John and he frequently shot together there and elsewhere.

The 1869 session of parliament was dominated by the Irish Church Bill, which disestablished the Irish Church. As mentioned in the last chapter, the subject had been debated at length the previous year, when Gladstone, then the leader of the opposition, had proposed disestablishment in a motion that was approved despite fierce opposition from prime minister Disraeli. Now the Liberals were in office Gladstone introduced a bill on 1st March which would immediately transfer all church property to new commissioners, and provide for the removal of the government's and queen's powers over the church. On 1st January 1871 the church's remaining established powers, including ecclesiastical courts and the ability of some of its bishops to sit in the House of Lords, would cease. In his speech of over three hours Gladstone went into great detail about the government's proposals, which included safeguarding the financial life interests of all existing Irish clergy, and the removal of the government's financial link to both the Presbyterian and the Catholic churches in Ireland. The latter was mainly represented by the annual grant of £24,000 to the Catholic training college at Maynooth, which would be replaced by a new endowment.

The bill had a long passage through the Commons, both its second reading and in committee, but the Liberals remained united in its support, and won most of the divisions by majorities of over 100. During these long debates there was one notable absentee from the list of opposition speakers – Sir John Pakington.

The Year 1869

In fact Sir John did speak, but only once, when the bill had already been in committee for several nights. The committee was considering a motion by the anti-Catholic campaigner George Whalley not to compensate Maynooth for the loss of its annual grant. Sir John seems to have felt particularly strongly on this point, and said "in my opinion, all the provisions with regard to Maynooth contained in the Bill are distinguished by undue favouritism of the Roman Catholic church and undue injustice to the Protestant church of Ireland…". The compensation was set at fourteen times the annual grant of about £20,000, but why should it be so much, asked Sir John, when students were there for a much shorter time? "To the Roman Catholics there is to be a remission of the building debt, but the Protestant clergy are to be compelled to purchase their glebes… I call, therefore, upon the Government to answer the charge I make against them – that their conduct is characterized by gross partiality and injustice".

Opposition to disestablishment was voiced both inside and outside parliament, and on 7th June Sir John was present at a demonstration against disestablishment at the City Terminus Hotel organised by John Allcroft. The bill had already passed the Commons, but Allcroft's resolution was that the House of Lords 'should refuse assent to this bill, so destructive of our national Christianity and so dangerous to the integrity and welfare of the United Kingdom'. Allcroft was a Worcester man, and later served a term as MP for the city. Only two days later Sir John was present at a meeting presided over by the Duke of Rutland, at which the speakers, including Sir John, spoke against Gladstone's bill.

But nothing could stop the progress of the bill, and it passed all its stages in the Commons and the Lords, despite the opposition of most bishops.

Since serving as first lord of the Admiralty in 1858-59 and in 1866-67 Sir John always took an interest in naval affairs, and he contributed to debates on the naval estimates in March. The same applied to army matters, after he had served as minister for war in 1867-68, and on 11th March he spoke at length on the army estimates which were being presented by his successor, Edward Cardwell.

But although Sir John's attention had been much taken up by these military affairs in the last eleven years, he still retained a strong interest in promoting education. His long held belief, much influenced by the fact that when he was a magistrate and chairman of quarter sessions he saw that most of the malefactors who came before him were illiterate, was that once educated they would be turned into moral law-abiding citizens. Proper education for the mass of children who still spent little or no time at school was therefore essential. In 1855 and 1857 he had promoted two bills that would have set up a national scheme and introduced a local rate, he had helped establish the Duke of Newcastle's education commission, and had chaired a select committee on the government's role in national education.

But religious opposition to a national scheme was strong in the House of Commons and no major legislation had yet been passed. One newly elected MP who shared Sir John's views was George Melly, the Liberal member of Stoke-on-Trent, and on 12th March he spoke about the large number of uneducated children in the large towns, and proposed a select committee to suggest a remedy. What was needed, said Melly, was "a scheme of national education capable of grappling with every class of children, with compulsory attendance and free municipal schools; but neither the government nor the House, much less the country, will be prepared to adopt a measure of so drastic and novel a character unless they are thoroughly convinced that the facts and figures will justify so extreme a course".

Melly described in detail the situation in the large industrial towns of Liverpool, Manchester and Birmingham. All these places had generous private provision for education of different types, yet, based on a survey of three streets taken at random, only a little over half the children were at school, meaning that in the whole city over 50,000 children were neither working nor at school. There was no lack of free school places of all denominations, so that could not be the cause. As a magistrate, Melly could see that all they were learning "were the habits of vagrancy, mendicancy and crime". He spoke similarly of Manchester and Birmingham, and concluded that, of the 251,710 children of school age in the three towns:

Born in 1830 to a Swiss Unitarian father, George Melly went to Rugby School, but, as a dissenter, could not go to university. Instead he continued his father's career as a merchant, and settled in Liverpool and travelled widely. He became active as a political liberal, and in 1858 was secretary of the National Association for the Promotion of Social Science, and was present at its Liverpool congress which Sir John Pakington also attended. A supporter of parliamentary reform as well as votes for women, he was MP for Stoke-on-Trent from 1868 to 1874, and promoted free secular education for all. Courtesy the National Museums Liverpool, Walker Art Gallery

only 56,261 are receiving education in schools recognized by the House of Commons and to which grants are made; not more than 125,000 can be put down as attending any school whatever; not more than 55,000 are at work; and there are no fewer than from 65,000 to 75,000 children in these three towns – and we have no reason to believe that they are, in proportion to their population, any worse than all other large towns – who are growing up unaffected either by the educational clauses of the Factories Act, the Industrial Schools Act, or by voluntary effort. This is the result we have arrived at by our laissez faire policy of leaving everything to be done by voluntary effort, and our want of courage in dealing with the sectarian differences which have so long retarded educational progress. The time has come to put out the strong hand of the law to teach and, thus to save this vast number of children.

Melly linked the large army of illiterate children with the increase of petty crime – in 1861 only about ten per cent of those arrested in the three cities could read and write well, and by the last year (1868) this proportion had fallen to under five per cent. If the high costs of the police and gaols in these cities could be reduced the burden on ratepayers would be much less.

He argued at length that providing more schools alone was not the answer, as it was the indifference of parents to educating their children that was the chief problem. The Factories Act and Industrial Schools Act provided for educating children who were at work; but those children who chose to, or who were allowed to, roam the streets were not covered by them. So he argued that it would only be by compulsion that the poorest class of children would go to school. Melly outlined his own proposals for creating a new class of free municipal secular schools, and concluded by moving for his enquiry.

Sir John was in the chamber, and would have agreed with most of what Melly said in his well argued speech, indeed he had stressed the poor state of children in the new industrial towns in many of his own speeches. The principal and important difference between Sir John's proposals and those of Melly was that Sir John had never suggested that attendance should be compulsory. Some of his opponents had argued, like Melly, that it was not the lack of schools that was the problem, but the indifference of parents. Sir John may have had sympathy for this view, but he clearly believed that going that far was politically impossible in the 1850s. Indeed the scheme put forward in his 1855 bill was also only permissive, allowing poor law unions to impose a rate and form an education committee if voted for locally, but if the bill had been passed one wonders how far it would have been adopted, and whether voluntary attendance would really have had the impact on education standards that he wished for.

The minister responsible for education at that time was William Forster, and he replied to the debate. While welcoming the contribution of George Melly and others, he felt the time for enquiries was past, and that now was the time for action. Unfortunately it was not practical to bring in a measure in the present session, but it was to be hoped that a bill would be brought forward in 1870, and it would probably be the most important measure of that session. He said the two great questions to be resolved were whether the measure would centre round the provision of free schools, and whether attendance would be compulsory. He was not prepared to give any definite opinion at present, although from the tone of his observations it seems Forster at that time thought free schools might kill off the present denominational system, and that compulsory attendance would not be necessary.

Sir John's contribution to the debate was quite short, and he largely supported what Forster had said. A further enquiry was not needed, and the matter was best now left till the following year when the government would bring forward their bill.

Sir John was also involved in the Endowed Schools Bill. The Duke of Newcastle's education commission, which had reported in 1861, had devoted a section to endowed schools, where it considered reform was needed. Some of the schools in this category were large and prestigious, but many were small and the endowment not always used as the founder had intended – many of these dated back to the sixteenth century. So the government put forward an Endowed Schools Bill, which was given its second reading on 15th March.

It was introduced in a long and detailed speech by William Forster, who said that there were nearly 3,000 endowed schools with a total income of nearly £600,000, but of this amount only a little over half was spent on education. He gave examples which illustrated the need for reform.

The head master of one of the schools told an assistant commissioner that "It was not worth his while to push the school, as with the endowment (about £200 a year) and some other small sources of income he had enough to live on comfortably without troubling to do so". Another master of a large endowed school, having an endowment of £651, put his nephew and son into the respective positions of second and third masters. The assistant commissioner 'Found the discipline most inefficient, and the instruction slovenly, unmethodical, and unintelligent; there was no one subject in which the boys seemed to take an interest, or which had been taught with average care or success'. At another school with an income of £610 a year – 'There were thirteen pupils, and it appeared as if even this number would be reduced; the school rooms were in a shameful state, and the scholars, though showing signs of having had teaching, were in a thoroughly bad state of discipline, and apparently only stayed on to qualify for the school exhibitions'.

The assistant commissioner in Suffolk found that at one school the master 'Did no work whatever, but supports an old age in the comfortable schoolhouse;

at another he was almost helpless from age and paralysis; at a third he was honest enough to declare that he was no longer fit for work; at a fourth he was deaf; while at three others he was no longer in the prime of life, and was languishing under his work. That is to say, more than a fourth of the grammar schools in one county were suffering from the bodily infirmities of the master'.

Forster also found that education at these schools was still very much centred on the classics, and he thought that this was increasingly inappropriate, particularly for boys who left at 16 and who were often going to enter one of the professions.

The bill would give power to commissioners, appointed by the government, to alter these endowments and to make new schemes for their application. These would first be put out for consultation locally, then laid on the table of the House for final approval.

As was usually the practice with complicated bills, at the end of the debate on the second reading a select committee was appointed to consider the bill in detail. William Forster was its chairman, and Sir John was one of the members. Sir John attended all eleven meetings, and the committee recommended many changes to the bill, but were by no means unanimous, dividing on many issues. In one respect the committee proved forward looking – they recommended that a new clause be added to the bill, which had hitherto only applied to boys, with the words 'In framing schemes under this act provision shall be made, so far as conveniently may be, for extending the benefits of endowments equally to boys and girls'. This was accepted unanimously, but Sir John seems to have thought that 'equally' was rather strong, and proposed that it be replaced by 'as well as', but this was negatived by the chairman's vote!

On 31st March the Worcestershire Conservatives held a grand dinner in the Shirehall. The hall, Berrow's reported, 'had seldom looked so pleasing as it did, or had had within its walls so influential an assemblage. Messrs Turley's decorative staff exhausted their art in the transformation of the usually dreary hall into a banqueting chamber resplendent with flags, banners, flowers and evergreens… Over the hall doors were the names: Beauchamp – Northwick – Coventry – Pakington in white letters on a blue ground'. The Earl of Coventry presided, with the Earl of Shrewsbury on his one side, and Sir John Pakington on his other. Sir John's elder son John Slaney Pakington who, like his father we will henceforth call Johnny, was also at the high table. It had been hoped that Disraeli would be able to attend, but in the end he had had to decline. Sir John spoke twice – firstly in response to the toast to the Conservative representation for the county. He thanked his own supporters in Droitwich for standing by him in a difficult contest, and said how proud the county should be to have increased its representation from five out of the twelve members before the election to seven out of eleven now (the county had lost one seat in the 1867 Reform Act when Evesham was reduced from two members to one).

Sir John's second and longer speech was in response to the toast to the health of the Conservative leaders coupled with the name of Sir John Pakington. He took the opportunity to attack the Irish Church Bill, which the week before had received its second reading. The measure would, he said, impoverish the Protestant church, and how would having both a poor Protestant and a Catholic church help establish equality? However, having made the mandatory attack on Gladstone and the Liberal party, Sir John did show a measure of a desire for a compromise when he said:

> Now, gentlemen, in my opinion, if financial equality is desirable – if you wish really to raise the Christian tone of the country – it may be worth your consideration – and I throw out this suggestion in perfect consciousness that it may not suit the views of all who hear me – it may be well worth while, in the crisis in which we stand, to consider whether it might not be better to make grants to Roman Catholics to enable them to conduct their religious duties properly and respectably rather than to despoil the Protestant church, and to throw the whole into one mass of confusion.

Sir John added that all reports reaching him were suggesting that the Protestants of northern Ireland 'were now labouring under a feeling, a sense of deep injury, a feeling of irritation, which is most dangerous to the tranquillity and the good feeling of the country'.

Although parliament sat until 11th August, Sir John was back in Worcestershire well before that, and was able to attend the prize giving at Malvern College on 27th July. He had presided when the foundation stone had been laid six years before, and had remained a vice-president, and his son Johnny had also served a term as governor in the early 1860s. The school had

George William, 9th Earl of Coventry, 1838-1930. He inherited the earldom in 1843 when he was five and retained it for 87 years, and was succeeded by his grandson. The family descended from Thomas Coventry, keeper of the great seal 1625-40, and have been seated at Croome Court until recent times.

The Year 1869

Malvern College, from a nineteenth century photograph. Founded in 1865, John Slaney Pakington was an early governor. The Malvern Hills, with its spring water and open spaces, was a popular area for schools.

steadily grown since it opened in 1865, and in 1869 had 170 pupils. During the prize giving, to emphasise the importance of learning modern languages as well as the classics, boys had performed short scenes from plays in foreign languages, and in his speech, Sir John emphasised the importance of this part of the curriculum. He had earlier been on record as criticising the traditional public schools for restricting their curriculum mainly to the classics, and he was clearly pleased to see the importance of French and German at Malvern. Although he did not mention maths, the existence of several maths prizes shows that this subject was also given importance.

Another school with which Sir John had formed a connection was Wellington College. Sir John himself had gone to Eton, and he had also sent his first son there in the early 1840s. But his ideas on education were developing rapidly at this time, and, as can be seen from his speech at Malvern and an earlier one at the Birmingham and Midland Institute in 1862, he had become something of a educational modernist.

Wellington College had been founded after the death of the Duke of Wellington as a national memorial to him, and admitted sons of deceased officers without charge as 'foundationers'. A national subscription list was opened, but the sum raised, around £100,000, was not enough to pay the building costs and provide a sufficient endowment for the foundationers, so it was decided to admit sons of serving officers paying fees as well, and also from the outset boys whose parents had no connection with the army were taken, paying a higher level of fees.

From the beginning the governors were chosen by their status rather than educational knowledge. The president, Prince Albert, took an active role, as did the 14th Earl of Derby. In the early days before the appointment of the first headmaster, the young Rev. Edward White Benson, the purpose of the school was somewhat ill-defined. Some thought that Prince Albert wanted to model it on German military academies, whereas others, including Lord Derby, himself a classicist, wanted it to be more like a traditional English public school. However, it did not open as a military academy, and it accepted boys with a wide range of academic achievement, and aimed to give them an education that would fit them for a practical career in later life. Initially no boy stayed after he was 16, but after the school opened in 1859 Benson started to steer it in a more academic direction, based on his experience as a master at Rugby. He instigated minimum academic standards for entry, and restructured the school so that boys could proceed to university.

Sir John would have known about Wellington College from his association with some of the governors, and also the fact that the Patriotic Fund, of which he was a commissioner, had added capital to the school's endowment in return for

Wellington College, from an early photograph. Although originally founded to educate the sons of army officers, today it is a fairly traditional public school.

the allocation of eighteen foundationer places to them. Nevertheless, when Sir John sent his second son, Herbert Murray Pakington, whom we shall henceforth like his father call Herby, to Wellington in 1861 rather than one of the better established public schools, it was a courageous act. The fees for non-military boys were £110 a year, which was said to be in line with other similar schools, unless Sir John had been somehow able to obtain a reduced rate. In his first year there Herby complained to his father about some of the masters, and Sir John passed on the complaint to Benson, writing that 'they were incompetent and had a distressing tendency to oversleep in the morning, causing them to cancel classes'. Benson replied firmly, listing all the qualifications of the masters, and we can perhaps put Herby's complaint down to youthful exaggeration. By the time he left, Herby seems to have done well at Wellington, and in 1867 was admitted to Merton College, Oxford, where he obtained his MA degree, before becoming a pupil at the Inner Temple, and eventually being called to the bar. In the course of time Herby sent his own son Herbert Stuart to Wellington. Sir John's nephew Sir John Hanbury Williams and his sons John and Charles all went, as did Herbert's son-in-law Roger Bertie-Roberts, so there developed quite a connection between the Pakington family and Wellington College.

In 1869 Sir John was appointed a governor of the college, and, as with all things with which he became connected, he attended meetings regularly, and took a close interest in the school. There is a note in the school archives that Sir John attended speech day every year after he was appointed a governor, unlike many of the other governors. Headmaster Benson left in 1873 after a difference of opinion with the governors, and a sub-committee of the governors appointed Rev. Edward Wickham to succeed him. Wickham soon made recommendations for changes to be made in the school, and, as we shall see, Sir John chaired a committee to consider and report on these changes.

Returning to Sir John's autumn in Worcestershire, on 28th July, the day after the prize-giving at Malvern College, he attended the first meeting that year of the Worcestershire Archery Society. This had been founded in 1846 by Baroness Windsor, and their meetings were great society occasions held at the leading country houses in the county. This meeting was held at Kings End, the home of John Slaney Pakington, in Powick parish west of Worcester. Berrow's wrote enthusiastically about the occasion:

> For a first meeting it was remarkably successful. This result may be attributed to several causes, not the least of which is the esteem in which the Pakington name is held throughout Worcestershire. The élite of the county were numerously represented, and as far as a large and fashionable attendance contributes to the success of a meeting, Wednesday's gathering may be classed among the best meetings with which the society ever opened a season.

LORD HAMPTON – HIS LATER YEARS

One of the attractions of archery as a society event was that the ladies took part, and it was traditional for the lady of the country house to be the Lady Paramount for the day. Shooting started at 1.00 p.m., and at 3.00 dinner was served in a large marquee. There were the usual toasts and speeches, kept short, according to Sir John, by the rules of the society. Sir John proposed the toast to Baroness Windsor, and, remarking that the society was flourishing and prosperous, hoped it would never be 'disestablished'! Neither Sir John nor the host for the day took part in the shooting, but the name Herbert Pakington does appear as a contestant – he was Sir John's son by his second marriage, then aged 21, although judging by his score he had yet to hone his skills as an archer! However, at the next meeting on 18th August at Bricklehampton Hall Herby returned a much better score, though his elder brother scored badly.

On 9th August the annual meeting of the Severn Navigation Commissioners was held under the chairmanship of Sir John. The improvement of the navigation, by the construction of weirs and dams, had been authorised by an Act of 1842, but in the 1850s an extra weir was constructed at Tewkesbury as the depth of water often proved inadequate south of Diglis weir in Worcester. Due to the unreliable navigation in the early days, and the increasing competition from railways, receipts from tolls had never been enough to pay the commissioners' outgoings, particularly capital and interest on the loans. In 1848, the first full year of operation, the tolls had exceeded £11,000, but had since dwindled, and in 1868 were just under £8,000. However, in the last year the finances of the commissioners had been transformed, according to Sir John. "Every commissioner who paid attention to the affairs of the Commission must have been struck by the immense contrast – the gratifying contrast – between the financial statements of the last few years and the financial statement of the present year". What had happened was that the Staffordshire and Worcestershire Canal Company, which had provided much of the original capital for the project, had written off over £20,000 of the money owing, in addition to the substantial arrears of interest. For reasons not entirely clear, the Great Western Railway had also become involved, and had guaranteed to make up the tolls to £14,000 a year.

It was also proposed to make further improvements at Gloucester by constructing a new weir and also a new cut that would make the navigation there more reliable, and which would, Sir John hoped, further improve the revenues. He said that, once these works were complete, not only would the navigation be able to compete in terms of cost with the railways, but he had recently been informed by the engineer, Leader Williams, that it could even compete 'in terms of time'. But unfortunately Sir John's optimism was not to be borne out – the navigation continued to attract insufficient tolls, and money owing on the capital and interest account started to mount again.

The Year 1869

Sir John had always enjoyed music, and in his younger days had been an amateur singer, even taking lessons. Those days were now past, but he had always been a regular attender of the Three Choirs Festival, having been a steward twice, and standing at the cathedral door with a plate seeking donations to the charity supported by the Festival for widows and orphans of the clergy. The 1869 Festival was held in early September in Worcester, and Sir John was noted in the great crush finding their seats on the opening morning, 7th September, when Mendelssohn's Elijah was performed – the service which used to precede the opening concert seems to have been dropped. Sir John, his wife and two sons were also noted as being present at the final ball held in the Guildhall on Friday, although the attendance was not so good as had been expected – 'the succession of gaieties during the week appeared to have tired out the visitors', thought the Daily News.

On 21st September Sir John and Lady Pakington attended the opening of a new school in Elmley Castle. In fact the school had largely been paid for by Lady Pakington, whose first husband, Col Henry Hastings Davies, had been a large landowner in the parish, and they had lived in Elmley Park, a country house near the church. The estate was now owned by a Mr Jones, who had given the land for the school, but Lady Pakington's fond memories of the village and its people, encouraged no doubt by her husband's enthusiasm for promoting education, had led to her long-standing ambition for the village to have a new school.

The opening was a great day for the village, as the Bishop of Worcester, Rt Rev. Henry Philpott, came to lead a procession into the church, where he gave a sermon. Afterwards the procession reformed and went to the new school, which could accommodate between 70 and 80 pupils, and Sir John gave a speech. In it he talked about the prospect of a new education bill being brought forward the following year, and although he admitted that he was not of the same political persuasion as the present government, he had a great respect for William Forster, who was charged with bringing forward the new scheme. His support for his political rival was widely reported in the press.

When Sir John had finished, the party assembled for dinner in a marquee, and the day concluded by there being a comprehensive round of toasts, presided over by Sir John, who spoke a number of times more.

Sir John had always been a keen traveller, and in 1829 had undertaken an extensive tour of Scotland. He had gone on a long tour of Europe on honeymoon, had visited the USA and Canada, and had made many shorter tours of the British regions and Europe. But no record of an Irish trip has survived before 1869, when he is recorded as arriving in Kingstown, the modern Dun Laoghaire, on 23rd September, so he must have left immediately after his day in Elmley Castle. Later he was recorded with his younger son Herby 'and suite' in

LORD HAMPTON – HIS LATER YEARS

Killarney. Whether his 'suite' included Lady Pakington is not clear – perhaps not, as the journey across England and Wales, the Irish Sea, then Ireland itself would have been arduous. Late autumn was traditionally a time when leading politicians and aristocrats stayed at each others country houses, and on the way back to England Sir John was amongst the guests of Col and Mrs Thomas Taylor, Conservative MP for Co. Dublin, at their home Ardgillan Castle, on the coast north of Dublin. He would have known Col. Taylor well, as he had served as a whip, then chief whip, in the 1850s and 1860s.

As a magistrate since 1824, Sir John had been a member of the Court of Quarter Sessions, and had been a long standing chairman from 1834 to 1858. Despite his many other activities, after his retirement he still made a point of attending when possible, and was in attendance at the Michaelmas court on 18th October, immediately on his return from Ireland.

A few days later an event occurred that would have caused Sir John great sadness. The leader of the Conservative party after the split with the Peelites over the corn laws had been Lord Derby, who had served three times as prime minister. Sir John had served in Lord his cabinet in each administration, and it seems that Derby was one man who commanded Sir John's unqualified respect. They may not have been close socially, but the correspondence between Sir John and his prime minister is always business-like and easy going. Sir John was disappointed that Derby did not make his educational ideas party policy in the 1850s, but he would have accepted that opposition within the party made this impossible, and that Lord Derby was doing his best to keep the party together.

This contrasts with his relationship with the leader in the Commons, Benjamin Disraeli. They both first entered the Commons in 1837, and regarded themselves as comrades in arms in the political struggle. But Disraeli was from a very different background to most Tory MPs, and while he admired Disraeli's debating skills and leadership, Sir John found him a difficult man to communicate with, and complained more than once that he tended to make policy 'on the hoof', and failed to involve his colleagues in policy decisions. Disraeli's attitude to patronage also differed from Sir John's. The Tory party had not had an overall majority in the Commons since 1846, and therefore Disraeli was also anxious to increase his support by whatever means was available, including the use of patronage. Sir John, on the other hand, claimed to make appointments in the best interests of the nation, which Disraeli criticised as not necessarily the best thing for the Conservative party. Nevertheless, Sir John was not averse to advancing family interests, and, when a minister, appointed his first wife's nephew Herbert Murray, and later his own son Johnny Pakington, to posts within his office.

Lord Derby had been a martyr to gout for a long time, and in 1868 finally decided to resign from his position as party leader. Disraeli had taken over that role and also that of prime minister, and now, only a year and a half later, Lord Derby died on 23rd October. Fulsome tributes were paid in the national press, and Sir John would doubtless have been greatly saddened by the loss of his former colleague.

On 1st December Sir John had been asked to address a public meeting in the Worcester Guildhall to publicise the activities of two charities for the blind: The society for providing cheap literature for the blind, and the proprietary college in Worcester for the blind sons of gentlemen. The Bishop of Worcester presided, and in a thoughtful speech praised two Worcestershire clergymen, Rev. Robert Blair, and Rev. William Taylor, for the work they were doing. Rev. Blair ran the college for the blind sons of gentlemen (not for the sons of blind gentlemen, as the 1871 census has it!), which at that time occupied the Commandery in Worcester, and had thirteen pupils. But the bishop said that the college's continuation was entirely dependent on Rev. Blair, and it was now proposed to establish a joint stock company to put it on a more permanent footing, and subscriptions were invited for the shares.

One of the problems regarding the books available to the blind, the bishop said, was that at that time no less than five different systems of embossed characters were in use, which was obviously most unsatisfactory. However, he said that, as a member of the committee of the society for providing cheap literature for the blind he had come to the conclusion that the system using Roman letters was the most preferable, if only because these books could be read by the sighted and unsighted. (We may presume that this system was not the same as modern Braille.) The bishop was followed by Rev. Blair, who made an impassioned plea for more books to be made available, as at present there were not only extremely few, but very expensive. Finally, Sir John spoke, and said there was little he could add to the fine sentiments expressed by the Very Reverend and Reverend gentlemen who preceded him. Sir John was not sure whether the privation of being blind was the greater for those who had earlier had their sight, or for those who had never had it;

> But at all events, we must feel that the best way, the only way, in which we can soothe and allay the misfortune of him who has never enjoyed it is by cultivating his intellect and furnishing his mind, and so far giving him the best and only compensation which is possible under such circumstances.

Emphasising the value of books for the blind to read, Sir John quoted the example given him by Rev. Blair of a man aged 51 with rough hands, who learned to read embossed Roman type in a very short space of time, and was soon able to read the book of Ruth. Sir John said he had been told that people could learn to read in as little as six months, but of course such benefit was restricted to those fortunate enough to pass through a suitable institution, so not only was there a need for more books, but also places where these skills could be taught. As a footnote, the college for the blind continued to slowly expand, and still exists as New Worcester College on the London Road.

On 14th December Sir John was involved in a third function in which the Bishop of Worcester played a part. This was the dedication of the new church of St Nicholas, near the railway station in Droitwich. St Nicholas had been an ancient parish, and before the reformation had its own chapel, which was allied to the nunnery at Westwood, situated somewhere close to where Sir John's seat at Westwood Park now stood. But the nunnery was closed at the reformation, and no subsequent record of the chapel has been found. So for a considerable period the inhabitants of the parish had no church or minister, and to remedy this the parish had been united with that of St Andrew, but pressure from parishioners eventually resulted in the building of this new church.

The Bishop of Worcester led a procession with other clergy to the church, and the service of dedication was performed, with the bishop giving the sermon. Afterwards a cold collation was served in the George Hotel, and Sir John was in the chair when the time for toasts arrived. Responding to the toast to the bishop and clergy of the diocese, the bishop told the history of the project, and paid tribute to the efforts of Sir John and Lady Pakington to raise funds for the building, including throwing open their park in 1866 for a three day grand bazaar, which had been most successful.

Chapter 3
1870 – Education, Education, Education

Sir John seems to have spent Christmas in London, as he left Westwood immediately after the Elmley Castle event, and appeared in public meetings there in January. He had lived at 41 Eaton Square since a short time after his marriage to his second wife Augusta Murray in 1844, but for some reason moved at about this time to no. 9, at the south western end of the Square. Perhaps his stay in London over Christmas was to accomplish this move. On 11th January he presided over a public meeting to discuss the Endowed Schools Act. The select committee on which he had served the year before had recommended that the government bill be divided into two: an Endowed Schools Bill to establish the commission that would produce schemes to reform the ancient endowments, and another bill to determine the qualifications of teachers at endowed schools, who would henceforth be subject to examination. The Endowed Schools Bill had been enacted, but the government had yet to produce the second bill.

The meeting on 11th January was mainly to discuss the qualifications of teachers, and was attended by many headmasters of endowed schools. The first and principal resolution, proposed by Rev. Edwin Abbott, headmaster of the City of London School, was that 'This meeting expresses its entire concurrence in the proposal to register and classify teachers who have passed an examination held by the Educational Council... as affording means whereby the public may distinguish qualified from unqualified teachers, and as an inducement to future teachers fully to prepare themselves for the duties of their office...'. This was adopted.

The following week on 19th January Sir John was present at a meeting presided over by John Talbot, MP for west Kent, and a nephew of the Earl of Shrewsbury. The meeting was to discuss the appointment of bishops, and had been triggered by the appointment the previous year of Frederick Temple to the see of Exeter. Temple had long been interested in the education question, and had served a term as headmaster of Rugby School, and, although beginning his life as a Tory, had become a Liberal and supporter of Gladstone.

What caused all the controversy was that he had contributed an essay in 1860 to a publication called 'Essays and Reviews'. It was not his own contribution that caused controversy, but some of the other six essays, which advocated a more rationalist and scientific approach to the Bible and Christianity. Many thought this heretical, and two of the authors were convicted of heresy. They appealed to the privy council, and, despite the Archbishops of Canterbury and York voting against, the appeal was successful. Thereafter many traditionalists continued to view Temple with suspicion, and his appointment to Exeter in 1869 caused a storm of protest. At his institution in Westminster Abbey in December 1869 the Bishop of London, standing in for the Archbishop, had to adjudicate in a side chapel of the Abbey on objections to the consecration by some other provincial bishops. Lengthy legal arguments took place, with references to acts of Henry III and of Henry VIII, not to mention the First Council of Nicea held in 325 AD! Eventually the Bishop of London held that as only a minority of the provincial bishops had objected to the consecration he had no authority to postpone or stop it, and, considerably delayed, the ceremony at last got underway with no further problems.

At the January public meeting a paper was read by Dr Goulburn, Dean of Norwich, which criticised the present mode of appointing bishops. Then, as now, the prime minister recommended a name to the sovereign, who had the final right

A cartoon entitled 'The Modern Guy Faux', showing Edward Pusey and Anthony Ashley-Cooper, 7th Earl of Shaftesbury, attempting to blow up Frederick Temple when Bishop of Exeter. Pusey was a high church Anglican and tractarian, and Shaftesbury was a strict Evangelist, opposed to modern biblical scholarship. Both were enemies of Temple.

of appointment, and this name went forward for the dean and chapter of the diocese to elect. This election was only a formality, and Dr Goulbourn's paper recommended that the law be changed to give the church authorities at least some say or power of objection when an appointment was made. Sir John spoke next, and in thanking the dean for his paper, said the recent appointment of Dr Temple "had created a period of great danger to the church… Why", he asked, "had Dr Temple been appointed a bishop? Was it was because he was sound in faith (laughter)? His notorious connection with Essays and Reviews rendered it impossible to regard him as one who had any claim to be 'sound in faith (hear, hear)'. Unless he had been misinformed, Dr Temple had acted as chairman of the election committee of the radical candidate for Warwick (a laugh). And would any assembly of sober Englishmen, whether Conservative or radical, say that was a proper stepping stone to the episcopal bench (hear, hear)?" Sir John continued some time in similar vein and referred to the disgraceful scenes in Westminster Abbey, concluding that the appointment 'was one of the most singular unwisdom'.

However, once he was secure in his see, Temple renounced his association with the other essays in Essays and Reviews, and went on to be a highly regarded Bishop of Exeter. Later he was transferred to the see of London, and ended his career as Archbishop of Canterbury. As to Sir John's complaint that he had meddled in radical politics, the Birmingham Daily Post pointed out that the clergy on the whole were strong supporters of the Conservatives, much to the benefit of Tories like Sir John. And how could the bishops refrain from being political when a number of them sat in the House of Lords?

A few days later on 23rd January Sir John presided at the weekly meeting of the Social Science Association, when a paper was read on the need for compulsion in education. Sir John then spoke, and explained why he had kept himself independent of the Birmingham Education League (which advocated free secular schools), and the Manchester Education Union, which campaigned for the retention of denominational religious schools. Sir John said there was much in these two bodies' aims that he supported, but also some that he disagreed with, and he wished to keep himself free to advocate whatever he felt was the best policy for the country. He was sure that William Forster, who would be coming forward with a government bill on the subject shortly, would do what he felt was the best for the country. He would rather wait to see what was proposed before making any detailed comments, but he did feel strongly that we needed an education minister and an education department. As to whether schools should be free, his own current view was that this was not necessary, and that the £0.5m now paid every year in fees should not be wasted. Surely there was no hardship in paying that small sum, but if it could not be afforded, the state should provide relief.

On the question of compulsion, he said that his own views had changed somewhat, and he now believed that some degree of compulsion was necessary if we were to reach such a degree of education as was desired.

Sir John made a brief return to Droitwich for a meeting of the Droitwich Benefit Building Society, of which he was president, on 31st January. He spoke of the satisfactory progress of the Society in promoting the building of new workmen's dwellings in the town. The Society had acquired 22 acres of land, divided each acre into roughly eight plots, and by loaning money had allowed 150 new houses to be erected. The site was just south of the modern Saltway along Burrish and adjoining streets, where the houses can still be seen. A few days later he attended the annual meeting of the Bromsgrove Literary and Mechanics Institute, where he spoke about the forthcoming legislation on education and proposed the motion 'That the Bromsgrove Literary and Mechanics and all similar institutes are deserving of increased patronage and support, as they tend not only to assist the industrial classes in self-improvement, but also promote mutual sympathy and friendly intercourse between different sections of society'. Sir John said he had only just heard of the establishment of a working men's club in the town – would it not be better if the two institutions joined forces? Johnny Pakington was also present, and both father and son were present at a meeting of the Worcestershire Union of Literary and Mechanics Institutes held the same day – Pakington junior was president of this Union.

Sir John returned to London on 5th February, ready for the opening of parliament on 8th February, but, ever ready to address meetings debating education, Sir John spoke at meeting of the Society of Arts the day before, proposing one of the resolutions encouraging more education with some degree of compulsion, and the maintenance of fees, very much as he had advocated in his speech to the Social Science Association.

In the evening of the same day Sir John was one of forty guests who dined with Disraeli at his house at Grosvenor Gate for the traditional pre-session get-together. Sir John was no doubt anxious to see what form the promised education bill would take, and he had not long to wait, for the following week on 17th February the vice-president of the council responsible for education, William Forster, was to propose the bill's first reading. The session commenced at 4.00 p.m., but members had to wait while a division took place on a Scottish bill, and listen to a discussion on the Marriage with a Deceased Wife's Sister Bill, a matter that was to engage the Commons, on and off, for over 50 years, before Forster was able to rise.

He began by underlining the importance of having a proper system of popular education; whilst it had the prospect of doing great good it also had the potential for harm. He thought there was never a measure that had a greater need to be considered impartially, with no ingress of party spirit, and he was confident there was never "a House of Commons more disposed so to consider it than the House I am now addressing". (Sir John must have turned his mind back to 1855, when his own education bill had been met by opposition and religious prejudice from all sides.) Forster had noted the increased interest in the subject manifested in many recent public meetings, and said participants were divided broadly into two camps: those who believed that education should continue to be provided voluntarily, whilst others believed the government should step in and provide a national scheme to ensure education was available to all children. He said he wished to emphasise that the bill had not been brought forward as a compromise between these differing views, but as an attempt to learn from the past in introducing a new scheme. However, it soon became clear that the bill was very much ploughing a middle furrow, making as much use as possible of existing resources, whilst adding to them in the least controversial way possible.

Sir John had been fond of quoting statistics when speaking of education, but Forster said he did not intend to weary the House with many of these, although he did produce a few to show the lack of education. He said that in 1869 government aid went to schools in England and Wales with about one and a half million children on their registers, although at any one time only about two

William Edward Forster, 1818-86, was brought up in a Quaker household. As a young man he went into the wool business with T S Fison in Bradford, and became wealthy, taking a benevolent attitude to his workforce. He married Jane, daughter of Thomas Arnold, one-time headmaster of Rugby School, and because of that had to leave the Quakers. He became nominally an Anglican, but seems to have lost any religious enthusiasm he might have had. He was much influenced by a visit to Ireland in 1846 to view the destitution caused by the famine. Regarded as a radical, he was first elected to Parliament in 1861, and became particularly interested in education. Under Gladstone in 1868 he was appointed vice-president of the council, and was widely praised for steering the 1870 Elementary Education Act through Parliament.

thirds of these were actually in attendance. This left about one and three quarter million children not on school registers at all. Admittedly, this did not include children going to unsupported schools, but with a few exceptions, these were the worst schools, and offered a very poor education. (It is difficult to get official figures from this period showing the population in different age groups, but out of a total population of 26 million my own estimate is that there were about 3.6 million children aged 6 to 12 inclusive, so this would roughly agree with Forster's claim that only about two fifths of children were on school registers.) He also referred to the report generated as a result of George Melly's motion the year before (see above page 28), which he said showed that of the 80,000 children in Liverpool between the ages of 5 and 13 one quarter were not attending any school, while another quarter were attending schools "where they got an education not worth having".

The two aims the bill sought to achieve were, said Forster, "to cover the country with good schools, and get the children to go to them". For the first of these objects, the country would be divided into school districts, equating with the parish or the municipal borough, and returns would be required from each district as to the number and quality of schools, and the number of children of school age. Inspectors would be sent to help make the returns. If it were found that the present provisions were adequate in all respects, then nothing further would be done in those districts, except to keep the situation under review. However, Forster thought that the "enormous majority" of school districts would be deemed insufficient.

What to do in these inadequate districts? First, keeping with the principle of using voluntary help where possible, it was proposed to give a year for local people to put the inadequate school provision right. But if that did not happen, then the bill would provide for these districts to elect a school board, which would have the duty to provide for adequate educational facilities. The boards would be elected by the town council in municipalities, and by the vestries in the country, and power would be taken to unite parishes for this purpose if necessary. Who, Forster then asked, would pay for these new schools? Firstly, he wanted to make it clear that the government did not want to do away with school fees and make them free; if they did that everyone would soon want free schooling, and the cost would escalate. "Why should we relieve the parent from all payments for the education of his child? We come in and help the parents in all possible ways; but, generally speaking, the enormous majority of them are able, and will continue to be able, to pay those fees", Forster said. But the boards would have special powers not to charge in two cases: where the district is exceedingly poor, and when the parents were unable to pay the fees the board could give free tickets for them to attend a fee-paying school.

Education, Education, Education

Most importantly, the bill would contain a provision for the board to impose a rate, part of the existing poor rate, for its own purposes, not to exceed threepence (1.25p) in the pound. Boards could also borrow for building purposes. Forster thought that all this would result in the cost of education being split in three roughly equal ways: parents; public taxes; and local rates.

Forster empathised that, while not wishing to interfere in the principles of denominational education, public elementary schools assisted under the act must subscribe to the so-called conscience clause, which the bill laid down as follows:

> No scholar shall be required, as a condition of being admitted into or of attending or of enjoying all the benefits of the school, to attend or to abstain from attending any Sunday school, or any place of religious worship, or to learn any such catechism or religious formulary, or to be present at any such lesson or instruction or observance as may have been objected to on religious grounds by the parent of the scholar sending his objection in writing to the managers or principal teacher of the school or one of them.

What about religious instruction in the new board schools? Forster said the government had considered whether they should be entirely secular with no religion taught at all, but surely that would be going too far in a Christian country. And it would not be right for government to lay down the details of religious instruction, because parents' wishes in this matter would vary from district to district. So this would be left to the school board, who would act as the school managers. After all, they were elected by the local people, so presumably would do what the electorate wanted.

Finally, Forster came to what he said was one of the most important aspect of any scheme – whether attendance would be compulsory. He said opinion on the matter had shifted in recent times, and it was now more generally recognized that to achieve the aim of a country with well educated children, some compulsion would be necessary. He discussed at length various indirect ways by which this could be achieved, but said in the end the government had decided to give the boards power to pass bye-laws, once the district was adequately provided with schools, to make attendance compulsory, with provision to fine non-complying parents up to 5 shillings (25p), although this would not be imposed if there was a reasonable excuse.

> What is our purpose in this bill? Briefly this, to bring elementary education within the reach of every English home, aye, and within the reach of those children who have no homes… It is the education of the people's children by the people's officers, chosen in their local assemblies, controlled by the people's representatives in Parliament. That is the principle on which our bill is based; it is the ultimate force which rests behind every clause.

LORD HAMPTON – HIS LATER YEARS

But education also had a more practical value for the nation, said Forster, as:

> Upon the speedy provision of elementary education depends our industrial prosperity. It is of no use trying to give technical teaching to our artisans without elementary education; uneducated labourers – and many of our labourers are utterly uneducated – are, for the most part, unskilled labourers, and if we leave our work-folk any longer unskilled, notwithstanding their strong sinews and determined energy, they will become overmatched in the competition of the world.

Finally, Forster dwelt on the moral side:

> We all know that want of education often leads to vice. Let us then each of us think of our own homes, of the villages in which we have to live, of the towns in which it is our lot to be busy; and do we not know child after child growing up to probable crime, to still more probable misery, because badly taught or utterly untaught? Dare we then take on ourselves the responsibility of allowing this ignorance and this weakness to continue one year longer than we can help?

First to reply from the opposition benches was Lord Robert Montagu, who had been William Forster's predecessor as vice-president of the council. He attacked Forster's statement that 'denominational inspection' would be ended. Under this arrangement, that dated back to 1851, it had been agreed that denominational schools could have the right of veto over their government inspector, which Forster said meant that different inspectors worked in the same district, leading to inefficiency. Montagu, something of a religious fanatic who was shortly to be received into the Roman Catholic church, claimed this would be a gross breach of trust with the different religious sects. Then he went on to complain that the bill appeared to sanction for the first time secular schools being provided at public expense; but he said that it was clear that secular schools were not popular, and the public much preferred schools in which the fundamentals of religion were taught and the Bible read.

Montagu then embarked on a rather rambling attack on the earlier Liberal government's 'revised code', which he said was designed to reduce expenditure and consequently led to the present want of education, and he queried the statistics that Forster had quoted in his speech about the situation in Liverpool. Then he criticised the proposal to give vestries the power to elect the school boards in country districts – if a rate was to imposed, he said, people in these small communities would simply be motivated by a desire to keep it as low as possible.

Finally Montagu came to the proposals to enable attendance to be made compulsory. This would bear very hard and oppressively on the labourer, on the poor widow, and on the sick and infirm, who often depended on the few shillings a week the children could earn to keep them from the workhouse. In any case, he said, if parents could escape the fine if they had a reasonable excuse for not sending them to school, what constituted a reasonable excuse would soon be so freely interpreted that the clause would cease to have an effect. Summing up, Montagu said:

> When educational destitution was so slight as it was at present, it would have been far better to foster the present system by removing all the deterring causes, by relaxing the onerous restrictions and requirements, and by giving more liberal grants. The success would then be much greater than they could reasonably hope for under this scheme of compulsion.

But Lord Montagu's somewhat vague criticisms of the proposals were not echoed by the other speakers. George Dixon, the reforming MP for Birmingham, generally welcomed the bill, but, as an advocate of secular education, he thought leaving the decision as to the religious nature of the new schools to the boards was unsatisfactory, although it was a step in the right direction. He also thought the proposal to leave to the boards decisions about compulsory attendance at school was a weakness. The House should decide whether children should be compelled to go school or not.

Other speakers generally welcomed the bill, although the lack of compulsion in it was referred to by more than one. Then Sir John rose to speak. His own bills of 1855 and 1857 had met with much hostility from members from both extremes in the debate, and it must have been gratifying for him to see that, at last, a bill which embodied many of his own proposals, was likely to become law.

George Dixon, 1820-98, was born in Manchester but spent most of his life running the Birmingham merchant firm of Rathbone Bros. He became active in local politics, and in 1867 was elected an MP for Birmingham. He was an ardent believer in educational reform, and in 1869 he became chairman of the new National Educational League, which campaigned for free rate-supported unsectarian national education. He resigned his Parliamentary seat in 1875, but was returned for Edgbaston in 1885, which he held until he died. His name is remembered in Birmingham schools today.

> The object of my rising is to state that I have never listened to a speech with more heartfelt satisfaction than to the speech of the right hon. gentleman in introducing this measure. I have worked for many years for the accomplishment of this object, and which I should rejoice to see settled under the auspices of my right hon. friend.

Consideration of the details would, of course have to wait for later, but his biggest regret at this stage was that the bill contained no provision for the appointment of a proper minister of education. Sir John had long thought that the present arrangements, where the education grant was managed by the privy council, which appointed a committee on education with a vice-president, was archaic and difficult to understand. By his speech that night, Forster had shown that he was totally in charge of his subject. But was he minister for education? No; schoolmasters all over the country daily received letters, not from the secretary of state for education, but from 'My Lords', and the Lord President of the Privy Council, Earl de Grey, who was the nominal head.

Sir John said he had come to regard the maintenance of school fees as desirable (although his 1855 bill proposed free schools) and he had also come to view some degree of compulsory attendance as necessary. But if, as Forster had proposed, living more than one mile from a school would be regarded as an 'adequate reason' for non-attendance, he thought this was far too short a distance. He knew of cases where children had to travel double that distance to school, and there was never any complaint at any season of the year. Furthermore, he thought it unsatisfactory to leave to bye-laws passed by boards the degree of compulsory attendance required in each district – for what period of the year would attendance to required? But Sir John did not wish to sound too critical at this stage, and concluded:

> I repeat the extreme satisfaction with which I have heard the statement of my right hon. friend, and my earnest hope is that by the wisdom of Parliament the measure may be carried to a satisfactory conclusion, and will give us that which my right hon. friend, in earnest, eloquent, and impressive language, enforced upon us at the close of his speech – namely, that real system of national education which is so essential to the prosperity and domestic happiness of the country.

The second reading of the bill came up on 14th March, but this was delayed by an amendment by the educational campaigner George Dixon to the motion for the second reading, that the bill would never be satisfactory if it left 'the question of religious instruction in schools supported by public funds and rates to be determined by local authorities'. Dixon, who was the chairman of the National Education League, said he would pass over for now the question of why the bill did not propose compulsory attendance and free schools, but wished to point out what he regarded as the very unsatisfactory idea of leaving the denominational character of the new board schools to the school boards. He felt that this would lead to jostling for position on town councils among members of different sects, and would increase rather than diminish denominational differences. He felt that schools should only teach secular subjects in their normal hours, and deal with religious issues outside these, leaving pupils free to attend or not as they wished.

William Forster made a long reply, saying that Dixon had not really put forward any straightforward alternative to the bill's provisions, and this led to a three day debate. At the end the government promised to take into account all the points that had been made, at which Dixon withdrew his amendment and the bill got its second reading.

The committee stage of the Elementary Education Bill was not to take place till mid-June, partly because the government were considering a number of changes, and partly because the Irish Land Bill, part of prime minister Gladstone's campaign to improve the lot of the Irish peasant, was the subject of lengthy debates before that. But Sir John did not take part in that matter, and restricted his interventions in the House of Commons to military or naval questions, based on his fairly recent experience as first lord and secretary for war. On 24th February the War Office Bill came up for its second reading – this measure created two new posts for under secretaries in the War Office, a clerk of the ordnance and a financial secretary. These would both be members of parliament, and were created to take the heavy burden off the secretary for war, at that time Edward Cardwell, member for Oxford, who had succeeded Sir John in that post after the last election. Sir John did not feel that enough explanation had been given for the need and functions of these new ministers, and pressed Cardwell for more information.

The War Office Bill came up for its third reading on 25th April, which was usually a formality. However on this occasion Joshua Fielden, Tory member for the west riding of Yorkshire, opposed the passage of the bill. It was, in his opinion, just an excuse for the government to increase the number of its officers, and it was quite wrong, at a time of national retrenchment of expenditure, to make these new appointments. However Sir John, although he did not still quite understand the exact duties of these new under secretaries, supported the bill. He could speak from personal experience that the duties of the secretary of state for war were the most onerous of all the secretaries of state, and that this burden told on the holders of the office; the House would recall that three previous holders of the office, Lord Herbert, Sir George Cornewall Lewis, and Sir Benjamin Hawes had all died relatively young. So Sir John was in favour of giving the secretary for war more support in the House, and after Edward

Cardwell, the present secretary of state, pointed out that the bill would create no new salaries, just transfer from the civil service to the government two senior positions, the House divided and only six members voted against the bill.

The lengthy debate on the second reading of the Elementary Education Bill had meant the postponement of a matter that Sir John had become involved in, and which had occasioned a number of comments in the press and elsewhere. This eventually came up after the Easter recess on 29th April, and concerned the resignation of Colonel Edward Boxer, superintendent of the Royal Laboratories, a department of the Royal Arsenal at Woolwich. Over several years Boxer had proved himself to be an able inventor, and several of his ideas had been adopted. Boxer considered that these inventions went beyond the call of his ordinary duties, and had applied for financial recognition, but this was turned down partly, so it was later said, because he had already applied for patents, which the War Office condoned, providing, of course, that Boxer did not benefit financially from any contracts with the British government. But immediately questions arose that were not clear cut, such as whether supplying the Indian army was covered or not, but the particular matter that led to the scandal concerned the cartridge manufacturing firm Eley Brothers. Boxer had developed a new type of cartridge, later called the Boxer cartridge, and in 1867 sold the patent rights to Eley. As the War Office were to order some millions of these cartridges, there was correspondence between the War Office and Boxer about the nature of his relationship. Eventually in January 1868 Sir John, who was then the secretary for war, sent a letter to Boxer telling him that he must not seek to benefit in any way privately from government contracts, and 'You must look for reward from the royalties or other remuneration you may receive as a patentee from private manufacturers'.

Col Edward Boxer. Although he saw no war service, the secretary of state declared that it was owing to Captain Boxer's efforts that the siege of Sebastopol in 1855 was pushed on and fire sustained as it was. When he left the service in 1869, he had designed shells, cartridges, fuses, and fittings that remained effective until the weapons for which they were invented became obsolete.

Education, Education, Education

Boxer and his supporters claimed that this letter sanctioned his receipt of royalties from Eley, a view which is understandable, although common sense should have dictated that, if it led to Boxer gaining financially from government contracts, it was wrong. But in the House on 29th April Sir John said that he had not agreed to this form of words, and indeed had shortly beforehand drafted a minute, which he had written in his own hand, confirming that government employees must never benefit from the placing of government contracts. The January letter to Boxer was written by Gen. Sir John St George, and Sir John said he did not agree with its wording.

Sir John's successor later received a letter from Kynoch, one of Eley's competitors, asking whether the War Office were aware that Boxer was receiving royalties from the government's contract with Eley, whereupon Cardwell wrote to Boxer asking him whether this was true. Boxer said he would not answer what he regarded as a private matter, as he did to a second similar letter. He was then asked to resign, which he did in December 1869. Some felt that he had been harshly treated (he was actually dismissed for insubordination), and in the House Major Myles O'Reilly, MP for Longford, proposed that a select committee be set up to look into all these matters – at the root of it was whether Sir John's letter condoned any arrangement by Boxer with Eley, as it was a private contractor. But both Sir John and Edward Cardwell spoke strongly against Boxer who, they claimed, had acted in a deceitful and ungentlemanly way, and at the end of the debate prime minister Gladstone said the government were not prepared to agree to such an enquiry.

But that was not quite the end of the matter, as on the Monday following Sir John was again on his feet in the House explaining the exact nature of the minute he had drafted on this matter, and the following day in The Times there was a leader commenting, in parts inaccurately, on the affair. This prompted a number of further letters from Sir John, General St George, Boxer, Eley, Kynoch, and others, putting their points of view and denying accusations made against them. Finally, on May 13th, The Times summed up the whole affair from the evidence of who said and wrote what and when, and neither Sir John nor the War Office came out well. To go into all the details would take too much space here, but, although Sir John had claimed to be against government employees benefitting financially from government contracts, he had also agreed to a report in which this had been sanctioned. Sir John's part in the affair was 'not very creditable' and 'inconsistent', and he seems to have been economical with the truth about what he learned, and when. None of this exonerated Col. Boxer, who seems to have had a grudge against his employer even though Sir John increased his salary from £500 to £800 in 1867. The Times concluded 'We do not meet with handsome dealing in any part of this unsatisfactory business'.

Even though we must sympathise with Sir John, as he had been in that office for barely twelve months, and, at 69, was probably finding that the pressure of work in the busy department did not always allow him the time to deal with matters (and this must not at the time have seemed a major matter) as carefully as he would have liked. That being the case it is understandable, but not excusable, that he went so far in destroying Col Boxer's character in the House on 29th April, but this final act in his ministerial career is the only one that has come to light in which Sir John played a less than creditable role.

After the Elementary Education Bill had been introduced on 17th February there had been many petitions and public meetings in which its provisions had been discussed, and it was the religious aspect that attracted most attention. These differences were reflected within the cabinet – Gladstone wished to keep a strong religious element, but Forster was in favour of a more liberal treatment. It was not until June that the cabinet agreed on the way forward, and the prime minister himself rose on 16th June to explain the changes made to the bill to the House. Although he took an hour and a half to describe these, he tried to make them sound relatively small, needing the elimination of two clauses and some extra words in a third. The changes were, however, fundamental to the religious aspects of elementary education. Probably the least satisfactory part of the original bill was leaving local boards to decide the nature of religious teaching in the new rate-supported schools, and Gladstone accepted that this might lead to local rivalry between different sects to achieve influence with the boards, and the objection of many people to paying for religious education out of public funds would remain.

Various proposals had been made to change this, but the government had accepted one made by William Cowper-Temple, the member for south Oxfordshire, a nephew of Lord Melbourne and probably the illegitimate son of Viscount Palmerston. Cowper-Temple thought that opinion was never going to be calmed on this subject unless the new board schools were made non-denominational, and the only way for that to be done in a way that had at least a hope of being enforceable at law was to insist that in all new board schools there should be no religious teaching at all, except for reading the Bible. But this led on to the fact that existing voluntary schools, which were mostly denominational, would also be receiving support from the rates. So it was finally decided not to allow boards to give financial support to voluntary schools, which would remain entirely funded by the Privy Council grant, and that this grant would be increased by about fifty percent to give a measure of equality with the board schools.

The only other change in the bill was be to make the conscience clause a 'timetable' conscience clause, meaning that in voluntary schools religious teaching

Education, Education, Education

William Francis Cowper-Temple, 1811-88, became MP for Hertford in 1835, and was private secretary to his uncle and prime minister Lord Melbourne. Thereafter he held a variety of government offices including in 1857 vice-president of the committee of council on education, and it was as a result of his experience there that he played a prominent part in the education debates of Gladstone's government. His famous amendment helped the 1870 Act pass after Gladstone had given way on the religious question. On the death of his step-father Viscount Palmerston he inherited much of his property in Ireland and Hampshire, and was later created Baron Mount-Temple.

would have to be done at certain times which would allow parents to withdraw their children if need be. Thus the bill would create a dual system of education.

How far the Conservative leadership had known of these proposals in advance is not certain, but in his reply Disraeli seized on the fact these major changes were being introduced at a late stage in the session, indeed he doubted whether there was time to consider the bill properly now. He criticised the government for taking four months to decide on these changes, when, he said, it was clear which way public opinion was going several weeks ago. Disraeli claimed that the country wanted a national education scheme with religion at its centre; but the bill now had departed from this, and would not satisfy public opinion. The proposed changes would put a great onus on teachers, who, if they chose could put a sectarian or religious gloss on passages from the Bible. That being the case, surely it would be better to allow clergymen to attend to this part of the education, rather than an unbeneficed teacher – they would become the new sacerdotal class.

Disraeli's speech was rather rambling and was criticised in The Times the next day for being negative, but Sir John's tone was different when he made a short contribution, and said that no time should be lost in reprinting the bill in its new form, and in starting the committee stage next week.

The motion to go into committee was debated the following Monday, and it opened with an amendment proposed by Henry Richard, member for Merthyr

Tydfil, who had at one time been a congregational minister, and was the informal leader of Welsh MPs. He proposed:

> That the grants to existing denominational schools should not be increased; and that, in any national system of elementary education, the attendance should be everywhere compulsory, and the religious instruction should be supplied by voluntary effort and not out of public funds.

His contention was that under the latest version of the bill an increased amount of state funds would go, via the committee of council on education, to the voluntary schools, the preponderance of which were Anglican. He concluded by saying that the state should look after literary and scientific instruction, and that Christian ministers should, by their trained minds, lead children to the knowledge and love of God. "Leave unto Caesar the things that are Caesar's, and unto God the things that are God's."

Sir John made a substantial contribution to the debate, and began by expressing his fear that the old arguments would continue indefinitely, and that the bill would never get passed. He pleaded:

> The discussion on the altered measure was opened on Thursday evening by the first minister of the Crown in a tone of charity and Christian feeling, which I hope may pervade the entire debate. I hope that we shall approach this subject remembering what is the real object we have in view. The object we have in view is the education of the children of the masses of this country. Let us bear in mind that it is not our object to give a triumph to one particular denomination or to inflict any injury or mortification upon another.

But there were, he said, two matters that he would like to bring to the attention of the government regarding the altered bill. One concerned that fact that, according to the 'timetable conscience' clause, religious instruction had to done at the beginning or end of the school day, which he regarded as impractical, and the second, much more general point, was that he thought that public opinion, which he fully supported, was still in favour of education being founded on religion, otherwise how could morality, which it was so important to instil in children, be taught? In view of the danger of interdenominational strife, he was not against the rule that no formularies or catechisms be taught in the new board schools, but that was too negative. Instead of this, we ought to adopt the positive proposition that the Bible should be read and taught. Henry Richard had proposed that this instruction could be adequately dealt with by Sunday schools and parents. But Sir John did not believe this could ever be adequate: "No man who knows what the cottage dwellings of England are like in the rural districts, or what is the character of the lodgings of the artisans in our great towns, will ever contend that the elements of religion can be taught in such homes, or that the children, in this regard, can be entrusted to their parents".

Sir John was followed by William Forster, who explained at length why he thought Richard's motion difficult to translate into practical action, and could be interpreted in different ways. As to compulsion he readily agreed that the present permissive proposal was not likely to achieve the long term goal of having all children attend schools; but it was a sensible beginning, and he was sure would in time lead to the desired result.

The debate continued for another three days, but after Gladstone wound up only 60 members could be found to oppose going into committee, and 421 voted in favour.

Once in committee on 27th June Sir John made occasional interjections, but he confined his proposals for change to the two matters he had mentioned in his earlier speech. The first was to allow managers more freedom in the timetabling of the religious instruction periods, rather than have them at the beginning or end of the day. This may seem a matter of detail, but probably what Sir John wanted was to allow these periods to be placed more centrally in the timetable, so that more children might attend them. In this he was supported by the member for Westminster, William Henry Smith, the newsagent who was at the beginning of a long and distinguished parliamentary career and who, like Sir John, was keen on furthering education, but believed religion should remain at its centre. Sir John claimed he was backed by a petition signed by 2,000 teachers, by a memorial from Leicester, and from the results of a survey of teachers in south Wales.

However, Forster opposed Sir John's proposal, mainly on the grounds that it would offend those who thought that religious teaching should be kept separate from education, and, once school attendance became compulsory, which looked increasingly to be the way things were going, there would be strong objection to making children attend school, in which religious education was mixed up in the curriculum. Sir John's motion was defeated by a majority of one hundred.

On 30th June, proposed adding these words:

> The Holy Scriptures shall form part of the daily reading and teaching in such schools, but no religious catechism or religious formulary which is distinctive of any particular denomination shall be taught therein.

This was Sir John's last-ditch attempt to nudge the new system in a more religious direction, but it was greeted by cries of 'withdraw, withdraw', and he must have realized that it stood no chance of being accepted. He said that he had deliberately not taken up much of the committee's time so far, keen as he was to see the bill become law, but he hoped that they would allow him now to explain why he had made this proposal. In deference to the non-conformist interest, he had already accepted that no religious catechisms or formularies should be taught; but in return Sir John stressed that the "whole country" wanted the Holy

Scriptures to be taught in schools, and asked whether it was consistent with their duty to pass an act in which there was no provision that there should be religious teaching in our schools.

Schools supported by the committee of council for education had, under the revised code, to be run by a distinct denomination, or have the scriptures read daily, yet for whom were these new board schools being established? For the poorest and humblest, so there should be some positive provision demanding that the children should be instructed in the Holy scriptures.

However, although Forster paid tribute to Sir John's "consistent, disinterested and useful support for the bill", it was with a good deal of pain that he felt compelled to oppose this insertion. He did not believe it would further the cause of religious education to force school boards in this way. When the committee divided only 81 members supported Sir John, while 250 opposed him.

The bill continued in committee for several more evenings, and on 14th July the election of school boards by secret ballot generated a heated debate. The use of the secret ballot for parliamentary elections had been pushed by more liberal members for decades, but most Tories were against. So the debate strayed from the Elementary Education Bill to the use of ballots more generally. Sir John evidently found the debate frustrating, as it was impeding the progress of the bill. He said:

> Why should the present measure be complicated by the introduction of a mode of voting which was strongly objected to by many hon. members – not on party grounds, but on principle? I have always opposed the ballot on principle, being of opinion that all public functions ought to be discharged openly and in the face of day. I cannot conceive any greater unwisdom than the complication of the bill by unnecessarily importing into it a mode of voting which formed the subject of differences between different classes in this House.

Those opposed to the ballot tried hard to have it removed, and put the committee to no less than fourteen divisions, but in the end the government had their way.

The bill finished its committee stage on 21st July, and the following day was read a third time. Opponents of the bill were determined to have a final say, and the bitterest opposition came from the dissenters' champion Edward Miall who, like Forster, was a member for Bradford. Miall complained that dissenters had supported Gladstone at the last election on the basis of promises he had made toward their causes, but now they felt badly let down, both in respect of the Education Bill and other recent measures. He was wholly against giving public money for denominational education.

Gladstone was highly critical of Miall, and then Sir John spoke. Although a political opponent of the prime minister, he quite agreed with Gladstone's

Edward Miall (1809-81) was a Congregational minister and leading non-conformist, who campaigned for the disestablishment of the Church of England, and founded 'The Nonconformist' magazine. He was against any state interference in religion, and opposed the government grant to voluntary Anglican schools. He also campaigned strongly against church rates. He entered parliament in 1855 as member for Rochdale, and was later the member, with William Forster, for Bradford, and the two differed in their attitude to education.

rebuke, and said "My feeling and my hope is, that men of all parties may concur in regarding it as the first duty of the country to give this great measure a fair trial". He said everyone agreed that the bill had short-comings, and no doubt in the course of time would be amended, but for now he supported it. He repeated that the great regret he, and many of his colleagues, had of the bill was that there was no mention of religion except in a restrictive sense, and that it was unfortunate that the Holy Scriptures were not required to be taught in schools. He also regretted the introduction of the ballot into the bill, which he felt had been done by the government to keep its own back-benchers on-side. But Sir John concluded on a positive note:

> I, therefore, say, whatever may be the defects and shortcomings of the Bill – and I do hope that hon. gentlemen below the gangway will remember that those defects and shortcomings exist in the opinion of both sides of the House – that I accept the measure with thankfulness and with joy. As time passes, in all probability this measure, like all great ones, will need amendment, and correction, and adaptation to altered circumstances; but I believe it will supply a want which has long been a scandal in English legislation; it will tend in a very large degree to promote the welfare of the country; and I cordially agree with the words which have just been spoken by the right hon. gentleman the first minister of the crown, that the gratitude of the country and of all parties is due to my right hon. friend the vice-president of the council for that happy combination of great ability with fine temper which has enabled my right hon. friend to bring this measure to a successful conclusion.

However, after the debate the Elementary Education Bill was given its third reading without a division.

LORD HAMPTON – HIS LATER YEARS

Sir John had only left his office of minister for war 18 months before, and he continued to take an interest in military affairs. He was watching the progress of his successor, Edward Cardwell, in reducing military expenditure. England had not been involved in a war since the Crimean war of 1854-55, but the continental states had not been so peaceful, and in 1870 the unification of Germany led to conflict with France, which started in late July. In fact the Franco-Prussian war was quite short lived, and led to France's complete defeat in January 1871, a revolutionary change of government there, and the loss by France of her eastern provinces, not regained until 1918. Emperor Napoleon III was exiled to England, where he died three years later.

There was a fear that England might be drawn into the war, and on 2nd August 1870 the government proposed a motion of supply that 20,000 more troops be added to the army. The first speaker, the radical and pacifist Sir Wilfred Lawson, was totally against even contemplating intervention, and spoke against any increase in the army. But Sir John, who spoke next, quickly dismissed these arguments, and said he quite agreed with the proposed strengthening of the army. However, he had been watching the substantial reductions in military expenditure with concern, and he chose that moment to attack what he thought was the irresponsible course being taken by Gladstone and his government. His main point was that under Cardwell the number of serving soldiers had reduced by 24,000 to 113,000. Sir John spoke at length about all aspects of the situation, including the use of the reserves, and thought that:

> An idea prevailed among foreign nations that we were devoted to trade, that we wished to live cheaply, and that we cared little about our national honour. From the time of what I would call that most weak and pusillanimous policy of our Government not to interfere when Denmark [the German speaking states of Schleswig and Holstein] was crushed by Prussia, the position of England in the eyes of the world has been changed. In my opinion, the reputation of England on the continent fell from that moment, and had never revived.

Cardwell gave what reads now like a sensible reply to Sir John's criticisms – the government's policy mainly rested on bringing troops that were garrisoned in our colonies back to be stationed at home. However, an editorial in The Graphic made fun of Cardwell, who had a very unmilitary bearing, and thought that Sir John and other opposition speakers 'tore his statement to threads'.

During the summer of 1870 Sir John was much occupied with the restoration of Worcester cathedral, raising money for the third appeal, but that matter will be dealt with in a later chapter. He was certainly back at Westwood by 27th July when he attended an archery society meeting at Grafton Manor near Bromsgrove, and in August he played a part in a great county social occasion, the visit by Prince and Princess Christian to Malvern during August. Prince

Christian of Schleswig-Holstein had married Princess Helena, Queen Victoria's third daughter, in 1870. One of their visits was to the Lechmeres of Rhydd Court, when Sir John and his son and daughter-in-law were among the guests. After lunch the party enjoyed a boat trip on the Severn – Leader Williams, engineer to the Severn Navigation Commissioners, was in charge to make sure there were no accidents! The Prince and Princess also visited Madresfield Court (where they presented the prizes at an archery society meeting), the Earl of Coventry's estate at Croome, and Hagley Hall, and Sir John was present on all these occasions. Finally, after lunching at Hagley, the Prince and Princess honoured Sir John by visiting Westwood on 20th August. They were met at the station by Sir John at 5.00 p.m., and after a drive in the park a large party was assembled for dinner. The guests included the Lyttelton, the Sandys, the Lechmeres, and the Amphletts from Wychbold, as well as Sir John's son and daughter-in-law, so the royal couple must have become quite familiar with the Worcestershire county families before they left for the Three Choirs Festival in Hereford the following week, whence they proceeded to Balmoral.

With the Franco-Prussian war raging there was not only a fear that Britain might become involved, but also sympathy for the wounded soldiers and bereaved families on both sides. On 27th August Sir John attended a meeting of the Worcestershire Society for the Sick and Wounded in War, and proposed the launch of a subscription. When he spoke at the annual dinner of the Worcestershire Agricultural Society a few days later he was pleased to report that the prospect of Britain becoming involved had lessened. In early September when proposing the loyal toast at the harvest home at Rushock, a village near Droitwich, Sir John referred to the difficult position the queen was in, as, while she rightly supported her government's policy of neutrality, she had two sons-in-law "constantly in the ranks of the battle, and from day to day she could not tell what domestic sorrow each telegram might bring upon her".

Chapter 4
The years 1871 and 1872

Sir John began the year by continuing to support the campaign against local taxation by raising it in quarter sessions. The 1871 Epiphany sessions were held on 2nd January, and Sir John, bringing a petition with 200 signatures, had given notice of a motion he wished to put forward. It read:

> That, inasmuch as many of the charges now paid out of county rates such as police, lunatic asylums, militia stores, coroners, gaols &c are rendered necessary, not for the benefit of one particular class, but for the community at large, it is just and politic that the national exchequer should contribute more largely to these charges, if not altogether defray them, and that a petition to this effect be presented to the House of Commons.

Sir John had carefully prepared his speech, which was peppered with statistics: rates, which were levied only on real property, which was worth £100 million a year, yielded £16 million, whereas income tax was levied on income worth £300 million a year, but as this went to the national exchequer, contributed nothing to the national items in his resolution. Of the £16 million, he reckoned that only £5.5 million was spent on local services, the rest on 'national items'. Rates, he said, yielded four times as much as manufacturing property. The costs of education and of road maintenance would also soon become a burden on the rates. Roads, Sir John said, should be paid by those who used them. Quoting two local towns, he said large numbers of invalids travelled to Cheltenham in the hope of improving their health "by putting water into their insides, and at Malvern other invalids expected to derive benefit by putting water on their outsides", but they paid nothing to the maintenance of the roads. Education too was a national question and should be paid, not by a section, but by the whole population. The motion received much support, and after the deletion of the words 'if not altogether defray them', was agreed.

On 20th January Sir John formed part of a deputation from the Society of Arts to the education secretary, William Forster. They wished to broach two subjects, the first being the advantages of introducing drill into schools. Lord Lennox was the principal speaker on this question, pointing to "the habits of discipline and order which drill produced, and the increased value of the services produced by drilled youths in every department of work when they had left school". Edwin Chadwick endorsed these remarks, speaking of "the benefits young men derived from drill, which formed a counter-attraction to the beer house".

Sir John endorsed what had been said about the drill, but also had to report the decision of the council of the Society of Arts that the teaching of singing should be made compulsory in all primary schools. He paid tribute to Forster in bringing the Elementary Education Act into being, and deplored the regrettable scenes earlier in the week when Forster had addressed his constituents in Bradford. A large and noisy meeting had passed a resolution disapproving the Act, and the means employed to secure its adoption in a Liberal House of Commons. Many felt that the Bill had been watered down to secure Conservative support, but Sir John said this did not represent public opinion, and that the "calm deliberate feeling of the intelligent classes would heartily condemn and repudiate it".

Apart from serving twice as first lord of the Admiralty, Sir John had been president of the Institute of Naval Architects (now the Royal Institute) since its inception in 1860, and would remain so until just before he died. In the 1860s and 70s there was a continual succession of shipping disasters, and in the early days of the Institute the loss of the 'London' in stormy seas in the Bay of Biscay had had much publicity. Sir John had suggested that it had been over-loaded before leaving England. Other losses followed, including that of the 'Captain', the first Royal Navy ship with a gun turret. In his opening addresses to the Institute's annual meetings Sir John had spoken on a number of occasions about this scandal, and supported moves to give the Board of Trade increased powers to ensure that ships were sea-worthy, and not overloaded.

Sir John's first speech in parliament in 1871 was on 22nd February during the debate on Samuel Plimsoll's Merchant Shipping Survey Bill. Samuel Plimsoll was a leading campaigner on this subject, and in introducing his bill he gave a detailed account of the problems of marine insurance. He claimed that ship owners were encouraged to over-insure unseaworthy ships, which then foundered with loss of life to the sailors, but profit for the owners. He gave examples he knew of ships with rotten masts and sails, and pointed out that in the last few years over 1,000 sailors a year had been lost round Britain's coasts. The purpose of the bill was a requirement that all ships be inspected before being allowed to go to sea, not just those about which there were complaints, and that every ship should have a load line marked on the side enabling a quick visual check to ensure it was not overloaded. He also pointed to the injustice of the law of the time by which sailors could be forced to go to sea on vessels that proved to be unsound, on pain of imprisonment.

Samuel Plimsoll (1824-98) went into business as a coal merchant, but conflict with established interests led to his bankruptcy. He developed a keen sense of social justice, and at his second attempt entered parliament in 1868 as an 'advanced liberal'. Initially keen to promote safer coal mining, his interest in ships came from James Hall, a Tyneside shipowner, who abhorred the loss of life caused by sending overloaded sub-standard ships to sea. This became Plimsoll's main campaign, and although on occasions he went too far in his condemnations, he was eventually successful when load lines gradually became mandatory.

Sir John spoke in brief but strong support of the bill, saying he "felt bound to express his deep regret at the shameful manner in which life and property had been sacrificed by the overloading of ships". He said that not only was legislation needed, but he repeated a request he had made the previous year for a royal commission of enquiry. But Chichester Parkinson Fortescue, president of the Board of Trade, said that the government had its own Merchant Shipping Bill, but it was so long and cumbersome that it was currently in abeyance. However, if Plimsoll agreed to withdraw his bill, the government would extract those clauses from its own bill that dealt with safety at sea, and introduce them as a separate measure. This was later done, although the measure did not prove very effective.

The subject of local taxation came up in the House on 28th February, when the Tory member for South Devon, Sir Massey Lopes, put forward a motion similar to that which Sir John had presented to quarter sessions, and asked for an enquiry. Lopes was an agricultural improver, and believed the farming interest was over-taxed. In his long-running campaign, he put forward similar motions annually. His long speech showed his command of the figures (although some were later disputed), and he concluded that national taxation accounted for £40 million net of interest on the national debt, and local taxation £30 million. National taxation bore, he thought, fairly on the whole community, whereas local taxation, principally rates on real property, bore too heavily on just one class, the owners and occupiers of houses and land.

The Years 1871 and 1872

Sir John spoke in favour of the motion, and mentioned the petition from quarter sessions that he had presented that day. He pointed out, as he had at Worcester, that new burdens were constantly being added to the rates – the maintenance of turnpike roads last year, and the new education act from next year, and he claimed that local rates had increased almost fourfold in the last 30 years. But in response, prime minister Gladstone found many of the arguments fallacious, saying that it was untrue that rural land owners bore an unfair burden, as occupiers of houses in the towns also bore a considerable share. But in any case the government had its own measure on the subject ready to be brought forward. He preferred action to another enquiry, and the motion was lost.

In fact the government did introduce a Rating and Local Government Bill on 3rd April, which proposed wide-ranging reforms in the rating system, the Poor Law Board, and the incidence of local rates, which would have gone a little way to meet the demands for reform. But the House was much occupied with army reforms and the introduction of the secret ballot that session, and, beyond renaming the Poor Law Board the Local Government Board and giving it extra functions, there was no time to enact the other provisions.

A major reform being introduced by the government was the Army Regulation Bill. This formed part of what are known as the Cardwell reforms, which together made major changes in the army, learning lessons from the recent success of the professional Prussian army in France, and putting right some of the major deficiencies that had been revealed during the Crimean War and Indian

Edward Cardwell, 1813-86, entered parliament as a Peelite in 1842, but for his later political career was Liberal MP for Oxford. In the 1860s he held a variety of political offices, but his greatest achievements were as minster for war in 1868-74, when he re-organised the war office, abolished purchase, devised the split battalion system and increased the reserves. Pressured by Gladstone on the one hand to reduce expenditure even more, but lacking enthusiastic support from some of his own colleagues and the Duke of Cambridge, passing the reforms put great stress on Cardwell, whose health suffered.

Mutiny, which had hitherto been resisted by the ultra-conservative army and its commander-in-chief, the Duke of Cambridge.

The debate on the second reading focused on the proposed abolition of the purchase of commissions, and on the third night of the debate Sir John, who acted as the opposition spokesman on army affairs, opened the debate by speaking for over an hour in defence of the purchase system. When minister for war in 1868 he had defended the system in a debate triggered by a leading opponent of purchase, George Trevelyan. Sir John had then admitted that, if he was starting from scratch, he would not allow commissions to be purchased. He did not repeat this admission in 1871, but set out the arguments in favour of purchase as clearly as he could, although he must have realised that, under reforming prime minister Gladstone, its days were numbered.

His main attack was financial – purchased commissions would have to be bought back, and the regulation value of all commissions at that time was thought to be around £8 million, but Sir John thought the final cost, including the cost of non-regulation prices, might be over £10 million. What advantages to the country had the government put forward to justify such an enormous expenditure? Very little, Sir John thought. Here was a government under a prime minister intent on economising expenditure, yet proposing to spend all that money to abolish a system that, Sir John thought, still held many advantages. If officers were not to enter by purchase, what did the government propose as alternatives? One was to make it easier to enter the army from the militia. But how were militia officers appointed? By lords lieutenants, so surely this system was just as liable to be subject to social, and even possibly financial, influence. At least when officers purchased their commission it was done openly and social position did not come into it;

> The point I wish to press upon the House is that under this system we are free from patronage and favour, jobbing and political influence. A young man gets his name put down for purchase, and when his turn comes round he is brought up for examination – which is most fairly conducted, for in my own personal experience I have known cases where men of very humble position have come out at the top of the list, and where the sons of noblemen have either been at the bottom or failed altogether, and were unable to enter the Army.

Sir John also pointed out that officers would certainly be more reluctant to leave the service if they could not sell their commissions, which could block the promotion of younger men, or necessitate an expensive retirement scheme to control.

Sir John was followed by George Trevelyan, who, with Sir John, took up most of the evening's debate. Trevelyan thought Sir John's estimate of the cost was exaggerated. Commissions would not always have to be purchased back, and in any case the cost would be spread over several years. He reminded the House that the purchase system in the Royal Navy had been abolished in 1688, as was the purchase of all other offices under the crown except in the army, and he thought this had clearly been to the manifest advantage to the nation.

A few days later Sir John and George Trevelyan crossed swords again, when Trevelyan proposed that the system of honorary colonelcies be abolished, and no new appointments made. The award of an honorary colonelcy to an officer added between £1,000 and £2,000 a year to his pay but involved no active duties, and was simply an out-dated way of giving him a sinecure. Trevelyan made some comparisons between the British and Prussian armies. In the former, the cost of each general (many of whom also had honorary colonelcies) far exceeded that of the latter, which had a much more rational and straightforward system of pay. But the minister for war, Edward Cardwell, said this question was bound up with the whole system of pay and pensions, and should not be considered in isolation. Sir John agreed with much of what Cardwell said, and thought it quite wrong that a back-bench MP should attempt to interfere with the army's organisation in this way – this was a question for the executive. But he admitted that he had always thought the system of honorary colonels "an anomaly and a most objectionable way of paying for the services of officers".

The following day a matter came up touching safety at sea. Lord Claud Hamilton, MP for Kings Lynn, proposed that a harbour of refuge be built at Filey, on the east coast of Yorkshire south of Scarborough. The provision of harbours of refuge had been investigated by a select committee which reported in 1858, and Sir John, who was then first lord, appointed a commission to make recommendations. But successive governments had not implemented the recommendations, mainly for financial reasons, but also because it was felt that improvements to shipping and to existing harbours had somewhat reduced the value of special harbours of refuge.

Lord Hamilton made a carefully argued case for Filey, saying there were no similar harbours between the Firth of Forth and Sheerness, and that the ships engaged in the important coal trade often became trapped by storms in that area, and that there had been regular shipwrecks and loss of life. He also pointed to what he saw as the growing threat to our national security from Prussia, and that we needed a Royal Naval station suitably placed to guard that coast, now that the threat from France was much reduced.

But the president of the Board of Trade, Chichester Parkinson-Fortescue, resisted these arguments, saying it would not be right to deal with the question piecemeal, and in any case thought there were better ways of spending the £1 million or so the Filey project would cost. But Sir John made a contribution in strong support of Hamilton, and first made a reference to prime minister Gladstone, with whom his relations were sometimes tetchy:

SIR JOHN PAKINGTON

> It is my intention to support the motion of my noble friend, even at the risk of again incurring the imputations of the present prime minister, who attacked me during his celebrated Lancashire tour for the extravagance I had shown in supporting former motions upon the subject of the shipping interest…

> I take part in this debate from the consideration – and from that consideration alone – that it is our duty to do what we can to save human life, and to protect the commercial interests of this country. Upon this broad and simple ground I am disposed to assent to the strong words of the hon. member for Leeds [an earlier speaker], and say that I am ashamed of the manner in which year after year this subject has been evaded by ministers of the crown.

That provoked an intervention by Gladstone, who pointed out that Sir John had been a minister himself. Yes, replied Sir John, but he had been active when first lord in appointing a commission to make recommendations. He accepted that harbours of refuge were not the complete answer to loss of life a sea, but pointed to the fact that the loss of life on the east coast was higher than the south coast, where there were more harbours. This led to a bad tempered exchange with Parkinson-Fortescue about the exact figures involved.

But Sir John was not to be put off, and said:

> I feel great regret at the line Her Majesty's government are taking on this question; and I regret it at this moment more than at any other, because the time is gone when the government may use the argument that they are unwilling to incur expense. A short time ago the motto of the present government was 'economy', now it appeared to be 'money no object'.

Sir John was, of course referring to the great expenditure proposed to be incurred in abolishing the purchase of commissions, and concluded:

> I, for one, shall give a hearty vote in favour of the motion of my noble friend, thanking him for having brought it forward in so able a manner, and, in conclusion, I wish to express my conviction that the day is not distant when the shipping of England will have some protection afforded to it on our dangerous eastern coast.

Gladstone, who is reputed to have had a quick temper, did not at all like Sir John saying that ministers should be 'ashamed'. Sir John retorted that he had merely been repeating the words of another speaker, but Gladstone said that when repeated by Sir John "they acquire tenfold force"! He said that when he had pointed out that Sir John himself had been a minister, he was not referring to 1858, as Sir John had thought. He continued with a heavy note of sarcasm:

> I will venture to remind the right hon. gentleman, who is so 'ashamed' that any minister in this country can allow such a question as this to sleep, and be so unmindful of the sacred duty of rescuing human life from danger, that he sat in great contentment in the position of minister during part of the session of

The Years 1871 and 1872

1866, the whole of the session of 1867, and the whole of the session of 1868. Whether he was 'ashamed' or not we cannot tell; whether he was struggling in the agonies his mind may have endured we are unable to tell; but external evidence of such agonies there was none. During that period the right hon. gentleman appeared to me to enjoy as much comfort and satisfaction as fate ordinarily allows to anyone in the position of a minister.

Gladstone then carefully explained the difficulties of the question, including how it might be possible to get both local communities and the shipping interest to help finance the harbours. Before the debate ended Parkinson-Fortescue felt he had to reply on behalf of Sir John to Gladstone's jibes about the Derby government of 1866-68. That government, he said, had principally come into office to pass a reform bill that Gladstone himself had been unable to do. The government party had been in a minority in the House, and Parkinson-Fortescue was sure that had it tried to pass any measure such as was now being proposed, Gladstone would have been the first to pounce on it and stop it.

The last speaker was the chancellor of the exchequer, Robert Lowe, and he was equally dismissive. He said rather sarcastically that Sir John thought his appointment of a commission in 1858 "which the right hon. member for Droitwich was so proud of having appointed that he seemed to think that its appointment placed him on a pinnacle of merit". These words angered Sir John, who rose and said "I hope that when the right hon. gentleman refers to me he will not grossly misrepresent me...", at which there were cries of "order", as members were not allowed to speak twice in the same debate. However, the speaker calmed things down, and Lord Hamilton's motion was defeated by a majority of 35.

William Gladstone, 1809-98, led a reforming government between 1868 and 1874, In addition to the army reforms and the 1870 Education Act the secret ballot was introduced, the Irish Church disestablished, and an attempt was made for Irish land reform. Some thought these reforms went too far too fast, which led to Gladstone's defeat in 1874.

SIR JOHN PAKINGTON

The Army Regulation Bill spent some time in committee, and Sir John made a number of interventions, but realised that the Bill would pass. However he did feel strongly enough to reassert his views against the principle of the abolition of the purchase of commissions.

Sir John was a long-standing member of the Patriotic Fund, properly called the Royal Patriotic fund. This had been established during the Crimean War in October 1854 to help the widows and dependents of dead and wounded soldiers. It was established by royal decree, which appointed commissioners, and the subscribers' list was headed by the queen, who gave £1,000, and Prince Albert and the Duke of Wellington who each gave £500. Prince Albert was the first chairman, followed after his death by the Duke of Newcastle, then by the Duke of Cambridge. The list of forty initial commissioners included leading aristocrats and statesmen, including Sir John Pakington. The commissioners had to arrange for meetings to be held throughout the country to open subscription lists, and gave their services freely, to keep operating costs to a minimum.

The funds, which included generous donations from the empire, approached £1.5 million, and it soon became clear that surplus capital would be available beyond the claims of widows and orphans. In July 1857 Queen Victoria laid the foundation stone of the Royal Victoria Patriotic Asylum for Girls, as it was called, in Wandsworth, in a grand ceremony attended by Sir John. Its purpose was to care for and educate girls orphaned in the conflict. A similar establishment for boys was also built nearby.

As the commissioners only met a few times a year, an executive committee was formed, of which Sir John was a member, to deal with more routine matters. A house committee was also formed to oversee the running of the asylum, but nevertheless in 1863 it was found that gross mismanagement of the school had led to abuses, including the burning to death of a girl in solitary confinement, and arbitrary and sadistic punishments. The matter reached the Commons and in June Sir John had had to explain in detail what had happened, and what steps had been taken to prevent a recurrence.

In 1867 the Fund was re-organised by an act of parliament. New commissioners were appointed, and its remit was widened to include victims of other later wars. Up till then the commissioners had been responsible only to themselves, which had led to complaints about a lack of transparency in their work, but the act now made the commissioners ultimately responsible to parliament. Sir John continued as a commissioner and his work on the executive committee, and ultimately must have become one of the longest serving commissioners.

Another organisation that Sir John had been a long standing member of, although in this case in a rather passive role, was the Trinity House Corporation. He had been appointed an 'elder brother' of Trinity House in February 1858 when he was first lord of the Admiralty, and remained so until his death. It had been traditional to have both 'active' and 'eminent' elder brethren who did not take an active part in the management of the corporation, and Sir John belonged to this latter category, but nevertheless he regularly attended Trinity House functions, including their dinner on 24th June, when the Duke of Cambridge presided.

On 7th August 1871 a matter came up in the House that Sir John had taken a great interest in, both because of his concern for increasing safety at sea, and his previous connection with the Admiralty. HMS Megaera was an iron ship launched in 1849, and on 22 February 1871 had left Devonport bound for Australia with about 300 men on board, including army recruits for Australia. It was soon found that in rough weather the portholes allowed water into the main deck, spoiling the men's possessions. The ship therefore put in at Cork to remove some cargo to increase the freeboard and to move some badly stowed cargo. She reached the Cape without further incident, but about half way across the southern ocean bound for Australia she began to leak. As the situation deteriorated the captain decided to head for the nearest land, the small unpopulated island of St Paul's, and there the ship anchored on 17th June. It was soon found that the iron plates under water were disintegrating, and after three anchors had been carried away the ship was beached by driving her hard onto the sand. All the crew could do now was to wait to be rescued. Fortunately there were plenty of stores aboard and abundant seafood and wild goats, and temporary shelters were erected against the stormy southern winter.

Almost a full month elapsed before the ship was spotted, and on August 1st a telegram was despatched that alerted the world to the crew's plight, but it was not until the end of August that the last of the crew were taken off the island.

These dramatic events were widely publicised in England. On 5th August a letter appeared in The Times, in which Edward Reed, who had resigned as chief constructor to the navy the year before, wrote that 'some years ago' he had examined the Megaera, and found her plates to be wearing thin. He reported that she was only fit for a short time of further service. In his letter he wrote that the fact that his report had been ignored was typical of the Admiralty, and, rather dramatically, that 'the present administration of the Admiralty is utterly inconsistent with the safety of Her Majesty's naval officers and seamen and, if it is continued, can have before long but one result – that of the refusal of brother officers and men to embark in Her Majesty's ships'.

Two days later Sir John Hay asked a question about the Megaera in the House. Hay had served in the navy before going into politics, and was always ready to criticise the government's handling of naval matters. In a long statement he said he was familiar with the Megaera from his naval days, and in his view she should never have been sent on a voyage to Australia. George Goschen, member for the City of London, who had only recently been appointed first lord of the Admiralty, replied for the government. He described at length the events at Cork, although, as he pointed out, these were probably not relevant to the loss of the ship. He had gone through all the information he could find on the Megaera, and nearly all the reports about her found that she was a good seaworthy ship, despite her age. As to Mr Reed's statement about her thin plates, there was no official report about this. It seems that Reed had given this information privately to Hugh Childers, a lord of the Admiralty, in 1866, but as Reed had not wanted to make his report official, it had not become a public record.

Towards the end of the debate Sir John spoke. He said the whole affair was very discreditable to the Admiralty, and there were several aspects that needed looking into further. How was the ship allowed to sail from Plymouth in such an unseaworthy condition, even if that was not connected to her loss? From his time at the Admiralty in 1866 he knew that the Megaera was known as an 'worn out old ship', and, whatever the truth about Reed's report, the ship was utterly unfit to be sent to Australia, and the whole system that had allowed this to happen must be examined. Sir John was followed by Gladstone, who said he agreed entirely that a thorough enquiry must be held.

HMS Megaera was launched in 1849, one of the earliest iron ships in the navy. It was subsequently found that she was made of iron which splintered badly, making her unsuitable for use as a warship. Instead she was used as a storeship and troop ship.

When Capt. Thrupp returned to England he and his fellow officers were court marshalled and totally exonerated, after which a Royal Commission under Lord Lawrence investigated the whole affair. It found that HMS Megaera had not been fully inspected since 1864, partly because parts of the interior were inaccessible without removing the engines, and that those who should have done so had various excuses for not so doing. The dangers of corrosion in iron ships were by 1871 well known, and one method to protect them was by applying a cement or concrete to the interior surfaces. One such was 'Spence's cement', and this was applied to the Megaera. Later this composition was found to be ineffective, but nothing was ever done to replace it in the Megaera. The commissioners mainly blamed the navy controller, Sir Spencer Robinson, but many others were at fault as well. They were critical of the workings of the Admiralty, where the keeping of reports was inefficient, and the reports themselves lacked detail. Edward Reed's report of 1866 was never found, and it was concluded that it was only made verbally.

Shortly after, the loss of another Royal Navy ship, HMS Captain, was brought up in the House by Lord Henry Lennox, who had served as secretary to the Admiralty under Sir John in 1866. This ship was an experimental 'turret' ship, having its guns on two revolving turrets rather than the traditional 'broadside' layout. Its construction had been campaigned for by Captain Cowper Phipps Coles over many years, and pressure from public opinion and the press persuaded the Admiralty in 1866 to finance the construction of a ship to Coles' design. The Duke of Somerset was then first lord, and had almost got to the point of signing the papers when Sir John took over in July 1866. The ship was subsequently built, and seemed to perform well in her early voyages. However, in strengthening winds off Cape Finisterre during the night of 6th to 7th September 1870, despite shortening sail, the ship capsized, with the loss of nearly 500

Capt. Cowper Phipps Coles, 1819-70, saw naval service in the Crimea, when he was promoted captain. While in the Sea of Azov he designed and constructed a shallow draft gun-raft, which carried a heavy gun protected by an iron shield. From this evolved the idea of a revolving protected gun turret on ships. Due to the weight of the turret the ships would have a low freeboard, and after securing the support of Prince Albert and large sections of the press, the Royal Sovereign was converted to a mastless turret ship, Coles having sold his patent to the Admiralty for £5,000 and was paid £100 for every turret built. A further ship, HMS Monarch, was built with turrets, but Coles was still dissatisfied, and eventually the Admiralty agreed that Lairds should build a ship entirely to Coles' designs, with tragic consequences.

souls including Coles himself and sons of both Hugh Childers, first lord of the Admiralty, and Thomas Baring, under secretary of state for war. Sir John also lost a relative in the tragedy. He was Herbert Francis Murray, a midshipman aged 20, who was the younger son of Rev. Francis Henry Murray, rector of Chislehurst, Kent, the brother of Sir John's second wife Augusta Murray – Sir John had probably got him into the navy when he was first lord in 1866.

The cause of the tragedy was discovered to be that calculations of the Captain's freeboard and stability had not been done accurately, and it was found that at a roll angle of over 18° she became unstable. Although revolving turrets became an essential part of battleship design, Coles' insistence on having a full rig as well made the ship top heavy.

Lennox's motion was to set up a select committee to investigate the loss, but it seems his main motive was to show that the mistake was not made during his own tenure of office, but by the next first lord, Hugh Childers, who accepted the ship and put her to sea. Childer's own loss, and the disputes that followed the tragedy, which some blamed on him, caused a breakdown and he resigned office. George Goschen, who had succeeded Childers as first lord, spoke, and tried to absolve Childers from blame. Then it was Sir John's turn, and he explained in detail what happened when he took office. The ship was about to be ordered

HMS Captain. As can be seen, the two turrets are on the main deck, and the masts and rigging are mounted on the hurricane deck above. Her early trials promised well, but her career at sea lasted just over four months before she foundered, her full rig making her top-heavy.

from Lairds of Birkenhead, and Sir John had to decide whether to go ahead with the construction. At that time he felt it was entirely right that Capt. Coles' ideas should be tried out – after all the concept of low-freeboard ships had already been proved a good one for coastal defences, and it was now just a question of whether a sea-going ship to the same design would be successful. The public were clamouring to know, Coles had proved himself a good designer, and Lairds were a well respected yard.

Sir John asked to see Coles' final designs, and this was his reaction:

> I am sure that I and all my colleagues vividly remember the day when we met in my room at the Admiralty to consider the design. Let me mention that the first thing that struck me with doubt and hesitation as to the design was that it only gave a freeboard of 8 feet to so large a vessel as 4,000 tons... I remonstrated with Captain Coles, but finding him unshaken in his opinion that 8 feet 5 inches was sufficient, after reflection the conclusion I came to was this – that although I thought it a very doubtful proposal, it would be better and fairer to adhere to the principle I had laid down, and to leave Captain Coles to construct his own ship in his own way.

Grave reservations had already been expressed within the Admiralty about the safety of low freeboard ships, but as the 'new boy' in the Admiralty Sir John lacked the confidence to stop a project about which there had been so much favourable publicity. In any event he left office before the ship was complete (George Goschen was the fourth first lord in five years), and therefore felt free to criticise the Admiralty's actions after she was launched. Sir John vented his 'astonishment and dismay' when it was found that her freeboard was not 8 feet 5 inches as predicted, but only 6 feet 7 inches. For this reason he thought the Admiralty ought never to have accepted the ship. Lairds had suggested further trials at Portsmouth to determine the centre of gravity, but in the end this was not done.

In retrospect, the heart of the problem was the fact that although the Admiralty ordered the ship, and inspected it for materials and workmanship, they had no control or even say over its design, and the court martial found it had been ordered because of the pressure of public opinion. Whether, if the freeboard had been as originally specified, the tragedy would not have happened will never be known, but we hope that Sir John was correct when he ended his speech:

> I can only say, in conclusion, that while I have no desire to speak harshly of anyone concerned in the affair, and more especially the right hon. gentleman the late first lord, who has himself suffered so grievously, I deeply deplore this calamity. But I do not regret taking the step I did...

Sir John was back in Worcestershire by 14th August, a week before the end of the session, and was able to attend, as usual, an archery society meeting at Ham

Court, and at the annual dinner of the Worcestershire Agricultural Society he replied to the toast to the House of Commons. It was, he said, his fate in the House to see most of those who sat opposite him, and he had looked at them so long it was delightful to him to come down there and look at the jolly agricultural faces of Worcestershire! At the end of the month he and Lady Pakington held a garden party at Westwood, entertaining about one hundred of the county élite, and at the beginning of September he attended the Three Choirs Festival in Gloucester. Later in the month he was at the annual army manoeuvres at Aldershot in the company of the Duke of Cambridge and Prince of Wales, when 33,000 troops were reviewed.

As Sir John had not had a ministerial position since 1869 he was relying mainly on his estates for income. There were many mortgages including £9,500 on his estate in Bishop's Cleeve, which he had used to repay a loan from George Banks of Hanbury, who had recently died. In September he sold these estates for £20,000 to the Gloucester coroner, and this must have been a very welcome influx of capital.

Sir John's most important engagement that autumn was in the Leeds Town Hall, where he was to give the opening address to the Social Science Association, of which he was president that year. On the way he attended the opening of the new Bradford Mechanics Institute on 2nd October, where he met the two Bradford MPs, William Forster and Edward Miall. In his speech at the lunch, Miall, a long time campaigner against state involvement in religion and therefore against parts of the Elementary Education Act, complained about the slow progress of business in the House last year, which he mainly put down to "the

The Bradford Mechanics Institute dates back to 1832, but the building in Bridge Street was opened in 1871. This building was demolished in the 1970s, but the Institute still functions as a subscription library.

immense quantity of inane speeches". He did not specifically blame the opposition of some Conservative MPs to his colleague's education bill, but thought that parliament would loose public respect unless things could be improved.

Sir John replied to the toast to 'The Visitors'. After paying tribute to Forster's Education Act, Sir John referred to Miall's remarks, and denied that Conservative MPs had anything to do with the slow progress. But with regard to inane speeches, Sir John said "I am an older member of the House than Mr Miall. I have sat there between thirty and forty years and during that time I have never met with a member who would acknowledge his own speech to be inane!".

In the evening there were further speeches, and Sir John spoke admiringly of the building. He had always been a supporter of mechanics' institutes, and he felt that the passing of the Endowed Schools and Elementary Education Acts would provide a proper elementary education and enable children to benefit more fully from secondary education, which mechanics' institutes could provide.

Sir John travelled the next day to Leeds, where on 4th October he was to give the inaugural address to the Social Science Association. The Association had been founded by Lord Brougham and Worcester-born George Hastings, to bring together those interested in various aspects of social reform. It held an annual congress in various cities (Sir John had addressed the first one in Birmingham in 1857). He began his speech by paying tribute to William Forster for his work in getting the Endowed Schools Act and the Elementary Education Act through parliament. However, Sir John wanted to register his disappointment that the Act did not provided for the appointment of an education minister. Forster's time that year had been almost entirely taken up by steering the Ballot Bill (introducing the secret ballot) through parliament, leaving him little time to oversee the working of the two new education acts. He regarded this as farcical. He also regretted that there was still evidence of interdenominational disputes, which ran counter to his belief that "the religious question in education should be settled on the basis of liberal consideration for the views of all". He had met with "much of that narrow and intolerant spirit too often the result of excessive zeal and implicit faith in the correctness of ones own opinions". He also regretted that school boards would only pay the fees for poor children to attend board, but not denominational schools. Surely it would be grossly unfair not to allow a poor Catholic child to attend a Catholic school? And he followed by making a further plea that more religious instruction should be allowed in board schools than had been provided for in the act.

Sir John concluded his speech with a passage that attracted criticism from the press. He touched on the question of compulsory attendance at school, which he now regarded as "indispensable" and then stressed the importance of technical education.

> The enemy is at our gates, not in the shape of fleets or armies, but in the shape of a rivalry with manufactures and trade, in which, if we failed to maintain the position we had hitherto held, our national prosperity would be undermined, and England's wealth, power and greatness would be a thing of the past...

Sir John then rather strayed from his brief, and touched on the possibility of revolution if our standards did not improve.

> Skilled workmen, comparing their position with that of skilled workmen in other countries, would become dissatisfied; and there are not wanting men who devote themselves to attempting to inspire the minds of the working classes with feelings of discontent and disaffection, and so to make them instruments for the accomplishment of revolutionary objects. The question of a workman's home is a very serious one; it involves not only the discomfort and discontent of the parent but the physical and intellectual inferiority of the child. The self-help of the people would no doubt do much to ameliorate their position, but it could not do all. The government had the necessary information; let them act upon it.

This last reference to a workman's home no doubt referred to a movement that had originated earlier that year and came to be known as the 'New Social Movement', which was supposed to have been kept secret, but had leaked to the press during the summer. This memorandum appeared in the Birmingham Daily Post on 25th October signed Salisbury, Carnarvon, Lichfield, Sandon, John Manners, Sir John Pakington, Sir Stafford Northcote and Gathorne Hardy, all members of the Conservative party:

> Early in the summer Mr Scott-Russell applied to one of the gentlemen whose names have been mentioned in connection with this matter, on behalf of a representative council of working men, of which he [Scott-Russell] was chairman, and he expressed a strong wish that some leading members of both Houses should consent to act together in considering the reasonable requirements of the working classes and such legislative measures as might be proposed to them. He urged that friendly relations between the two bodies so constituted might have the good effect of averting alienation of feeling between the classes. He offered to be the medium of communication, and he wished it to be understood, if the plan proceeded, that it was to be wholly unconnected with party or political designs, and strictly limited to the promotion of an object of national importance...

What seems to have happened is that the council of representative working men had already come up with a scheme for what we would call today 'new towns' which would provide working class families with an almost Arcadian existence. It had a seven point plan, under which parliament would give powers to set up new settlements outside the overcrowded cities, where workmen's cottages would be built. There would be technical schools, a limit of eight hours to the working day, a market selling produce at wholesale prices, places of 'public entertainment, knowledge and refinement', and railways owned by the state and run for the public good.

This scheme was picked up in the press in August, and quickly got short shrift – the Birmingham Daily Post (usually supporting radical ideas) called it 'state communism', and The Times 'mischievous and unreasonable'. Most of the politicians who had signed the letter referred to above were quick to disassociate themselves from this scheme, but it is clear from his speech that Sir John not only knew about it but supported at least some of its objects – for example, in his speech he had also referred to the need for wholesome food to be available at affordable prices. This led the Birmingham Daily Post on 19th October to claim that Sir John had been the only politician supporting the plan. It does seem that he increasingly regarded himself as a social reformer. In his diaries Lord Derby described him as 'intoxicated with the prospect of being one of the regenerators of society, and reconciling the people with the aristocracy'. Early the following year an official letter from Scott Russell outlining the scheme did appear in the press, but little more was heard of it. The following year the Liberal MP Henry Fawcett accused Sir John of saying the government should provide food at reasonable prices, and comfortable dwellings for the working classes. Sir John was not present when this was said, but he subsequently appeared in the chamber and denied that he had said any such thing, which would have been 'very erroneous'. What he had said was that if the legislature could do anything that would facilitate these desirable objects, that would be very good.

Sir John was in London in December, but travelled to Worcester for the Epiphany quarter sessions on 1st January, and joined in an argument about the Powick Lunatic Asylum. This large institution had to be funded out of the county rates, and some regarded its expense as too great. In 1870 a plan to extend it had met with opposition. Eventually the court had agreed to this expenditure, but on one condition – that the inmates be classified, and those regarded as 'idiots' and incurable should be put on a more basic dietary, similar to that in workhouses. Earl Beauchamp said he thought the asylum diet 'luxurious', and, he had calculated, cost eight shillings and sixpence (42.5p) per head per week against one shilling and ten pence (9p) in the workhouse. However, the commissioners in lunacy had told the court that they were against this discrimination, and when the report of the asylum sub-committee was read at the 1872 quarter sessions, this proposal was dropped. Earl Beauchamp, however, was still in favour of 'classification', and proposed that the report be rejected. Eventually his motion was put to the vote and defeated by a large majority.

From Worcester Sir John travelled to Lancashire to address the Rochdale Conservative Association, then on 12th January he was back in London and presented prizes at the Birkbeck Literary and Scientific Institute. The following week he returned to Worcester for meetings of the Archidiaconal Church Extension Society and the Diocesan Board of Education, and, two days later, a meeting of the Worcestershire Chamber of Agriculture, which had arranged a meeting to discuss tenants' rights. While he was in Worcester Herby sung in an amateur charity concert, an interest he shared with his father.

As the new session of parliament approached Sir John would have considered the state of the Conservative party, and its future in parliament. The period after the party split in 1846 had not been a good one, as the party had never had a majority in parliament, despite providing three short-lived governments under Lord Derby. But these had all foundered for the same reason, and, with the Liberals having a working majority of around 80, there seemed no prospect of this changing. The next election would take place in a year or two, and would be conducted under the secret ballot for the first time, and Sir John must have thought this would hardly advantage his party. Then there was the question of the leadership. Disraeli had been the leader in the Commons since 1848, and of the whole party since 1868, but had never been really liked by the members. He was considered an ambitious and unscrupulous adventurer without any real policies of his own, and many still remembered his merciless destruction of Peel in 1846. After the Tories' defeat in 1868 he had not been so prominent in the Commons as before, and instead had devoted his energies to writing a new novel, 'Lothair'. But his parliamentary brilliance still meant there was really no other viable contender for the leadership.

In an article in The Leeds Mercury in September 1871 the writer referred to the discontent, which it was thought had surfaced under the leadership of William Bentinck, MP for West Norfolk. An example was quoted when Sir John and others objected to arranging a morning sitting to consider the Army Bill as it clashed with quarter sessions, but Disraeli suggested an equally inconvenient alternative, quickly accepted by the government. 'Mr Bentinck, Sir Rainald Knightly and Lord Elcho interchanged looks of mutiny and words of disgust. It was another instance of Mr Disraeli's arbitrary leadership and disregard for the opinions of his followers… The Mutineers were supposed to be looking to Sir John Pakington as their future leader, and this was how Mr Disraeli, with a certain grim contempt, threw over the 'man of war from Droitwich". Sir John had been spoken of after the death of Lord Bentinck in 1848 as a possible party leader, but now he was 72 not many would have thought it sensible to turn over the attack against the all-powerful Gladstone to someone nearing the end of his parliamentary career.

Since his election in 1868 Gladstone seemed to be unbeatable, with a substantial parliamentary majority, and popular in the country. However, as Lord

The Years 1871 and 1872

Hurd wrote in his 2013 biography of Disraeli, politics is always a see-saw, and during the winter an event occurred that Hurd thinks changed the public mood. This was the severe illness of the Prince of Wales, who caught typhoid and at one stage was thought to be close to death. But in December he rallied, then recovered, and on 27th February 1872 a thanksgiving service was held in St Paul's cathedral. Not only did these events serve to restore the popularity of the royal family, which had suffered badly from the queen's withdrawal from public life after the death of Prince Albert ten years earlier, but at the same time Hurd wrote that the popularity of Disraeli, who was cheered much more strongly than was Gladstone on the way to St Paul's, dates from this time, as in the public's mind he was more associated with the monarchy than his opponent. The public were getting tired of Gladstone's constant reforms and self-righteous stance, and became more in tune with Disraeli's chauvinism and larger visions.

Benjamin Disraeli c. 1878.

As we have seen, the 1870 Elementary Education Act was something of a compromise with regard to religious education. Sir John would have liked to see more religion in board schools, but the National Education League led by Birmingham MP George Dixon continued to promote secular education free from the influence of religion. On 5th March in the House of Commons Dixon proposed that school attendance should be compulsory, and in particular that public money should not be used to pay for poor children to attend denominational schools. The motion was heavily defeated, but although Sir John did not participate in this debate he did speak at a public meeting in London about the same time organised by the National Education Union, which wished to promote religious education. Sir John proposed the first resolution, which called Dixon's motion unjust and uncalled for. He said it was a matter of deep regret "to find the friends of education arrayed in hostile camps". He continued:

> I believe the Education League commenced their organisation with a sincere desire to promote education in this country, but their position had now

> assumed the character of a plan for the attack and destruction of the Church of England. I desire, above all thing, to see charitable and kindly feeling exist between the different denominations of Christendom, and I deprecate the feelings of bitterness now existing between sect and sect as a disgrace and stain upon our common Christianity.

Perhaps talking about the destruction of the Church of England was going rather far, but it illustrates how far it was seen still to dominate education, at least by dissenters. Later in the House there was an attempt to bring in a Bill repealing clause 25 of the Elementary Education Act, which gave power to boards to pay for poor children to attend a school of their parents' choice, which could include Anglican schools, but this, too, failed.

As part of the reorganisation of the army England was being divided into military districts, of which the counties of Worcestershire and Shropshire formed one. Each district would have a military centre, and Shrewsbury had provisionally been designated for that district. However a number of Worcester people felt that it would be to the advantage of the city if it were chosen instead, and therefore lobbied the government to that effect. At a city council meeting on 19th March the mayor, alderman Willis, explained the background, and said that Sir John and the Lord Lieutenant, Lord Lyttelton, had introduced him and other local officials to the secretary of state for war, Edward Cardwell. They had explained the advantages that Worcester possessed over Shrewsbury, and had been courteously received.

However at the meeting many councillors spoke against the proposal, fearing that the presence of soldiers might bring immorality of different kinds to the city, and other supposed problems. These fears were taken up by a number of councillors, and 19 councillors voted against the idea and only 11 in favour.

When news of this got about the mayor was petitioned to hold a public meeting, and this took place on 27th March. Sir John was unable to attend but expressed his views in a letter to the mayor, which was read out at the meeting. In particular he wrote:

> I am unable to express the astonishment with which I learned that a large majority of the council voted against making Worcester one of the military stations. I rejoice to hear that a meeting of citizens has been convened in the hope of over-ruling this extraordinary and short sighted decision…

And Sir John pointed out, in answer to those who had apprehensions about the military being billeted in the town, that 'one of the objects of the new system is to put an end to those evils and inconveniences and to substitute a well-disciplined station'.

At this crowded meeting most speakers were much in favour of the idea, and the motion 'was carried with every demonstration of approval'. The evidence of popular feeling prompted a further meeting of the council, and this time they gave it their undivided support. At quarter sessions held on 8th April the court unanimously passed a resolution in favour of the scheme, and, armed with this, Sir John and other leading citizens again led a delegation to the war office to support the claims of Worcester. Berrow's reported that Sir John read the quarter sessions' resolution, and made Worcester's case on national rather than local grounds. He denied any antagonism towards Shrewsbury, but did say that there was a rumour that an officer in a high position with connections in Shrewsbury had been responsible for its initial selection. Although Sir John said he discounted the idea, he urged Cardwell to ensure that an unbiased officer would be responsible for making the final decision.

In the end Sir John's efforts were rewarded, and later in the summer it was announced that Worcester had been chosen. Another of Sir John's suggestions had also been adopted, which was that Worcestershire should be joined with Herefordshire to form a military district rather than Shropshire.

Sir John returned to Worcestershire in August. On 17th an embassy from the King of Burma, the modernising Mindon Min, visited the county. The king, it seems, wished to advance his country in industrial and commercial affairs, and wanted the delegation to investigate these matters in England. Dressed in national costume, they were shown round the Royal Worcester Porcelain works, then they took the train to Droitwich, where they were met by Sir John. After a tour of the salt workings in the town, the party were entertained to lunch at Westwood .

On 28th August Sir John spoke at the annual dinner of the Worcestershire Agricultural Society. In 1872 the Union of Agricultural Labourers, founded in

Norton Barracks. Following the decision to make Worcester the centre of the Worcestershire and Herefordshire military district, in 1872 20 acres of land was purchased at Norton for the new barracks, which were completed in 1877. Initially it housed the Worcestershire and Herefordshire Regiments and militias. Siting them some distance away from the city was probably deliberate.

Warwickshire by Joseph Arch, was becoming a force that could not be ignored. One of their demands was a minimum wage of two shillings and sixpence (12.5p) per day, and this was very much a topic of the day. Sir John said:

> I am one of those who think that labourers should be fairly met. My strong belief is that if labour be fairly met, then the agitator will appeal to him in vain (applause). I think there have been respects in which the agricultural labourer has not been so well off as we should wish to see him. We must remember that provisions are now dear, and that fuel is dear. We must remember that under certain regulations in which I have humbly born some part, and in which I feel a deep interest – I mean the improved education of the masses of England – the labourer will in many instances not be able to augment his earnings by the earnings of his children, to the extent he has hitherto done... I wish too that we could see the labourers occupying better homes (applause) and obtaining better food at more reasonable rates.

Sir John said he had been accused of proposing that parliament should legislate directly to improve the labourer's situation. But this was not so – his belief was that "men of all classes must depend mainly for their prosperity on their own individual exertions". But he did believe that parliament could assist by passing legislation to make this more achievable, and he wished that it spent more time on this, and less on "party struggles".

Joseph Arch (1826-1919) was born in Barford, Warwickshire, the son of a shepherd. After a short time at school he worked on local farms, becoming an expert hedger and ditcher. He also educated himself, and, helped by the fact that he owned his own cottage, became a Primitive Methodist preacher. In the 1860s he became active in Liberal politics, and on 7th February 1872 he addressed a meeting in Wellesbourne which led to the formation of a farm labourers' union. This grew rapidly with Arch at its head, but in 1874 a dispute in East Anglia cost the union dearly, and thereafter it declined. Arch became more active in politics and campaigned for the vote for the rural labourer and other agrarian reforms. He entered parliament in 1885 representing North West Norfolk, but his oratory, so effective at mass meetings, proved less so at Westminster and he retired in 1900.

But although Sir John was sympathetic to the needs of labourers in respect of housing and food, he had little sympathy for the new trade unions. On 26th September he was invited to the Hanbury harvest home, held in the grounds of Hanbury Hall, the seat of Harry Vernon. He congratulated the labourers in that parish for not, as he was informed, joining any union, and he said:

> You might rely on it, these unions were not for the promotion of your happiness… They should remember the good advice given them in that day's excellent sermon, that happiness did not depend on wealth. Happiness depended upon something far higher, upon a thankful spirit, a contented mind; and the poor man possessed of these attributes had within him elements of happiness which the rich man was entirely destitute of if he did not properly discharge the duties of his station. In my belief the labourers have no occasion to be led by any union or be led astray by any discontented agitator. I apprehend that what they mainly stood in want of were three things, viz. better education, better homes, better food (loud applause). If these requirements were looked to and legislated for and promoted, labourers would cease to be the dupes of those who fostered a spirit of discontent, and would lead far better lives.

Again Sir John was returning to the themes of the 'New Social Order' started the year before, although he was never very clear about the legislation needed for these benefits to happen. Sir John's views must have become known to members of the union, as on 10th October it held a meeting in Worcester to explain its aims to labourers, but Berrow's reported that 'very few of that class were present', most of those present being curious locals. Cllr Airey presided, and 'contended that no class of men in this country could make out a better case than they could for an alteration in the present condition of things. They were ill-fed, under-paid, badly-housed and altogether an ill-used class of people, and he condemned the views expressed by the Duke of Marlborough, Earl Beauchamp, Sir John Pakington, the Bishop of Gloucester and others…'. Joseph Arch himself was present, and said they determined to persist in their demands until they had obtained more money, the franchise, and two or three acres of land for each labourer. But they were not republicans – when they had obtained their rights they would give three cheers for the queen and the happy homes of England.

The subject came up again when Sir John spoke at the dinner of the Worcestershire Agricultural Society's annual show on 26th October. He again deprecated the union 'going round amongst the labourers and endeavouring to excite feelings of discontent and dissatisfaction', but at the same time felt that more action could be taken to improve the lot of the labourer. An 'Association for the Improvement of the condition of the Agricultural Labourer' was being formed. The Association felt that every labourer should be lodged in a decent house, with land enough for the purposes of himself and his family. Another proposal was that labourers should be encouraged to keep a cow. They might have saved enough to purchase one, or be able to rent one from the farmer. But when Sir John said that 'the pecuniary advantage to the labourer would be considerable', dissent was voiced. Thirdly, Sir John said that working for piece work often showed a big advantage over day work. In this way the labourer could gain 'full advantage of his own industry', and Sir John quoted an example when a man had succeeded in raising his earnings from ten shillings a day to fourteen, without any disadvantage to the farmer. His fourth suggestion was that labourers should be able to buy their food at co-operative stores at cheap prices, and that the co-operative principle may perhaps be extended to farming itself.

It is clear that not everyone at the meeting agreed with him, and subsequently there was adverse press comment. The Times was somewhat scathing, and even Berrow's, normally a friend of Sir John, thought these ideas utopian, and gave its opinion that the labourer was not so badly off as was sometimes represented. After all, farmers generally did not lay off workers during the slack season but provided year round employment, and as for the idea of allowing each man to keep a cow, there would be practical disadvantages and it might be the subject of jealousy between neighbours; 'The labourer is entitled to fair treatment and kindly feeling from his employer', Berrow's concluded, 'but not to sacrifices on his behalf which only a rich philanthropist can be expected to make'.

Finally, Sir John spoke about the landlord and tenant question, and expressed himself much in favour of the tenant being allowed compensation for unexpired improvements at the end of his lease – it was right that the landlord should enjoy protection under the lease of his land during the last few years of the lease, but in the same way tenants should be encouraged to invest, and not lose the value of their investments at the end of the lease.

Sir John's suggestion that every labourer should be encouraged to keep a cow was the subject of some controversy, and Robert Woodward, a prize wheat grower, in a speech to the Severn Valley Farmers Club on 5th November called it 'impractical and undesirable'. The only way to improve the labourer's lot was to pay them the highest wages that could be afforded. He followed it up with a letter to the Worcester Chronicle, and this prompted Sir John to reply at some length in Berrow's. His main point was that it was common for labourers to keep a cow in many parts of this country as well as in Scotland, and he quoted a farmer writing about the Duke of Rutland's estate: 'It is quite remarkable what effect the possession of a cow-gate has upon the labourer – he seems quite a different person; he does his work much better, in an almost cheerful way, as if conscious that he was not forgotten by those who employed him'.

But when Sir John addressed the Worcestershire Agricultural Society again the following year, he still had to take pains to deny that he had ever said that every labourer should have a cow. "I never expressed or entertained any opinion if that kind. It would, in my judgement, been a very nonsensical opinion... But where the agricultural labourer was a prudent, well-conducted man, who had saved sufficient money to buy a cow, it was desirable for his own benefit and that of his family and neighbours, that he should enjoy the privilege of having a cow".

Earlier in autumn the Three Choirs Festival had been held in Worcester, and Sir John had been, as always, an enthusiastic supporter and had been chairman of the executive committee. Earlier in the century the Festival had had six stewards, three lay and three clergy, and they were responsible for meeting any deficit which occurred, which it then usually did. When Sir John was last a steward he had had to find £47. But since then two things had changed – there was now a much larger number of stewards, and the festival finances had improved to the extent that in 1872 there had been a surplus of £678. On 19th October a meeting of the stewards was held under the chairmanship of Earl Beauchamp, and the main discussion was on a suggestion of Sir John's about the disposal of the surplus. Traditionally money raised had gone to the widows and orphans of the clergy, and even if the festival had incurred a deficit the money donated at the collections held at the cathedral door went to this charity. But, Sir John explained, this charity was now well funded – not only were demands on it tending to decrease, but it had received a £10,000 legacy from Miss Kilvert, the daughter of the late Canon Kilvert. So Sir John thought that it would be sensible to apply the surplus towards other local charities, and he suggested that £400 be donated to the Infirmary, £100 to the cathedral clock and bells fund, £100 to the orphan's asylum, and £70 to Mr Done's festival class (a music school).

The only objection to the principle was whether it was legal – reference was made in the printed programme to the widows and orphans of clergy, but Sir John thought that as long as the collection money went to widows and orphans of the clergy he could see no problem with disposing of the surplus as the stewards thought fit. There was general agreement on this, although it was thought wise to get counsel's opinion. But the chairman objected to the suggestion that £100 be given to the orphan's asylum – he said this was 'unsectarian', and many people objected to that. However, Sir John's proposal was at last accepted.

Sir John's last major engagement of the year was at the inaugural dinner on 3rd December for Worcester's new mayor, Edward Wall. When the toasts were proposed after dinner the mayor proposed the toast to the Houses of Parliament, and said how pleased they were that Sir John had honoured them with his presence that night. Replying, Sir John chose the occasion to speak about the House of Lords, unique in the world he thought. Reference had already been made that night to unrest in France, and Sir John referred to the "miserable state to which that great nation was reduced from want of stability of her institutions". That contrasted with England and our House of Lords, "which for centuries had been rooted in the affections of the people... and how every national question was discussed in that chamber". But perhaps Sir John went a little far when he said that "there was no man in the country, however lowly his position, who, if he had the talent and opportunity, might not hope to rise to a seat in that House". There had been recent suggestions that the House of Lords should be abolished, but Sir John hoped that it would be, for a long time to come, as it had been in long time past, one of our most valued institutions, one of the most cherished bulwarks of our national liberty.

Sir John was followed by William Laslett, MP for Worcester, who paid tribute to Sir John. But, he said, it was only natural that from time to time the hon. baronet should make a little slip. He said that when Sir John recently referred to labourers keeping cows he mentioned Northumberland and Scotland, where farms were much larger than in the midlands. In Worcestershire, which was divided into small farms, it would not be possible for labourers to keep cows.

William Laslett (1801-1884) trained as a lawyer and practised as a solicitor in Worcester. In 1852 he entered parliament as a Liberal representing Worcester, but resigned his seat in 1860 when his views differed from those of his party. He re-entered parliament in 1868 for Worcester, but in the general election in 1874, contrary to the national trend, he was defeated. He lived at Abberton Hall near Pershore and in 1842 married Maria, daughter of Rt Rev. Robert Carr, the late Bishop of Worcester. They had no family, and he was a generous benefactor, founding Laslett's arms houses in Friar Street, Worcester, on the site of the old gaol, and giving the city land for a new cemetery. From a portrait in the Guildhall.

Sir John could not let this remark pass without rebutting it, so in the next edition of Berrow's a letter from him appeared, expressing surprise that Laslett had turned from wine to milk, quite inappropriately, during his speech! He thought the best way of showing him that he was not correct about it being impossible to keep cows, was to meet a labourer of Sir John's called Eggerton. He rented about one acre of land at Cutnall Green, and his wife would tell Laslett that they had kept a cow for four years, and that the milk is a blessing to the family with its two young children, and that they also make up to 10lbs of butter a week. Selling the surplus has added five or six shillings a week to his income. Eggerton has rented the grass along the railway for a short distance to make hay, and had built a little shed for the cow's winter quarters.

Chapter 5
The Contagious Diseases Acts

In 1864 Sir John was one of the sponsors of the Contagious Diseases Bill. 'Contagious diseases' was a euphemism for sexually transmitted diseases, the prevalence of which was proving a serious problem in various towns where soldiers or sailors were based. The act would give police, after getting the approval of a justice, the power to detain any female thought to be carrying a venereal disease and to take her to a certified hospital for examination. If she was found to be infected she could be detained until medically discharged. The bill passed through parliament with little opposition, and there are no reports of the debates in Hansard, possibly because of the indelicate nature of the subject.

The 1864 act was only valid for three years, and was replaced by a more wide-ranging one in 1866 which gave the police the power to have any common prostitute (not just those thought to be diseased) examined, and if necessary detained in hospital for a maximum of six months. Although not a sponsor of this bill, Sir John was a member of the select committee appointed to examine it in detail. In 1869 another select committee was appointed to assess the results of the 1866 Act, and Sir John was again a member, attending all but one of its meetings. The report, published on 8th July, found that 'although the act has only been in operation for two years and a half, strong testimony is borne to the benefits both in a moral and sanitary point of view, which have already resulted from it. Prostitution appears to have diminished, its worst features to have been softened, and its physical evils abated'. One table showed that during the year to 31st March 1869 over 18,000 prostitutes had been examined in all the districts covered by the Act, and a little over one quarter had been found to be infected.

The 1866 Act had applied to women living within five miles of any of the military or naval towns specified in the Act, and the committee's report recommended that this be increased to fifteen miles, as many prostitutes had based themselves just outside the five miles, and were thus not covered. It also recommended a tightening of the rules covering women who voluntarily submitted themselves for examination, but who subsequently could not be forcibly detained. It also identified six additional towns where soldiers or sailors were stationed that should be covered. But the committee felt that the question of whether the act should be extended to cover London or even the whole nation needed separate consideration. So in 1869 another act was passed based on the recommendations of the committee, and extended to nine months the period during which women could be kept in hospital.

By now the acts had aroused much opposition. In 1869 the tireless campaigner Josephine Butler founded the Ladies National Association for the Repeal of the Contagious Diseases Act. It was probably the first well-organised national movement in support of women's rights, and members of parliament found themselves somewhat unprepared. In January 1870 a letter was published in The Daily News condemning the Acts. In particular it stated that 'As far as women are concerned, they remove every guarantee of personal security which the law has established and held sacred, and put their reputation, their freedom, and their persons absolutely in the power of the police; and because it is unjust to punish the sex who are the victims of a vice, and leave unpunished the sex who are the main cause, both of the vice and its dreaded consequences; and we consider that liability to arrest, forced medical treatment, and (where this is resisted) imprisonment with hard labour, to which these acts subject women, are the punishment of the most degrading kind'. The letter was signed by, among others, Josephine

Josephine Butler (1828-1906) was born Josephine Grey, a distant relation to the Whig prime minister Earl Grey, and her family had a strong feeling for social justice, even republicanism. As a teenager she developed a powerful feeling of having a religious destiny, which pervaded all her later campaigning. In 1852 she married John Butler, an Anglican clergyman, but she disliked their early married life in Oxford as the society there was very misogynistic. After a spell in Cheltenham they went to Liverpool, where she worked among the female paupers in the workhouse. In the 1860s she widened her campaigns to include votes and higher education for women. When she became involved with the National Association, she actively participated in parliamentary elections, favouring candidates in favour of repealing the CD Acts against more reactionary Liberals. Later in life she widened her campaigns to continental Europe, and in the 1890s campaigned on behalf of Indian women. She was a prolific writer.

Butler, Florence Nightingale, Harriet Martineau, Elizabeth Wolstenholme-Elmy, and Ursula Bright, wife of Jacob and sister-in-law to John Bright.

The controversy forced the government to investigate, so in November 1870 a Royal Commission was appointed under the chairmanship of William Nathaniel Massey, a former under-secretary in the Home Office. Sir John was one of the commissioners. The report was published in July 1871 and ran to over 800 pages and 80 witnesses had been examined. It began with a review of the legislation and presented a balanced discussion of the evidence, with arguments for and against the acts. They were agreed on the bad effects of venereal disease, particularly syphilis, which could affect innocent people, even new born children. Most of the evidence pointed to a significant reduction in venereal disease, both among soldiers and sailors and in prostitutes, although some thought this was not necessarily as a result of the acts. All the medical evidence indicated that the forced periodical examination of prostitutes, so greatly reviled, was essential to the effective control of disease. It also seemed that the number of prostitutes had diminished, although many may have escaped the notice of the police by contacting their clients in a more clandestine manner. But even if this were true the commissioners thought that

> the absence of public solicitation is a material gain to public decency and morality. It is hardly to be disputed that a sensible improvement has been observed in the streets in the conduct and demeanour of the women since the acts came into operation. Soldiers and sailors under the influence of drink are no longer importuned and seized upon by filthy prostitutes as in the past…

Although the reclamation of fallen women seems hardly to have entered into the original conception of the acts, it soon became recognised as part of the system. A chaplain is attached to each of the certified hospitals. The matrons

William Nathaniel Massey, 1809-81. Trained as a lawyer, he was elected to represent Newport, Isle of Wight, in parliament in 1855. He was a moderate liberal, and in 1857 defeated the unpopular Sir Elkinah Armitage in Salford. In 1855 he was appointed a Home Office minister, and later a deputy speaker and chairman of ways and means. From 1863 to 1867 he served as financial member of the government of India, and on his return represented Tiverton until his death. He did not hold office again, and was thought to lack drive and ambition.

are mostly of a superior class... The influences brought to bear on the inmates of the Lock [venereal disease] wards through these agencies are not without effect. Many of the women on their discharge from hospitals have been induced to enter the refuges and homes which are ready for their reception... some of them, weary of a life into which they have drifted from neglect and poverty rather than from wantonness, have gladly embraced the opportunity offered to them of returning to a regular life, or rather perhaps of entering upon it for the first time.

The report then discussed the objections to the acts raised by their opponents. Firstly, by ensuring that prostitutes did not suffer from contagion, it might be thought that the acts were designed to provide sound prostitutes for soldiers and sailors and might thus be thought to increase immorality and encourage males not in the armed forces to visit these 'safe' areas. The commissioners answered this by saying that the main purpose of the acts was to maintain the physical abilities of the members of the army and navy, and that 'we are of the opinion that these reasons are sufficient to justify exceptional legislation, but that such legislation should be strictly guarded'.

Another objection was that 'subjecting prostitutes to periodical examination for the purpose of ascertaining whether they are in a fit condition to follow their trade is in itself an outrage upon public decency and morality'; another that it is 'unfair to exempt men from the restraints and regulations to which women are subjected'. The report does not really answer the first objection, but of course it would not be practical to extend examination to men, as, unlike the female sex, illicit sex is not confined to one easily distinguishable class of person. The report also considered the question of whether the acts should be made to apply to the whole country, as some people proposed; but it was thought this would be 'hardly practical'.

The report concluded, somewhat unexpectedly, that the 1866 and 1869 acts should be repealed, and that the provisions of the 1864 act should be reinstated. That act provided for no compulsory examination of prostitutes, but where they came forward voluntarily, or were known to be suffering from disease, then they would be treated at the public expense, and only discharged when cured, subject to a maximum retention of three months. The report suggested that any town or city in the country could have the act applied if it requested it.

It then went on to suggest ways that the law on brothels could be tightened up, and ways in which the Vagrant Act 1825 could be used to remove prostitutes from the streets, and also to give more protection to girls under 16.

This part of the report was signed by all twenty one commissioners, but then there was a further section entitled 'Reasons for dissenting form Parts of the Report'. This was signed by seven commissioners, at the head of whom was Sir

John Pakington. They entirely agreed with the main thrust of the report that 'legislation with the object of diminishing the terrible evil of venereal disease ought to be maintained'. But the evidence given to the commission was quite clear, and as the main report says 'the medical witnesses are nearly all agreed that the periodical examination of the public women is essential to the system'. Thus 'we have been irresistibly led to he conclusion that it is only under a system of periodical examination that either venereal disease can be speedily detected and effectively checked, or police be safely entrusted with duties which must be admitted to be, under the most favourable circumstances, of a difficult and delicate nature, requiring every safeguard which prudence can suggest'.

After referring to the mass of statistics in the report's appendix to strengthen their case, Sir John and his co-signatories recapitulated the good moral effects which these acts have produced, and which, in their opinion far outweighed any moral objections which have been or can be alleged against them. They cite:

> Religious and moral influence has been brought to bear upon large numbers of women, a great portion of whom had been from infancy familiar only with scenes of debauchery and vice; towns and camps have been cleared, or nearly so, of the miserable creatures who were formerly to be found in their streets; the sad spectacle of juvenile prostitutes of tender age, so rife in such localities heretofore, has been greatly diminished, in some instances almost removed; and the temptation by which young men of all classes have been hitherto assailed have been to a great extent taken out of their way, and morality has been thus promoted.

Sir John did not make it clear what the evidence for this last benefit was.

They pointed out that any woman who felt aggrieved by her treatment under the acts 'has it in her power to emancipate herself from such a consequence of her mode of life'. Referring to the opponents of the acts, they said:

> We see no adequate reason why we should yield to a clamour which we do not believe to be well founded or deep seated and which we believe to have been for the most part artificially excited by means, the discreditable character of which has been stigmatised with just severity in the foregoing pages, and which we may reasonably hope will be silenced by the force of facts.

Finally they thought the procedures under the acts for examining women could be improved, and that acts 'should be gradually and cautiously extended, as circumstances may render possible and advisable'.

There originally had been as many as twenty three commissioners (all men of course), but two dropped out early, and they had clearly been chosen to represent a wide spectrum of opinion. It was therefore probably inevitable that when considering such a controversial subject as this the commissioners would not come to a single opinion, and not only did Sir John and his group dissent, there were no less than eight other dissenting reports. As far as Sir John's was concerned, as can be imagined his group were mainly Conservatives. The second name was Lord Hardinge, who had served with Sir John in Lord Derby's second administration of 1859-59, Sir John Salisbury-Trelawney, Liberal Member for East Cornwall, Sir George Paget, a prominent physician and leader of the Conservative faction within Cambridge University, Samuel Wilks, another leading physician, Timothy Holmes, a leading surgeon, and George Woodyatt Hastings, a social reformer who, as we have seen, was president of the Social Science Association. Although not a doctor himself, he was son of Dr Charles Hastings who was the founder of the British Medical Association.

The second dissenting report went in the other direction and opposed a re-enactment of the compulsory powers of examination and treatment contained in the 1864 act. They approved all measures designed to lessen prostitution, but were against any compulsion. This group was led by William Francis Cowper-Temple (see page 54), Anthony Mundella, the radical MP for Sheffield, the well-known theologian and leader of the Christian socialism movement Rev. John Maurice, Holmes Coote, a surgeon who had published a report on syphilis and was himself to die of the disease the following year, Robert Applegarth, a trade unionist and reformer and the first working man to be appointed to a royal commission, and Peter Rylands, the radical MP for Warrington, who was later to lead the campaign against the acts.

It was mentioned above that Josephine Butler was one of the leading campaigners against the acts. Some of her correspondence has survived, and on 8th July 1871, just after the report was published, she wrote:

> Dear Friends all over the country
> I must try and tell you how extraordinary is the state of affairs. It is not unhopeful at all, but it is a life and death struggle. The result of the commission is as good as possible for the cause of truth. I remember at the first praying to confound their deliberations, and to make the result like the confusion of tongues at the tower of Babel – not a very Christian prayer perhaps, but it has been answered. I was at the House of Commons yesterday & saw many people. The report had been signed and it is all open and above ground now. You will be amused to hear that six reports have come out – so much for those who waited for the report. First Mr Massey's, which is a hateful compromise, and signed by the majority. Then a minority report drawn up by Cowper Temple (who has been completely converted in the course of his work) is signed Mundella [&c]… Then a third minority report has been drawn up by Sir John Pakington in favour of the acts, Mr Massey's not being strong enough… Mr Mundella told me that Sir John Pakington regards the acts as almost divine. He said that it is disgusting to hear that man talk of prostitution. He seems to think that men's souls cannot be saved without it [Butler must have meant 'the acts' by 'it'].

When the report was published in July 1871 the government promised to give it careful consideration, and to introduce a measure the following session. Accordingly on 13th February 1872 the home secretary, Herbert Austin Bruce, rose to introduce a new Contagious Diseases Bill. He went over the history of the legislation, and pointed out that a Lords committee in 1868 had proposed that the 1866 act could be extended to cover any town whose inhabitants applied. This led to a movement led by medical men to extend the act more generally, and it was this threat, Bruce thought, that had led to the campaign for repeal. He continued:

> The campaign was founded first of all on the opinion that these acts invaded private liberty; secondly, because they appeared to give legal sanction to prostitution; thirdly, because they tended to promote immorality among men; and lastly, because they had a tendency still further to harden and degrade fallen women themselves. There was no doubt but that these objections elicited the sympathies of large numbers of persons of serious and thoughtful habits, but it was equally certain that many who opposed the acts dealt in exaggerations and appeals which were calculated to give a false impression as to the manner in which the law was carried out… Anyone who knew the facts of the case would bear me out in saying that the acts had worked in a most satisfactory manner.

He said that although the moral effects of the acts had been controversial, there was no denying that they had been successful in reducing prostitution and venereal disease, and in very much reducing the number of juvenile prostitutes. The commission had come out against the forcible examination and treatment of prostitutes, yet they proposed the re-enactment of the 1864 Act, which Bruce thought was inconsistent. But he said that the government had come to the conclusion that it was impossible to maintain legislation that applied only to some parts of the country and was not capable of extension to the whole nation.

So the new bill would totally repeal the 1866 and 1869 Acts, but would include a number of measures, as proposed by the commission, to strengthen the law on brothels, to make the Vagrant Act more applicable to prostitutes, and take various steps to protect juvenile women, including raising the age of consent. At the conclusion of his speech the House must have been a little confused by Bruce's position on the bill, as his remarks made it clear that he thought the campaign for repeal misplaced, and that the acts had had many beneficial effects. Yet he was now proposing to repeal them.

The next speaker was Jacob Bright, brother of John and a campaigner for women's rights, who began by saying "the right hon. gentleman the secretary of state for the home department ought to be the object of the sympathy of the House, because it was his cruel fate to propose the repeal of acts which he believed to have been highly successful!". However, Bright questioned some of Bruce's statistics, and thought some of the claimed benefits of the acts could have been achieved by other means. He pointed out that if women could become members of parliament no such acts would ever be passed in future.

Sir John also spoke, in terms of great regret. "The course adopted by the government on a subject very painful in its details, but deeply important to the health and welfare of the people, was at once timid and unworthy. I look upon it as a triumph of prejudice and clamour over reason and truth; nor do I believe it possible for anyone who has heard or read the evidence taken before the commission to come to any other conclusion".

Apart from making a few observations on the army estimates, Sir John made little contribution to parliament in 1872, determined to do what he could to stop the new Contagious Diseases Bill from being passed. On 11th May Sir John led a delegation to the home secretary consisting of seven peers and about 150 members of parliament, drawn from both parties. They had with them three memorials signed by over 2,500 medical men pleading that nothing should be done to weaken the present laws respecting contagious diseases, which had, they claimed, reduced by more than one half the more serious forms of the disease in the districts in which they applied. The memorialists specially protested against the 'erroneous suppositions spread about as to the degrading or repulsive action of the acts', and, Sir John said, the acts had been found to contribute to raising classes from a degrading position and restore them to paths of virtue, and the opportunities to do this were given by a temporary seclusion in a healthy moral atmosphere.

Home secretary Bruce must have been impressed by this show of force, particularly as it corresponded in some degree with his own feelings, and 'promised to present the matter to his colleagues with all the force with which it had been laid before him'. A considerable number of petitions were presented to parliament, both for and against the government bill, but nothing more was heard of it until on 15th July when the prime minister was asked how the government proposed to deal with all the outstanding measures before the end of the session. Gladstone admitted that several items would have to be dropped, and this included the Contagious Diseases (Prevention) Bill, which, he said, 'involved a great difficulty' – at that there was some cheering. One of the principal opponents of the acts was the member for Cambridge, William Fowler, and on 21st May 1873 he moved the motion for the second reading of his own bill to repeal the acts. As an aside, it is interesting that on an earlier occasion when he tried to introduce a similar bill, a member cried 'I spy strangers'. This referred to visitors and the press in the galleries, and by custom the speaker was obliged to have the galleries cleared at that injunction. The member felt that the subject was

SIR JOHN PAKINGTON

too indecent to be reported in the press, and there may have been women in the galleries. On that occasion, despite resistance from other members, the galleries were cleared, but full accounts of the proceedings had been given to the press by members, which appeared in The Times and elsewhere.

On this occasion, however, the galleries were not cleared, and Fowler spoke about his bill, and was seconded by Anthony Mundella. But Sir John led the opposition to the bill, and when home secretary Bruce spoke, he summed up the mass of statistics quoted during the debate, and said the great weight of evidence, even if some of the figures might be queried, showed that there had certainly been a reduction in prostitution in the districts covered by the acts.

There had not previously been a division in the house on the subject, and when one was held at the end of the debate, it showed that there was a large majority of nearly two to one in favour of keeping the acts, and it was to be over ten years before they were eventually repealed. Berrow's, as usual a supporter of Sir John's, was fulsome in its praise:

> The country may be congratulated upon the overthrow of Mr Fowler's movement against the acts, and upon the triumph on the question that was gained by Sir John Pakington, who led the opposition... The subject is not one on which we care to dwell, for the opponents of the acts have done enough to disgust the nation with it by obtruding their repulsive particulars upon our breakfast tables, and they have not scrupled to send, amongst other petitions in parliament, one which bore the signatures of 22 young girls who are now at school. When zealots do not hesitate to run the risk of polluting immature minds in order to achieve their prudish ends they must expect to meet with contempt...

William Fowler, 1828-1905, was born to a Quaker family, connected to the Gurneys and Lloyds. He trained as a lawyer, but became a director of Cunliffe Alexander & Co, a London bank and discount house, and was financially embarrassed by the 'great crash' of 11 May 1866. In 1868 he was elected as a Liberal for Cambridge, lost his seat in 1874, and regained it in 1880. He had a liberal interest in many subjects including prison reform, and his speech against the Contagious Diseases Act was published.

The Contagious Diseases Acts

A large number of women, Berrow's thought, had had their lives transformed after being taken off the streets, and concluded 'we congratulate Sir John upon his signal success in the House of Commons'.

A number of letters to Sir John on this subject survive in his archives, and show the strength of feelings on both sides of the argument. Edwin Kell, a non-conformist minister from Southampton, who clearly felt that the acts had actually led to an increase in prostitution, wrote:

> Allow me to express my surprise and regret that anyone professing himself a friend to education and interested in the progress of social science should have come forward to support one of the most immoral and irreligious measures ever introduced into a Christian country. The increase of vice both here and at Plymouth is such as to shock every man possessed of any feelings of the sanctity of marriage, and the laws of poverty and chastity. I am prepared to show you what the least acquaintance with the laws of human nature and the experience of history would have pointed out as the inevitable consequences, that the increase of vice still continues in Southampton and that now under the superintendence of the police and the medical doctor there is here nightly a seraglio of women on places of public resort where men may make their selection without any danger of end consequences, and vice and wickedness run riot from the result of the infamous measures.

A totally different point of view came from Rev. Henry Canham of Suffolk:

> Dear Sir John, I beg to congratulate you and sincerely thank you for you great victory on behalf of humanity last Thursday. As a workhouse chaplain of some twenty years standing I can say without the slightest hesitation that of all diseases of which flesh is heir, that for the alleviation of which you made so bold a stand, it is the most painful horrible & revolting. I have witnessed scenes that would make your hair stand on end, & the agonising screams of some of the poor sufferers still ring in my ears & will as long as memory lasts. Not the least distressing cases are those inherited – of which I have seen several.

Strong support also came from James Knight, the proprietor of the Worcester Chronicle, not always a political friend of Sir John's, who wrote: 'I cannot deny myself the satisfaction of expressing to you my thorough appreciation of the moral courage and steadfastness you shewed in standing up against Mr Fowler's attempt to procure the repeal of the Contagious Diseases Acts… I congratulate you on the triumph of reason and common sense against slanderous falsehood, blind bigotry, and sanctimonious tartuffism.

At the end of this book I have speculated as to why Sir John might have been so interested in this subject.

Chapter 6
1873 and the Droitwich Brine Baths

Sir John remained at Westwood over Christmas, and on 22nd January addressed the annual meeting of the National Education Union in Manchester Town Hall. The Union had been formed to support the principle that religion should be at the heart of education, as opposed to the National Education League which supported secular education. He began by saying that "it is with deep pain that I witness the unfortunate position of the country, with the sad spectacle of the thoughtful men of England split and divided into two hostile camps because they cannot agree upon the mode and manner in which the children of this great country are to be taught their duty to God and man". He attacked the views of Samuel Morley, MP for Bristol, who had recently chaired a meeting of the League:

> If Mr Morley were to go through schools opened all over the country he would find the children of non-conformist children and the children of Anglicans sitting side by side, and receiving the blessings of a good education and, what is more, the blessings of a religious education, given to them with the most scrupulous respect for their respective religious opinions, doing violence to the conscious of no-one, but bringing up those children as a harmonious body, who are learning their duty to God, and preparing to go forth into the world as Christian men.

On 31st January Sir John joined a distinguished delegation from the National Education Union to see prime minister Gladstone. It was led by Edward Akroyd, MP for Halifax, although Sir John was the main speaker. He explained the resolutions passed at Manchester Town Hall, and voiced his fear that the League would try and get the 1870 Act changed to the detriment of denominational schools. Every parent, he believed, should have the right to send their child to a school of their choice. The Union also felt that school attendance should be made compulsory, enforced by school boards, or in their absence by the poor law guardians.

Sir John and his household moved from Westwood to London in the first week of February, and the following week he was part of another educational delegation, this time from the Worcester Diocesan Board of Education, led by the Bishop of Worcester. They saw the Marquess of Ripon, lord president of the council, and their spokesman George Hasting made the board's case that school attendance should now be made compulsory, and should be enforced by school boards, or in their absence by an enforcement officer appointed by the magistrates. Hastings added that in Malvern, where he lived, the appointment of school boards had proved expensive, and in some places it was difficult to find suitable members of the boards. Sir John also supported Hastings' views.

Samuel Plimsoll was continuing his campaign for better safety at sea, and early in 1873 had published a book entitled 'Our Seamen: An Appeal'. It contained many rather sensational claims, but The Times said 'the writer showed, by his ignorance of technicalities, that he was dealing with a subject that he did not know in detail, and was not entitled to speak with authority'. Nevertheless it caught the public attention, which added further pressure for an enquiry. On March 4th Sir John seconded a motion in the House by Samuel Plimsoll for a royal commission to look into 'certain practices, and the condition, of the mercantile marine'. Sir John quoted many statistics about the loss of life and foundering of vessels, both of which he considered wholly excessive. Chichester-Fortescue, president of the Board of Trade, agreed to the commission in principle, although he thought some of Plimsoll's claims somewhat exaggerated. Sir John returned to the theme when he gave his presidential address to the Institute of Naval Architects on 3rd April. He said he was well pleased with the terms of reference given to the commission, and was particularly pleased that the secretary of the Institute, Charles Merrifield, was to be one of the commissioners.

He also said he was very sorry to have to refer, for the third year running, to the dreadful loss of a ship incurring much unnecessary loss of life. On 22nd January the Northfleet, a merchant ship bound for Australia, was lying at anchor off Dungeness, when, in the darkness, she was struck by another ship, later identified as the Murillo, and soon sank, with the loss of all but 86 of the 379 on board. The Murillo, disgracefully, did not stop and Sir John was pleased that it was now proposed to make it a criminal offence not to stop after an accident at sea.

On 17th April Sir John was in Worcestershire during the Easter recess, and spoke at a dinner to mark the retirement of Henry Allsopp as master of the Worcestershire hounds. Allsopp, then 62, ran the Burton on Trent brewery Samuel Allsopp & Sons Ltd, but since 1860 had lived at Hindlip Hall near Worcester. As, apart from his hunting, he later became an MP and deputy lieutenant, Henry must have left the day to day management of the brewery to

SIR JOHN PAKINGTON

The Burton on Trent brewery of Samuel Allsopp & Sons can trace its roots back to the 1740s when Benjamin Wilson established a brewery. His son, another Benjamin, took his nephew Samuel Allsopp into partnership, and in 1807 relinquished his share. Samuel died in 1838, and his son Henry, 1811-87, (right) succeeded. The company got into financial difficulties in 1911, but it survived and eventually became part of Allied Breweries. The family lived at Hindlip Hall near Worcester from 1860 till Henry's grandson Charles' widow moved out after the last war.

the local management. He was later ennobled as the 1st Baron Hindlip. After paying tribute to Allsopp, Sir John, who had been a keen huntsman himself in his younger days, spoke in praise of the new masters, the Earl of Coventry and Frederick Ames of Hawford Lodge. The hunt would now be divided into a southern section under the mastership of the Earl of Coventry, and a northern section under Mr Ames.

Sir John said how pleased he was that the Earl and Countess had recovered well from their recent 'narrow escape' in the hunting field. Two weeks previously they were both riding fast to hounds, and the Earl saw a fence ahead of him which he prepared to jump. But too late he realised that on the other side there was a quarry face, a drop of twenty six feet according to Berrow's, and the Earl had a nasty fall. The Countess followed him, and was more seriously hurt about her face. Her horse had had to be put down, but it seems the riders suffered no lasting damage,

Apart from leading the campaign against the repeal of the Contagious Diseases Acts, described in the last chapter, Sir John made no major contributions in parliament that session, although he did support Lord Claude Hamilton's further but unsuccessful attempt to get funding for a harbour of refuge at Filey. However Sir John regularly attended, and spoke at, various functions in London. On 3rd May he spoke at the dinner at the launch of the annual exhibition of the Royal Academy, responding to the toast to the navy. He said, no doubt with his tongue in his cheek:

It is with a pang of regret we no longer see depicted on your walls by Stansfield, by Turner, and many other marine artists, those beautiful picturesque ships which used to contribute alike to our artistic tastes and our national pride. Those ships are now ships of the past. If we turn to the ships of the future I am afraid that there is no chance that any artist will ever be induced to give us the portrait of the Devastation. (Hear, hear, and laughter.) The ships of the future will have no canvas upon them, and I fear we shall never see them on canvas (laughter).

These ships were unsightly monsters, Sir John said, but will be better adapted to protect our shores.

The following Wednesday Sir John was one of the main speakers at a 'grand Conservative banquet' held in Willis's Rooms in London. He attacked Gladstone's reforming agenda, saying "the legislation of the last four years has been bold and sensational to the extent of rashness and danger. I have no confidence – and I do not believe any man present has the slightest confidence – in the minister now at the head of affairs". He pointed to the fact that for many years Gladstone had sat on the Conservative benches, and "during that period any man would have been thought mad if he had expressed an opinion that he would live to see the day when Mr Gladstone, as prime minister of England, would propose measures for the destruction of the Irish Church, for dealing a heavy blow at the rights of property, and for the adoption of the democratic and dangerous system of the ballot".

Sir John concluded with an attack on Sir Charles Dilke, who had been promoting republican ideas – the queen had been almost invisible during her period of prolonged mourning. Earlier that week Dilke had proposed a motion in the Commons that the inequalities in the distribution of electoral power in England should be addressed, and in his speech he had mentioned Droitwich, in which the numbers of electors was falling off; but, he said, the right hon. member showed no falling off at all! At the end of the debate Dilke's motion attracted 77 votes, all members of the Liberal party and supporters of Gladstone, Sir John pointed out. What was the remedy for this state of affairs, Sir John asked at the end of his speech? You must trust to the people's good sense, and he forecast that after the next election the House of Commons would have many more Conservative MPs.

The following week Sir John was back in Willis's rooms when he spoke at the annual dinner of the Friends of the Clergy Corporation. This charity was established in 1655 to help the many clergy dispossessed under the Commonwealth, and subsequently supported poor clergy and their families. Sounding a little more moderate than he had the previous week, he again referred to the Irish Church and said: "whether or not the destruction of that church was a wise measure, it had given something of an impulse to those who desired to weaken and attack the Church of England". This was demonstrated by the springing up of many church defence associations. He also thought that inclusiveness in the Church of England, while one its strengths, could be taken too far.

On 4th June Sir John returned to Worcestershire to distribute the prizes won by candidates for the Cambridge Local Examination in Malvern. George Hastings was in the chair, and in his speech Sir John spoke about the two recent education acts. However he added that advances were not confined to those acts, and he referred to the establishment of Malvern College, and another in Cheltenham for the education of the upper and middle classes, due to the 'exertions of individuals'. Sir John also spoke in favour of women's education: "the admission of both sexes to the examinations was a matter which they all ought to regard with satisfaction, for it was most desirable that young women, to whatever class they belonged, should have as good an education as their respective powers would permit". However, at the end of he meeting Rev. Isaac Smith, a prebendary of the cathedral, struck a rather different note when he made this distinction: "a difference there must be, and ought to be, between the education of boys and that of girls – between the training for a public life and that for private, domestic life".

In 1867 Sir John, as a senior member of the government, had been much engaged by the state visits of the Viceroy of Egypt and the Sultan of the Ottoman Empire, and in 1873 another eastern grandee, Nasser al-Din, Shah of Persia, visited England after progressing through Europe. He had a retinue of fifty, and it is said that he depended on foreign loans to undertake this expensive visit. He was joined at Ostend by a large naval escort and arrived at Dover on 18th June, where he was met by the Duke of Cambridge and Prince Arthur. At Charing Cross he was welcomed by the Prince of Wales ('the queen herself, of course, was unable to be present', wrote The Times) and the party drove through London to Buckingham Palace, greeted by large crowds and numerous troops, undeterred by heavy rain.

On the same day Sir John was at Wellington College for a meeting of governors, and his return train arrived at Charing Cross shortly before the Shah's, so Sir John may have stayed to witness the grand arrival.

The following day the diplomatic corps and members of the government, were presented to the Shah, and in the evening the Prince of Wales gave a dinner at Marlborough House. The next day, Friday 20th, the party was received by the queen at Windsor, and in the evening they attended a ball given by the Lord Mayor and Corporation of London. On Saturday the party visited the Woolwich Arsenal – the Shah was regarded as a moderniser, and desired to see European industry at first hand, and Sir John was in the party at Woolwich answering questions posed by the visitors.

1873 and The Droitwich Brine Baths

The Shah of Persia leaving Charing Cross station en route for Buckingham Palace. He was met by the Prince of Wales, the Duke of Cambridge and other members of the royal family, and Sir John Pakington also happened to be present.

On Monday there was a review of the fleet at Spithead, which Sir John viewed with the Prince and Princess of Wales from the Royal Yacht Victoria and Albert, and on Tuesday there was a review of the troops in Windsor Great Park. On Wednesday the party was taken down river from the Tower of London to Greenwich to view the port of London and be entertained at a banquet by the first lord of the Admiralty, and on Thursday evening there was a grand state ball at Buckingham Palace. Sir John and Lady Pakington were present at the Lord Mayor's ball, at the Greenwich banquet, and at the final grand ball in Buckingham Palace, as well as being presented to the Shah at Buckingham Palace on 30th June.

On Friday the Shah went on a short visit to Liverpool and Manchester, where he visited some cotton factories, and returned the next day, staying at Trentham, the seat of the Duke of Sutherland. More events took place in London the following week, before the Shah and his retinue embarked at Portsmouth for France.

The Shah of Persia (holding glasses) at the Albert Hall, on June 24th 1873. On his right is the Princess of Wales, and on her right the Tsesarewich (heir to the Russian throne), and at the end the Duke of Edinburgh. On the Shah's left is the Tsesarevna (sister of the Princess of Wales), and on her left the Prince of Wales.

Page 105

Sir John was back in Worcestershire by the beginning of August, and on 4th chaired a meeting of the Droitwich Benefit Society, of which he had now been president for 13 years. He spoke of the satisfactory progress of the Society, the achievements of which were mentioned above (page 44). He said that "if a working man began by paying 2s 2d above his rent, reducing to 4d a week, he would in 14 years become the absolute owner of his house".

Later in the month Sir John went to stay with Sir Massey Lopes, Tory MP for South Devon, at his seat, Maristow House in Devon, where they were due to watch the autumn manoeuvres at Roborough Down attended by the Prince of Wales. But Sir John became ill and was not able to see the manoeuvres, but a few days later it was reported that he had recovered and returned to Westwood.

On 4th September Sir John attended an event that must have given him great pleasure. This was the opening of the new Worcester board school in Hounds Lane, a poor part of the city lying between Deansway and the River Severn. The chairman of the board was George Hastings, and at an earlier board meeting they had decided on the school hours, 9.00 a.m. to 12.00 noon, and 2.00 p.m. to 4.00 p.m., and that the day would begin with a religious service and instruction for 30 minutes. There would be a further religious instruction period during the last 15 minutes of the day. The chairman said how pleased he was that these matters had been decided 'with a unanimous feeling, that in other boards had agitated the minds of the members and caused a good deal of controversy'.

A survey of the local Worcester children had shown that between 600 and 700 did not attend school, which is why the board had been set up to provide for them. The new school was divided into three sections, all with separate entrances, for infants, girls and boys. Each section had a large schoolroom, 73 feet long for the infants, and 86 feet for both the boys and girls (whose accommodation was on the floor above the boys), and each had two smaller classrooms as well. Provision had been made initially for a total of 700 pupils, but there was space to increase this if necessary.

The city council and board members processed from the Guildhall to the new school, and gathered for a short service in the infants' schoolroom, culminating with the hymn 'Work, for it is a noble thing'. Then George Hastings opened the proceedings by paying tribute to the guest of honour, Sir John Pakington, who had campaigned so long for a national scheme. In his reply, Sir John said:

> Having lived through what has been a long life in the immediate neighbourhood of this city, it is impossible for me to feel indifferent to anything that concerns the welfare of the citizens. I strongly believe that nothing can tend more to promote the welfare – regarded in its best and soundest aspect – of this or any other city than the establishment of a system of education which should reach every child among that great population.

1873 and The Droitwich Brine Baths

He said he was very pleased with three aspects of the new school. Firstly, that attendance would be made compulsory. Secondly, he had 'unqualified satisfaction' from the mode in which the school was being inaugurated, with a degree of religious solemnity which he thought highly appropriate, and thirdly he thoroughly approved of the decision about the religious instruction that would be provided. He had always believed that "no education could be complete without impressing on the minds of the young their duty to God and man as well as imparting the ability to read and write".

During 1873 Sir John became involved, not for the first time, with efforts to improve the brine baths in Droitwich, which were becoming renowned for their curative properties. Natural brine springs occur in the town, and due to its heavy concentration of salt (ten times that of sea water) salt can easily be extracted by boiling. This had been done in Droitwich since at least Roman times, and continued well into the twentieth century, and the furnaces situated behind the High Street in Vines Park made the town centre a smoky dirty place. But it was not until the 1830s that the curative properties of brine began to be noticed – it was even said that during the 1832 cholera outbreak some had tried successfully to cure themselves by immersion in the brine.

The first brine baths were established by William Gabb in 1836, who previously had a draper's shop in the town, and who also took over the George Hotel, situated on the corner of Queen Street and Hanbury Road. He built the baths adjacent to the hotel, but by the 1850s the buildings were in a poor state, which, together with the dirty smoky town nearby, did not attract visitors, particularly from the upper classes, who would have preferred the fashionable spas of Europe, or perhaps the increasingly popular Malvern. Gabb wished to improve the facilities, but lacked capital himself. He therefore enlisted the help of some notable local people including Sir John and the Worcester physician Dr Charles Hastings, in setting up a company and inviting subscriptions for £20,000. A public meeting was held in 1855 and enthusiastically addressed by the promoters, and subsequently Sir John chaired several meetings of the directors. Unfortunately the fund-raising fell well short of its target, and

The George and Royal Hotel c. 1875. The entrance to the baths was through the doorway to the right of the building.

the company was liquidated. William Gabb remained at the George Hotel managing the brine baths, but by 1871 he had moved to Ombersley Street, where he was a colliery agent. Possibly looking after and accommodating his eleven children in a small hotel had proved difficult. William Walker took over the hotel.

About the same time a retired surgeon moved to Droitwich, and took up residence in St Peter's manor house near the church. William Bainbrigge FRCS had been a senior surgeon in Liverpool and elsewhere, and soon took an interest in the brine baths. He could see great medical possibilities in them, and negotiated a new 21 year lease with the Earl of Dudley, the freeholder. He decided to form a joint stock company with some leading local figures, and Sir John agreed to be chairman, and George Hastings his deputy.

The formation of the company was announced in 1872, and at a public meeting on 29th September 1873 Sir John was able to report progress. The company planned to build new baths to replace the dilapidated ones then existing, to take over the George Hotel and convert it into a private establishment for first class patients, to instal Turkish baths, to add more grounds and landscape them into a pleasure garden, and, perhaps in the longer term, to build a new public hotel. At the same time the George Hotel would be renamed the Royal Hotel, and the brine baths the Royal Brine Baths.

At the meeting Sir John recounted the history of the undertaking, including the failed attempt of twenty years before, since when the whole thing 'had lingered and languished'. But now, with the enthusiastic involvement of Dr Bainbrigge, Sir John felt optimistic, although he had to admit that only about £3,000 had been raised. This was sufficient for the construction of the new baths and Turkish bath, but to buy the George Hotel they had had to take out a mortgage of £3,000. They had also been able to buy extra land, the Herriot Pools, and the whole now amounted to over 8 acres, which had been nicely landscaped. Work on the new baths was almost complete, and Sir John looked forward to the benefits of the saline waters being much more widely known. He, and other speakers, gave examples of patients seriously afflicted with rheumatism who had had remarkable recoveries. These included a Glasgow merchant, Mr Jack, who was present that day. "For seventeen years Mr Jack had been afflicted with chronic rheumatism of a character that I had hardly ever witnessed, but, to my great surprise, I have seen that gentleman walking across this room without any support of any kind".

Some speakers referred to the value of the baths for the poor, and Sir John said good provision would be made to help this class of patient, but he emphasised that the company must be successful financially, and, after going over figures for the accounts, he predicted a surplus sufficient to pay a six percent dividend.

1873 and The Droitwich Brine Baths

On 25th October Sir John addressed a further gathering at the Queens Hotel in Birmingham, again giving examples of the cures that had been effected. He anticipated great interest in the baths in Birmingham, and he hoped many Birmingham residents would add their names to the subscription list.

The official opening of the new baths took place on 15th December. Berrow's printed a detailed report of the occasion, beginning with an unflattering description of Droitwich. 'The begrimed walls of the present shops and dwellings; the thoroughfares with their chronic state of dinginess and dirt; the continual subsidence of the soil on which it stands; and the vapours rising from the salt works which overhang it and permeate every part of it. By contrast, the new baths are very pleasantly situated in the midst of extensive and picturesque grounds and overlooking a country justly famed for its beauty and variety of landscape'.

The new buildings, in the Italianate style, housed four first class, three second class, and three third class baths, each with its own entrance. Each bath room had two dressing rooms, to speed the flow of patients. The natural brine was too strong to bathe in directly, so it was diluted two parts water to one part brine, the water being heated so the baths were at about 100°F.

After a tour of inspection led by Dr Bainbrigge, the official guests sat down to lunch, after which toasts were proposed. Sir John declared that he was gratified by the presence of so many medical men, which he believed "indicate their concurrence with the opinion which I, as a civilian, venture to express, that the company is engaged on a work which will mitigate and remove a vast amount of human suffering". He regretted that the Turkish baths were not quite finished, but they would be shortly, and he thought that the added use of brine in them would make them even more effective. The company was well aware that

The Royal Brine Baths, situated behind the George and Royal Hotel.

there was a shortage of good class accommodation in the town, and intended to enlarge and improve the hotel that they now owned. He understood that more accommodation was now being offered in the town, and that other new hotels might be built. The company also hoped to add a large swimming bath to the facilities.

William Bainbrigge then recounted how in 1870 his attention had first been drawn to the baths, and how "in a very short time I was thoroughly convinced of their value and importance". But he wished to dispel one great misconception about the baths: that there were only efficacious in the treatment of rheumatic or gouty conditions. He went on to explain:

> Digestion is the natural means for renewing, nourishing, and sustaining the body. If perfectly carried on, growth and health result; if imperfectly performed, derangement ensues, and misery and wretchedness become the lot of the unhappy sufferers… All diseases and disorders we know of are wholly dependent upon an abnormal condition of the digestive functions… Pure blood is the mainspring of nutritive life; impure blood the exciting or predisposing cause of all diseased action, producing the many varied symptoms commonly called disease. Now, when this is the case, we immediately endeavour to relieve the system of its impurities by correcting the condition of the digestive functions, but at the same time we want some further assistance to enable us to eliminate quickly these impurities alluded to. In ninety nine cases out of one hundred the skin is the organ first implicated.

The varied temperature and moisture of our climate affect the skin, Bainbrigge explained, and, because it is the most important organ of digestion, the internal organs are affected. So, he concluded,

> Through the skin we have the means afforded us by the judicious use of these incomparable Droitwich waters, in conjunction with the hot air bath, a remedy both safe and effectual; the powerful salines are rapidly absorbed, the capillary circulation is restored, and the skin at once recovers its healthy action. In producing this result, while at the same time relieving the other internal organs which have naturally sympathised with the skin, the stomach resumes its normal condition. The health of the patient becomes re-established and all the symptoms – whether gout, rheumatism, neuralgia or many others which are legion – disappear.

The local Dr Roden spoke next, giving more examples of the relief of suffering of rheumatic patients. "Within the last seven weeks a lady, who had long been unable to move without assistance, even to sit down or rise from her chair, had called upon me, and after using the baths she was able to walk across the room without help".

George Hastings, the vice-chairman, also spoke, and said his post was almost superfluous as Sir John had given the most assiduous attention to the project from its commencement. But he had assented to join the board as he considered he was carrying on the work of his late father, Dr Charles Hastings, who 40 years ago had investigated the salt water and analysed its composition, and had first advocated its use for medical treatment.

In concluding and declaring the baths open, Sir John paid tribute to the Earl of Dudley, unfortunately unable to attend that day, who had come forward with a magnificent donation of £500 "at a time of embarrassment".

At the end of the following year Bainbrigge purchased the whole enterprise and repaid the shareholders, and the company was put into liquidation. Bainbrigge then ran it himself till the early 1880s, when new proprietors took over. He died in 1884. Thanks to the efforts of Sir John and Bainbrigge Droitwich gradually became better known as a health resort, and the accommodation was improved when, in the 1870s, The Raven and Norbury House were opened as hotels. The wealthy and fashionable started to come in greater numbers, and Berrow's started to publish the names of arrivals. Although Sir John's connection was ended when Bainbrigge took over, he was the chairman of St John's Hospital, which opened in 1877 for poor patients. Ten years later John Corbett, 'The Salt King', built new brine baths adjacent to the Salters Hall, and these survived until modern times. Four years later, in 1891, the Worcestershire Brine Baths Hotel was opened with sixty six suites and rooms. But as local residents will know, the baths are no more. Brine baths were built as part of the new private hospital in the 1970s, but more recently closed for financial reasons. The Worcestershire Brine Baths Hotel has been replaced by flats, and the Raven Hotel is to be redeveloped into other uses. But even if some of the claims for the curative properties of bathing in brine were exaggerated, it does seem a pity that such beneficial treatment has been lost.

Bathers in the brine baths, kept afloat by the natural buoyancy of the brine.

Chapter 7
The 1874 Election

The Liberal government lost some by-elections in 1873, and on 24th January 1874 Gladstone, to much surprise, decided on an immediate dissolution. In his statement he admitted that the government had lost some authority, and he wanted a new mandate to support his radical legislative programme. Rather than disrupt the session with a spring election, he had decided to call one now. The government anticipated a £5m surplus that year, and therefore if re-elected they would abolish income tax and modify local taxation.

Sir John was now in his 37th year representing Droitwich, and had been unopposed until the last election in 1868. Although he was now nearly 75, and he knew that John Corbett, 18 years his junior, would oppose him again, he had no plans to retire. As soon as he heard about the dissolution he sent his election address to the newspapers. 'I therefore lose no time in expressing my confident hope that the support I have received from my neighbours in this borough for 36 years will not now be withheld' he wrote, and that his politics were so well known that there was no need to go further into that.

Corbett's address was much longer, and expressed general support for the measures taken by the last government, and its continuance. It mostly consisted of vague generalities, and Berrow's commented that all his aspirations had been supported by Sir John as well in the past. Corbett emphasised that this was the first election to be held using the ballot, which 'gives to all classes, and especially the working man, the opportunity of voting according to the dictates of his conscience. The honour I covet is to be elected by your free and unbiased votes…'.

Berrow's wrote of Corbett's address:

> Not a single political reason is assigned why the choice of the electors should be transferred from Sir John, whose brilliant career has reflected such marked honour upon the borough he has so long and faithfully represented. Personal ambition alone accounts for the candidature of a man who issues such an address as that of Mr Corbett. The defeat of Sir John Pakington would give

regret and pain to thousands of all parties in this country, and would be deplored throughout the length and breadth of the land. His return to the seat he has filled with distinction will save the borough from disgrace, and will be welcomed with rejoicing by the entire kingdom.

Meanwhile Herbert Goldingham, the Tory election agent, was watching the voters' registration, and predicted that Corbett would probably win, so it was perhaps understandable that when Sir John addressed a meeting at the George Hotel on 28th January, he sounded rather bitter. There was a large crowd, with many having to stand – no doubt the interest was spurred by the knowledge that it would be a hard contest. Edward Bearcroft of Mere Hall, Hanbury, a long time supporter of Sir John, was chairman, and when Sir John spoke he said this was the thirteenth time he had put himself up for election in Droitwich, and he asked why he was meeting, for the first time, such strong and vehement opposition. He had, he said, always made a point of attracting support from all shades of opinion, and on four recent occasions had been nominated at the election by a member of his own party, and seconded by a supporter of the Liberals. These included John Bradley (a magistrate and salt manufacturer) and Thomas Grove Smith, another magistrate, yet both these gentlemen were now acting in support of Corbett. Sir John then read a passage from a newspaper, reporting what Smith said about him in 1868 when he had seconded Sir John's nomination. After paying many compliments to Sir John, he ended 'I hope and trust that the friends of Sir John will rally round him tomorrow morning early at the poll, and that they will record their votes in his favour; and, you may rely upon it, the victory will be ours by a triumphant majority'.

Sir John was clearly stung by Smith's change of sides, and had written to him saying that in the circumstances Smith was bound, in fairness, to state his reasons. Smith had replied that 'I believe the interest of the salt trade will be best represented by a gentleman like Mr Corbett, who is deeply and intimately interested therein'. But Sir John did not accept this, and in any case 'no reason exists now against my return that did not exist with equal force at the last election'. He pointed to his long-term support for the salt industry, and his successful motion in 1853, which was opposed by the government, for removing the monopoly on salt production enjoyed by the East India Company, thus opening the way for the import of salt from England. Fearing that the influence of the Droitwich Salt Company might be used against him, Sir John had also written to John W Lea, its chairman, who had assured him that this would certainly not be the case.

Sounding somewhat plaintive he continued to address the meeting:

> I have lived among you for forty years, and represented you in parliament for thirty six years, and have sat in nine parliaments. I make no boast for anything I have done, or any reputation I have acquired, but I only say this,

that during that long period of public life I have taken an honest, honourable and straightforward course, and I have a right to complain, after a long public life and good neighbourhood, that those who praised me to the skies at the last election are now ready to condemn me.

After another attack on those who had changed sides, Sir John referred to his age. He said that Bearcroft had said he was an old man;

But perhaps I am hearty and vigorous still for an old man (loud applause). I cannot hope to act for many years longer as your representative, but the time has not yet come (hear, hear) when I would be compelled to relinquish active work (hear, hear) and I feel just as able as ever to go into the House of Commons and even to make another motion on the salt trade (laughter and applause).

After this lengthy introduction, Sir John turned to more political matters, including the relationship between landlord and tenant, and the welfare of agricultural labourers. These, he said, deserved a fair wage, a good house, and a garden to cultivate if they were to be happy and contented, and he referred again to the possibility of them keeping a cow. He said that this question, like so many others, had attracted extremes of opinions, and, as always, he saw the solution as a compromise. After touching on other current political subjects, and promising to campaign to introduce more religion into education, he sat down 'amidst a storm of applause'.

However, when the returns were in on 3rd February, Sir John's worst fears were confirmed – out of the electorate of 1,541, only 401 voted for him, whereas 787, nearly twice as many, preferred Corbett. Interest in the election is shown by the high turnout – less than 25 per cent did not record a vote, which was good even for a time when turnouts were much higher than today.

Predictably, Berrow's was scathing: 'Droitwich has brought upon itself a disgrace that will be long remembered against it – one of which the entire county of Worcester is ashamed'. There was much more of the same, calling Corbett a 'local nobody' and a 'nouveau riche'. By contrast, Sir John 'was revered in all assemblages for the ability and urbanity that characterise him, and for the exalted conscientiousness with which he has discharged for many years his public and private duties… the electors of Droitwich have taught the country their true value, and the finger of scorn will long be pointed against them'.

It is ironic that in 1868, when the Tories generally did badly in the election, Sir John easily overcame his new opponent, whereas in 1874 the Tories did much better, and for the first time since they split in 1846 they had an overall parliamentary majority of about fifty, although the Liberals still polled about twenty per cent more votes than the Conservatives – the fact that many Conservatives were unopposed contributed to this. Yet Sir John did badly, being the only member

The 1874 Election

of the opposition front bench to lose his seat. John Corbett had become a well known and popular local figure by that time, having just completed his new house, Impney Manor, now called the Chateau Impney, and was highly regarded in Stoke Works among his employees. He was becoming a philanthropist having just built the new school in Stoke Works village, although most of his major works – Wychbold church, and his various projects in Droitwich – were still to come. By contrast, Sir John, although still well-known locally, would have been seen as at the end of his long career, and, although he had taken a great interest in many local organisations, it was not thought that he had much to offer the community in future, in contrast to the wealthy Corbett.

Shortly after the election there were press reports that another seat would be found for Sir John, so he could join Benjamin Disraeli's new Tory government. The new member for Chatham, Admiral Elliott, was said to be ready to resign his safe seat in favour of Sir John if necessary. But it seems Disraeli wanted a new younger looking cabinet, and he probably also remembered the battles he had had with Sir John over expenditure when he was first lord, and secretary for war. Accordingly on 20th February he wrote:

Stoke Works school. Opened in 1872 as the village school, much later it became a school for children with special needs, before being more recently converted into flats. It was among the John Corbett's local 'good works', making him popular with the electorate.

SIR JOHN PAKINGTON

> My Dear Pakington, I obtained from the queen on Wednesday a peerage for you. I did not immediately communicate this, as I was in hope of having combined it with something else, but in that I have failed after many efforts. This may be a disappointment to you; to me it is a mortification.
>
> I trust, however, you will not consider your active political career to have terminated, as I shall take every opportunity to prove the contrary.
>
> Let me have at your convenience the title that you wish to take, so that I may put affairs in train, & believe me always, most sincerely yours, D

Disraeli would probably have liked to find his old colleague a position of some sort, if only to give him a salary as it was known that Sir John's financial position was not good, with his estate being heavily mortgaged. But Disraeli had always been keen on using patronage for party political purposes, and would have given such posts as were in his gift to aid the Tory party, and he probably thought Sir John was well down his list in that respect. Whether Sir John hesitated before accepting the peerage we do not know – when in 1866 there had been rumours that he was going to raised to the peerage, he said when seeking re-election in Droitwich:

> I am by no means insensible of the honour of the peerage, and I do not think well of any Englishman who would seek to deprecate the great institutions of our country, of which the peerage is one; but we have all the right to hold our personal views, and I beg distinctly to state that I have never had the least desire to be raised to the peerage. I am perfectly contented to remain in the position in public life which it is my fortune to occupy, and as far as my public life is concerned I desire for the remainder of my days to enjoy nothing more than the support of my constituents of Droitwich.

But now he no longer had the support of his constituents in Droitwich, Sir John may be excused for accepting the honour. In any case, as will be seen, he still wished to play an active part in politics, and the upper house would provide that platform. Sir John decided to style himself Baron Hampton of Hampton Lovett and Westwood, so we will in future refer to him as Lord Hampton. On Tuesday 10th March he took his seat in the House of Lords.

Letters of congratulation flowed in, but he must have been particularly pleased when, at a meeting of the Worcester city council on 7th April Alderman Edward Webb rose to speak of his recent elevation. He said that Lord Hampton, whether for his national or for his local achievements, "had commanded the respect of all who knew him". He pointed to the many occasions he had put himself "a great deal out of his way" to help those who sought his assitance, and mentioned his work as a Severn Commissioner. He proposed that a congratulatory address be presented to him. This was his address:

The 1874 Election

> *We, the mayor, aldermen, and citizens of Worcester in council assembled, beg to offer to your lordship our sincere congratulations upon the honour which Her Majesty the Queen has been graciously pleased to confer in adding to the peerage of England the name of one who has served his country in some of the most distinguished offices of the State.*
>
> *We take this opportunity of expressing our grateful sense of the many acts of kindness, courtesy, and valuable assistance at all times willingly rendered by your lordship to the citizens of Worcester during your long and honourable parliamentary career, and we pray that Divine Providence may permit you long to enjoy the new honour you have so well merited.*

Another speaker recalled how, when he was mayor, Sir John 'had kindly afforded the citizens of an opportunity of receiving such distinguished visitors as Lord Napier of Magdala and Mr Reverdy Johnson' (the American ambassador).

As discussed above, Lord Hampton's defeat at Droitwich went against the national trend, as the Conservatives made widespread gains. Among these were in East Worcestershire, where the Liberal candidates, Hon. Charles Lyttelton and Arthur Albright, were unseated by the Conservative candidates, Henry Allsopp and Thomas Eades Walker, giving the eastern division two Tories for the first time for thirty years. To celebrate, a banquet was held in Bromsgrove on 7th April at the Golden Cross Hotel, at which Lord Hampton presided, with Messrs Allsopp and Walker on either side. All the usual toasts were drunk, and the chairman gave a review of the political scene. He said it was the second time that the electorate had brought in a Tory government after some years of Liberal misrule – the previous time was in 1841 when Lord Melbourne's government were defeated on a vote of no confidence by a majority of one, an occasion at which he had been present.

He thought that the calling of the election at very short notice was an attempt by Gladstone "to surprise the country, and by doing this to obtain some advantage". He also referred to Gladstone's 'bribe' when he proposed the abolition of income tax, having said the public finances should show a surplus of £5,000,000 that year. But in fact, Lord Hampton said, the latest estimates were that the surplus would be smaller at only £3,500,000, so the prime minister had made an exaggerated promise. Both new MPs spoke, and admitted to being 'new boys' in the House. Walker lived in Studley Castle in Warwickshire, and said that when he first put his name forward it was said he was not wanted in Worcestershire. But he now found this was not so, and he looked forward to doing his best for his new constituency. Walker, just 31, was in fact shortly to become the son-in-law of his fellow MP Henry Allsopp, as he married Allsopp's daughter Elizabeth. But Walker did not stand for parliament again.

Henry Allsopp, 63, has been referred to before (page 101). He was defeated at the next, 1880, election, and was eventually raised to the peerage in 1886, a year before he died. In his speech he said that his brief parliamentary experience had shown him that all taxes were disliked, and that "the income tax is certainly one of the most obnoxious taxes ever imposed on the people of this country, and I think there might be improvements effected with respect to local taxation. The malt tax is a great burden upon the country, and I would like to see it repealed".

The following day Lord Hampton attended the grand re-opening of Worcester cathedral, which will be described in a later chapter.

Later in what was a busy week a similar celebratory event was held in the Town Hall, Birmingham, presided over by the Earl of Dartmouth. It was well attended with members of both houses of parliament, and 'the side galleries of the hall were set apart for the accommodation of ladies and gentlemen not guests proper, most of the ladies appearing in full dress'. Lord Hampton proposed the toast to the armed forces, and referred to the recent successful termination of the Ashanti war (in modern Ghana). The soldiers from the West Indies and India fought side by side with the British, he said, facing not only the ordinary dangers of war, but the pestilential climate of West Africa. Sir John recalled that he had had the high honour of being connected with both the great services, and that he felt a personal, as well as a national, feeling of admiration.

Henry Allsopp was also present and reminded the meeting that, although there had been Conservative gains in many of the areas around Birmingham, the three members representing Birmingham itself (George Dixon, Philip Muntz, and John Bright) were all Liberals. In fact there had only one Conservative member for the town since 1832, and that only for three years. But Allsopp hoped that the work done by his friend Sydney Gedge would eventually change this. Gedge, a London solicitor, had proposed standing for the borough, but had withdrawn when it was clear he would not succeed, but he had worked hard to increase Conservative support.

The 1874 Election

The day after the Birmingham meeting Lord Hampton attended a meeting of the Worcester Diocesan Board of Education when prizes were presented, and he spoke about the effects of the 1870 Act, which he called a 'Great Act'. But its one fault was that, although it had very much increased the number of Church of England schools, it had abolished diocesan inspection and examination of schools. So the diocese had to rely on its own system of examinations, and it was the results of that that they were marking that day. The bishop pointed to the poor results from the candidates for teacher training colleges when examined in religious knowledge. Over half the candidates only attained the third class, and nearly one fifth failed. Lord Hampton said that the 1870 Act did not make proper provision for religious education, and he still hoped it might be changed.

One subject on which Lord Hampton had long held strong views was that of local taxation, and reference was made in an earlier chapter to his resolution to the quarter sessions, and the debate in the House of Commons in 1871 on a motion by Sir Massey Lopes in which he spoke. In fact Lopes made this an annual campaign, and in 1872 proposed a similar motion:

> That it is expedient to remedy the injustice of imposing taxation for national objects on one description of property only, and therefore that no legislation with reference to local taxation will be satisfactory which does not provide, either in whole or in part, for the relief of occupiers and owners in counties and boroughs from charges imposed on ratepayers for the administration of justice, police, and lunatics, the expenditure for such purposes being almost entirely independent of local control.

Sir John had not spoken in that debate although he cast his vote in favour, and in the division the motion attracted a majority of 100. The Liberal government, however, had taken no action on the matter, and now there was a Conservative government the agricultural interest hoped that local rate payers would be offered some relief. In 1873 Sir John had joined the Central Chamber of Agriculture, and later that year was invited by the secretary, John Algernon Clark, to become vice-chairman in 1874, which would lead to him being chairman the following year. Sir John attended his first meeting of the Chamber in April 1873, when there was a long report on local taxation from Sir Massey Lopes.

Lord Hampton was duly elected vice-president on 3rd March, and after a discussion on the topics of the day – local taxation, and the landlord and tenant bill – it was agreed that a deputation should be sent to the new prime minister, Disraeli, to emphasis the importance of the reform of local taxation. This took place on 23rd March, when Lord Hampton led a large delegation to Downing Street. He began by saying the delegation was not a political one, having representatives of all political views, but on one thing they were united: the need for reform of local taxation. He reminded the prime minister of the debate in the House in 1872, a debate in which Disraeli himself had taken a distinguished part, and the large majority by which Sir Massey's motion passed. Lord Hampton was sure that if a similar motion was proposed today, it would command an even bigger majority. Now the new government were considering their financial arrangements, Lord Hampton hoped this matter would be brought into consideration, and that the delegation would not leave the room without some hope that, for example, the cost of the police and of lunatics would be taken over by the state. Other speakers included the president of the chamber, George Frederick Muntz, the son of the late Birmingham MP of the same name.

The prime minister responded with a lengthy and sympathetic speech, and said he himself had first introduced the matter in the House in 1848. But he refrained from giving any actual commitments, saying "I cannot say that your views thus expressed differ from those of Her Majesty's government (cheers), but at the same time allow me to exercise that reserve which we must all exercise in the business of life, and if I confine my expressions to those of sympathy, and do not show it in a practical form, it is not that I do not feel it". The deputation expressed its great thanks to the prime minister for seeing them and listening to what they had to say, but must have felt disappointed that Disraeli did nothing more than give an historical review and express his sympathy. Nevertheless, in that year some burdens were transferred from local rates to the national exchequer, and indeed this trend continued over many years, when central government increasingly took over the burdens of local authorities by giving them grants.

The Central Chamber of Agriculture formed a separate committee to lobby on local taxation, and they were successful over a number of years in opposing new legislation that put extra burdens on the local rates.

Lord Hampton led another deputation from the Central Chamber in April when he saw the home secretary with Lord Lyttelton on a technical point regarding the law on industrial schools, and again in May, when they went to see the Duke of Richmond, Lord President of the Council. This time it was about the implementation of the Contagious Diseases (Animals) Act, under which the privy council could produce regulations. It was thought that firm enough action had not been taken to stop the spread of disease, and George Muntz, who was the main speaker, thought that more powers to slaughter diseased animals, and to compensate the farmers, were needed.

The third agricultural question that occupied the attention of the Central Chamber was that of the relationship between landlord and tenant, particularly the question of unexhausted improvements, that is to say long lasting improvements in the farm that would endure beyond the end of the tenancy. It had already been legislated that buildings erected by the tenant should be compensated for by the landlord at the end of the tenancy, but there remained many other improvements that the tenant might make including drainage and soil improvement. The Central Chamber produced a long report on this, investigating what the local practise was in different counties, and at its June meeting the matter was debated, and Lord Hampton was generally in favour of legislation, although this would have to be carefully considered. Others were against any government 'interference' in what they saw as a mater that should be negotiated between landlord and tenant. Lord Hampton thought long leases would also help solve the question, but admitted that many farmers did not want to commit themselves to these.

In May Emperor Alexander II of Russia visited London. He had come to visit his daughter, the Grand Duchess Maria Alexandrovna of Russia, who earlier in the year had married the Duke of Edinburgh, the second son of Queen Victoria. Lord Hampton had had dealings with the duke when he was first lord of the Admiralty in 1866, when, at the request of the queen, he had arranged for the Duke, then an RN captain, to go on a long cruise to Australia to keep him away from the female delights of London. The duke had survived an assassination attempt in Sydney, so perhaps he was not Lord Hampton's greatest admirer, but he was nevertheless invited to receptions held for the emperor and his family by foreign secretary Lord Derby, and the lord mayor's banquet at the Guildhall.

Despite regularly attending the House of Lords, Lord Hampton did not make any major intervention until May, when on 22nd he introduced a motion on a topic about which he had long campaigned – that there should be a secretary of state for education (or minister of public instruction, as he proposed to call it). Education was the most important responsibility of the privy council. The president of the council thus had overall responsibility for education, and the vice-president of the committee on education was his subordinate, and in day-to-day charge of education. Lord Hampton had always regarded this as anomalous – why should education be different from other great departments, such as the war office, home office and foreign office, which had their own departments and responsible ministers?

Lord Hampton went over the history of the committee of council, which dated back to 1839 when it was formed to administer the annual education grant, then £30,000. In 1865 Lord Hampton had moved for a committee to be appointed to enquire into the working of the committee of council. He chaired the committee, which drew up a report. Unfortunately the report was never finalised as a change of government took place at that time, but the draft (no doubt largely drawn up by its chairman) recommended the establishment of a separate department of education. But Lord Hampton said that much of the evidence revealed great disparities in the way different ministers saw the working of the committee of council – some saw the position of the vice-president as little different to that of a secretary of state, others thought the committee itself was useless, knowing little about the matters they had to deal with. He continued:

> Now, such discrepancies of opinion on such a matter among statesmen who had actually filled the office either of president or vice-president, were hardly consistent with the proper organization and useful working of a great public department; but the climax of anomaly was reached when, in the late government, the president and vice-president of the council happened to sit side by side as members of the same cabinet, each representing the department of education.

In support of his argument Lord Hampton pointed out that the president of the council had many other duties to perform; matters of public health, quarantine, cattle disease, the Channel Islands "and many other subjects sufficient to engage his whole energies". Before sitting down, he also mentioned the subject of religious education, hardly relevant to his motion, and thought that "the great body of the nation desired that the education of the people should be based on religious grounds".

The lord president of the council, the Duke of Richmond, opposed the motion. His main contention was that the present system worked well, and that if education was taken away from the privy council, what would there be left for it to do? After all, the lord president ranked third in the government after the prime minister and lord chancellor, but without education he would become "a first class veterinary surgeon". It was true that Lord Hampton had been to see him recently on matters concerning both education and agriculture. But he could

Charles Henry Gordon-Lennox, 1813-1903, 6th Duke of Richmond. He was MP for West Sussex from 1841 until he inherited in 1860, and after Lord Derby died in 1869 he became Tory leader in the Lords. He was loyal and hard working, but a man of limited ability, and Disraeli made him president of the council when he formed his government in 1874. Richmond had long taken a special interest in agriculture, so had some knowledge of cattle plague, the prevention of which came under his charge, but he knew little of education.

speak both for himself and his deputy Lord Sandon when he said that they "did not exhibit any ignorance of what was going on in either subject, and I can say that I felt quite equal to my noble friend on all these occasions". However, Paul Smith in his book on 'Disraelian Conservatism' wrote that Richmond was 'a man of little calibre with no particular interest in education, an aristocratic amateur of the old type, whose main concern seems to have been to get the business of the session over and depart to the Scottish moors', so perhaps we may take what Richmond said about his mastery of all these subjects with a pinch of salt.

Only one other speaker supported the motion, and Lord Hampton did not press it to a division, and it was 'negatived'. In its editorial, The Times did not think Lord Hampton had put the case very well, but thought there was a strong case to be made. At present, with both the president and vice-president having responsibility, who was in overall charge? The Times agreed with Lord Hampton that it was unsatisfactory that the privy council had many other unconnected matters to deal with, and thirdly, and this was not a point that Lord Hampton made, that the administration of various aspects of education were currently scattered among different departments, and, as education was bound to increase in importance, surely it would be sensible to bring all these under one roof.

In fact little change took place until 1900 when an education board was established, but it was to be another 70 years before the first minister of education was appointed.

On 29th June Lord Hampton again rose to ask the Duke of Richmond questions about education. Firstly, in line with a recent deputation to the lord president, he asked whether it was not time that the government gave more attention to the training of teachers for the schools of the middle and upper classes. There was now a system of training colleges for teachers of the 'humbler classes', but it was just as important, if not more so, that teachers in the schools for older and better off children were competent. Secondly, what was the committee of council going to do about the recent statement by Lord Sandon, the vice-president, that of the 2,200,000 children on the books of elementary schools, 500,000 had attended for less than the half year necessary to count for grants. In reply, the Duke of Richmond said that he did not think the country was ready for a scheme of compulsory certification for teachers of these schools, but his department were well aware of the poor attendance figures, and his department was looking "with great anxiety" at the whole subject.

Also towards the end of June Lord Hampton went to hear the judicial committee of the House of Lords consider a case with which he had a distant personal connection. His second wife, Augusta Murray, had a sister Caroline who, in 1834, had married Sir John Mordaunt of Walton Hall, Warwickshire. Sir John had died in a tragic shooting accident not far from his home in 1845, leaving a son and heir Sir Charles Mordaunt. In 1866 he married Harriet, one of fourteen children of Sir Thomas Moncrieff from near Perth in Scotland. Unfortunately Harriett became involved in a 'fast' London set, and, aided by her husband's absences in Norway and elsewhere, she mixed freely with the Prince of Wales and others, and, as it later emerged, had dalliances with some of them. On 15th July 1868 her husband returned unexpectedly from abroad, and was astounded to see Harriett in the company of the Prince in front of the Hall showing her how to drive a carriage with a pair of white horses. The Prince quickly made his excuses and left, and Sir Charles, disgusted at the Prince's behaviour at visiting a married lady uninvited by her husband, got his groom to shoot the two horses dead and burn the carriage, all in front of his wife.

About the same time Harriett became pregnant, and when the baby, later named Violet, was born Harriett behaved in a peculiar way, frightened that the

Georgina (left), 1846-1929, and Harriet, 1848-1906, two of the eight daughters of Sir Thomas Moncrieff. Georgina, a noted beauty, in 1865 married William Ward, 1st Earl of Dudley of Witley Court, Worcestershire. Harriett married Sir Charles Mordaunt of Walton Hall, Warwicks in 1866. Lord Hampton was related to Sir Charles Mordaunt as his second wife Augusta's sister Caroline had married Sir John Mordaunt, Sir Charles' father, and he was related to Harriett Moncrieff as her mother, Louisa Hay-Drummond, was a cousin of Augusta. After her divorce Harriett spent the rest of her life being cared for in various asylums. Her daughter Violet turned out to be free of disease, and married Viscount Weymouth, and their son Henry, 6th Marquess of Bath, founded the popular safari park at Longleat.

baby might be suffering from 'the disease'. Shortly after she called her husband into her room, and said the baby was not his, but Lord Cole's, and she mentioned other names including that of the Prince of Wales.

Adultery by the wife was a reason for an automatic divorce, and Sir Charles started proceedings. But Harriett's family came to her aid, and made out that the confessions were made when she was mentally disturbed, and that she was, in fact, insane. When the court proceedings started it was ruled that the case could not continue as the wife was unable to defend herself, and this sparked off a lengthy series of court cases, and the retention of Harriett in various asylums while her family tried to prove her insane. But Sir Charles made out that she had been put up to feigning her insanity by her family. The case dragged on for a long time, and in one hearing the Prince of Wales was called to give evidence, and denied that he had ever had an improper relationship with Lady Mordaunt. Sir John Pakington, as he was then, was also called upon on one occasion to try and persuade a doctor, who said she was insane, that she was not. On 22nd June 1874 the case reached the House of Lords, and Lord Hampton and Lord Lyttelton spent the day listening to the submissions. At the end of the day the judges found, by a majority of three to two, that if adultery was proved then the wife's insanity should be no bar to a divorce. It was inequitable that the husband should be permanently deprived of his rights for that reason. The case was remitted back to the divorce court, where Sir Charles eventually obtained his divorce, and in 1878 remarried and had six more children. The story is told in great detail in 'The Warwickshire Scandal' by Elizabeth Hamilton, a descendent of Sir Charles Mordaunt.

On 6th July the question of the best way to train naval cadets came up in the House of Lords, and Lord Hampton always had views to express on naval matters. There was a training ship, HMS Britannia, at Dartmouth, but Lord Hampton doubted this was the best place to site it, as "I would not hesitate to say that of all the places to be found along our coasts the very worst situation for a training ship was the port of Dartmouth, for, although it was one of the most beautiful as regarded its scenery, it was, at the same time, one of the most relaxing as regarded climate!".

A matter that had been causing, and would continue to cause, Lord Hampton much difficulty, concerned Spanish bonds. At some stage in the past he had personally invested in securities issued by the Spanish government, no doubt because they offered a better rate of interest than British government bonds. But internal problems in Spain had caused the government to default on the interest and capital due in 1873, and Lord Hampton was asked to head a committee of bondholders to seek redress. After negotiations with the committee, which represented a large number of both British and foreign bond-holders, the Spanish government had agreed to deposit shares in the new Rio Tinto mine and another mine with the Bank of England, which would be used to settle with the bond holders. The securities had been duly deposited, but after a change in the ministry in Spain they had been withdrawn, and an order by the Court of Chancery that they should not be touched came too late to save the bond holders.

On 21st July in the House of Lords Lord Hampton explained the background to the default, and asked whether the government could use its influence to get the Spanish government to make satisfactory arrangements with the bondholders. The foreign secretary, the Earl of Derby, expressed sympathy with Lord Hampton and his fellow creditors, but said that, as the British government was not directly involved, he had no official knowledge on the matter, but would continue to use such friendly influence as it could to get the matter settled. He pointed out that the ultimate sanction for the Spanish government was that they would find themselves shut out of the money markets after making a default, but this would have been small comfort for the bondholders.

The parliamentary session ended on 7th August, and Lord Hampton was soon back at Westwood. The main events of that autumn concerned the Three Choirs Festival, when Lord Hampton led the campaign against the dean and chapter's refusal to allow a festival to take place in 1875, and this will be described in the following chapters.

Chapter 8
The Restoration of Worcester Cathedral

In the early part of the nineteenth century Worcester Cathedral, like so many other medieval English religious edifices, was in a sorry condition, despite spasmodic and sometimes botched attempts at repairs in the eighteenth and early nineteenth centuries, and by the 1840s it was clear that the building itself was in danger. When it was finally re-opened in 1874 Berrow's published a long account of the work, and described the cathedral before the restoration thus:

> Almost surrounded by buildings and old walls, the fine proportions of the sacred edifice were not apparent to the passer-by, while the immediate vicinity of the building was desecrated by nuisances and other unseemly consequences of domestic establishments reared beneath the shadow of its walls... One by one these have disappeared, to the great regret of the antiquary and historian but to the vast improvement of the conditions affecting the external appearance of the Cathedral, and to the entire realisation of our estimate of the propriety in the surroundings of the house of God – the great and principal temple of the diocese.
>
> Although, therefore, that unique building, the Guesten Hall, has disappeared, St Michael's church and (long ago) the old clochium or campanile have departed; the charnel house vaulting has been almost entirely destroyed... When we look at the restored fabric as it now stands, free from all unsightly excrescences, surrounded as far as possible by a beautiful green sward, and its noble tower richly renovated, a cherished landmark 'for all the country round', we cannot but feel thankful that it has been put into the hearts of the present generation thus to atone for the guilty neglect of their predecessors, and to commence and complete a glorious and magnificent work for the honour and praise of God.

The major restoration work had started 20 years before in 1854, under the dean, the Very Rev. John Peel DD, who had been appointed to the deanery under the premiership of his brother, Sir Robert Peel, in 1845 and who was to remain in that office throughout the restoration. Some of the buildings mentioned above were taken down, as well as a house against the west end of the cathedral, allowing the great west doors to be reopened. The ground level around the cathedral, which had risen over the centuries causing damp problems to the building, was lowered, which 'added to its apparent height and general effect'.

Having improved the surroundings of the cathedral, the restorers turned their attention to the structure itself, using the local architect Abraham Edward Perkins (1809-73). Perkins had trained under the gothic revival specialist Thomas Rickman in Birmingham, and had already designed some local churches and public buildings. He was appointed in 1848, and started by doing some minor repairs, but by 1854 he realised that major reconstruction was needed, both at the west end where the end wall needed support and a new window, and, particularly, at the east end, where he replaced the 'great and unsightly' east window with five Early English lancets. At the same time much of the upper parts of the Lady Chapel and east transepts were taken down and rebuilt, again with lancets.

However, by 1863 the capitular funds were exhausted, and, wishing to see the great work completed, the dean decided that a public appeal was needed, and approached the lord lieutenant, Lord Lyttelton. Lyttelton seems to have readily agreed to take the initiative, and in February 1864 had a letter printed for circulation throughout the diocese. It began by outlining what had already been done, which he summarised as follows:

An engraving of the north side of Worcester cathedral in 1673. Note the campanile, the domestic buildings up against the cathedral walls, and the late gothic windows. It had suffered particularly badly during the civil war, when parliamentary troops were stationed in the city.

The Restoration of Worcester Cathedral

Externally, the whole of the fabric east of the tower has been restored, and the east end and two eastern transepts have been in great measure rebuilt. All the windows have been altered, and new buttresses and pinnacles erected. The two western transepts have been thoroughly repaired, and a large new window inserted in the north west transept.

Internally the whitewash and plaster have been removed from the walls both of the choir and the nave, the whole of the vaulting repaired, two large piers rebuilt, two unsightly walls removed: the marble shafts and carved work restored: the bosses re-gilt: and part of the ancient painting removed. Some ancient rooms have been converted into vestries, and the chapter house restored within and without.

Lyttelton's letter continued that the cost so far had been £31,000. Some of this had come from the capitular funds, now in the hands of the ecclesiastical commissioners, 'but much the larger portion of the expenditure involved a proportionate and very considerable personal sacrifice of income on the part of the present members of the chapter, and in some degree also on the part of their successors'. However, it should be noted that figures given later showed that this was not quite correct – £15,000 had come from the ecclesiastical commissioners, £7,200 from the cathedral fabric fund, and the rest from the dean and canons. Indeed there were anonymous letters in the local papers from writers who had gone into the finances carefully, and who claimed that the cathedral clergy had not made any personal sacrifices, and who noted that, in contrast to the public

John Peel, 1798-1875, one of eleven children of Robert Peel 1st bart, and brother of the prime minister. Educated at Christ Church, Oxford, where he received his doctor of divinity degree, in 1828 he was presented to the living of Stone near Kidderminster, which he retained until his death, and there is a memorial to him there. He was Dean of Worcester from 1845, and gave generously to the restoration. His gift of the reredos was in memory of his wife Julia, who had predeceased him.

meeting in Worcester on 8th April, described below, when a similar meeting was held in Warwick (much of that county was in the diocese of Worcester) it was just stated 'that the capitular funds had been exhausted'.

Lyttelton then went on to explain what still needed to be done, which, he wrote, could be divided between external and interior work. Externally, the north west and south sides of the nave and the north porch needed repair, stained glass for the new large west window was needed, and the cloisters needed thorough repair. Internally, the choir was to be remodelled, the stalls improved, the nave re-floored, the building heated and lit, the organ reconstructed, and a new screen and reredos provided.

Lyttelton explained that Perkins would continue as architect, but on the internal work would collaborate with George Gilbert Scott, who had already submitted a report on the building. Scott, born in 1811, was then at the height of his powers, having just been selected to design the memorial to the late Prince Consort. He had designed new churches, and had been involved in the restoration of very many gothic churches, including most of the English and Welsh cathedrals, as well as many important civil projects including the new Foreign Office, and St Pancras station. He worked with tireless energy, and his practice was among the largest in Europe. Spending a lot of his time travelling, Scott had the ability to work while on the move, and was adept at producing detailed

George William, 4th Baron Lyttelton of Hagley Hall, 1817-76. In 1839 he married Mary Glynne, sister-in-law to William Gladstone, who died in 1857 after the birth of their twelfth child. In 1869 he married a second time and had three more children. He was a strict Anglican and his religious beliefs led him to oppose the use of the cathedral for the music festivals, although, like the Earl of Dudley, he had been a steward of the 1842 festival. He died in tragic circumstances, as described later in this book.

sketches of his designs which could be passed on to be worked up by his large team of assistants.

Lyttelton concluded by writing that these proposed works were estimated to cost just under £22,000, which, he wrote, was comparable with sums raised for the restoration of Lichfield and Hereford Cathedrals, and less than the £40,000 proposed for Salisbury Cathedral. He had made enquiries in Worcestershire, and it seemed that 'an appeal for assistance would be cordially entertained'; but he was less able to speak for the part of the diocese that was in Warwickshire. Finally, he announced that a public meeting would be held in the Worcester Guildhall on Thursday 8th April, when the appeal would be launched.

Most of the great and good of the county were present at the meeting, including the bishop, the Earl of Dudley, Earl Beauchamp and Sir John. Lord Leigh, lord lieutenant of Warwickshire, sat next to Lyttelton. In his speech, Lyttelton said that he was there at the invitation of the dean and chapter who had taken the initiative in the project, and said how generous they had already been with their own funds. But now it was up to the counties of Worcestershire and Warwickshire to fund the project through to its conclusion, which would need another £22,000, plus, if it was agreed, £8,000 for the restoration of the tower. He felt this was particularly important, since another clergyman, Rev. Richard Cattley, had launched a separate bells and clock appeal, so that the cathedral would be endowed with a fine peel of bells which would also mark the time. Restoration of the tower would involve raising the pinnacles by seven feet, and the parapets two feet.

George Gilbert Scott, or Sir Gilbert Scott as he later called himself, lived from 1811 to 1878. The most famous restoration architect of his day, his work at Worcester was among his last work, and it is believed he was responsible for a total of nearly 1,000 completed projects. One of the most famous is the Albert Memorial. He was buried in Westminster Abbey. Two of his sons, George Gilbert Scott and John Oldrid Scott were also architects, as was his grandson Sir Giles Gilbert Scott, architect of Liverpool cathedral.

LORD HAMPTON

Lord Lyttelton said that hitherto the dean and chapter had managed the restoration and taken all the decisions, but henceforth trustees would be appointed to manage the subscribed fund and the work, although of course it would be done to the plans of the dean and chapter. Lyttelton then named the various people who had already subscribed or promised to do so, including the Earl of Dudley, who had already promised to add £1,000 for every £10,000 subscribed.

The meeting was then addressed by the bishop, Earl Beauchamp, and, at somewhat greater length, the Earl of Dudley. Lyttelton had referred to the fact that the subscriptions would be staged over three years, as the restoration would take many years, and he had even referred to timescales measured in decades. But Lord Dudley wanted the work to be finished in five years, and would certainly include the tower in the new appeal. But he felt that to be successful the finished cathedral should be seen as a place for all to worship in, not just a 'limited number of persons' as at present. He was keen for the nave to be properly floored and brought back into use for services, at least on Sundays. Comfortable seating there with boards to kneel on should be provided. An important need was for the building to be heated – he knew from personal experience how cold it could be at all seasons of the year, and "how can you have a warm heart with cold feet?". The Dean may have allowed himself to have extra warmth at his feet, but how could the poor organist play properly with freezing hands?

Lord Dudley then referred to what had from time to time been somewhat controversial, and was to become even more so later, that of holding the Three Choirs Festival in the cathedral every three years. The newly arranged nave would, Lord Dudley thought, put the holding of a festival there out of the question, and there was such a thing as fitness of place, "and to make a cathedral,

William Ward, 1st Earl of Dudley, 1817-85. He inherited the Ward barony from his father John Ward, and became the 1st Earl of Dudley of the second creation in 1860. The family fortunes were based on the mineral wealth of their Black Country estates, and Dudley was by far the largest contributor to the restoration of the cathedral. Although he became an implacable opponent of the music festivals, he had been a steward of the 1842 festival. From a picture taken c. 1865.

which ought to be a place of prayer, the spot for holding a music festival was unbecoming". No-one, he continued, attended a concert with a sense that it was a divine service – they even kept up every-day conversation during the performance. He said that the Town Hall in Birmingham was one of the finest places to perform music in the country, and it would add little to the inconvenience of those attending the festivals to go to Birmingham instead.

Sir John also spoke, proposing a resolution for the formation of a fund raising committee to be chaired by Lord Lyttelton, and to include the mayor of Worcester, the county sheriff, Sir Charles Hastings, and Sir John's son Johnny. In fact, although this committee met on a number of occasions, their meetings were largely a formality, and John Slaney Pakington is recorded as only attending once. Sir John referred, as some other speakers had done, to the fact that some may object to the fact that the present generation was being asked to make up for the deficiencies of past generations, but he pointed to the greatly increased prosperity of the nation over the last generation, as was shown by the national returns of income for the income tax. Hereford, a much less populated county than Worcestershire, had, he believed, raised over £40,000 to restore its cathedral, and he was confident that the same could be achieved here.

Before the meeting was concluded it was agreed to open an account at the Worcester Old Bank in the names of the Lord Lieutenants of Worcestershire and Warwickshire, the Earl of Dudley, Sir John Pakington, and Sir Edmund Lechmere, who would also form the main restoration committee.

Soon after the meeting it was announced that the subscription list had already reached over £12,000. The Earl of Dudley had offered £5,000 towards the restoration of the tower, and £2,000 towards the heating, the Dean had promised a further £1,000, and Earl Beauchamp, the Hon. and Rev. Canon Fortescue and Lord Leigh £500 each. Among other early promises Sir John's £100 indicated that his help would mainly be as a trustee rather than in cash.

The restoration committee got down to business with little delay, and Sir John was able to attend most of the meetings – there were sixteen in 1864. In view of the Earl of Dudley's offer of funds towards the restoration of the tower and the installation of heating, these items were given priority. In June it was decided to investigate the new heating systems installed in various cathedrals, and in the October meeting, on a motion from Sir John, it was decided to install stoves produced by the inventor Goldsworthy Gurney, which had been successful at York. These were quickly installed and led to an improved attendance in the cathedral during the winter, although there was trouble with some of the stoves emitting a 'sulphurous vapour'.

Perkins was asked to prepare designs for the restoration of the tower, and in August a tender from the Worcester builders Messrs Wood for £6,985 was accepted. But at a meeting the following month it was found that Wood's tender had omissions, and instead the contract was awarded to Messrs Hughes of Bristol for £9,997, somewhat above the £8,000 suggested at the public meeting. As this was an important contract, references were sought from leading architects, including Thomas Wyatt and Edward Habershon, and these were satisfactory.

But the main matter the committee had to attend to was the organ, screen, and choir stalls. According to Scott's report, in monastic times the choir stalls extended westward under the tower and into the nave; under the Protestant reforms during Edward VI's time the stalls were removed and stowed away; during the Catholic revival under Queen Mary they were re-installed, but only east of the tower. At the same time, new canopies and other work were added in the renaissance style. Scott also wrote that neither the altar screen nor the screen between the nave and the choir, which also supported the organ, were of architectural or antiquarian merit.

There were, Scott wrote, four main questions to be decided by the committee in dealing with the choir. Firstly, whether to open up the choir from the nave by replacing the present solid screen with an open one; secondly, whether the organ should be moved, and if so where to; thirdly, whether to replace the renaissance canopies of the stalls with work in the style of the fourteenth century; and lastly whether to replace the altar screen with a suitable reredos.

As to the screen and organ, Scott was in favour of opening up the nave by removing the existing solid screen; however, he felt there was 'a certain dignity in the appearance of a finely designed organ standing upon the rood loft betwixt

A Gurney stove, now in the cloisters at Worcester. The main cathedral is now heated by more modern appliances, but at Hereford they are still in use in the cathedral. Goldsworthy Gurney (1793-1875) began life as a surgeon but his interests broadened to cover very many subjects, including steam carriages, which were successfully used around 1830, but they met with much opposition and high tolls. He later worked in the fields of heating, lighting and ventilation, and was appointed to improve the ventilation in the newly reopened House of Commons. His work was cut short when he became paralysed in 1864, but the Gurney Co. continued to exploit his inventions.

the nave and choir of a great church'. After considering alternatives, he wrote that his personal preference would be to have two separate organs, retaining some part of it above the new open screen, while the remainder would fit neatly into an eight foot gap between the north eastern tower pier and the first arch of the choir, where it would be invisible from the nave. Although this would mean the screen would have to be double to support the organ, he did not think this would be any more obstructive than a single screen. As to the other questions Scott made suggestions for the committee to consider.

Turning to the choir vaulting, Scott said it had been found impractical to remove the present plaster coating. So this would have to be decorated in colour 'in a quiet and modest tone, and should be executed by first rate artists'.

In the report as finally printed, there is a postscript dated June 1864, in which Scott dismissed any idea (as had been suggested) of reducing the size of the choir. At the end he emphasised again that his whole scheme is based on the idea of opening up the nave to the choir, and that if that idea was not followed, he would resign from the work.

In fact the committee were fully in agreement with that idea, but it was the position of the organ which caused much discussion and disagreement. By the end of 1864 the old screen had been dismantled and the organ placed temporarily in the first north bay of the choir, but the committee spent all the following

A print of 1823 showing the nave, screen and organ before the restoration. The stone screen was deemed to be of no architectural value, and, with the organ mounted on top, completely divided the cathedral into two parts. The nave, which had no seating, was little used except for special occasions, and services were held in the choir. Scott wished to retain part of the organ above a new open screen, but the restoration committee wished to have the cathedral as open as possible with seating in the nave so the congregation there could participate in services.

year trying to decide where its permanent position should be. In April, on a proposal from Sir John, the committee agreed that 'for the provision of increased facilities for public worship, to architectural beauty, and to musical effect, it is not desirable to replace the organ on the screen between the choir and nave'.

Before making a final decision the committee consulted the well-known London organ builder, Thomas Hill, and William Done and John Corfe, Worcester organists, and James Turle, organist at Westminster Abbey. They were unanimous on one point – that it would be wrong to have a small organ in the choir for services there, and ideally there should be large organs in both the choir and nave. The committee also received a long letter from Scott, which began by analysing the different services that would take place in the cathedral, and from this the desirable positions for the organ.

Scott repeated that his preferred arrangement was to have part of the organ on an open double screen, and the remainder on the blank walls in the choir before the first columns. This had now been rejected, but 'this is personally humiliating to myself, as it is the only one I have firmly recommended, and the only one definitely rejected by committee'. Scott then went on to discuss the other possible positions.

The committee met on 15th January 1866 to make a final decision, and six possible positions, including that already rejected on the screen, were put to the vote. Other than this, all the other five positions had their adherents, but the committee was united in their second choices, which were to re-erect the present organ in the second bay of the north choir aisle. Dean Peel approved of this, but the bishop opposed all the suggestions, although his own preference was not recorded.

While these discussions on the organ were continuing, the Earl of Dudley created further controversy by reiterating his opposition to holding the music festivals in the nave. In August the committee had before it a copy of a letter from Dudley to the dean offering to pay for the entire completion of the work in the nave – its flooring and furnishing, the erection of a large organ in the Adelaide (south west) transept, and the glazing of the new west window, providing that a majority of the committee voted in favour of his proposal to end the festivals. The use of the word 'majority' implies that Dudley knew that some of the members were in favour of the festivals, and these would certainly have included Sir John. No formal response to Dudley's letter is recorded in the minutes – Dudley himself was present – and the committee would have to await the decision by the dean and chapter.

Once the organ position had been settled, the committee formally commissioned Scott to prepare a scheme to restore the choir, and by the April meeting Scott's proposals were ready. The restoration of the cloisters was also going to start – in December 1865 the dean and chapter had offered to pay for this work as long as the restoration committee contributed £1,500 towards it, and, on a motion from Sir John, this offer was gratefully accepted. In May a tender for £3,290 from Messrs Collins & Cullis of Tewkesbury was accepted.

Meanwhile work on the tower was progressing, but Perkins, who was supervising this, was not happy about the fact that the work by Hughes the contractor was not being done equally on all sides, which would put a differential load on the wall and might cause unequal settlement. In fact there were several disputes with Hughes, mainly about his accounts, and at one stage Perkins suggested that a new contractor be brought in. Hughes had also been commissioned to carve new statues for the niches in the north porch, but these were not considered satisfactory by the committee, so Hardman & Co of Birmingham, best known for their stained glass, were asked to produce samples.

By the end of 1866 Scott had been able to show his plans for the remodelling of the choir which he estimated would cost around £10,000, and the committee took stock of the financial position. Although the appeal initially had gone well, the receipt of subscriptions had much slowed, and by the end of 1866 only a little more than half the £30,000 target had been promised. So at a committee meeting on December 15th Sir John proposed that a further public meeting should be held in Easter week 1867 to relaunch the appeal, and suggested that public interest would be enhanced if Scott could produce drawings of his plans for the choir for public display.

So Lord Lyttelton wrote another letter for public consumption, describing the progress made since 1864, and what remained to be done. 'Great progress' had been made, he wrote, and he detailed the major contributions to the fund including £6,000 from the Earl of Dudley, £1,500 from Dean Peel to pay for the reredos in memory of his late wife Augusta who had died in 1861, and £500 from Canon Fortescue for the new west window. The general subscriptions from Worcestershire had now nearly reached £13,000, and from Warwickshire £2,778. The committee must have regarded both these sums as rather disappointing, as the figure for Worcestershire included the Earl of Dudley's £6,000.

What now remained to be done, Lyttelton wrote, consisted of the new nave floor, the lighting, and, by far the most important, the remodelling of the choir, including the organ and screen. To complete this work would require another £15,000, and the letter ended by inviting subscriptions in five annual instalments.

The well attended meeting was duly held on 25th April 1867. Lord Lyttelton presided, and the bishop, dean, Sir John and Lord Leigh were also on the platform. After introductory remarks from Lyttelton, the dean gave a detailed résumé of the work done in the last three years, and the cost of each item. The bishop then proposed the first resolution, which was that the meeting approved of what had been done, 'and sanctions the further attempt now to be made for its full completion'. In his speech, the bishop made reference to the somewhat disappointing support from Warwickshire, particularly from the archdeaconry of Coventry which had been transferred to the Worcester diocese relatively recently. But he pointed out that the cathedral founder, Bishop Wulstan, had come from Warwickshire, and he hoped that "not withstanding all the old associations of Coventry with the see that used to be there, they will look upon the cathedral church of Worcester as their present mother church". Lord Leigh seconded the resolution, and confessed that he had not visited the cathedral until today since he was at the 1864 meeting "and I must say that I was not only gratified but greatly surprised at the marked change that I witnessed in that noble edifice". He regretted the small attendance that day of Warwickshire people – perhaps this was due to the poor railway links between the two counties! He said he would like to have seen a longer subscription list from his county, and "promised to do my utmost to stir up my neighbours and endeavour to get as good a subscription list as I possibly can".

Sir John proposed that 'this meeting authorises the attempt to raise a further sum of £15,000, payable in three annual instalments, for the completion of the restoration' (after Lyttelton had written his letter, it had been decided that five years was too long a time scale). He referred again to the successful appeal to restore Hereford cathedral, and hoped that "equal success will attend the efforts in this diocese, and that the day is near at hand when we may see the cathedral of Worcester as a splendid Protestant temple of Christian worship".

The next resolution was that the trustees appointed at the earlier meeting to act as a joint committee with the dean and chapter should be re-appointed,

William Henry Leigh, 2nd Baron Leigh of Stoneleigh, 1824-1905. Stoneleigh Abbey was acquired by the Leigh family at the dissolution, and after the 5th baron died in 1786 his distant cousin Chandos Leigh, father of William Henry, was made 1st Baron Leigh of the second creation. William Henry was lord lieutenant of Warwickshire from 1856 till his death, and made one unsuccessful attempt to enter parliament as a free trader in 1847. His efforts to raise subscriptions for the restoration of Worcester cathedral were not as successful as they might have been. From a painting in Warwick Guildhall.

The Restoration of Worcester Cathedral

but with the addition of the names of Earl Somers and the mayor of Worcester. Harry Vernon of Hanbury Hall seconded this resolution, and introduced a note of controversy when he said that there was one blot in Scott's plans, which was the continued inclusion of the tomb of King John "which destroyed the view of the choir", and he hoped the committee would take steps to remove it – Berrow's recorded that there were loud expressions of dissent at this point.

The dean then spoke to propose the continuation of the finance committee, and said that among their duties would be a direct appeal to the citizens of Worcester. So far not many of these appeared on the subscription list, which was because it was decided early on to leave this until the restorations plans were more advanced. But this should now be done, and the following speaker, Sir Edmund Lechmere, said he thought the proposed inclusion of special seating for the mayor and corporation would help in this respect. But Lechmere was against the removal of King John's tomb "as being connected with one of the greatest periods of our English liberties".

During the meeting the bishop had made reference to the clock and bells that were the subject of a separate appeal and were part of the scheme for the restoration of the tower. The leader of the appeal, Rev. Cattley, immediately wrote to Berrow's to enlarge on the scheme, saying that the clock would satisfy a 'citizens' want most strongly felt by all – an unerring timekeeper on which all might with certainty rely'. The clock would be linked with that in the Palace of Westminster, which the astronomer royal said did not vary more than one second in ten days. But he also said that the Earl of Dudley had made it a condition of his offer to pay £5,000 towards the restoration of the tower that it should not be 'disfigured by an external dial'.

The new appeal brought in new subscriptions, but all the evidence shows they were coming in more slowly than hoped. A subscription list in Berrow's in July showed that a further £4,500 had been promised, and on 24th October a public meeting was held in Stratford-upon-Avon to raise money, presided over by Lord Leigh. He admitted that support from the county had been disappointing, and wondered whether appeals in the county from the Church Extension Society and Poor Benefice Fund had had an adverse effect. Lord Lyttelton proposed the resolution in support of what had been done, and 'to re-affirm the obligation on the diocese generally to maintain the fabric in due order and architectural beauty', an obvious reference to Warwickshire. Sir John was one of the speakers, and made his usual reference to the success of the Hereford appeal. Berrow's reported that nearly £50 was collected in the room, bringing the total from Warwickshire in response to the second appeal £641.

Using these new funds, work continued during 1868 and 1869, and was almost complete, apart from the choir and the flooring throughout the cathedral.

But by the beginning of 1870 the committee could proceed no further, as their funds were exhausted.

At this point the Earl of Dudley decided to take the initiative. He offered the dean and chapter £10,000 to complete the work, on condition that they did not allow any more festivals. What had turned Lord Dudley so strongly against the festivals is difficult to say. According to an editorial in the Birmingham Daily Post he had been a strong supporter of the festivals in his younger days, and it was only earlier in the 1860s that he let his opposition be known, including at the public meeting held in 1864 referred to above. But, the Post thought, he now sought to achieve his ends 'by means of a golden bribe'.

Dudley's offer was made known to the restoration committee, at which he was present, on 29th January 1870, and the minutes simply record that this decision would have to be made by the dean and chapter. Sir John must have been greatly shocked by this announcement, and at once fought back. A letter from him appeared in Berrow's, in which he stated they had exhausted their funds. He then explained the Earl of Dudley's offer, and wrote:

> I was present, as a member of the committee, when the offer was made, and met it at once by an earnest protest and a declaration that I should do everything in my power to prevent such an arrangement.
>
> But as an individual I am powerless, unless I am supported in the opinions I entertain. I can only appeal to public feeling, and express my hope that it will not sanction the sudden and unnecessary destruction of an institution by which for no less than 146 years many a widow and orphan has been rescued form sorrow and distress, and the public have annually heard the most sublime compositions by which the genius of man has enabled us to sing the praise of God... I am confident that all those whose sympathy and co-operation I hope to receive will join me in a feeling of extreme regret that, after the truly generous and munificent aid which our work of restoration has received from the Earl of Dudley, his lordship should have taken any course of which we cannot approve.

Sir John went on to write that he thought the £10,000 offered by Dudley was rather more than would actually be required, and also that the dean and chapter had offered to make further contributions from their maintenance fund, and he thought that if a further appeal was made to the diocese 'it will be met with a response so general and so generous as to put an end to any excuse for discontinuing our ancient festivals for the sake of the price that can be obtained for their abandonment'.

At their monthly meeting on 1st March, the Worcester City Council were asked by Cllr Woodward to suspend standing orders to consider an urgent resolution concerning Lord Dudley's offer, namely 'That the council desires respectfully to express to the dean and chapter their earnest hope that they will not be induced to deviate from the practice of nearly 150 years of allowing the use of the cathedral for the celebration of the triennial music festivals'. An amendment was proposed by Ald. Webb, who disliked the beautiful building being given over to 'carpenters and logs of timber every three years', to add the words 'unless some equally suitable building for the performance of oratorios be provided for that purpose', but this was greeted with cries of 'no, no'. The original resolution was passed unanimously.

On Saturday 5th March a public meeting was held in the Guildhall. The object was 'to give the inhabitants of the city and county of Worcester an opportunity of adopting a memorial to the dean and chapter, urging them not to allow any influence to lead them to withdraw their consent to the use of the cathedral for the triennial music festivals which have been celebrated with so much benefit to the cause of charity for 150 years'.

After an introduction from the mayor, R E Barnett Esq, Sir John was the first and principal speaker. He evidently felt very strongly on the subject, and made an impassioned speech. "I do not rise with pleasure on this occasion;" he began, "on the contrary, during the long period of years that, on various subjects and in various ways, it has become my duty to address my neighbours on public occasions, I do not remember one when I felt so deeply sorry as I do at this moment". After regretting the absence of the high sheriff, he said "I have here a letter from Lord Leigh, who is himself a member of the restoration committee, and who has requested me to add his name to the memorial to the dean and chapter which I hope will be the result of this meeting". Then Sir John repeated the same formula several times, substituting the names of Lady Emily Foley; of the Earl of Coventry; and of Lord Sandys. Then Sir John referred to the bishop. He was not, he said, authorised to make any statement on behalf of the bishop, and it was understandable that he did not want to enter into the controversy; "but any communication from the bishop is totally unnecessary... since the bishop succeeded to the see of Worcester several music festivals have been held, and on every one of the these occasions he was president of the festival. On every one of those occasions he has himself been present to hear the sacred music performed within those walls".

Sir John then read out the lengthy memorial it was proposed to send to the dean and chapter. It was polite but firm, and ended:

> We are therefore of opinion, while we share your anxiety to complete the restoration of the beautiful temple committed to your care, that an institution so ancient, so popular, and so good ought not to be abandoned, and, above all, we deprecate an unfavourable decision on your part, on any other ground than a deference to a manifest preponderance of public opinion. We hope that

you will seriously consider that the views we have thus expressed are widely entertained by your neighbours in town and country, and we respectfully and earnestly beg you to decline the proposal you have received.

Sir John then said he would like to consider the nature of the objections to the festival. Many, he said, were so trivial that they were hardly worth discussing – he had heard, for example, that the behaviour of the audience in the aisles was not always what it might have been – someone had once been seen eating a sandwich! But who could blame those who, not being part of the distinguished company entertained by the dean and chapter, needed some sustenance during the long hours of the performances. Another objection was the presence of workmen preparing for the festival and clearing up afterwards; but, said Sir John, "if it is right to do it, it is right to prepare for it". There was no need why there should be any other than minimum disruption of divine services, and of course care must to taken not to damage the fabric. Sir John then came to the main objection:

> There remains that objection which, if it is sound, is fatal. I mean the objection, which, I believe, is honestly entertained by some minds, but which I not only cannot share, but cannot even understand: that the performances within these consecrated walls of those grand sacred compositions amounts to desecration. I would only ask anyone who is disposed to complain of the desecration of those sacred walls 'Did you ever hear the chorus of the Hallelujah resounding through the aisles of that great church? Did you ever hear that splendid composition of Mendelssohn 'Holy, Holy, Holy is God the Lord'? Did you ever hear that resounding through the walls of the cathedral without feeling devotional emotions of a most serious character?

After continuing in the same vein, he concluded:

> If anyone tells me that this is desecration I can only say that I do not understand the feeling of that man's mind, be he whom he may. I say it is no desecration; I say it is the proper place for those compositions, those songs of prayer and praise, to be heard and to be sung. I listen to them with pleasure whenever I hear them; they are the grandest compositions of human genius. I hear them in the Birmingham Town Hall; I hear them in Exeter Hall in London; but never do I hear them anywhere with those feelings and with that sympathy than when I hear them within the sacred walls of this grand cathedral.

Public opinion, thought Sir John, was important.

> Why should the dean and chapter now change a practice which had lasted so long unless public opinion thought they should? But what is public opinion now? What do I infer from the state of this room at this moment?... I say that it is perfectly clear that public opinion does sanction, fully and entirely sanction, the continuation of these festivals, in the same manner, in the same place, and upon the same footing which they have been hitherto held.

The Restoration of Worcester Cathedral

Sir John pointed out that the Earl of Dudley had made a similar objection to the festival in 1866, and a memorial signed by 300 or 400 prominent citizens had been presented to him, and he thought feeling was now still as strong. He had had a report that the Earl of Dudley would be present at the meeting, but looking around he could not see him. Sir John was sorry, as if he had been present, he would have appealed to him directly. Lord Dudley was in most respects a good and kindly man –

> but is it for any one man – I care not how good his motives are, I care not how elevated his position – to endeavour to force his own views upon a question of opinion in violation of those views which are entertained by the great bulk of his neighbours… If Lord Dudley does not like these festivals, he is perfectly welcome to stay at home. The last few years he has refrained from attending, and I mean no respect to Lord Dudley when I say that the festivals have gone on extremely well without him… If he thinks these meetings are wrong let him stay at home, but do not let him make us all stay at home.

> From my childhood I have attended these festivals. I hope that those who come after me will have the power to attend them as I have done, and to listen year after year to those songs of devotion which are performed within the walls of one or other of the cathedrals in the three dioceses.

What made it worse, Sir John continued, was that fact that it had come down to a question of money:

> From the moment that offer of Lord Dudley's was made – that unfortunate, that mistaken offer as I venture to think it – on right and left in London and in the country I have been met by everybody with this: there may be difference of opinion about your festivals, there may be those who think they had better not be held in the church, but, whatever may be thought, they ought not to be sold and parted with for money.

Finally, Sir John said that the public should not be afraid that, without Lord Dudley's money, the restoration would not be completed. Of course it would take time – great works always do – but if the dean and chapter turned down Lord Dudley's offer and a new subscription list was opened now, he was convinced that the public would give even more generously.

Sir John's motion was seconded by Thomas Rowley Hill, who echoed exactly Sir John's feelings, and would just quote the Psalmist: 'Praise Him with the sound of the trumpet; Praise Him with the psaltery and harp; Praise Him with stringed instruments and organs; Praise Him upon the loud cymbals; let everything that hath breath praise the Lord'. If it was desecration, he did not know what worship was.

Then a solicitor, Hyla Holden, rose to propose an amendment. He was sorry he lacked Sir John's eloquence, and realised that his amendment would be defeated, but he owed it to his conscience to express his views. He did not wish to enter into the money side of things, but could not divest his mind of the idea that the festivals were turning the noble cathedral into a concert room. As regards the widows and orphans charity, the sum raised was only small, and he was quite sure other ways could be found of raising this (to be fair, Sir John had not made much of the charity in his speech). So his amendment was 'that the use of the cathedral church for other than devotional or strictly ecclesiastical purposes is objectionable. Therefore it is desirable to ask the dean and chapter not to continue the triennial festivals as at present conducted'.

The feeling of the meeting was clearly not with Hyla Holden, and he was hissed during his speech. The amendment was seconded by Rev. William Rayson, a minor canon. He brought the meeting down to earth when he pointed out that after Lord Dudley had made a similar proposal in 1866, the city and county had the opportunity of coming forward with the necessary funds then, but failed to do so, so it was possible the same would happen again. But the main question was: was it right or wrong to hold the festivals in the cathedral? The object of a cathedral was the dignity of the worship of almighty God, and the second was the edification of man. But the worship of Almighty God was put into a corner and sometimes even stopped in order that the festivals might take place. That was wrong. It should also be considered what was lawful and what was not lawful, and he did not think any lawful justification could be found for holding the festivals as they were. If, in what was the model church of the diocese, the front seats were charged 15s, second seats 7s 6d, and others 3s 6d, how could they prevent in course of justice every village church holding a scared concert in the nave? This he would very much deplore. "The festival has been called a very grand and impressive musical sermon. I ask, upon the principle of scripture, upon the principles of church rule and church practice, ought the seats be charged for, and God's poor cast out from that sermon? No; the cathedral service ought to be open to the poorest of the land". Rev. Rayson believed that every church should have free and unappropriated seating. He also cast doubt on the importance of the widows and orphans charity. People did not attend the festival in order to benefit the charity – that was a small by-product of the affair.

Sir John spoke again, and concluded that he believed that nothing they had heard from Messrs Holden and Rayson "will for a moment influence the judgement of this great meeting". The mayor then put the amendment to the meeting, and only about a dozen hands went up, whereupon the original motion was carried with only one dissenting vote, by Rev. Thomas Smyth, rector of Hindlip. It was proposed and agreed that Sir John, the sheriff and the mayor should present the memorial to the dean and chapter.

Lord Dudley must have felt the need to put his own case over to the public, and on 26th March and 2nd April two long letters appeared in the press. In the first he made much of the disruption caused during the weeks prior to the festival during the installation of the seating – during this time the services had to be confined to the choir only. And he regretted that, in order to maximise revenue, the audience was now also accommodated in the choir rather than in the more public nave. Dudley also referred to the charity, which he thought could easily be replaced if the festivals ended.

He also considered the legal aspects of the festival, and had sought counsel's opinion as to whether the dean and chapter had authority to allow musical performances in the cathedral. A lawyer, Sir Robert Phillimore, opined that, after due consideration, 'I am unable to understand how it can be legally competent for the dean and chapter to allow a music festival wholly unconnected with the service of the church, to be celebrated in their cathedral. I have always thought that the services contained in the prayer book, together with the sermon and anthem and hymns, which the prayer book contemplates as being incorporated with the morning and daily prayer, are the only services which can, according to law, be performed in any consecrated church'. It was up to the bishop, as visitor, to admonish the dean and chapter, and explain that it was contrary to law. If this was disregarded, 'he should visit with proper censures those who had set his authority, and that of the law, at nought'.

This legal opinion was countered by Sir John in a letter to Berrow's, based partly on the long and uninterrupted use of the cathedral for the festival, sanctioned by the bishop, dean and chapter, for nearly 150 years, partly on the fact that meetings other than divine services were in fact regularly held in the cathedral, and partly on an 1850 act which specifically allowed churches to be used for 'a charitable object, or some other purpose approved by the bishop of the diocese'. However, a later letter from 'An Observer' accused Sir John of selectively quoting the Act, the main purpose of which was to prevent certain types of meetings in churches. This led to a further exchange of letters, with Sir John vigorously defending his view, and in 'An Observer's' last letter he wrote:

> I regret that my criticism should have caused a little unnecessary irritation upon the usual equanimity of the right hon. baronet, whose public services and personal affability I freely admit and admire; but I cannot refrain, while taking leave of the subject, to notice Sir John's parting words, viz: 'I will only say there are two ways of conducting an argument', in which we are agreed. One is by fair and legitimate deduction; and the other is by skilful, yet futile, evasion.

However, given the sanctity of long usage, the legality of the festivals does not seem to have ever been seriously challenged, and they have continued, of course, to the present day.

The Earl of Dudley's letter the following week made a completely new proposal. At present there was an impasse: public opinion was strongly against the cessation of the festivals, but on the other hand without his £10,000 the restoration, which was now completely stopped for want of funds, could not be completed. So he would make an offer that he hoped would provide a way out: his opinion was that the completion of the work would cost rather more than £10,000, and he would offer £5,000 towards this, on the condition that the city and county of Worcester would each raise a further £5,000 or enough to see the work completed. He would then give the other £5,000 he had promised to the widow's and orphans' fund. If the further £10,000 failed to be raised by the public subscription, then the public would have to agree not to press their objection to the acceptance of his present offer by the dean and chapter. His hope was that once the restoration was complete 'I hope that the general feeling of the whole diocese will be that no such use shall ever be made of the beautifully restored cathedral as in times bygone', and everyone then would be content.

Sir John Pakington, wrote Dudley, could surely rally round him those he had enlisted in opposition to the offer made, and, with some three or five more, 'form such a body of gentlemen as would take the responsibility of the county's share of the amount required'; similarly Cllr Woodward for the city.

In its editorial, Berrow's called Dudley's offer clever, as he had taken away from the dean and chapter the making of difficult decisions, and put the onus entirely on the city and county to raise the remaining funds. If they did, the future of the festivals would be entirely in the hands of proper authority. The only comment that Berrow's allowed itself was that so far the public had not shown any serious inclination to provide the necessary funds.

Sir John responded to Lord Dudley's offer in approving terms in a letter to Berrow's. He wrote that he was confident that the amount needed above Dudley's gift of £5,000 would be raised, but disputed that this would come to a further £10,000. After deducting the money promised by the dean and chapter, Sir John believed that less than half this amount would have to be raised. On April 19th the dean and chapter considered both Lord Dudley's offers – presumably they considered the first one still open, despite Dudley's admission that opinion was strongly against it. Reluctant to make a final decision, they decided to see whether the city and county really could raise the necessary funds. They also decided to donate an extra £2,500 from capitular funds.

Meanwhile Sir John took the lead not only in preparing for yet another appeal, but in investigating whether the remaining work could be reduced in cost. He wrote to Scott to see whether he could suggest cost reductions and if the work could be put out to competitive tender, but Scott would have none of it.

The Restoration of Worcester Cathedral

> I am convinced that no part of the work then designed is in any degree extravagant, on the contrary I think it fully as simple as the dignity of the cathedral will consistently permit. You have gone liberally through the repairs to the fabric and now that you have reached the very heart of the work, the choir itself, where the sacred services will be celebrated, it will never do to begin with economising upon what was at first approved and has been waiting so long while the more ordinary works have been progressing. As to going out to tender, no! Must be my own carvers working under my own eye.

The committee met Scott in May, and he seems to have relented a little in that he agreed to examine all the estimates again, and soon came back with an estimate of £14,444 for the remaining work, which, after deducting Lord Dudley's £5,000 and the dean and chapter's £2,000 left, in round figures, £8,000 still to find. Lord Dudley had asked Sir John to raise the money, but according to a later description of the meeting, Lord Lyttelton offered to join Sir John in the appeal. But Sir John later said that the only part Lyttelton played was to sign the appeal letter, which was dated 13th June and duly circulated.

Remarkably, by the end of July this sum seems to have been raised, and work could start again. A neatly written list of all the 185 subscribers to the third appeal is kept among the committee's papers. After Lord Dudley's £5,000 and the dean and chapter's £2,500, Dean Peal gave £600, Lord Lyttelton, the Bishop, and the Worcester bankers Berwick & Co gave £500 each, the Earl of Coventry and a Miss Porter £300 each, and Sir John, Harry Vernon, Lea & Perrins, Henry Allsopp and John D Allcroft £250 each. The subscriptions totalled just over £16,000, but the committee must have been disappointed to see that the total from Warwickshire was only £325. Lord Leigh's name does not appear.

Unfortunately Scott fell seriously ill in October 1870, and his work at the cathedral stopped. Work on the new choir stalls had already started but there was no proper contract, and Scott's designs for the choir roof were still awaited. However, by the end of the year a cost of £3,065 for the stalls was agreed with Farmer & Brindley, the well-known London firm. It seems that John Hardman Powell, a grandson of the founder of the Birmingham firm Hardman & Co, was commissioned to produce designs for the choir roof, and by the end of January 1871 the committee was able to examine Powell's three suggested designs, and send them to Scott for comment.

Another important part of the work was the paving of the choir, and at a meeting in April 1871 Sir John proposed that Scott's ideas be laid out on a large scale and in colour for examination by the committee, and at a meeting in June at Dudley House in London Scott's designs were considered, and some modifications requested. They were approved the following week.

The final major part of the work was the new screen between the nave and the choir. In October Scott wrote to the committee that the screen was an essential part of English cathedrals, separating the two distinctly designed apartments of nave and choir. Without a suitable screen the interior would become a 'magnificent corridor'. His design at Worcester was 'perhaps more open than any which at present exists'. It consisted of a shallow marble base, which supported metal columns with tracery of oak above, crowned with open metal work. 'I flatter myself that so beautiful a screen has hardly been erected and none so unobstructive to sound or sight', Scott wrote.

Sir John seems to have been unhappy with Scott's design, and proposed a resolution that is not entirely clear, but indicated that there should be the marble base only, with no upper work, but he was heavily outvoted, and Scott's design accepted. By the beginning of 1872 the decoration of the choir vault was complete, and, once the scaffolding had been removed Scott requested some

The new screen at Worcester, designed by Sir Gilbert Scott and made by Francis Skidmore of Coventry. On a stone base, it is made of brass and wood. From an original drawing by Frances Rogers.

strengthening of the colours. Perkins had produced designs for the flooring of the nave and the choir, where he proposed using both marble and encaustic tiles, and the committee asked him to refer these designs to Scott. Perkins had also found a slightly less expensive stone for flooring the choir aisles, tower, nave and transepts, and, as other costs were constantly rising, the committee gratefully accepted his suggestion. Another small bonus was that the government agreed to contribute £250 towards the restoration of King John's tomb and Prince Arthur's chantry, as these were national monuments.

It had been hoped to re-open the cathedral at Easter 1873, but inevitably there were further delays, with irregular walls in the choir, and a workmen's strike in London contributing to them, and in November, 1872 during an inspection of the new choir floor, Sir John pointed out that the some wrongly coloured marble had been used and it was agreed that this should be put right. Shortly afterwards he also discovered that tiles had been used in place of marble in the altar steps, and this had to be corrected as well. There were also delays to the new organ being put together by Thomas Hill, using part of the old organ, and the case was also delayed, but at that stage the committee were still hoping for an Easter 1873 opening. The committee agreed to spend an extra £392 to use brass instead of wrought iron in the screen, but asked Perkins to produce less expensive metal gates for the north porch.

Early the following year, Lord Dudley made an inspection visit, and was disappointed when he saw the stone it was proposed to use to floor the nave. The stone was from Hopton Wood, and was a fine almost marble-like limestone. Although it had been used in the new Houses of Parliament and in Westminster Abbey, Lord Dudley did not think it good enough for the Worcester cathedral nave, and offered to pay for black and white marble, which would cost over £4,000. He offered the unused limestone to the committee, and they used it to re-pave the cloisters. To complete what he wanted to be a magnificent nave, Dudley also offered to pay for the stained glass in the new west window.

The committee wished to discuss the nave floor with Scott, and met in London a few days later. But there was no problem – Scott thought that marble would be fine for the nave, comparing it with Amiens cathedral. In April there was a setback, when Abraham Perkins died unexpectedly, aged 65. At the time he was still architect to the dean and chapter and in day to day charge of the work, but the work was fortunately sufficiently far advanced to be carried on without him. The re-opening date was postponed on three occasions, but finally, at a meeting on 11th October, it was fixed for 8th April 1874. Meanwhile the committee found themselves short of funds again – inviting donations over three years made it possible for donors to promise larger sums, there was always the danger that they might fail to make all their payments, as was the case in 1873.

So Sir John, Sir Edmund Lechmere and Canon Wood were asked to investigate the financial position in detail. They reported that a deficit of over £1,000 remained, despite the fact that Lord Dudley had agreed to pay for the nave seating, and enclosures for the north and south nave doors, and Lady Dudley to pay for the altar rails. The committee disputed some of Scott's bills, as they thought charges for drawings should be included in his percentage fee. By the end of the year the committee had incurred an overdraft of £287, and they expressed great dissatisfaction with the progress of the remaining work in the choir and choir aisles. The fact that they had to pay Abraham Perkins' widow £50 in interest demonstrates how dilatory they had become in settling outstanding accounts.

But somehow or other the work was completed and the remaining bills paid. Over £2,000 was due under the subscription scheme in August, and this would have helped the committee to close their books. So at last all was set for the grand opening, and as well as giving credit for the generosity of the Earl of Dudley, future generations should give due credit to Sir John, who not only took an active part in the joint committee's proceedings but also played a major role in the third appeal of 1870. And, of course, he was also responsible for leading the campaign to keep the triennial festivals, but that story was not concluded and will be continued in the next chapter.

There is a note in the committee's minute book to the effect that the final cost of the restoration, taken from its beginning, was £114,295 – it is claimed that was the most expensive restoration of any English cathedral. This included voluntary subscriptions of nearly £38,000, capitular funds of £27,500, Lord Dudley's gifts worth £20,300, other gifts of £11,000, and £17,300 from the ecclesiastical commissioners.

A detail showing Scott's decoration of the choir vault.

The Restoration of Worcester Cathedral

(Right) An early C19th engraving by John Buckler of the choir. The photo below shows the same view today. Note the replaced east window, the new reredos, and the plain stalls. The old plain ceiling was decorated by Scott, and the flooring replaced.

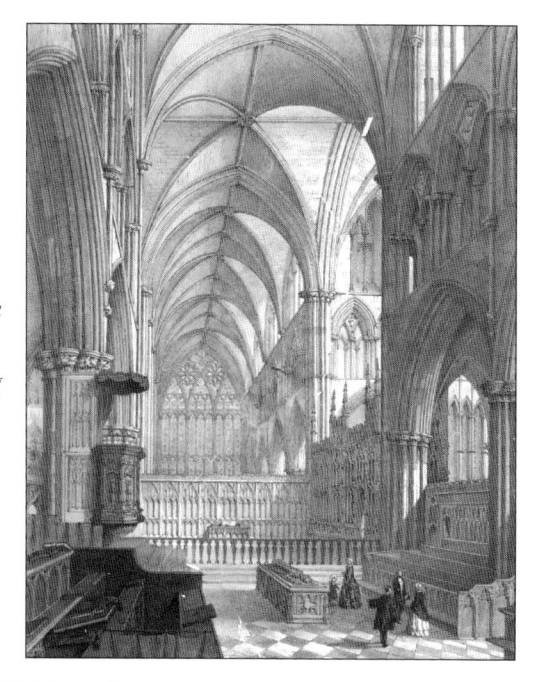

(Left) The new reredos and screen, with a modern cloth in front. The back of the reredos is inscribed IN MEMORY OF JOHN PEEL DD DEAN OF THIS CATHEDRAL FROM AD 1840 TO 1874 WHO ERECTED THIS REREDOS IN AFFECTIONATE REMEMBRANCE OF AUGUSTA HIS WIFE. THIS CROSS IS INSCRIBED BY THE DEAN AND CANONS AND OTHER FRIENDS AD 1877.

Chapter 9
The Cathedral Restored

The joint restoration committee made an inspection of the cathedral on 4th April 1874, and everything was deemed ready for the opening four days later. The only work in progress was the glazing of the great west window, but it would be some time before this was finished, and it was not necessary to delay the opening on this account. There was also the new organ in the south transept that the Earl of Dudley had proposed and would pay for, to improve the sound for the nave congregation, but this had not yet been started.

The mayor, Worcester solicitor Herbert Goldingham, announced that in addition to encouraging citizens to put up appropriate decorations on their own premises, a committee would be formed to decide on what public decoration could be mounted, and workmen were soon busy putting up three triumphal arches at the main entrances to the city, and 'Venetian masts' along the main streets. By the day before the opening, Berrow's reported, 'the effect far surpassed anything ever seen before in the city. The fronts of many houses were wreathed in evergreens and flowers… Inscriptions indicative of joy at the re-opening of the cathedral, and of gratitude to munificent contributors to the restoration fund, were displayed, and from nearly every house in the principal streets flags were suspended'. The day of the opening, Wednesday 8th April 1874, was blessed by fine weather.

The day began with a breakfast hosted by the mayor, and attended by councillors, officers and about 200 freemasons of the province of Worcester. After the breakfast the mayor gave a speech of welcome and proposed the loyal toast. The company formed a procession: the freemasons in their robes, the mayor with his gold chain and robes, the aldermen in their scarlet robes. Large crowds watched the procession on its way to the cathedral, where the mayor and corporation sat in reserved seats in the north aisle, and the masons in the south aisle, from where they could admire the window they had presented some time previously. At 11.00 o'clock the clergy went in procession from the chapter house into the

The Cathedral Restored

cathedral. The procession was led by the Kings School masters and scholars, about 300 members of the diocesan clergy, archdeacons, canons, the dean, and finally the bishop, attended by the chancellor, registrar and chaplains, and the bishops of Oxford and Derry, singing psalm 68 as they went.

The bishop gave the sermon on the text 'Lord, I have loved the habitation of Thy house, and the place where Thine honour dwelleth'. After the service the dean and chapter entertained those who had been chiefly involved in the restoration, including Lord Hampton (as he now was), to lunch in the college hall. The dean was the first to speak, proposing the loyal toast, and was followed by Lord Lyttelton, who proposed the health of the bishop and clergy of the diocese. In his speech he paid tribute to Lord Hampton who had proved so valuable when they had to raise funds at a difficult time, and said he might have described Lord Hampton's elevation to a well-earned repose on the soft red benches of the House of Lords 'if it had not been that the noble lord seems endued with perpetual youth, and in more sense than one was among the junior members of the House'.

The bishop, dean, and the Earl of Dudley were the next speakers followed by Rev. Canon John Ryle Wood, since 1872 secretary of the joint committee. He also paid tribute to Lord Lyttelton and Lord Hampton, who had been so active and successful in the fund raising. However, Wood said there was still a deficiency estimated at about £4,000 – the £1,092 collected in the first four days' services would have helped. He thought the committee was

The stained glass window in the north transept, representing the twelve apostles, was presented to the cathedral during the restoration by the freemasons of the province of Worcester, and made by Lavers & Barraud of London.

right in not stinting on some aspects of the restoration, which led to the present deficit, and there would be a liberal response to the application that must necessarily be made for the remaining funds that would be required. When Lord Hampton spoke, he said the response to the appeal had been very creditable, and that, if a return could be made of all the expenditure on church restoration that had been made, he thought "it would be in a remarkable degree creditable to the piety and liberality of the Protestant church of England. And I am proud to believe that there is no part of England where that liberality is more conspicuous and more successful than in this diocese… Today has been a day of thankfulness and joy", he concluded.

The luncheon concluded by Lord Lyttelton proposing the health of Sir Gilbert Scott, as he was by then known. Scott replied that most of the credit was due to the late Abraham Perkins, and his teacher Rickman. Scott sought to play down his own part in the work. Celebrations continued with a service in the evening, when the Bishop of Derry gave the sermon. Further services were held on Thursday and Friday, with sermons by the bishops of Hereford, Rochester, and Oxford, and the Dean of Chester.

Now the cathedral had been re-opened, the dean and chapter decided to charge sixpence (2.5p) for public admission to the choir and east end, except for services, which led to some critical comment in the press, and an appeal from the city council. The council, however, received a polite reply in July that the dean and chapter found the present arrangements, which were similar to those at York, Westminster and elsewhere, satisfactory, and would not be making any changes. One reason for the imposition was that if too many visitors were allowed in, some who belonged a class that did not appreciate the fine new decorations might cause some damage!

On 23rd June Rt Rev. John Peel resigned as Dean of Worcester, as he was allowed to do under a recent act of parliament. Peel had not been in good health, and, now the restoration was complete, he was glad to give up this burden. He was to die early the following year after a fall. It was soon announced that the new dean would be Rev. Grantham Munton Yorke, who had been rector of St Philips, Birmingham, for thirty years. This church is in the centre of the town, and was to become the cathedral of the new diocese of Birmingham in 1905. A a supporter of the Conservative party, Yorke, who was the brother of the 4th Earl of Hardewick, had worked hard to improve education in Birmingham, and, when he left, the churchwardens opened a subscription list in appreciation of his work in the town. But he was described by a contemporary as 'a poor reader and preacher, lame, not handsome, and deaf as a post… He took little notice of anyone, and no-one took notice of him. He was, in fact, unpopular'.

The Cathedral Restored

The other figure in what was to become a battle between the dean and chapter, and Lord Hampton and the general public, was Canon Alfred Barry, a son of the architect Charles Barry. Dr Barry had been made a residentiary canon by Gladstone in 1871, and it was known that he had reservations about the way the festival was conducted. He gave the sermon at the opening service of the 1872 festival, and spoke of its history and objectives. Although in his sermon he went on to analyse and praise the great oratorios, saying that they were a way of bringing the religious feelings of their composers to the present day in a way that great preachers could not, he did say that the nature of the festival had changed. Originally, Barry said, the festivals celebrated the worship of God with the united force of the three great cathedrals. But this objective has been "too much encroached upon, thrust out to a far too secondary position in later times'.

But no-one who heard the sermon, and that included Lord Hampton, would have thought it would lead to such radical changes as Dr Barry was later to propose. But of course Dean Peel still held sway in 1872, whereas even if the description above of Dean Yorke is somewhat biased, it can be imagined that he was no match for Dr Barry, as in his entry in the Dictionary of National Biography Barry was said to have been 'an innovative and energetic, even pushy' head of King's College, London, and that he had 'a fine presence and with a sonorous voice, and was an effective speaker and preacher'. By contrast Yorke, at the age of 66 was clearly past his prime, and was to die four years later.

So, probably at the initiative of Dr Barry, a meeting of the deans of the three cathedrals was held in the week before the opening of the 1874 Gloucester festival,

Very Rev. and Hon. Grantham Yorke, 1809-79. After a short military career during which he helped put down the chartist riots of 1839, Yorke entered the church, and for a time was chaplain to Rt Rev. Henry Pepys, Bishop of Worcester. Pepys then presented him to the rectory of St Philips, Birmingham, in which he remained for thirty years until he was appointed Dean of Worcester in 1874. During his time in Birmingham he was active in promoting education, and was a governor of the diocesan training college at Saltley.

to discuss the future. Dean Yorke was accompanied by Dr Barry. Although the meeting was private, news soon leaked out, and Berrow's reported:

> The changes contemplated are, we believe, such as will entirely do away with the enormous expenses now incurred for the services of professional artistes, and that in future the festivals will assume more of a strictly religious character, none except cathedral or church choristers being permitted to take part in them. We understand that it is proposed to model them on the services recently observed in celebrating the restoration of Worcester cathedral.

The Worcester festival stewards, who would be responsible for promoting the 1875 festival in Worcester, must have been aware of Dr Barry's proposed changes, which he had set out again in a sermon on the last day of the Gloucester festival, and which he had caused to have printed. His chief objection was to the 'commercial character' of the festival, the fact that the cathedral ceased to be considered a church, and the degradation of the element of worship to a merely secondary place. He wished to return to the original objects of the meetings of the three choirs, viz. the cultivation of the noblest church music.

> There is, I believe, a very important function which these festivals might fulfil, and which now they entirely miss. They might supply to the cultivated and scientific music of our cathedral service exactly what the meetings of choral associations supply to the simpler music of our parish churches – increase of knowledge, increase of earnestness, a higher conception of the beauty of worship, a more glowing enthusiasm for its realisation.
>
> The three choirs should meet together, strengthened as is usual by assistance from the best choirs in the kingdom, and their first object should be the

Alfred Barry, 1826-1910, was one of the sons of Sir Charles Barry, architect of the new houses of parliament. Before coming to Worcester in 1871 he served terms as headmaster of Leeds Grammar School, Cheltenham College, and in 1868 principal of Kings College, London, in which position he continued while at Worcester. He was regarded as a progressive in education, promoting its extension to women, so his opposition to the festivals at Worcester seems rather out of character. He later served five years as Bishop of Sydney.

conduct of services with the greatest possible excellence, so as to raise the musical standard in Divine service… The aid of good instrumental performers should be called in. The greatest masterpieces of ancient church music, absolutely unknown to many in our generation, should be reproduced, but at the same time each festival should be made the opportunity for the production of new church music of the highest and most scientific character. There are living composers who, if called upon, could produce compositions worthy to be placed on a level with the greatest works of the past.

This would give great impetus to church music everywhere, said Dr Barry. But the religious character of the festival should be strictly preserved. There should be a daily early morning Holy Communion, and the greatest preachers of the day should preach at the grand festival services. Thus it would be a real church festival, not an inferior copy of the London or Birmingham festivals and which rarely ventured on any novelty. 'It would bring home, not to the few who could afford to pay for seats, but to all church people, the real grandeur and beauty of worship of the church'. He did not wish to banish oratorios, but bring them to the poor and those of moderate means – the oratorios should be used as an adjunct to divine services. After the grand services in the morning, oratorios could be performed in the afternoon or evening, with outside soloists if necessary, but Dr Barry said again that the opportunity should be taken of sponsoring newly composed church music. And admission to these performances should be absolutely free, those who came would be a congregation not an audience.

Immediately after the Gloucester festival ended, the Worcester stewards for 1875 met under the chairmanship of the Mayor, and Henry Goldingham and Lord Hampton was among those present. The committee had no intention of abandoning the festival, and resolved to invite the bishop to become president, as he had been at the last festival, and, after his expected affirmative reply had been received, to write formally to the dean and chapter for permission to use the cathedral.

At the same time, as a counter to the publication of Dr Barry's sermon, Lord Hampton published an account of his own side of the story. The main point of his pamphlet was the third appeal, which took place in 1870 after the dean and chapter had declined to accept Lord Dudley's condition for paying for the rest of the restoration himself. The appeal had been based on a letter which he drafted and which both he and Lord Lyttelton signed, and explained that Lord Dudley had withdrawn his condition, and continued: 'every question of opinion, whether with respect to music festivals or otherwise, is left entirely open and unprejudiced, as before any such question was raised'. No doubt these words were carefully chosen, as, unlike Lord Hampton, Lord Lyttelton was opposed to the festivals.

LORD HAMPTON

Lord Hampton's pamphlet set out the course of events in 1870, and referred to 'one of the greatest and most influential and enthusiastic meetings I ever saw in Worcester', which resulted in an address signed by 'seven or eight hundred of the leading inhabitants of the city and county' being presented to the dean and chapter, which led to Lord Dudley's withdrawal of his 'unpopular condition'. Lord Hampton and Lord Lyttelton then signed the new appeal letter, but apart from signing the letter 'Lord Lyttelton took no part in the matter'. (Lord Hampton later had to modify this rather bold claim – he admitted that Lyttelton had been responsible for bringing in some of the donations.)

As far as the festivals were concerned, the matter reverted to the status quo.

> What was the status quo? Why, we had a performance of the finest sacred music every third year, and we knew of no reason at that time, Lord Dudley's conditions being out of the way, and the cathedral being completed, why the music meetings should not be continued for another century and a half. My address called forth a subscription not of £5,000, but of £11,000! If the list of subscribers is examined, there will not be found more than one or two, if any, who were not supporters of the festival.
>
> I say without fear of contradiction that had it not been for the desire to save the festivals, a large portion of that money would not have been subscribed. I declare for myself, that I would not have made the effort I did, if I had thought it possible that the chapter, having received our money and completing the cathedral, would now turn round upon us, and say 'the question was left to be settled on its own merits, and we will now either refuse the use of the cathedral, or insist on mutilating the festivals'.
>
> I admit the chapter to be free from expressed conditions, but I do contend that the facts I have stated constitute an implied condition which cannot fairly be disregarded.

Lord Hampton went on to write that he regretted very much the disturbance of friendship and good neighbourliness that has been caused by Dr Barry's proposals. And what was behind the dean and chapter's wish for change? Do they really have such confidence in their judgement that they condemn the 'views and conduct of all their predecessors for 150 years', the views of the other two chapters of Gloucester and Hereford (which had told Dr Barry that they did not wish to make any changes), and their own bishop, who had already said he would be pleased to be president of the 1875 festival? Lord Hampton then pointed to what he regarded as inconsistencies, particularly between what Dr Barry said in his moderate sermon of 1870, and his latest more extreme views.

He said he recognised that Dr Barry did not want to destroy the festivals but to reform them. 'Or rather he would kill them by degrees, instead of putting them out of their misery, as Lord Dudley would do'. He then attacked the idea that the oratorios would be free to all comers. Did he really think, asked Lord Hampton, that 'decorum could be maintained if the cathedral, during an oratorio, were open for all, high and low, who might chose to come?' And as far as people who have heard the oratorios before are concerned, 'they would have to submit to hearing them performed by inferior musicians, and we must submit, whenever we hear an oratorio, to hear a sermon also! Now I like to hear a good sermon, and I like to hear a good oratorio; but I think they had better be kept distinct'.

Finally, Lord Hampton said there was one suggestion made by Dr Barry with which he agreed. It used to be the practise to open the festival by a religious service with a sermon, with admission by cheap ticket, followed by a performance of Handel's 'Dettingen Te Deum'. But more recently the service had been relegated to a different time, and a fourth oratorio performed instead, which he, like Dr Barry, regretted.

The bishop duly assented to being president, so the provisional stewards' committee wrote to the dean and chapter asking official permission to hold the festival in 1875. The application contained the usual statement as to how disappointed the public would be if the 150 year old festival tradition was now terminated, but it did contain one conciliatory note: that, in view of the need to protect the new work in the cathedral, the committee would act in conjunction with the dean and chapter in deciding on the physical needs of the festival. In the past the dean and chapter had more or less handed over that part of the building which was to be used for the festival, and the long drawn-out work of erecting and dismantling the seating and platforms had been one of the reasons put forward by the anti-festival faction.

At the same time Sir Edmund Lechmere, who had been a member of the joint committee and was religious enough to have a chapel built in his park, and whose uncle was a canon of the cathedral, wrote to the dean expressing his own feelings. He had not, he wrote, attended any recent festivals because of his reservations about them, which he detailed, and which followed those already expressed by other festival opponents. However, Sir Edmund did not go as far as wishing the cessation of the festivals, just some modification that would go further to recognise that they were being held in the sacred house of God, and were not just concert performances. He made four suggestions that would overcome his religious scruples: that the dean and chapter retain control of the cathedral during the festivals; that there should be evening as well as morning services during the festival, to retain the 'daily routine of prayer'; that no construction be permitted in the cathedral without the permission of the dean and chapter; and that each performance of the oratorios, as part of a special service, should be preceded and closed by prayer offered by the bishop or dean. If these suggestions were adopted, wrote Sir Edmund, 'we may have oratorios performed and listened to with such reverence as to be worthy of being acts of solemn worship'.

The dean and chapter met on 19th October, and quickly reached their decision. Their reply to the provisional committee, signed by Dean Yorke, began by rejecting the assertion that the appeal of 1870 was made on the understanding that the festivals would continue, and 'claim for themselves the entire freedom to deal with the question on its own merits'. While recognising that many would be disappointed by the cessation of the festivals, they also felt 'there is a large and increasing class who are prevented from attending the festivals by a conscientious objection to the system on which they have been conducted for many years'. So they 'deeply regretted' that they could not comply with the request of the provisional committee. The main grounds were that they did want to give the control of the nave, now it had been newly restored, to other hands. Secondly, 'they are of the opinion that musical performances unconnected with any religious service, and to which admission is given only by purchased tickets, should no longer take place in the cathedral'.

However, the dean and chapter wished to keep up the meetings of the three choirs for the cultivation of sacred music, and that they should 'resort to the general form under which the meetings of the choirs were originally conducted'. They continued:

Sir Edmund Anthony Harley Lechmere, 3rd bart, 1826-94. He lived at The Rhydd, south of Worcester, and was a member of the ancient family of that name which lived at Severn End, Hanley Castle. He served as Tory MP for various Worcestershire constituencies, and played an active part in the restoration committee. He was a founder member of the Venerable Order of St John, having travelled several times to Jerusalem. His uncle Rev. Anthony Berwick Lechmere was an honorary canon of the cathedral and vicar of Hanley Castle. Sir Edmund had reservations about holding the festivals, and suggested some changes.

The Cathedral Restored

> We propose, therefore, in the month of September next to hold, on two or more days, a festival of religious services, which shall contain the performance of sacred music of a high class by the united choirs, with adequate assistance, vocal and instrumental, and sermons by preachers of eminence, advocating the cause of the charity… We see nothing in this proposed change which will prevent them from co-operating with the chapters of Gloucester and Hereford for the support of the charity in which they have a common interest… We trust that this course, when considered by the public under all circumstances of the case, will meet with general approval, and that they may obtain the support of the inhabitants of the city and diocese in carrying it out.

Immediately after printing the dean's letter, Berrow's commented:

> The document signed by the dean exhibits no sufficient ground whatever for the abolition of the festivals, and wholly fails to justify the braving of public opinion or the cruel disappointment of thousands who wish well to the church of England, and desire to see the cathedral of our city productive of the largest possible benefit to the diocese in a spiritual and a secular point of view.

It pointed out that in 1870 Canon Barry was unconnected with the chapter, so why did he think he was in a better position to know how the appeal was carried out than Lord Hampton, the then high sheriff Thomas Rowley Hill, or the mayor Mr Barnett? And why did the public quickly subscribe £11,000? Not to restore the cathedral, as Lord Dudley was prepared to pay for that himself, so the conclusion must be drawn that the response to the appeal was mainly by those who gave so that the festivals might continue. As to the dean's assertion that there were a growing number of people who objected to the festivals as they used to be carried out, Berrow's thought this was simply untrue – where was the evidence? – the support for the last festival in 1872 had been as great as ever.

Berrow's concluded that to end the festivals would be 'truly lamentable' and was likely to alienate the sympathies of the people from the cathedral as completely as the restoration had won their sympathies. The provisional stewards' committee, which had so far acted in a most moderate manner, should now again approach the dean and chapter in attempt to get them to change their mind, and:

> We hope that this will meet with success, otherwise the position of dean and chapter will be seriously prejudiced in the minds of those amongst whom they are centred… The festivals have been abolished under the rule of a dean who has had no personal experience of them and a canon who is a comparative stranger, whose arguments are inconsistent, and whose facts have been contested by those whose experience should carry weight.

After this personal attack, Berrow's threw an even more explosive assertion into the argument: that those who contributed in 1870 under the impression that this would save the festivals, might now ask for their money to be returned by the dean and chapter.

LORD HAMPTON

A few days later the provisional committee met to consider their response. The mayor presided, and Lord Hampton proposed that the reply should be placed before the 'eighty noblemen and gentlemen who have consented to act as stewards' for consideration at their meeting the next day. This duly took place, again with the mayor as chairman, and, helped by Lord Hampton, the meeting agreed on a long letter with seven resolutions to be sent to the dean.

The letter covered familiar ground, the main bone of contention being whether those who donated in 1870 did so on the understanding that the festivals would continue. The chapter's second reason was also attacked:

> This is an objection of a religious nature, about which, therefore, there may of course be different opinions. But when five clergymen, united as a cathedral chapter, undertake by an arbitrary exercise of power to destroy an institution supported by a prescription of 150 years – to endanger an excellent charity, to disregard the wishes of their neighbours, and to interrupt the harmony and good feeling of a whole district – they need to have stronger support of a religious character than their own opinions.

Finally the stewards tried to be conciliatory by offering to abandon the platform for the orchestra, to close the festival with an extra divine service on Friday, and to submit all the music to the dean and chapter for their prior approval. On that basis, the stewards hoped, the dean and chapter may even yet be induced to reconsider their decision, and thus avert a breach of those amicable relations between the chapter and the citizens of Worcester.

The dean and chapter's reply was equally forthright, and began by regretting that the stewards seemed to be accusing them of obtaining money under false pretences in 1870. They said that the restoration committee would certainly not have wished to accept money given under a misunderstanding, and wondered whether the committee should now offer to anyone who gave money in 1870 thinking they were securing the future of the festivals a return of their subscription; in which case the dean and chapter would undertake their own contributions. The dean and chapter rested its case on the undisputed fact that the appeal in 1870, contained the words 'every condition [of Lord Dudley's] is withdrawn, and that every question of opinion, whether with respect to the music festivals or otherwise, was left entirely open and unprejudiced', in the letter signed by Lord Lyttelton and Lord Hampton. To support their case they got both the retired dean John Peel, and the bishop, to write confirming that this was the case. So the reply contained no hint of a change of mind, and concluded: 'we trust that the stewards will see the propriety of withdrawing a resolution which is virtually an imputation to the dean and chapter of a serious breach of faith'.

Berrow's was, of course, disgusted by the whole affair, and quoted editorials from The Times, The Musical World, and others disagreeing with the dean and chapter. The Hereford Journal wrote that it was 'a monstrous anomaly that some half a dozen men, who have positively nothing to do with the county, (except enjoying its sinecures) can block the festival against the bishop and all Worcestershire...' Only the Guardian, the Hereford Journal wrote, supported the dean and chapter, 'but the influence possessed by certain members of the chapter in this quarter renders the opinion of the Guardian on this subject of very little value'!

At the same time there was a war of words in the letters column of Berrow's between Lord Lyttelton and Lord Hampton about the meaning of the 1870 appeal letter. Although so far he had held back from taking an active part in the controversy, Lord Lyttelton now came out as an opponent of the festivals as they had been held, and said that in 1870 it was clear that the matter was left entirely in the hands of the dean and chapter. Lord Hampton, on the other hand, claimed that the understanding was that the appeal was made to save the festivals, and it was on that basis that subscriptions were made.

A petition, probably organised by Mayor Goldingham and Lord Hampton, containing nearly 300 signatures, was got up, requesting the mayor to hold a public meeting, which took place on 28th October in the Guildhall. Lord Hampton, the mayor, and others on the platform were greeted 'with every demonstration of enthusiasm, the whole audience standing and cheering again and again'. The mayor opened proceedings by going over the history of the dispute from 1870, and he asked the audience to avoid intemperate speeches, which would not accomplish the object they had in view. He paid tribute to the late dean, Dr Peel: "there was a great current of courtesy running through his whole conduct; he had the most kindly feelings towards the city and the citizens, and there was general regret that advanced age and infirmity compelled him to retire".

He then read a letter he had received from Earl Beauchamp, who was unable to attend. He had written 'I cannot say how deeply I regret that the dean and chapter of Worcester should disregard the traditions of their body, and lay rude hands upon an institution which has done so much to keep alive provincial interest in one of the highest branches of sacred art'. When the cheering had died down the mayor read a short supportive letter from John Slaney Pakington, and referred to a number of others.

An important point made in support of the Worcester festival was that if it was discontinued, then it was likely that the other two festivals would also cease, certainly in their present form, and delegations from both Gloucester and Hereford had been invited to the meeting. The Rev. Canon Samuel Lysons spoke for the Gloucester delegation, and told of the extreme disappointment that there would now be a divorce between the three dioceses. The Gloucester stewards had already sent a memorial to Dean Yorke expressing their 'extreme regret' at the dean and chapter's decision. He said he had an hereditary connection with the festivals – the meetings started in 1718 in the house of his great great great grandfather, and his father had published a history of the festivals, so he knew a little about their history. A great deal of nonsense had been spoken about the early festivals; "the idea of returning to what was said to be the original scheme, namely a meeting merely of the three choirs, was moonshine… there had never been a time when the three choirs alone were employed". He said the discontinuation would very much damage the charity; he knew it was said that gentlemen would continue to give anyway, but, as treasurer of the fund, he could say that he had "never seen the colour of their money".

John Arkwright of Hampton Court near Leominster spoke for Hereford, and expressed similar sentiments. He spoke for the great majority of Herefordshire people when he said they approved of the festivals as at present conducted. He had been connected with six festivals, and of those invited to become stewards not more than one or two per cent declined on the ground of objection to the manner in which the meetings were held.

But the main speaker was Lord Hampton, 'who was received with loud and prolonged applause, the audience rising, waving their hats and cheering enthusiastically'. He moved the first resolution, which regretted the imperilment of the friendly relations between the dean and chapter and the people of Worcestershire, and of the intense regret with the refusal to allow a festival in 1875. He started by sounding moderate, reminding his audience that the dean and chapter "were men of high position and high personal character. They may be mistaken in the decision they have come to, but we have no right to question their motives". He continued:

> I have again and again, in a period of a little under 50 years, addressed my neighbours upon various subjects, but never did I rise with such strong feelings as I do now – feelings in which I cannot deny that there is some measure of indignation, mingled with deep sorrow.

He then reminded the audience of what took place in 1870, and that when Lord Dudley made his second offer why was Lord Hampton asked to raise the balance of the money for the restoration? Why did he undertake this difficult task? "For this one reason: I had advocated the festivals and I desired to continue them". Why, he had been asked, had he not asked the dean and chapter for an undertaking on this point? But this would have been insulting, he said, as there was an understanding – he did not put it at anything but an honourable understanding – which was clear, conclusive and binding. The appeal letter, which he had written with Lord Lyttelton, stated that 'I am sanguine that, whenever an appeal may be made to the diocese to subscribe the remainder, the appeal will meet with a response so general and so generous as to put an need to any excuse for discontinuing our ancient festivals for the sake of the price that can be obtained for their abandonment'. What could this mean other than that the appeal would save the festivals? Lord Hampton then quoted a letter from Whitmore Isaac, the treasurer of the festival fund, who congratulated Lord Hampton when the total raised had reached over £14,000 'on the successful accomplishment of your work – you have saved the festivals'. Obviously his understanding was that this was the purpose of the appeal.

Lord Hampton contrasted this with the behaviour of Lord Dudley, whose second offer was made in response to public opposition to his first, and who merely hoped that when the restoration was complete public opinion would turn against the festivals. But it was clear that the public still wanted the festivals, and "I would ask the dean and chapter whether this is really the moment for a body of clergy to set themselves against the festivals, and to disregard the wishes of a large body of laity". He then quoted the first reason given by the dean and chapter for its refusal: that now the restoration is complete, and the nave as well as the choir brought into use for worship, music performances unconnected with any religious service should no longer take place. But what, asked Lord Hampton, had the fact that the restoration was complete got to do with it? Winding himself up for an emotional appeal, he continued:

> Are we to be told that because that edifice has been beautified it is no longer right that the praises of God should be sung in it in the best way? Are we to be told that we are no longer to listen to the Hallelujah, with all the strength and force that can be given to that grand chorus? That the chorus in Elijah so wonderfully calculated to inspire us with devotional feeling 'Holy, Holy, Holy', is not to be sung, and that such music is not a religious service, one that raises the thoughts to heaven and inspires devotion more than most dry forms of praise could do. Are we to be told that because the church is beautified we are to hear 'I know that my redeemer liveth' sung by some inferior artist?
>
> Every man is entitled to his opinions, but is our dean a better man than the deans of Hereford and Gloucester? Is he a better man than our respected and beloved bishop? Even Lord Lyttelton, who is opposed to the festivals, in one of his letters admitted that 'public feeling is an element in this question'. May I accept that what I see before me as a proof of this? (Loud cried of "yes", and cheers.)

So Lord Hampton concluded by entreating the dean and chapter to reconsider the grave mistake they had made.

Thomas Rowley Hill, the newly elected MP for Worcester, seconded the resolution, and his fellow MP, Alexander Sherriff, proposed a similar one, seconded by Cllr Woodward. He said that he could not conceive anything more unfortunate than that a body holding a brief authority should set up their private opinions in utter defiance of the wishes of the whole population of the three dioceses – that five gentlemen should set themselves up in direct opposition to a million of their fellow Christians. The Earl of Coventry moved another resolution that the cathedral was specially suitable for performing oratorios, which was seconded by Alderman Josiah Stallard. He said he hoped that the modifications adopted by the stewards and offered to the dean and chapter would give them a way out of their decision, and allow them now to discuss the arrangements with the stewards. Finally, George Woodyatt Hastings proposed a resolution appealing to the dean and chapter to change their minds, and said that surely the period of 150 years during which they had been held gave them unchallengeable legitimacy.

After some more speeches Lord Hampton concluded proceedings by thanking the mayor for so promptly convening the meeting, and for his help in presiding over the meetings of the provisional festival committee.

Various letters appeared in Berrow's the following week on the subject. The Earl of Dudley defended the dean and chapter who, he said, had decided on the side of 'conscience'. But in the same edition this was attacked by the newspaper, saying that there is not a single proposition that cannot be defended under the plea of 'conscience', and that this excuse will not satisfy the public. This was followed by a letter from the stewards, complaining that a letter from the bishop to Canon Wood had been only partly quoted by the dean and chapter. The bishop's opening paragraphs confirmed that it was his understanding that the third appeal gave no guarantee that the festivals would continue, but his last paragraph was not quoted, or any indication given that the letter was incomplete. In fact the bishop concluded 'I have always enjoyed the oratorios, and that they are edifying and profitable to the great mass of people who attend them. I do not see any objection to such use of the cathedral, nor to the admission of bearers by paid tickets'. But the bishop objected strongly to the turning of the cathedral into a carpenters' shop before and after the festival, and wrote that some other way must be found of conducting them.

Next, Berrow's published a letter from Dean Yorke in which he listed eighteen names, mostly clergymen, who had written to him objecting to the festivals. But Berrow's pointed out that eighteen names were not very many, and that not one of them came from anywhere near the three counties! Finally, Berrow's quoted words by Dean Peel when the window donated by the freemasons was accepted. He said "it is a great mistake to suppose that the cathedral belongs exclusively to the dean and chapter. It belongs to every person in the diocese, although we are appointed guardians and custodians…".

Berrow's also quoted an amusing poem in Punch magazine, making fun of the dean and chapter.

The Cathedral Restored

> *When music, heavenly maid, was young,*
> *O how delightfully she sung!*
> *Then Deans and Chapters liked full well*
> *To have her in Cathedrals dwell,*
> *But now it seems they can't endure a*
> *High ut de poitrine* [high note], *shrill bravura,*
> *And strive to banish lute and lyre*
> *From heavily fruitaged Worcestershire.*
>
> *Wherefore, O Dean, this change of fashions?*
> *Has music now revived the passions?*
> *Is it a back-recoiling fear*
> *Lest song than sermon prove more dear?*
> *Or does a too cacophonous clangour*
> *In decanal ear arouse some anger?*
> *Or is it possibly despair*
> *Of rivalling music anywhere?*
> *The list's too long to investigate –*
> *It may be love, it can't be hate;*
> *But clearly Worcester's fair Cathedral*
> *Is ruled by men with no polyhedral*
> *Angles. No enemies are apter*
> *To hurt the church than such a Chapter.*

The following week more letters appeared, including one from the bishop regretting that only part of his letter had been quoted by Canon Wood, but absolving the dean and chapter from accusations of doing this deliberately to mislead. But a new factor was now rearing its head as an impediment to any further discussions between the dean and chapter and the stewards. This was the statement by the stewards, already referred to, that the dean and chapter were guilty of bad faith in allowing money to be collected during the 1870 appeal, even of 'obtaining money under false pretences', if there was any question of them still disallowing the festivals. They objected strongly to this, and insisted that the stewards withdraw it. The stewards had sent an explanation which was a sort of half apology, but the dean and chapter, stung by the fact that the phrase had been repeated in other newspapers, insisted on its withdrawal. There was also a copy of a letter from the bishop, ever the conciliator, to Lord Hampton, admitting that 'the feeling in favour of them has been so strikingly manifested, that we must not despair, I think, of finding conditions under which the dean and chapter may still permit the performance of our great oratorios in the cathedral, if this charge of breach of faith could be abandoned'.

On 17th November the town council had a regular meeting, and, despite the fact that they had already memorialised the dean and chapter in favour of continuing the festivals, Cllr John Bozward moved that a further deputation should see the dean and chapter in the hope of getting them to change their minds. That Bozward was not an admirer of the dean and chapter came out clearly as he proposed his motion. First the chapter had appealed to the chapters at Gloucester and Hereford to 'curse' the festivals, "instead of which they blessed them altogether". Then the dean and chapter said that it would be wrong to transfer the newly restored cathedral to the charge of other people. But did the restoration make the cathedral more sacred than hitherto? The nave had always been used for services since the cathedral's foundation; now the dean and chapter were trying to exclude worshippers from the choir altogether, and he had noticed at some recent services that some of the congregation walked away just before the sermon "as if they did not wish to listen to the rhetorical efforts of the capitular body". Heaping more criticism on the canons, Bozward continued:

> Then there is the objection to the manner of admission. Anyone not acquainted with the facts would be led to imagine that the capitular body knew nothing of emoluments. What did it matter whether people paid for tickets or paid when they had a plate thrust at them? The dean and chapter were paid for their services as were the lay clerks and all who had to do with the cathedral. What ground of objection then could there be to the singers at the festivals being paid?

> Then something was said as to 'conscience'. If the dean and chapter were told that they were not the true successors of the apostles how much offended would they be. But, if the apostles came to life and visited Worcester, would they be likely to look to the capitular body receiving large emoluments, say £800 each, as their successors? Would they go to the most squalid dwellings in the city and expect to find their successors sitting by the bed of sickness and administering consolation to dying men, or would they go to large mansions filled with richest furniture and decorations, and expect to see them clothed in purple and fine linen and faring sumptuously every day? Talk about conscience!

Bozward continued in similar vein for some time, and particularly attacked Canon Barry.

> It was not for Canon Barry to sneer at what he called the commercial principle. Upon what principle did he receive his preferments and emoluments? Would he, scorning the commercial principle, resign his canonry and its emoluments? It was not for him to attempt to slander the tradesmen of Worcester by saying that they regarded the question in a commercial spirit. It would be better for Canon Barry to look to his own affairs than to twit tradesmen of this city with commercial selfishness.

Bozward also pointed to the difference between what he preached in his late sermon at Gloucester, "yet at Worcester this doctrine is condemned. Were there two Dromios – a Canon Barry of Gloucester and a Canon Barry of Worcester?"

The council had also been offended when on a recent occasion the dean and chapter had not been present to welcome the mayor and civic dignitaries when they attended a service, as had been customary. The dean said the omission was due to his ignorance of this custom, but the council was not very pleased. So Bozward's motion was carried unanimously, and a small delegation duly met the dean and Canons Lewis, Wood and Barry. The new mayor, Mr Longmore, led the council delegation, which, perhaps fortunately, did not include Cllr Bozward. Instead J W Scott was chosen to be the main spokesperson. He said as a non-conformist he could speak with perfect neutrality, but he and other non-conformists had contributed to the 1870 appeal on the definite understand that this would save the festivals. As to the religious question, he would leave this to higher authorities, but "he would only point attention to the subject as concerned its social and commercial influence, in respect of which he felt it would be a great calamity if the festivals were abolished". Cllr Jones also thought that the way the festivals were managed could be modified so as to satisfy both the dean and chapter and the public, and the mayor added that perhaps a large conference could be held attended by all interested parties to find a solution. But the dean had nothing to say except that all these points would receive the most attentive consideration.

But the dean and chapter were not to be moved, and on 25th November the dean sent a final reply to stewards. The letter began by implying that the stewards had apologised for accusing the chapter of a breach of faith, although in a comment Berrow's wrote that they had not, but merely explained what they meant by it. But on the main question:

> They adhere to their already expressed opinion that sacred music of the highest character should be combined on these occasions with religious services, open to all classes of the community, and they feel sure that with the assistance of the principal gentlemen of the diocese, and with the co-operation, which they hope to retain, of the choirs of Gloucester and Hereford, a festival of prayer and praise worthy of the occasion could be held.

Berrow's was, of course, disgusted by this final decision, and could only hope that a future chapter, not containing those who had until recently proclaimed the grandeur of festivals and yet have more recently vetoed them shall revive this ancient and honoured tradition.

But although it was generally assumed that this was the dean and chapter's last word, on 3rd December the dean wrote to Lord Hampton saying that they had not intended to close the door on a meeting with the stewards, and that 'even now by a free and friendly interchange of our respective views, we may arrive at the means of holding a festival at once carrying out the principles on which we desire it to be based, and such as the stewards would unite with us to perpetuate'. Eager to seize any chance that the festivals might yet be saved, Lord Hampton replied immediately, and said he would put the letter to a meeting of the stewards the next day.

A meeting was duly held between the stewards and the dean and chapter on 19th December. The stewards had two proposals that they wished to put forward and which they thought might satisfy the other side. One has already been referred to, suggesting that church services should be held at the beginning and end of the festival, that the band and performers should stand on the floor of the transepts rather than on a temporary platform, and that the chapter should vet all music to be performed. The second proposal was, it was thought, even more closely aligned to the proposals of the dean and chapter, which was to have a service every day at 10.00, followed by the oratorio at 1.00. There would also be a service on the last evening.

Having put forward these ideas, the stewards asked what plans the dean and chapter had. But, according to the stewards' report, 'they had not matured any plans, and only vague and general ideas were thrown out'. So the stewards asked the individual members of the chapter what they thought, but this did not get very far, as there was disagreement among the canons on some points. The only thing that united them was their opposition to the sale of tickets, but the stewards countered this by saying that they had to have adequate funds to pay the performers. The dean and chapter admitted the need for funds, 'but suggested no mode of raising them'. So the meeting ended inconclusively.

The stewards and the town council had already considered one further step they could take, which was to petition the queen as head of the Anglican Church, but had awaited the outcome of the meeting on the 19th. The town council brought this up, and asked Lord Hampton how it should be presented. He replied that he would have to take advice about that, and in any case it was doubtful if the queen would wish to interfere with the decision of the dean and chapter. But he thought nevertheless that it was worth doing, if only to show the citizens of Worcester that all efforts were being made. The petition rehearsed all the familiar arguments in favour of the festivals, and asked the queen to use her influence with the dean and chapter. When finally submitted to the home secretary on 25th January it had nearly 3,400 signatures according to Lord Hampton's diary – Berrow's reported double that number. In fact three similar petitions were presented: one from the mayor and corporation of Worcester, one from the citizens generally, and one from the mayor and corporation of Droitwich.

The Cathedral Restored

At the end of 1874 the Earl of Dudley wrote to Berrow's, putting forward some new proposals. He seemed to think it desirable that the continuity of the festivals with those of Gloucester and Hereford should be kept up, and also accepted that the performance of oratorios needed high class professional singers. As the dean and chapter had ruled out charging for entry in the cathedral, Lord Dudley suggested that a new music hall should be built for the festivals, which would take them entirely away from the interference of the dean and chapter. It was too late for a new hall to be built for the 1875 festival, so he suggested that a temporary structure be erected, to be followed by a permanent hall for the longer term. Alternatively, the 1875 festival could be abandoned to save the cost of a temporary hall as long as an amount was paid to Gloucester and Hereford in lieu of Worcester's usual donation to the charity. Lord Dudley wrote that he would willingly attend any meeting called to discuss this idea.

There had been similar suggestions by those who wished the festivals to continue, but not in the cathedral – one correspondent suggested using the Shirehall. But most festival supporters regarded hearing the oratorios in the cathedral to be an essential element in their enjoyment, and although this idea received the support of Berrow's it was never followed through – people probably thought it would be better to wait for a change in the make-up of the capitular body.

On 31st March the dean and chapter convened a meeting to discuss what was now to be called a 'festival of services'. Present were the bishop, the dean, canons Wood and Barry, Lord Lyttelton, Sir Edmund Lechmere, and various clergymen including Rev. Henry Douglas of Hanbury, mostly, excepting the bishop, opponents of the old-style festival. A letter was read from Cllr Goldingham, chairman of the stewards committee, saying, in effect, that the stewards would have nothing to do with the proposed festival. The meeting decided to appoint a committee to make arrangements under the chairmanship of Lord Lyttelton, and this was the proposed shape of the festival:

1.   To hold a festival of church services on two days in September, in the course of which such music as the Dettingen or Utrecht Te Deum, new music by living English composers, and (in place of anthems in the afternoon services) Mendelssohn's Lauda Zion or Hymn of Praise, &c, to be rendered by a full choir and orchestra (if the choirs of Gloucester and Hereford agreed to take part). The charity would be advocated by distinguished preachers.

2.   Admission to such services, whether by ticket or otherwise, would be without any charge whatever, and all collections would go to the charity.

The chapter's funds, the statement concluded, would not be sufficient to meet this expenditure, therefore the scheme would be dependant on subscriptions from those who approved the general outline, to an amount of £700 or £800. To further the appeal a general committee of clergy and laity would be required.

However, a week later another meeting was held, and it was decided not to go ahead with an appeal, but instead to confine the music to that which could be paid for out of the normal capitular funds, which would probably mean that there would not be an orchestra or large chorus.

Berrow's and other Worcester newspapers, continue to campaign for the dean and chapter to change their minds, but in a brief notice on 12th June, defeat had to be admitted. The following month further details of the festival were announced – it would last three days, the first of which would be devoted to rehearsals and open to the public. The services would consist of hymns, anthems and choral selections sung by the Worcester and neighbouring choirs. Berrow's called it 'farcical'. Lord Dudley had subscribed £100, and the dean and chapter £150, towards the charity – this contrasted with over £1,000 which had been raised in past years. By 14th August the details of the festival were decided. It would take place on 22nd and 23rd September, there would be services at 11.00 and 3.30 each day, there would be a 'full choir of 100 voices' accompanied by the grand organ. Details of the anthems were given, and although admission would be free, tickets should be obtained for the reserved portions of the cathedral.

At the same time Dr Barry wrote a long letter to The Guardian about the festival. He wrote that it would be on the principle that all music performed in the house of God should be associated with divine services, and that all admission should be free. They had endured a painful six months, when attacks had been made against them, and he had even heard that some of his opponents would be deliberately avoiding the festival, and doing what they could do damage it. So his letter was mainly an appeal to all churchmen to support the festival by attending. He also regretted that, as a public appeal would not have been successful in the prevailing atmosphere, there would be no orchestra that year, but he hoped very much to reinstate this when public sentiment had become calmer.

Shortly afterwards a letter appeared in Berrow's from Earl Beauchamp, examining the two principles that Barry had laid down in his Guardian letter. He examined both in detail, arguing that neither stood up to scrutiny. The Earl ended his letter 'those who suddenly invent a new order of things, and fortify themselves by arguments which if tested produce what Dr Barry will forgive me for calling grotesquely sanctimonious results, must not complain when the principles to which they appeal become the subject of examination'. Beauchamp's letter provoked another from Barry in the Guardian, which Berrow's called a paraphrase of his first, and 'weak, prolix and ineffective'.

In an attempt to maximise attendance, Dr Barry also wrote to the mayor asking the council to put aside the differences which had arisen in the last year, and attend the festival. But although the mayor was asked to politely acknowledge the letter, no-one came forward to take the matter any further.

Frederick, 6th Earl Beauchamp (1830-91) was the grandson of the 1st Earl, whose marriage to an heiress founded the family fortune. Frederick was preceded by two uncles, his father, and his brother, before coming into the title in 1863. During his time at Oxford, when he was a fellow of All Souls, he adopted tractarian views, and represented the high church view on various commissions, and in articles in the press. He served as a Tory MP between 1857 and 1863, and was briefly a lord of the Admiralty when Sir John Pakington was first lord. Friendly with Disraeli, he was appointed lord steward in 1874, and later served under Salisbury. He continued the reconstruction of Madresfield Court started by his brother, and was keen on promoting both education and music locally. From a painting in Worcester Guildhall.

The festival duly took place, and Berrow's devoted almost a whole page to a detailed description. In its comment column it pointed to the very wet weather and lack of decorations in the city that made it a very low-key affair, and a few people and traders wore black arm bands. 'Regarding it simply as a 'festival of services', not admitting of comparisons with the festivals of the past – the gathering has been a success', Berrow's grudgingly admitted. The choir, which included singers from the three dioceses as well as singers from some top national choirs, 'did their part creditably', and the Bishops and Worcester and Hereford took part as well as about one hundred clergy, so the processions into the cathedral must have been impressive. The Earl of Dudley and Lord Lyttelton were the leading laymen present. One of the visiting preachers, Rev. MacLagan, vicar of Kensington, did not seem to have been well briefed when he spoke of the change having provoked 'some little opposition', and hoped that old prejudices and predilections would soon be put aside. Attendance was variable, with the nave over half full for some services, but others only had a congregation in the choir. It was evident, Berrow's thought, that many of those there were showing support for the dean and chapter, 'but no interest whatever was manifested by the general public. But why should they?' Although the music was well done, despite the poor sound from the new organ put in the south transept by Lord Dudley, 'there was little more than might have been expected at ordinary services in a well-conducted cathedral'.

Lord Hampton recorded the 'mock festival' in his diary, but it has to be assumed that he did not attend, preferring on Wednesday to attend the regular morning meeting of the Droitwich poor law guardians instead.

The great west window in Worcester cathedral. The window was part of the earlier restoration, and the stained glass by Hardmans of Birmingham was added in the 1870s at the expense of Lord Dudley.

Berrow's somewhat unenthusiastic report of the 1875 'mock festival'.

> The city presented a most gloomy appearance on the two days of the Three Choirs' Meeting. Rain fell, with little intermission, throughout each day; and the degree of indifference manifested by the citizens amply testified to their deep-rooted aversion to the Dean and Chapter's substitute for the Worcester Musical Festival. In the beginning of the week handbills were issued, recommending the citizens to display tokens of mourning. We are glad to say that this suggestion met with little favour. On Wednesday morning three or four black flags were to be seen, and at a few shops shutters were put up. The great bulk of the citizens adopted a far more effectual way of showing their dislike of the change which has been made. They did not attend the services at the Cathedral, but allowed room to be made for those who favoured the project of the Dean and Chapter and felt it a duty to support that body by their presence at the meeting. There was an entire absence of decorations, and in every respect a most striking contrast with the interest displayed in former years was presented.

Chapter 10
The Year 1875

Lord Hampton remained in Worcestershire over Christmas, but at the end of December went to London to preside over a meeting of the Spanish bondholders at which an agreement with the Spanish finance minister by which the bondholders would be compensated by the issue of shares in the Rio Tinto mine was accepted.

When the purchase of commissions in the army came to an end, the promotion prospects for junior officers were seen to be much reduced. Accordingly a royal commission was appointed in November 1874 to investigate and recommend how the 'rapidity of promotion' could be maintained. The commission chairman was the lawyer James Plaisted Wilde, since 1869 Lord Penzance, who had already investigated claims of unfairness in the compensation given to officers on the abolition of purchase. There were six other commissioners, Lord Hampton being one. He had faced similar problems in the Royal Navy, and although he had opposed the abolition of purchase in the army, this was mainly on financial grounds, and he had once said that if he was organising a new army now, it would not include purchase. The commission also included three major generals: Edwin Johnson, Arthur Herbert, and Charles Foster.

The commission did not begin taking evidence till April 9th, but they started meeting in the new year to plan their modus operandi. Lord Hampton attended nearly all the meetings, and the report was not published until July 1876, and will be described later.

Lord Hampton's diary for 1875 has survived and gives a good picture of his day to day activities, although more days are left blank than in his earlier diaries. On 2nd January he travelled to Kings End in Powick, the home of his son Johnny and his wife Lady Diana, and, not for the first time, we learn that Johnny was poorly. This matter will be discussed later. On 6th January the household travelled to London – the servants and horses in the morning, the family in the afternoon, and when they arrived at 9 Eaton Square, dinner had already been

LORD HAMPTON

James Plaisted Wilde, Lord Penzance, 1816-99. He had a successful legal career, ending as a judge in the court of probate and divorce, and after being raised to the peerage took an active, and usually liberal, part in the House of Lords. After he retired in 1872 he took a position in the court of arches in Canterbury, but he was not able to successfully assert his authority, and the court transacted little business. He served on various commissions including the marriage laws and the condition of Wellington College, as well as those to do with the army.

prepared. But Lord Hampton was only in London for a week before he returned, having various engagements in Worcestershire during the following week. After shooting on Friday, he attended the Worcestershire Agricultural Society meeting on Saturday, at which he complained about the amount of time wasted on proposing toasts, when they would all rather be outside watching the show jumping! On Monday he went to Kings End again to see Johnny, but did not join the theatre party in the evening out of respect for Gustavus Smith, who had just died. He was the second husband of Caroline Mordaunt, the sister of Lord Hampton's second wife Augusta Murray. The following day he went to the Hunt Club Ball wearing the colourful uniform of the Club with Johnny 'who bore it well', before finally returning to London on Friday.

Lord Hampton was a regular church-goer. In London his routine was to attend St Michael's, Chester Square, a short walk from his Eaton Square house, in the morning, and the Chapel Royal in St James' Palace in the evening. The vicar of St Michael's in 1875 was the recently appointed Rev. James Fleming, a leading London clergyman noted for his powerful preaching. He was a moderate evangelist, and a successful raiser from his large, fashionable and wealthy audience. On 24th January Lord Hampton heard 'a beautiful sermon by Mr Fleming in aid of schools'. In the afternoon he usually made calls – on 24th he called on Mrs Milner, a widow also living in Eaton Square, with whom he had had a close friendship thirty years before, and also Lady Sandys, and Lady Beauchamp – perhaps their lordships were out visiting too. At the Chapel Royal that evening he met Lord and Lady Dudley. Lady Hampton gets very few mentions in his diary,

The Year 1875

Rev James Fleming (1830-1908) was educated at Cambridge, and he soon became noted for his gifts as a speaker and preacher, and, judging by his portraits, his good looks. After several other appointments he became vicar of St Michael's, Chester Square, in 1873. He supported many causes and was a committed teetotaller, and while at St Michael's is said to have raised £35,000 from his wealthy congregation, including his patron the Duke of Westminster. He turned down appointments to deaneries and bishoprics, but did became a canon of York.

except when she is ill, and as he mentions other relations he went to church with, it must be assumed that Lady Hampton was not a frequent church-goer.

When at home in Westwood, Lord Hampton would normally go to Hampton Lovett church in the morning, and say prayers with all the family in the chapel at Westwood in the evening.

Having returned to London on 22nd January, on 25th he travelled to Burghley House, the seat of the Marquis of Exeter, for a country house party, parliament being not yet in session. Returning to town by early train on 29th, he only spent one night in Eaton Square before travelling to Worcestershire, where he had to attend another meeting in connection with the winding up of the Droitwich Saline Baths Company, after the establishment had been sold to Dr Bainbrigge. While there, he inspected the new organ in the south transept of the cathedral paid for by Lord Dudley, and found it 'less ugly than I expected'. After just two nights in Worcestershire he returned to London, where on 2nd February he attended the Central Chamber of Agriculture for the first time as president. The government had published a draft landlord and tenant bill, which was discussed at the meeting. The following day Lord Hampton was off again, this time to Birmingham where he was to inspect an exhibition of drawings done by pupils of the School of Design, of which he had been president for the past year. He was met at the station by two members of the Birmingham and Midland Institute, the leading Birmingham architect John H Chamberlain and Abraham Follett Osler, a meteorologist, and went to inspect the drawings. After spending the night at Osler's 'nice villa' in Harborne Road, Edgbaston, he left by an early train the next morning and was in London in time to attend a meeting of the army commission.

The following day, 5th February, saw the opening of parliament, and Lord Hampton attended both the Commons and the Lords to hear the speeches. The address was traditionally moved in the Commons by a junior member, and he thought the speech by Edward Stanhope, the newly elected member for mid-Lincolnshire 'remarkably good'. Stanhope went on to serve as a cabinet minister in the next decade. The next day he presided for the first time as chairman of the executive committee of the Patriotic Fund. Mrs Carr, a 40 year old widow and superintendent of the Royal Victoria Patriotic Asylum for Girls, and some of the other staff, had complained about the chaplain, Rev. Kyle, possibly because he was not giving enough time to religious instruction. After a lengthy discussion it was resolved that 'the committee see much to regret and disapprove in the course she adopted and in the manner in which she brought those charges under the

A print of c. 1840 of the Chapel Royal in St James' Palace, with Queen Victoria and Prince Albert attending a service. It was first built c. 1540, and restored by Sir Robert Smirke in 1837. It has always been noted for its music, which may be a reason Lord Hampton regularly attended services there. Many royal events, including Queen Victoria's wedding to Prince Albert and the recent christening of Prince George, have taken place there. Print courtesy of City of Westminster Archives Centre.

The Year 1875

The Royal Victoria Patriotic School for Girls in Wandsworth, south London. It was built to care for orphans resulting from the Crimean War, but later took in other orphans from the armed services.

notice of the committee', and this resolution was read to Mrs Carr when she was brought in. But in 1878 it was revealed that Rev. Kyle had managed to obtain money under false pretences, and had also misused the offertory money, and was dismissed. Other than these staff problems, and problems with the buildings and sanitation, the committee was mainly concerned with requests for grants and allowances by beneficiaries of the Patriotic Fund and their families, each carefully considered by the committee. The same night Lord Hampton hosted a dinner party with a guest list headed by foreign secretary Lord Derby.

When Lord Hampton had married his second wife Augusta Murray in 1844 there had been, as usual, a marriage settlement, of which her mother, Lady Sarah, was a trustee. Lady Sarah had died in July 1874, which meant that Augusta's fortune (she had died in 1848) could now be released, and on 8th February Lord Hampton and Herby, his son by Augusta, visited his solicitors and resettled the fortune on himself for life, and on Herby. The amount, £7,000, was invested in Brazilian, United States and Egyptian bonds to produce a yearly income of £418. One hopes that these bonds did not give the same trouble as the Spanish ones had done!

The same week there was a further meeting of the executive committee of the Patriotic Fund. The previous August there had been an outbreak of catarrhal fever in the Wandsworth Asylum, followed by a more serious epidemic of peritonitis which affected fifty two girls, four of them fatally. This had got into the press and occasioned adverse comment about the drains and sanitary arrangements at the asylum, and the executive committee had caused a thorough inspection to be carried out. Eventually the cause was discovered – most of the building was supplied by water from a tank in the tower, but a lavatory in the junior section, where the outbreak had occurred, was supplied from a rain water tank in the yard. During the dry summer this water had become 'impure'. It was found that the girls using this lavatory had been in the habit of drinking the water, which is how the infection spread. This was immediately put right, and the epidemic terminated. But there was another fatality – a doctor doing a post-mortem investigation scratched his finger, and died of the infection.

The committee took every action they could to ensure the health of the girls – later they even bought a house in Margate for use when it was thought that 'sea air' would be of benefit, and a later minute recorded that 'the medical officer reported… that the effect of the residence at Margate had been most beneficial on all the girls who had been there; in one or two instances it was truly remarkable'. Of course it is probable that it was not so much the sea air, but the removal from the polluted London air that was the main benefit. But sometimes the girls took advantage of the change of scene in Margate. At a meeting in June 1878 it was reported that two girls 'had got out of the upper windows and made all sorts of noises, until the neighbours complained. They refused to work, and incited the younger children to behave badly during grace before meals. When locked in they took off the lock'.

The committee was understandably keen to make sure the whole of the water supply, the drainage, and the disposal of the sewage (in cesspits) was without fault, so after another detailed inspection the medical officer gave regular reports to the committee on the health of the girls. At the meeting on 11th February he reported that the girls were mostly in good health, although a great many were suffering from chilblains, some severe. But he did admit that he had found some girls with very dirty heads, and 'others with their heads full of vermin'. This obviously alarmed the committee, which then sent for the superintendent Mrs Carr and questioned her about this, also an outbreak of rowdy behaviour earlier in the year.

This occasioned a further meeting the following week, at which Lord Hampton explained to those who had not been present at the last meeting what had happened, and the committee now decided that Mrs Carr be asked to resign. The committee felt it would be better for the institution to be managed by a married couple, but there was a difference of opinion as to whether the man should be a clergyman or not, and eventually this was left open. But at the next meeting on 3rd March one of the committee, E Carleton Tufnell, who had voted in favour of appointing a clergyman at the previous meeting, had now changed his opinion, and said he had found three couples, any of which might be suitable, and the committee agreed to see them the following week. But Lord Hampton became ill over the weekend with a cough and an inclination to gout, and could not attend the meeting. In his absence Mr and Mrs Richard Larcombe were appointed at a joint salary of £150

The Year 1875

Lord Hampton's birthday was on 20th February, and he made the following entry: 'Birthday – 76!! – & I am thankful to say, still blessed with health and activity little, if at all, impaired'. His diary makes it clear that he made full use of his good health. We have seen him travelling all over the country in January, and once settled in London he had a constant stream of engagements. He was a regular attender at the House of Lords, attended one or two meetings a week of the army commission, as well as meetings of the executive committee of the Patriotic Fund, and more meetings of the Spanish bondholders. In the evenings he had a string of social engagements – his own dinner parties, attendance at other social functions, and visits to the theatre and opera. Just before his birthday he went to see Midsummer Night's Dream at the Gaiety Theatre, taking Sabine, who was staying with them. This lady has not been positively identified, but she was probably a niece of his second wife Augusta, as other nieces also stayed at different times – Augusta had had at least sixty two nephews and nieces! There are frequent references to him going out with these nieces, and as Lady Hampton is rarely mentioned except in connection with various periods of indisposition, we must assume she stayed at home.

Lord Hampton had known John Scott Russell through the Institute of Naval Architects, and he visited Lord Hampton on the day after his birthday. Although best known as a ship builder, Scott Russell had turned his hand to many things, and this meeting with Lord Hampton was to promote his scheme for a new London bridge. Traffic congestion in London led to a demand for a new Thames crossing, but the problem was that shipping came up as far as London Bridge, preventing any low bridge being built downstream of it. But Scott Russell's proposal was for 'a bridge of one arch below London Bridge, so as to allow ships to pass'. If this was a fixed arch, then it is difficult to imagine a bridge high enough to allow ships' masts to pass underneath. A short time later a committee was formed to investigate the problem further, and eventually it was solved when, after a competition, Tower Bridge, with its lifting platforms, was built.

As we have seen, Lord Hampton seems to have got on well with Rt Rev. John Peel when he was Dean of Worcester, and it was only after his retirement that the new dean and chapter turned against the music festivals. Peel had been dean throughout the restoration, and Lord Hampton must have felt that great credit was due to him for his leading role. But Peel died in February, only eight months after his retirement, and Lord Hampton was due to be a pall bearer at his funeral on 26th February. But 'severe and snowy weather determined me to write and give up Dean Peel's funeral tomorrow…'. Berrow's still reported him as a pall bearer – presumably they had not been informed of this last minute change of plan.

On 2nd March Lord Hampton presided at another meeting of the Central Chamber for Agriculture. The chamber had produced their own draft Landlord and Tenant Bill, but they had just learned that the government would be introducing one in the House of Lords soon. Some felt it would be better to postpone further discussion until this bill was published, but Lord Hampton suggested that their own ideas should be made clear now, as there was still time to influence government thinking. So the draft bill was considered clause by clause. The main discussion was whether the compensation for unexhausted improvements should only be determined by the act if there was no provision for it in the lease or agreement, but an amendment was proposed that it should always be at least as good as provided for in the act. Lord Hampton was against this, and he recorded 'Compulsory principle adopted by narrow majority'. The same subject came up at a meeting the following week, and some felt that it was wrong for parliament to interfere in agreements made between one man and another, even with the intention of protecting the tenant, and when a division on the matter was held the vote was tied, and Lord Hampton made his casting vote against compulsion.

After suffering the cough and inclination to gout referred to above, on 10th March he had recovered enough to attend a levée 'held by the queen herself – her Majesty's manner very gracious'. However, a bad cold prevented Lady Hampton from accompanying him to the levée or the dinner with Lord and Lady Dudley in the evening.

Two days later, after a meeting of the army commission, Lord Hampton attended the House of Lords to hear the Duke of Richmond introduce the Landlord and Tenant Bill. The Duke explained that the subject of unexhausted improvements had been debated over many years, and he judged that public opinion on the matter was now so strong that a government bill was needed. The main reason was that a tenant would be deterred from making improvements unless he was compensated. This could lead to the holding becoming run-down towards the end, thus not making full use of the productivity of the soil, which was not in the national interest. The Duke discussed the various classes of improvements, and said the amount of compensation would be based on the increased letting value of the holding at the end of the tenancy attributable to the unexhausted improvements, to be determined by a referee, who, if the parties failed to agree, would be nominated by the county court. But under clause 44, Lord Hampton would have been pleased to note that nothing in the act would prevent a landlord and tenant from contracting together to cover the points in the act and to opt out of its provisions if so agreed.

The following week Lord Hampton presided at the annual meeting of the Institute of Naval Architects. In his opening address he referred to the report

The Year 1875

of the royal commission on unseaworthy ships. A preliminary published earlier the previous year came to no firm conclusions on the various matters they were studying, and, possibly because of this, Samuel Plimsoll, the long term campaigner for stricter rules governing ships going to sea, brought forward his own bill entitled the Merchant Shipping Survey Bill. Its main provision was that all British ships had to be surveyed for seaworthiness by surveyors appointed by the Board of Trade, and would not be allowed to proceed to sea without the appropriate certificate. It also made provisions controlling the carrying of deck cargo in the winter months. Under the existing Merchant Shipping Act the Board of Trade had extensive powers to stop unseaworthy ships sailing, but there was no provision for all ships to be automatically surveyed. Plimsoll's bill was given its second reading on 24th June 1874, and was defeated by the narrow majority of 173 to 170.

In his 1875 presidential address, Lord Hampton, who had been a long-time supporter of Plimsoll's campaign, said that although the royal commission report was important and valuable, its contents were disappointing. The Institute had given much attention to such questions as the marking of a load line, how far ships should be inspected while building and before leaving port on a voyage, and other similar subjects. "It is regrettable that the royal commission did not give any distinct recommendations with regard to these points that have attracted so much public attention" Lord Hampton said. He was particularly disappointed by the absence of any distinct recommendation on the difficult and most important subject of marine insurance.

> Now, I do not think I shall exaggerate if I say that there is one thing that has excited the public mind more than another... it is the humiliating and discreditable idea that under the mask of prudence... there should be existing in this country men so lost to the feelings of honour, propriety, and justice, so as to allow their ships to go to sea in an unseaworthy condition in the expectation – and indeed I am afraid there have been cases in which it has been done with certainty– that the insurance would answer their purpose better than keeping their ships honestly afloat, and without regard to the loss of life.

Lord Hampton quoted passages that showed that the commissioners were aware that there where cases were a ship that had foundered at sea could give the owners a pecuniary profit. Trying to sound as moderate as possible, he said that he "had not the slightest idea or intention of availing myself of my position in this chair at this moment to throw anything like censure on the decision of the commissioners, but I am disappointed that, instead of making any distinct recommendation, the commission contented themselves by saying that 'our whole system of insurance law requires a complete revision'".

Lord Hampton was perhaps being a little unfair to the commissioners. Early in the report they pointed out that in a recent seventeen year period 'only 60 ships were known to have been lost through defects in the vessel or in the stowage, whereas 711 ships were lost from neglect or bad navigation'. In other words, the claims of Plimsoll and his supporters somewhat exaggerated the seriousness of the problem. The report went into some detail into the possibility of marking ships with a load line, and whether all ships should be surveyed, as Plimsoll's bill had proposed, but found these ideas had many practical disadvantages, and did not propose any major change. However, Lord Hampton did approve some of the report's other recommendations, including one 'that the marine department of the Board of Trade should be revised and strengthened'.

As a post-script, the government brought in a Merchant Shipping Bill to give effect to the report's recommendations. However, when prime minister Disraeli announced in the House on 22nd July 1875 that there would not be time for the bill to complete its passage through parliament that session, Plimsoll, who was not well, lost his composure and started shouting. In an extraordinary scene he called Sir Edward Bates, MP for Plymouth and a ship owner who had lost five ships at sea, a villain and scoundrel. Pointing at Disraeli, he accused him of consigning some thousands of human beings to a miserable death. He was escorted out of the chamber and later apologised. Sir Edward Bates' son Sir Percy Bates was chairman of Cunard from 1930 until his death in 1946, and was responsible for the building of the two 'Queens'.

As usual, Lord Hampton went to Westwood for a few days over Easter, and on his return found his wife poorly, so she was unable to accompany him to a dinner with Mrs Milner on the day he travelled back. The following day her condition gave rise to alarm, and although she was better in the evening, Lord Hampton felt obliged to give up a short break he had booked in Richmond. Instead on Monday he took Sabine to see Tommaso Salvini in his celebrated role as Othello. The next day he presided at a meeting of the Central Chamber of Agriculture when the main discussion was on local taxation.

The same week the army commission reassembled after the Easter break, and started taking evidence – the first witness was the Duke of Cambridge, the commander-in-chief of the British army, and cousin to the queen. The Duke had become notoriously resistant to change – he is said to have observed "there is a time for everything, and the time for change is when you can no longer help it". This reputation was borne out in his evidence before the commission, as Lord Hampton wrote that he 'objected to all change'.

The following Saturday was a typically busy and varied day: 'Went to London in morning shopping. After luncheon went with Herby to Crystal Palace concert – saw octopuses & wonderful new creatures called horse shoe crabs. Dined

The Year 1875

The Crystal Palace after its move to Sydenham. It housed a large number of attractions, and was served by its own railway station. The tall water tower (one of two) was designed by Brunel to drive the fountains, and were later used for early TV transmissions. Not designed for a long life, the building deteriorated, and was destroyed by a disastrous fire in 1936.

with Disraeli – one of his great parliamentary diners – about 8 or 10 peers and 24 MPs – found pleasant neighbour at dinner of young Lord Lytton'. The Crystal Palace, now at Sydenham, had a number of attractions including an aquarium, and promoted regular popular concerts. At the same time his saddle horses, which had been kept at Westwood, were transferred to London now the weather was suitable for riding. Two of the nieces of Augusta, Lord Hampton's second wife, came to stay with him – they were Eleanor and Frances ('Fanny'), whose parents were Harriet, Augusta's sister, and her husband George Pratt, 2nd Marquis Camden, both of whom were now dead.

With his horses stabled in Eaton Square, Lord Hampton took every opportunity to ride – St James' Park, Green Park and Hyde Park were all nearby. Wednesday 21st April began with a ride: 'Beautiful day – rode in park in morning. Then went to Moody & Sankey with Sabine. Extraordinary & interesting scene & in every respect superior to my expectation. I dined with Greys & went to Ly Derby's party at Foreign Office in evening. Madre still too weak & ill to go out even to dinner'. Dwight Moody and Ira Sankey were American evangelists who had come to Britain to hold revivalist meetings, which had created great interest. Their four month London ministry started on 9th March in the Agricultural Hall in Islington. Incredibly, seating had been provided for over 20,000, and this was soon filled, and the service was interrupted by the noise from a further crowd trying to gain admittance.

The services were designed to appeal to all Christians, from Roman Catholics to Quakers, and they were assisted by a number of clergy. A large choir had been assembled, and the services consisted of preaching by Dwight Moody, and singing by Ira Sankey, accompanying himself on his harmonium. By all accounts, although Sankey's singing was very powerful, Moody's preaching was of no special merit, except that he professed a certainty about the power of prayer, which he illustrated by numerous anecdotes. No doubt his unrefined American speech also added to the interest. At some meetings individuals, who hoped for divine intervention, who had perhaps fallen into sin or poor health, were prayed for by

Dwight Moody (preaching) and Ira Sankey (at the harmonium) in Brooklyn, New York. They first met in Chicago in 1871, and started holding revivalist non-denominational meetings there, attracting mass audiences. They started their campaign in Britain in June 1873, and stayed for two years preaching throughout the country. The highlight was in spring 1875 when they held meetings in London where, in four different venues, they were reckoned to have preached to over two and a half million people.

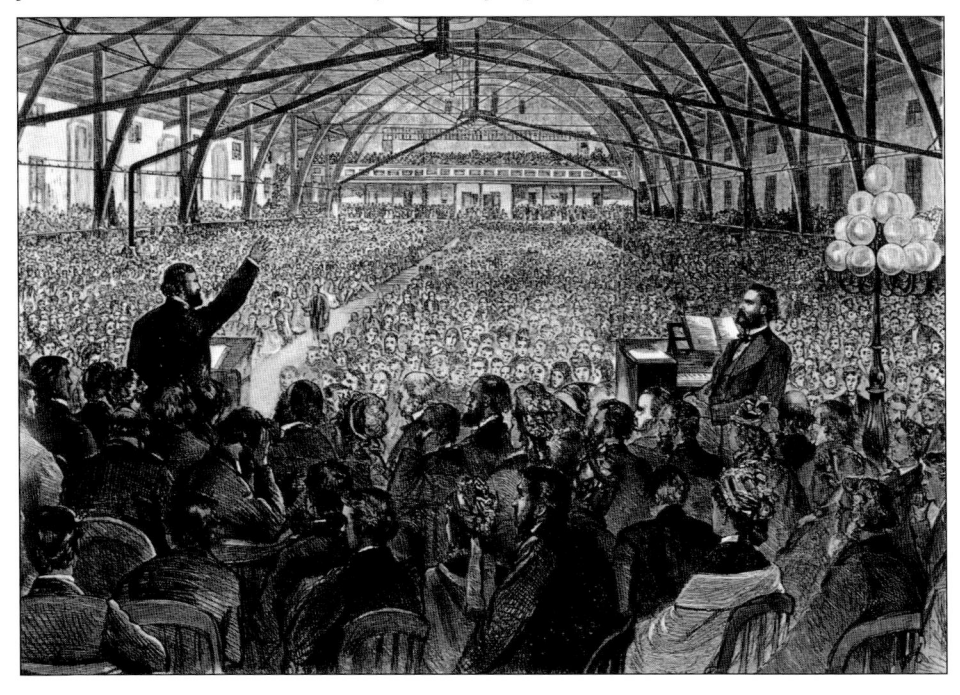

the masses. Moody and Sankey used a variety of venues, and after a season at the Exeter Hall in April transferred to Her Majesty's Theatre in the Haymarket, where prayer meetings were held daily at midday, and Bible readings in the afternoon. The meetings appealed to people from all walks of life. Many members of the aristocracy were recorded in the audiences, including the Princess of Wales who was present the week before Lord Hampton.

On Friday 23rd April Lord Hampton left to spend the weekend in Worcestershire. The purpose seems to have been to attend a meeting about the shortage of hotel accommodation in Droitwich. Mr Bainbrigge had taken over the old George Hotel to use as his clinic, so there was now no large hotel in the town to accommodate visitors to the brine baths. The following month the mayor arranged a public meeting on the subject. Lord Hampton was not present, but he was put on the committee to discuss the matter further, which he attended on 22nd May. One problem was the journey between the railway station and the baths. This passed along the High Street with its subsiding buildings and dirty smoky factories nearby, and it was decided to investigate the possibility of building a new road to run from the station directly to the Worcester Road. In fact little seems to have happened, and it was left to John Corbett, 'The Salt King', to build first The Raven Hotel, opened later in the 1870s, then in 1891 the Worcestershire Brine Baths Hotel, reputed to have been the largest hotel in the county at that time.

Although a regular attender, Lord Hampton made only a few interventions in the House of Lords. On 13th April he opposed a private members bill introduced by Lord Albemarle to widen the pool from which magistrates could be chosen. At that time magistrates had to hold land to the annual value of £100, which meant that many clergymen qualified, although some people felt it was wrong for clergymen to sit in judgement on their fellow human beings. The bill would widen this to include income from personal property of £300. Lord Albemarle pointed out that the current restriction excluded many who would make excellent magistrates – for example lawyers living on their fee income, and the younger sons of the land-owning class who were living on a settled income. This would reduce the need for clergymen to become magistrates

But Lord Hampton's conservative instincts led him to oppose the bill. Lord Albemarle had shown no good reason to change the present system, he said – if someone had a personal income of £300 a year, surely he would be able to purchase sufficient land to qualify. And he said that some of the best magistrates in Worcestershire were clergymen, and they were particularly valuable in cases such as poaching where it was thought that some land-owning magistrates might be prejudiced. However Lord Lyttelton, the lord lieutenant of Worcestershire who was responsible for appointments to the bench in the county, supported the measure, as he had often found it difficult to find sufficient properly qualified men to become magistrates. Despite Lord Hampton's opposition the bill was given its second reading, and it received the royal assent on 2nd August.

On Saturday 1st May, at the opening of the Royal Academy summer exhibition, Lord Hampton viewed the paintings in the afternoon, and attended the grand banquet in the evening mixing with the Prince of Wales, several other royals, prime minster Disraeli, and other members of the government. But his day was not yet over – after listening to 'beautiful singing' he left Burlington House and still had the energy to attend a party at Lady Beauchamp's.

The 29th May was a similarly busy day, when he visited the zoological gardens in the morning, and after lunch went to the Albert Hall for a performance of Verdi's Requiem, where he joined Lord and Lady Dudley in their box. In the evening he attended a reception at the Foreign Office. In the same week he and Herby attended two operas, and shortly afterwards he attended another grand dinner given by Trinity House, well attended by royalty.

Early in May there was a debate in the Lords on the second reading of the Army Exchanges Bill. Following the abolition of purchase in 1871 this bill would authorise officers to exchange places provided it was approved by higher authority. It would also be legal for the officer wishing to exchange to pay compensation, which was seen as a purely private transaction. The Duke of Richmond opened the debate and explained at length that this bill was not, as had been alleged, a way of bringing back purchase, but was to allow something that was to the benefit of the army. Viscount Cardwell, who had introduced the army reforms in the House of Commons, opposed the bill. Lord Hampton's view was that 'the debate was good & better division – 137 to 60. Opposition case absurdly weak. I cannot understand how they c'd have been so ill advised. 14 opposition peers voted with us'. He did not speak, but voted with the government.

On 14th June Lord Lyttelton introduced the following motion in the House of Lords: 'That it is expedient in the administration of the Poor Law to revert more nearly to the principles laid down in the Report of the Commissioners of Inquiry (1833), with a view to the ultimate discontinuance of out-door relief'. His purpose was to precipitate a general discussion on this subject, and opened the debate with a lengthy and analytical speech. His main theme was that outdoor relief (which was the money or supplies given to pauper families in their own homes as opposed to being in the workhouse) led to an increase of pauperism, as inevitably poor people sought to add this relief to their earnings – what Lyttelton called 'their little annuities'. He accepted that everyone had a legal right to be kept from hunger and the elements, and questioned the notion, as laid down by the first poor law commissioners, that conditions in the workhouse should be worse, or 'less eligible', than those enjoyed by the ordinary agricultural labourer.

The Year 1875

It was not the physical conditions inside the workhouse that deterred families from seeking 'indoor relief', "but the feeling of shame and degradation which attaches to it, and which does not attach, in the minds of the unskilled labourers as a class, to outdoor relief".

When the new poor law was first implemented Lord Hampton was on record as saying that he thought the new regime was likely to become unnecessarily harsh, and he certainly did not think that workhouses should be in any away akin to prisons. So it was only reluctantly that he became the first chairman of the Droitwich Board of Poor Law Guardians in 1836, but he remained chairman thereafter for nearly 30 years. His attendance, of course, was somewhat erratic due to his parliamentary duties, but surviving records show that when there were internal disputes over policy, he usually took the more liberal and enlightened view. However, in the House of Lords that day he seems to have hardened his opinions somewhat. He said that the topic of outdoor relief had come up at a recent meeting of the Central Chamber of Agriculture and "the opinion was unanimously expressed that they ought to revert to a more strict system of outdoor relief". Lord Hampton concluded:

> A period of 40 years has elapsed since the introduction of the present law, and I think there should be an inquiry whether there could not be a more strict administration of the system. What should be borne in mind in reference to the Poor Law was humanity on the one hand and sound principles of administration on the other. My noble friend opposite [the Earl of Kimberley] said that they must harden their hearts against the system of outdoor relief. I do not like to adopt that language; but I think that they must teach the labouring classes habits of self-reliance, and that they must not apply for outdoor relief. I hope that the government will turn their attention to the subject.

June and July were the height of the social season, and Lord Hampton seems to have had engagements most nights. On 25th June he went to Lady Derby's party for the Queen of the Netherlands, and 'I was presented to her and also again to Sultan of Zanzibar. Unusual sight to see an European queen and an African king sitting on the same sofa!' The following night the queen was entertained by the Archbishop of Canterbury, and Lord Hampton wrote 'Archbishop took me up to talk to Her Majesty & she was struck as I was with scene of night before'. The last day of June was another busy day:

> Meeting of governors of Wellington College at 11. Elected Col Talbot Vice-President, after awkward scene when D. of Cambridge proposed by D. of Richmond declined to accept. I moved for committee about the headmaster's salary, tutors' incomes &c. At 3 attended prize distribution by Lady Charles Wellesley at Wandsworth asylum. In evening dined at Goldsmiths Hall – freedom of company given to lord chancellor.

LORD HAMPTON

Sultan Barghash bin Said (1837-88) was the nominally independent ruler of Zanzibar, although heavily influenced by Britain. He inherited from his brother, who had been the first sultan after the territory split from Muscat and Oman, and he is credited with ending the slave trade, and modernising the infrastructure of Zanzibar city. (Right) Queen Sophie of Württemberg (1818-77) was married to Prince William III of Orange, but the couple were estranged. When she died she was buried in her wedding dress 'as that is when my life ended'.

Lord Hampton had not been able to attend the meeting of the Patriotic Fund executive committee, but arrived in time for the prize giving. Lady Charles Wellesley was the widow of the younger son of the 1st Duke of Wellington, and granddaughter of Henry Cecil, 1st Marquis of Exeter, and Sarah Hoggins, 'The Cottage Countess'. The committee had had to contend with problems in the management of the boys' asylum, as both the superintendent, Mr Hullah, and his wife, the matron, had fallen seriously ill, and they had been asked to resign.

A charity that Lord Hampton supported was the 'Home for Little Boys' in Farningham, Kent. It had been started in Tottenham to provide a home for boys that were 'destitute, homeless or in danger of falling into crime' in 1864, but its premises soon proved insufficient, so a new home was established at Farningham, with accommodation for 300 boys. To provide a homely atmosphere, the boys were accommodated in ten small houses of 30 boys, each looked after by a married couple. The boys were taken in at a young age, and generally left at 14. They were given a non-sectarian religious education and were taught various trades to provide for their future. On 10th July a special train brought Lord Hampton and other supporters to Farningham, and they toured the premises where a variety of activities had been organised, and he presided at the luncheon in the marquee. At 3.00 p.m. the Princess of Teck arrived and Lord Hampton accompanied her on a tour of the establishment. In the chapel boys were examined on scripture and arithmetic, and the Princess presented the prizes. Before they left, Lord Hampton proposed a vote of thanks to the Princess, and her husband the Duke of Teck said how impressed they had been and wished the charity prosperity. As the charity apparently had debts of £3,500, this was badly needed!

The Year 1875

The Home for Little Boys in Farningham. They were accommodated in ten small houses under the care of a 'father and mother'. Each house was gifted by a different person or organisation. The chapel, school, workshops and entrance lodge can also be seen.

The annual meeting of the commissioners of the Patriotic Fund was held on 20th July, and all twelve commissioners attended, presided over by the Duke of Cambridge. Lord Hampton presented the executive committee's report, which was adopted. He queried whether the fund should pay for holidays for the orphans it was supporting, but this idea was rejected. Discipline at the schools was strict. Visits from mothers and other relations were only allowed in the school holidays, and a proposal was passed by the committee that no food or drink should be allowed to be brought during these visits. The boys and girls lived permanently in the asylums till the time came for them to leave, and if a mother or other relation wanted to withdraw a child, the executive committee had to give permission. However the committee could give grants for a variety of purposes, for example for an outfit for a girl leaving to go into service (£5), and for the travelling expenses of a mother making a visit. The boys' school had a flourishing band, which was allowed to perform elsewhere if convenient, although a rule was passed that boys would only be allowed to join the band if they and their mothers undertook that they would join a military or naval band on leaving.

The following day Lord Hampton attended a meeting of the Wellington College governors under the chairmanship of the Prince of Wales, at which the Duke of Connaught and Lord Salisbury were elected governors. Lord Hampton had been chairman of a committee to report on various matters to do with the school, some originating from proposals from the new head master, Rev. Edward Wickam, who had taken over from the first head, Rev. Edward Benson, in 1872. The report covered proposals for new buildings, including a science laboratory and new boarding houses, tightening up the entry requirements, and a revision to the system of scholarships. A printed copy still exists in the school archives, and someone has written on the inside cover 'This committee laid the basis of much of the later history of the school'. Lord Stanhope opposed the report, but after the Duke of Richmond had supported it, it was adopted without a division.

Lord Hampton had long been a friend of the sugar producers in the West Indies, and had opposed the reduction in the tariff protection they enjoyed, partly because they were competing against other producers using slave labour. On July 22nd in the House of Lords he made further representations on their behalf. Negotiations had gone on for a long time with the French, Dutch and Belgians to agree a uniform system of duties and bounties, resulting in the Convention of 1864. But although Britain had promptly put in place their part in the agreement, the French had not, so Lord Hampton presented a petition from the British producers in the West Indies. In reply the foreign secretary, the Earl of Derby, thanked Lord Hampton for raising the matter, and explained in some detail the technical difficulties that lay behind the problem. Nevertheless he agreed that the French had not done what they had promised to do, and the matter was being taken up vigorously with their government.

The London season was nearing its end, but Lord Hampton still found time to entertain four of the daughters of George and Harriet Murray – Frances and Augusta accompanied him and Herby on a visit to the theatre, and Caroline and Eleanor went to the Chapel Royal with him on 24th. On Tuesday 3rd August Lord and Lady Hampton returned to Westwood, but the parliamentary session had not quite finished, and Lord Hampton returned to London the following Monday to speak on the Unseaworthy Ships Bill, which the government were rushing through parliament before the end of the session. As described above (page 184) the Merchant Shipping Bill, giving effect to many of the recommendations of the royal commission, had been dropped through lack of time to consider the large number of amendments, many proposed by Samuel Plimsoll. As a temporary measure to give some extra protection to mariners against going to sea in unseaworthy ships, this short bill was passed through parliament in the last two weeks of the session.

It was given its second reading in the Lords on 9th August. The Duke of Richmond explained that this measure would strengthen the powers of the Board of Trade. The Board was to appoint special officers with the power to stop unseaworthy ships leaving port and to order a survey. Furthermore, if one quarter of the seamen on a ship informed the Board or its officer that they considered the ship unseaworthy, 'proper steps' had to be taken in investigate the complaint. The only other provision concerned grain or other bulk cargoes, which, in a heavy sea, could move and cause the ship to list dangerously. The new rule was that if more than one third the cargo was of grain or similar, then it either had to be packed in bags or sacks, or protected from shifting by partitions or bulkheads.

The Year 1875

Lord Hampton generally welcomed the bill, but regretted one omission. This was the loading of cargo on deck, which in bad weather could be dangerous in a number of ways, and he referred to the opinion of the Institute of Naval Architects, which was that the carrying of deck cargo should be prohibited.

Before leaving London the next day, Lord Hampton attended another meeting of the Spanish bondholders to approve the latest proposals. The lack of interest paid on these bonds had evidently caused Lord Hampton some financial embarrassment, and in his diary he had noted the week before that 'Messrs Glyn placed £1,000 to my account for six months' – presumably this was temporary loan. In his annual summary at the end of his diary he explained that he should have received £600 a year from his bonds, and eventually received just half the amounts due for 1873 and 1874, with no prospect of any more payments till the end of 1875. Furthermore he had lost £100 a year from the rent of the Elmley Castle estate – this was now occupied by Henry Davies, a descendant of his wife's late husband's family, although what occasioned this loss is not clear. But all that was to change in November.

Lord Hampton was back in Worcestershire in time to speak at the annual dinner of the Worcestershire Agricultural Society, and Augusta and Eleanor Pratt came to stay at Westwood. His son Johnny was then in residence at Kings End, and hosted a garden party there the next day, attended by his father, half-brother and the Pratt girls. The same party attended another garden party the following day, and on Saturday Lord Hampton took the Pratt girls to Worcester where he showed them round the city and 'lionised' the newly restored cathedral.

On Monday he attended the thirty second annual meeting of the British Archaeological Society, which that year was meeting in Evesham. Lord Hertford of Ragley Hall presided and gave the inaugural address, and referred to some of the antiquities to be found locally. Lord Hampton had been asked to give a vote of thanks to the president, and said how grateful they were that Ragley

Kings End, John Slaney Pakington's house in Powick. Although it did not compare with his father's seat at Westwood, it had large grounds and provided comfortable accommodation for the couple when in Worcestershire.

LORD HAMPTON

Hall was once more occupied by its owner, after a long period when the Hall "had been only a name; now it was a reality". This referred to the fact that the 4th Marquess Hertford had lived all his life in Paris and never visited Ragley, and the estate became run-down. When he died in 1870 he left his magnificent art collection to his illegitimate son Richard Wallace, which later became the nucleus of the Wallace Collection. But the title and entailed estates descended to the 4th Marquess's second cousin Francis George Hugh Seymour, the present Lord Hertford. Lord Hampton attended the evening dinner, but did not join the Society for their excursions the next day.

There was more socialising during the week, including a wholly unsuccessful duck shoot with Harry Vernon of Hanbury, and neither Lady Downshire, a relation of Lord Sandys, nor Lady Georgina Vernon turned up for the dinner party in the evening. The next day seems to have been more successful: 'Lord & Lady Lyttelton & old Miss Lyttelton came for long day, lunched, dined and went home at night. Beautiful day, as fine as England is capable of. We boated and set trimmers & walked about'.

Lord Hampton was due to host a meeting of the archery society the following week, and as usual a house party would be assembled. But over the weekend Lady Hampton became ill again, and her husband feared she would not be able to act as hostess. But the event went ahead anyway, and on Tuesday the guests arrived. They included Lord and Lady Beauchamp from Madresfield, the Pratt girls, Johnny and Lady Diana Pakington, and the Swinton Isaacs from Boughton Court near Worcester. This was the third time that the archery society had met at Westwood, and, after a dull morning, the weather was beautiful, the attendance was good, and the event successful except that Lady Hampton was still too poorly to be present as Lady Paramount. Her place was taken by Lady Diana, Lord Hampton's daughter-in-law. Shooting started at 1.00 p.m., and luncheon was served at 3.00 p.m. Shooting resumed at 5.00 p.m., and after the prizes were awarded in the house, a dance was held in the marquee.

Augusta and Eleanor Pratt were still staying, and Lord Hampton took them to Hagley Hall and the Clent Hills the following Monday, and on Wednesday to the Malverns, where they lunched with Gen. Eardley Wilmot and viewed his lovely garden at Rose Bank near the centre of Great Malvern. Then on Friday they drove, taking Herby, to the Hundred House at Abberley, and, the day being fine, they all walked to the top of the nearby Woodbury Hill, where they were 'much pleased by beauty of scene'. By Lord Hampton's standards this was not a long walk, but the same week he had noted that while shooting 'I am not so keen on long continued walking as I used to be. I went out in afternoon and beat clover and turnip fields, but only got one shot and gave it up'.

The following week the Pratt girls went to stay at Madresfield for a few days, and they were replaced by Sophia Amphlett, the unmarried daughter of the local rector Joseph Amphlett, who had gone away, and who was a distant cousin of Richard Paul Amphlett of Wychbold Hall. When the Pratts returned Lord Hampton took them with Herby to Hanbury Hall to visit Harry and Lady Georgina Vernon – Harry would later become a baronet, but in 1875 only his wife had a title as the daughter of an earl. Another visit was to Spetchley Park, the seat of Robert Berkeley.

After they returned from Spetchley, a Mr Earle and Melville Moore came to stay for some shooting, but Lord Hampton's attempts to arrange a dinner party for them failed. But Mr Earle proved to be a poor shot – although the expression is lost to us now, Lord Hampton noted that he was a 'weak goat', and they gave up the shooting after a couple of hours. The next day was worse, as Earle became 'knocked up' by the heat, 'which was extraordinary'.

Lord Hampton's daughter-in-law's family had property in Scotland, and Johnny and Lady Diana were due to go there in September. Lord Hampton went to Kings End to say goodbye before they left, but they had to delay their departure as Johnny 'suffered a slight relapse' – this is further evidence of his health problems.

The 'mock festival' at Worcester referred to in an earlier chapter was to take place the following week, and Lord Hampton obtained a copy of a pamphlet which was circulating entitled 'The Mock Festival, or the Festival of Five Priests', written by 'A Layman'. Its sixteen pages is a closely argued attack on the dean and the four canons ('The Five Priests'). Firstly, the pamphlet attacked the notion that 'all music should be associated with divine service'. The fact that the service of prayer was separated from the service of praise (i.e. an oratorio) by a short interval was inconsequential, and allowed those who did not want to attend a service following Anglican rights to attend the oratorios. 'An oratorio, and a sermon commingled and continued without cessation, if such a course were practicable, would indeed be wearisome to the flesh', the author suggested.

The dean and chapter's second principle was that all admissions to the cathedral should be free of charge. But the pamphlet countered that by pointing out that all services there had to be paid for – the officials had their stipends, which came from endowments left by our predecessors. And indeed the cathedral itself, in its newly restored state, had been paid for recently by the citizens of the diocese. So why should not the public be allowed to pay to hear oratorios?

Then the author comes to what he regarded as the main point: 'How far are the dean and chapter morally right in taking the entire control of the Festivals into their own hands?'

The fatal error into which they have fallen, from which we suffer and of which we have a right to complain, is that of idolising their own private opinions and convictions, and asking the public to kneel down and worship them. It is this error that has been the cause of the whole mischief which they have effected, and has rendered them the most unpopular of all similar bodies in the kingdom.

If the dean and chapter should have considered their private opinions and conscientious views and scruples as distinct from their public capacity they would have saved themselves from the odium which they have incurred. This distinction should be most carefully borne in mind by all those who hold public offices and have authority vested in them by the State… All that was asked of them was the use of a national building for a few hours for a public purpose.

Let them reserve to themselves the liberty to stay away. Let us, on the other hand, have the liberty to attend. Let them absent themselves for these few hours once in three years; they manage with very clear consciences to do so for months at other times. But to oppose their individual wills against the opinion of their bishop, and the bishops, deans, and chapters of the neighbouring dioceses, and an overwhelming majority of churchmen is quite another matter.

The author then pointed out discrepancies between what Dr Barry had said in sermons, when he said how important cathedrals had been to the preservation and development of church music, and his attitude now, which was to provide second rate performances of sacred music accompanied only by the organ, an instrument that the author seems to have particularly disliked. He thought the large new organ recently erected in the south transept had been built specifically to dispense with the need for an orchestra.

> The baneful effects it is capable of are only equalled by its unsurpassed ugliness. Who that has the slightest knowledge or appreciation of the effects given by the various instruments of the orchestra in rendering the emotional effects intended to be produced by our composers, could wish or be satisfied with such a substitute? How is it possible to conceive that the mechanical action of one man struggling with both arms and legs on an instrument tuned to imperfect intervals can be comparable to the hundred minds at work separately upon the part assigned to each by the composer, under the direction of an able conductor, and giving to every phrase its right rendering and due expression, subduing or bringing out into high relief each note in sympathy with the author's meaning.

The pamphlet's author was not known, but George Hastings was suspected.

Lady Hampton's poor health has already been referred to, and, whatever her complaint was, she decided to try the saline baths. According to Lord Hampton's diary, she was 'wonderfully strengthened' by this and was able to go for a walk after church on Sunday. She had another bath a few days later, and whilst she was bathing Lord Hampton took the Pratt girls to see John Corbett's grand new house built in the French style just outside the town, initially called Impney Manor, but later The Chateau Impney.

On 30th September Lord Hampton set out, as he had done in some previous years, on a tour of the north. He first made a short tour of Derbyshire, where he was joined by Herby, and after arriving at Matlock showed that he was still fit by walking up the Heights of Abraham. The next day they toured the locality, stopping for a 'good look' at Haddon Hall, and the following day they went to Chatsworth, where they toured the park, but did not visit the house. Then they moved on to Buxton, preferring to go by road as they did not feel 'railway velocity was adapted to this pretty country'. There Lord Hampton had arranged to meet a notary from London with the agreements about the Spanish bonds to be signed.

Bad weather confined them to Buxton for a couple of days, after which Lord Hampton travelled to Leeds, where he was met by Mr and Mrs Town. This would be one of the brothers Joseph, John or William Town who managed the paper mill of Joseph Town & Sons. Lord Hampton stayed with friends in

Chateau Impney, the home of John Corbett 'the salt king', completed in 1875. His wife had been brought up in France, and Corbett employed the French architect Auguste Tronquois, who designed a building in the elaborate style of Louis XIII (early C17th). The English architect Richard Spiers supervised the work on site. Some said he built such an imposing home to out-do Lord Hampton's Westwood. Two men died in accidents during construction, which cost about £250,000.

LORD HAMPTON

Chapel Allerton, and the next day he was to take part in the inauguration of the new Yorkshire College of Science. The Duke of Devonshire formally opened the college, after which the party assembled in the Great Northern Hotel for a luncheon. The Duke proposed the loyal toast, and said that her majesty's long reign had not been characterised by a succession of military victories "but what would always make this reign glorious, and distinguish it in the annals of English history, is the immense development of British industries, British manufactures and commerce, and the great advance in scientific discovery and, perhaps above all, the application of scientific discovery to practical ends".

Lord Hampton proposed the toast to the scientific societies of Great Britain, and, in slight contrast to the Duke of Devonshire, sounded a cautious note.

> England is running a very great race, and for many years has been making play, and running in the hope that she has the race in hand. But it is time to put an end to this delusion, for she finds that her competitors are gaining ground upon her. If she means to stay ahead in the race she should use whip and spur, and she cannot use any whip or spur more effectively than by the formation of such an institution as this Yorkshire College of Science.

Lord Hampton also attended a large public meeting to mark the inauguration at the Victoria Hall, again presided over by the Duke of Devonshire, in the evening. The next day was 'most interesting and agreeable'. With some other people he drove to Farnley Hall, the seat of Ayscough Fawkes. Fawkes' ancestor Walter Ramsden Fawkes had been a friend of J M W Turner, who had spent much time painting in the district, and Fawkes had amassed a large collection of his paintings, drawings and sketches.

On Friday Lord Hampton was the guest of honour at the annual meeting and prize giving of the Keighley School of Science and Art in the Keighley Institute. The chairman, worsted spinner John Harper Mitchell, introduced him by paying tribute to his lifetime's work in furthering the cause of elementary education, adding that a few years ago we were the worst educated nation in western Europe. Now things had improved, but we had a long way to go before we could catch up with the likes of Germany, where elementary education, and scientific and technical education for the older boys, had long since been almost universal. It had been observed in the annual report that attendance at the evening science classes was disappointing, and this was put down to the long time neglect of elementary education, and Mitchell hoped this might now be rectified.

Lord Hampton talked about the history of national schemes for elementary education, and his own part in them, and like the chairman, said he was ashamed when comparing our education system with those in continental Europe. Mechanics institutes dated back to 1824, but the standard of those like the Keighley Institute was as different to those early ones as between chalk and cheese. He praised the Keighley Institute, but pointed to a couple of points that had come out of the annual report that he would like to see improved. In particular, like the chairman he was disappointed in the poor attendance at the evening science classes, and contrasted this to Germany. In one large industrial town, it was made a condition that all apprentices should attend the science and art classes of the town's trade school. This institute had provided excellent facilities for technical education, but, Lord Hampton observed, "you can take a horse to water but you can't make it drink". He hoped that if came here in the future, he would "find the men of Keighley more sensible than they were now, and the schools crowded with men anxious to cultivate their intellects and take advantage of the facilities offered them".

On Saturday 'the party went to see Mr Craven's great mill for making lady's stuff [woollen cloth]. Very wonderful, but not intelligible by ordinary uninitiated spectator'. This would have been Joseph Craven's Dalton Mill, noted as one of the largest in the area, which had remarkably powerful engines, employing around 2,000. The next day, after church in Keighley, Lord Hampton drove with the Towns to nearby St Ives, to visit William Ferrand, formerly MP for Devonport. He had been born William Bushfield, but changed his name after his mother inherited her brother's considerable property. The family would probably have been known to Lord Hampton, as Frances Ferrand, a cousin of William, had married Sir Richard Paul Amphlett of Wychbold Hall. Before returning to Westwood Lord Hampton 'drove in morning to see Mr Town's paper mill – much pleased, simple and intelligible and very pretty process'. This would have been the Turkey Mill in Keighley, bought by Joseph Town's father John Town in 1822, and, served by rags from a nearby rag mill, producing high quality paper, used, for

The Keighley Mechanics Institute was founded in 1825, and the building shown below was opened by the Duke of Devonshire in 1870. In 1962 it was destroyed in a fire.

example, for Indian rupee bank notes. The next morning he had time to see the Yorkshire exhibition in Leeds before catching the train to Birmingham.

Back at home visitors came and went, and he was pleased to note that his wife was better, and that she was able to drive into Worcester. In an underlined note, he said that they both called separately at the Deanery, the home of Dean Yorke, his arch-opponent over the music festivals, although only Mrs Yorke was in. His wife's improvement may have made her more assertive, as he noted two days later that there was a 'contretemps after dinner'!

Lord Hampton attended quarter sessions the following week, and there was a discussion on the outbreak of foot and mouth disease, which had affected upwards of 2,000 farms. But only a few animals had been slaughtered, and its incidence was now abating. Thomas Curtler said he had been told that putting Stockholm tar on the animals noses was a preventative, and Lord Hampton said a remedy had been given him by a Yorkshire friend who bred high-class shorthorns, and he would publicise it. It consisted of a mixture of chlorate of potash and camphorated spirits, which if given daily not only prevented the disease, but cured it! Richard Amphlett, the nephew and heir of Sir Richard Amphlett of Wychbold, was beginning his career as a barrister, and defended one of the prisoners at the sessions, unsuccessfully, and during the week stayed at Westwood.

On Monday 25th business called Lord Hampton to London again, and his first call was to see some improvements being made in his home at 9 Eaton Square. In the evening he went to the Lyceum to see Sir Henry Irving in Macbeth, but was 'disappointed'. It was there that Irving had established his reputation the

Henry Irving (1838-1905), probably as Macbeth. He was born Henry Bodribb, and developed an early interest in the theatre. From 1856 to 1870 he underwent a lengthy apprenticeship taking a wide range of roles in the provinces, and it was not until he played in John Albery's successful play 'Two Roses' that his career took off. He was then engaged by Hezekiah Bateman to play in his Lyceum Theatre, and his success there in 'The Bells' made him famous, reinforced by playing Hamlet in 1874. In 1878 he bought The Lyceum from Hezekiah Bateman's widow, and for the next 23 years ran it, playing leading Shakespearean roles and many others, in productions of a high standard.

previous year as Hamlet, but his Macbeth was less successful. On Wednesday there was a meeting of the Patriotic Fund committee in their offices in St Martins Place, and he saw Lord Penzance about the army commission. Later in the week he was back in Worcestershire, and he and his son Herby went to stay at Hagley, but Lady Hampton was not well enough to join them. Lord Hampton had probably been invited as both he and Lord Lyttelton were due on Friday to attend the annual meeting of the Saltley training institution in Birmingham, with which they had both been connected since its foundation in 1852. It had been established by the Church of England to train teachers from the dioceses of Hereford, Worcester and Lichfield partly by the generosity of Charles Adderley, 1st Baron Norton. Lord Lyttelton presided at the meeting, and Lord Hampton spoke next, pointing to the importance of the religious education that the teachers were being trained to provide, now that it had not been promoted by the 1870 Act. The following day he returned to Westwood, but not before he and Lord Lyttelton had visited the Blind College in Worcester, 'a very interesting and wonderful institution', Lord Hampton noted.

The following Monday he again travelled to London for meetings of the Central Chamber of Agriculture, returning to Worcestershire on Tuesday evening. The Agricultural Holdings Act was discussed, followed by a long debate on how to combat the prevalence of foot and mouth disease. It was believed that this was brought into the country by foreign cattle, and the Chamber's view was that all foreign cattle should be slaughtered at the port of disembarkation. The alternative of quarantining them was not thought to be effective, as the incubation period could be quite extended. One controversial point was how to treat cattle imported from Ireland. Some thought they should be included in the measure, but others, led by Lord Hampton, thought this was impractical, and that the United Kingdom should be treated as one whole country. He also strongly supported a motion for the better treatment of animals in transit. Quite apart from the general principle of avoiding cruelty to animals, weakened animals were more susceptible to infection. It was agreed to send a deputation to the prime minister on the matter during the Smithfield Show week.

The following Monday Lord Hampton travelled yet again to town to attend meetings of the army commission, at which finishing touches were being put to their final report. At the end of the week he attended the funeral of Catherine Lady Beauchamp, who had died on 4th November aged 68. She had been distantly related to Lord Hampton, as her first husband had been Henry Murray, the uncle of Lord Hampton's second wife Augusta, who had died after only four years of marriage. The funeral took place at Stanford near Rugby, the seat of Lady Beauchamp's mother's family, and Lord Hampton travelled down from London with Lord Beauchamp, Lady Beauchamp's great nephew, and others.

LORD HAMPTON

The weather was miserable, preventing a walking procession, and the mourners 'drove in flies with great coats &c. Inconsistent with aristocratic splendour of coffin, pall &c'. Lady Beauchamp is commemorated by a fine marble monument at the west end of the church. Lords Hampton and Beauchamp travelled back to Worcestershire together, and when they were delayed at Rugby and Birmingham they played chess – one of them must have carried a portable set for just such occasions!

On 22nd November Lord Hampton received a letter that would change the rest of his life – an offer of a government post by prime minister Disraeli. This will be discussed in the next chapter. Later that week he went to London again, as the report of the army commissioners had still not been finalised, and as Lord Penzance was indisposed Lord Hampton took the chair. He returned to Westwood on Saturday, then the following Tuesday the whole household moved to London, where the improvements at no. 9 Eaton Square had been completed. The same day he presided at the annual dinner of the civil service music society, and the following evening at a lecture at the Society of Arts on French sugar duties. A few days later he returned to Westwood, this time just for some shooting, and after more sport the following evening he returned to London.

The army commission report had still not been quite finished, and immediately on his return from Westwood there were two further meetings, and on 18th December Lord Hampton recorded that it was finished. One senses he was relieved that the long enquiry was at last over, particularly as his new duties would have made further attendance difficult. Herby was with him in London, and on 20th they both went to a performance of the Messiah at the Albert Hall. 'Singing both choral and individual both very good and attendance large, but I made up my mind that the hall is too large for full enjoyment of music' was Lord Hampton's verdict. For some reason he had been selected to buy the Christmas decorations for the Royal Victoria Patriotic Girls and Boys Asylums at Wandsworth, and on Christmas day he and Herby rode round there to view the results of his efforts. In the evening there was a large family party, and on new year's eve Lord Hampton and Herby rounded off the year by seeing Edward Sothern in 'David Garrick', Tom Robertson's long running play about the actor.

Lord Hampton ended his diary, as he had done on previous occasions, by writing 'And here I must record, as I have so often done before, my thankfulness for unnumbered blessings and mercies, and above all for still unbroken health and activity, throughout another year'.

Chapter 11
1876 – First Civil Service Commissioner

After Lord Hampton had lost the 1874 election Disraeli had written to him as mentioned above (page 116) that he had not been able, 'despite many efforts', to combine the peerage with the offer of a job, and he assured Lord Hampton that 'I shall take every effort to prove that your career is not terminated'. This letter sounded genuine enough, and Disraeli was certainly a believer in the power of patronage, but the Conservative party would have little to gain from doing the elderly Lord Hampton a favour. So perhaps we should give credit to Disraeli for living up to his word and helping his old campaigning colleague.

On Monday 22nd November Lord Hampton received the offer from Disraeli of the first civil service commissionership. He did not give a definite answer straight away, saying he was disposed to accept, but would delay his final decision till Friday. The pros and cons were fairly clear – as previously mentioned, Lord Hampton had not had a good year financially, and the salary attaching to the post would have been most welcome. Against that would have been the fact that his duties would involve regular attendance at the London office, with an even shorter summer break than he had had as an MP.

No doubt the question occupied his mind when out shooting on Tuesday. Wednesday was rent day, at which the tenants were wined and dined and then treated to a speech by their landlord about the new Landlord and Tenant Act, in which he advised them not to contract out of the Act's provisions. On Thursday he went to town, and attended further sessions of the army commission. Afterwards he went to the Carlton where he discussed the offer with three of his relations: Herbert Harley Murray, who had been a secretary to Lord Hampton when a minister and later a secretary to Lord Derby; George Herbert Murray, then a young but rising civil servant, and Herbert Domvile, who had also been a secretary to Lord Hampton.

The next day he went to see Sir Stafford Northcote, then the chancellor of the exchequer, who had been one of the authors of the Northcote-Trevelyan report which had led to the establishment of the civil service commission in 1855. Lord Hampton's diary recorded: 'Long talk with Northcote. Satisfactory – he wished to raise tone of commission – wd appoint a 3rd commissioner, wished first to be in parliament, and would raise salary to £2,000… and wrote Disraeli acceptance of commissionership'.

The civil service commission had been established to regulate entry into the civil service. Fifty years before, the service was, like parliament, dominated by patronage, and officials were remunerated by fees and gratuities rather than salaries. But in 1815 the government assumed responsibility for the payment of officials and most sinecures had been abolished, and the need for reform of the selection of officials was gradually being recognised. However reform of parliament took precedence over the civil service, but after 1832 the first steps were taken towards selection by merit, and the introduction of a superannuation scheme that covered the whole civil service was the first step towards regulating the service as a whole, rather than separate departments. The revolutionary year 1848 made the need to reform our own government more obvious, and the first major scheme to select candidates by public examination was introduced by the Indian Civil Service in 1853.

In 1853 Gladstone, by Treasury minute of 12th April, appointed his close associate Sir Stafford Northcote and Charles Trevelyan to investigate the civil service and make recommendations. They did not take long to complete their investigation, which was signed in November 1853, and although short it was uncompromising in its observations and recommendations. The report opened

Sir Charles Trevelyan (1807-86) was educated at Haileybury, then a training school for the East India Company, and at the age of 19 was appointed a writer in Bengal. After a successful career in India he returned in 1839 and was appointed assistant secretary to the Treasury. During his 19 years in this office he helped establish the Treasury in its leading role in the civil service, and was co-author of the famous report. In 1859 he returned to India as governor of Madras, later finance minister, and when he finally returned home in 1865 he became involved in many current issues, including army purchase.

1876 – First Civil Service Commissioner

by stressing the importance of having an efficient permanent civil service to assist the ever-changing composition of government ministers, and which should have 'sufficient independence, character, ability and experience to be able to advise, assist and, to some extent, influence those who are from time to time set over them'.

This is the report's view of the existing civil service:

> It would be natural to expect that so important a profession would attract the ablest and most ambitious youth of the country, and that the ablest would rapidly rise to distinction and public eminence. Such, however, is by no means the case. Admission into the civil service is indeed eagerly sought after, but it is for the unambitious, and the indolent or incapable, that it is chiefly desired. Those whose abilities do not warrant an expectation that they will succeed in the open professions where they must encounter the competition of their contemporaries; and those whom indolence of temperament or physical infirmities render unfit for active exertions, are placed in the civil service, where they may obtain an honourable livelihood with little labour, and with no risk; where their success depends upon their simply avoiding any flagrant misconduct, and attending with moderate regularity to routine duties.

Sir Stafford Northcote 1818-87, later 1st Earl of Iddesleigh, trained as a lawyer, but when he was 24 was invited by Gladstone to be his private secretary. In 1850 he advanced his career when he became a secretary to the Great Exhibition, and in 1853 was co-author of the report on the civil service. In 1855 he was returned as MP for Dudley, a seat where Lord Ward had much influence, but when his increasingly conservative instincts led him to vote against Lord Palmerston in 1857 they fell out, and Disraeli offered him a seat (Stamford) and a government post if he stood as a Tory. Thereafter he held a succession of government posts, being chancellor throughout Disraeli's 1874-80 government and enjoying a reputation for sound financial management. He was less successful as leader of the opposition from 1880 to 1885, his previous loyalty to Gladstone holding him back more than many would have preferred. In the Lords in 1885 he served a brief term as foreign secretary. One of his outside interests was reformatory schools, which he shared with Lord Hampton, and they were both members of the Reformatory Union when it was established in 1855.

Civil servants already had a superannuation scheme, and were protected against failing health;

> And this furnishes strong inducements to the parents and friends of sickly youths to endeavour to obtain for them employment in the service of the government; and the extent to which the public are consequently burdened, first with the salaries of officers who are obliged to absent themselves from their duties on account of ill health, and afterwards with their pensions, would hardly be credited by those who have not had opportunities of observing the operation of the system.

The appointment of poor quality junior clerks had a knock-on effect on promotion. As most promotion was by seniority, juniors did not have to work hard to rise, so the inefficiency spread throughout the service, and in cases where a really able person was needed to fill some senior position, an outsider had sometimes to be brought in, further lessening the need for ambitious candidates. Finally, the report attacked the fact that, although comprising 16,000 persons, the service was still run on an entirely departmental basis, and there was little or no interchange of personnel between departments, meaning, for example, that when one department was overstaffed and another understaffed, civil servants were not normally moved to achieve a balance.

To obtain a supply of suitably qualified young men into the service needed, the report said, 'the establishment of a proper system of examination before appointment, followed by a short period of probation'. Several offices had already introduced a system of examination, but each department set its own exams, and the system was subject to several problems. The examiners were too busy with their ordinary duties to give the setting and marking of papers much attention. Standards varied from office to office, and as the candidate was often known to the senior members of the department, the pass-mark could be adjusted to allow a favoured candidate to be accepted.

Accordingly the report recommended that a central board be established to conduct the examinations. The board should be entirely independent of the rest of the service, and should include men with experience of education as well as the needs of the service, and should be headed by a person of the rank of a privy councillor. No-one should be admitted to the civil service (except where it was decided no examination was necessary) without an enquiry first being made into his age, health and moral fitness, then, if satisfactory, being examined, and having a certificate to prove it. The report recommended that the exams should be conducted 'periodically' rather than when particular vacancies occurred, and in different parts of the country simultaneously. And, importantly, the examinations should be open to all-comers who were able to pass the physical and character tests referred to above. Applicants for inferior posts should be between

17 and 25, and for superior situations 19 and 25. It then discussed what might happen if there were more successful candidates than there were vacancies. It also considered the subjects to be covered by the exams: history, jurisprudence, political economy, modern languages, political and regional geography, besides the staples of classics and mathematics, were all thought worthy of inclusion, as well as tests to see how competent candidates were in composing their own letters, or précis.

The report then discussed the importance of promotion by merit rather than by seniority; but it recognised that promotion by merit could become promotion by favouritism, and to guard against this the process of promotion should be carefully recorded, with names and comments submitted to the head of department, who should make a record of why a particular individual was chosen. As to the annual increments in salary which were usually given automatically, these should in future be made subject to a satisfactory report from the man's superior as to his attendance and work. The report also considered it desirable that men should sometimes be promoted to a vacancy in another office; this would introduce fresh blood, and encourage men to seek further promotion.

Finally, Northcote and Trevelyan anticipated that their recommendations would meet with opposition:

> The existing system is supported by long usage and powerful interests; and were any government to introduce material alterations into it, in consequence of their own convictions, without taking the precaution to give those alterations the force of law, it is almost certain that they would be imperceptibly, or perhaps avowedly, abandoned by their successors, if they were not even allowed to fall into disuse by the very government which had originated them.

The government, however, decided, probably because it gave them more flexibility and avoided the possibility of an embarrassing defeat in parliament, to institute the changes by means of an order in council. This was issued on 21st May 1854, and appointed three commissioners, Sir Edward Ryan, John Shaw Lefevre, and Edward Romilly, whose job it would be to arrange examinations for all young men entering junior situations in the civil service, and to issue certificates of satisfaction. Additionally, before issuing a certificate, the commissioners should ensure that the candidate was within the age limits prescribed, that he was 'free from any physical defect or disease which would interfere with the proper discharge of his duties', that his character was 'such as to qualify him for public employment', and that he had sufficient knowledge for the proper discharge of his duties. They would then enter into a period of six months' probation, at the end of which satisfactory proofs of his fitness would be required for his appointment to become permanent.

LORD HAMPTON

The main difference between the order in council and Northcote and Trevelyan's recommendations was that, although the candidates had to gain the commissioners' certificate, there was no provision for making the examinations open to all. Instead, the previous practice of examining persons who had been nominated was continued. Two debates took place on this in the House of Commons. On June 21st, after a three day debate, a motion was passed without a division supporting 'the institution of judicious tests of merit, as well as by removing obstructions to its fair promotion and legitimate rewards'. However, on 10th July Vincent Scully, MP for Cork, introduced a motion which supported the order in council, but preferred that all examinations should be open ones, held in public. However, this was going too far for the House at the time, and the motion was defeated by 140 votes to 125. Sir John Pakington had voted against.

The commissioners quickly got down to business, starting the examinations and issuing certificates, which continued until a new order in council was issued on 4th June 1870, which directed that henceforth the examinations should be open to all persons. The commission had been led by Rt Hon. Sir Edward Ryan since its inception, initially with two other commissioners, although since 1870 there had only been one other. In line with the policy of gradually raising the profile of the commission, from 1862 the commissioners, who initially had been unpaid, were paid a salary, and the first commissioner's salary was raised from £1,500 to £2,000 in 1875 when Lord Hampton was appointed. Ryan, who had led a distinguished legal career, including a period as a judge in India, died on 22nd August 1875 just short of his 82nd birthday, creating the vacancy that led to Lord Hampton's appointment, and at the same time Theodore Walrond, who been the commission's secretary, was appointed a commissioner, so, with George Webbe Dasent already a commissioner, there were now three again.

Within a week of his appointment Lord Hampton had been introduced to his fellow commissioners by Stafford Northcote, and the following day invited them to dinner – 'I had a long talk, and dinner very successful'. Of the two, Dasent (58) was the best known, having devoted himself to ancient Scandinavian literature, and written several books. He had also been a deputy editor of The Times until his appointment as a commissioner, and had been called to the bar. Walrond (51), from Calder Park near Glasgow, was a classical scholar and best known for his biography of the Earl of Elgin.

The next day Lord Hampton went to the Civil Service Commission office to look over the premises and meet some of the staff, and later consulted Northcote about the secretaryship – Walrond had been secretary, and now needed to be replaced. Lord Hampton's rooms needed some attention, and he saw two gentlemen from the office of works to arrange this. But he did not allow new duties to spoil his occasional shoot, and the following day, after attending the office, then dining at home, he returned to Westwood. Over 100 head of game were accounted for on each of the next two days, and after spending two nights at Westwood he returned to town, and before the end of the week had ordered his first letter to be sent, which concerned the health of those working at the British Museum.

Thereafter he attended the office regularly till the end of the year, usually in the afternoon. It was closed for the Christmas holidays only on Christmas Day and Boxing Day. The diary for the first thirteen days of 1876 is blank, but from subsequent entries it seems that all was not well in the office. Commissioner Dasent seems to have been unhappy with his position and prospects, and Lord Hampton promised to speak to Northcote about this. A priority for Lord Hampton was the need for new rules about examinations, to fit in with the changes in the civil service recommended by the Playfair Commission of the year before. This divided the service into four divisions: staff officers (the most senior); a higher division of senior civil servants; a lower division recruited from candidates between 17 and 20 years old selected by examination; and boy clerks recruited between 15 and 17 years old and discharged when 19 unless they were successful in applying for a position in the lower division. An order in council had to be made covering all the examinations that had to be passed, mainly by candidates for the lower division, and Lord Hampton was busy on this in January.

He had arranged for some Worcestershire engagements to be grouped during the week commencing 17th January, when he attended the hunt club ball, the Worcester Diocesan Board of Education, and chaired a lecture by Dr Bainbrigge on physiology. He returned on Saturday.

Back in the office the week started well when he found his new furniture in place, but 'Later in day letter arrived from Treasury upsetting all our proposals and violating Northcote's promise to me that nothing should be settled till he had seen me. I wrote immediately requesting him to see me tomorrow.' Lord Hampton apparently regarded some action by Ralph Lingen, the abrasive permanent secretary to the Treasury, supported by William Henry Smith, the financial secretary to the Treasury, to reduce expenditure, as unwarranted interference. His diary entry for the following day reads: 'Went to Northcote by appointment at 12. Long talk about secretaryship, then saw Smith, then at Treasury long discussion with Lingen who stuck to their plan about secretaryship and I stuck to ours. Nothing finally settled. I found Dasent at office, who quite agreed with me, and I returned letter of last night to Lingen'. As successor to Walrond, Horace Mann, who had worked for the commission since its inception, had been appointed secretary in December 1875, and continued till he retired in 1887. The differences between Lord Hampton and Lingen were not clear, but they continued for some time.

LORD HAMPTON

William Henry Smith (1825-91) was, with his father, the founder of the well-known newsagents, selling books and newspapers to the travelling public. Initially he tried to get into parliament as a Liberal supporting Palmerston, but his first success was in 1868 as a liberal Conservative, representing Westminster. In 1874 Disraeli made him a Treasury minister, where he had dealings with Lord Hampton in the civil service commission. In 1877 he has made first lord of the Admiralty, when some, including Gilbert and Sullivan, made fun of him for his lack of naval knowledge. He later held other senior ministerial posts.

On Thursday 'I received back Treasury letter I had returned with unpleasant note from Lingen, desiring letter might be placed on record, but that ch. of exec'r reluctantly conceded our plan, to which Lingen and Smith were as much as opposed as ever, and requesting statement from us. This we directed Mann to prepare, and bring to us tomorrow'. On Friday 'In morning I wrote answer to Lingen's note and took it to office for consultation. I showed up break of promises, tho' perhaps unintentional, and on the whole wrote a severe and dignified rebuke. After much consideration this decided step was taken, and my indignant reply accompanied Mann's able reply to the official letter'.

But there was a change of tone on Saturday, probably because Stafford Northcote had stepped in and supported Lord Hampton against Lingen.

> Extraordinary fog all day in London. Intended to go to Westwood in evening, but it was remarkable day in office – I met Dasent there at 2.00 and found explanatory and satisfactory letters from Northcote and Lingen, with no apparent offence at my strong letter of yesterday – evidently the reverse, and my strong line was successful. We immediately obtained interview with Lingen, and found tone greatly improved, and most, if not all, our points conceded. Dasent greatly pleased – but we had to alter last Treasury despatch in one sense, by Lingen's request, and this took too long for me to leave town even if fog would have let me, which was very doubtful.

So Lord Hampton's visit to Westwood was delayed until Monday, and although he had to be back in town for Wednesday evening, when he had to respond to

1876 – First Civil Service Commissioner

a toast at a dinner of the Clothworkers Company, he managed to fit in some shooting as well as attending to estate business. But his diary makes it clear that he was busy most days in the office, so he must have been disappointed to learn that on 18th February, when the civil service estimates were being discussed in the House of Commons, the increased cost of the civil service commission was questioned. William Baxter, MP for Montrose Burghs argued that, although the work of the commission had not increased this year as against last, the cost had been increased, first by the appointment of a third commissioner at a salary of £1,200, then by the increase of the first commissioner's salary from £1,500 to £2,000. William Smith was the first to defend the appointment, as the duties had been growing in importance and magnitude for a long time past. He continued:

> The duties discharged by the commission are most delicate and responsible, and it is therefore desirable that the commission should be a strong one, having the confidence of parliament. The government, therefore, thought it advisable to appoint Lord Hampton to the position of first commissioner, as he is a statesman of great experience in public and official life, and it is desirable to have someone in parliament who would be able to account for the action of the commission, in case it should be questioned. The increase of salaries has for a long time been promised, and I believe is very well deserved by the officers of the department.

He was followed by the chancellor of the exchequer, Stafford Northcote, who said he wished to put the commission on a more important and independent footing, and repeated the points made by Smith. The expense was then attacked by Lord Robert Montagu, the maverick member for Westmeath who had been expelled from the Conservative party, and Alexander MacDonald, considered one of the first 'Labour' MPs, who made slighting remarks on Lord Hampton's age. Another radical MP, Anthony Mundella, joined in and said that what had been done was to create a sinecure. The late first commissioner, Sir Edward Ryan, had been very advanced in years, so why had it been necessary to replace him with two appointments?

The chancellor defended the commission again, and of Lord Hampton he said:

> It should be remembered that Lord Hampton, though of advanced years, is a man of energy, is every day at his office, and takes an active part in the discharge of his duties. I would have thought that anyone who sat in the House of Commons with Lord Palmerston would not have laid down the rule that men advanced in years are not able to work. Lord Hampton has by nature a great desire for work, and it has never before been suggested that he has ever flinched from it.

The discussion continued for some time, and the general feeling was that the appointment of Lord Hampton had been inappropriate. There were two divisions, but the whips ensured the government won both, though not by very large majorities. Ten days later Anthony Mundella again proposed a reduction of the vote by £500, and attacked the appointment. The chancellor again defended it, and said Lord Hampton

> would have to exercise authority in dealing with all the civil service departments as to questions which required the exercise of great tact, a good deal of firmness, and a good deal of authority. So far from Lord Hampton taking a new office in which he had to learn his business, it is exactly that part of the working of the civil service system in which his assistance will be invaluable. The noble lord has administered three public departments – that of secretary for the colonies, that of first lord of the Admiralty, and that of secretary for war. Besides that, he has acquired a large experience of public life, and great knowledge of the wants and necessities of the civil service, and their qualifications for the duties they has to perform.

There was another division at the end of the debate, but the government won by 159 votes to 126. In his diary, Lord Hampton wrote that the opposition could hardly have let the increased cost pass without comment, – 'it was only taken up by a few radicals', was his rather overly dismissive comment.

Although his diary indicates that he was a regular attender at the House of Lords, he is not recorded as getting involved in debates there in 1876, no doubt thinking his duties at the civil service commission were plenty to keep him busy. There were further meetings of the Spanish bond holders, and he led an active social life, where Eleanor Pratt seems to have been his usual companion, as well as his great niece Fanny Hanbury Williams, 15, for a visit to the theatre. Lady Hampton sometimes went out with her husband, as on 26th February when they dined with Sir Massey and Lady Lopes, but when they got back home Lord Hampton exchanged his wife for his niece, and took her to Mrs Sclater Booth's party. A few days later he took Eleanor to a 'spelling bee', a game based on spelling tests, at Lady Combermere's. Lord Hampton was much amused to record that there were 'three cabinet ministers – Lord Halifax, Lowe and self went up to spell – all flunked!!'.

Some of the issues that arose in the office are mentioned in his diary – some were of a general nature such as the possible introduction of Saturday half day's holidays (which were eventually granted from 25th March till 1st November) and new rules for the entry of senior clerks. Others concerned particular cases where the commissioners were required to adjudicate. All three commissioners had to be present for an official decision to be reached, and on one occasion, when there was a difference of opinion as to whether a clerk had to be examined for a new position, Lord Hampton felt sufficiently strongly to overrule his colleagues: 'my colleagues both said yes, I said no, we had long argument, but I was firm though conciliatory, and they yielded'!

1876 – First Civil Service Commissioner

Reading his diary, one is continuously struck by how much Lord Hampton managed to fit into his days, making light of the fact that he had recently turned 77. On Monday 6th March he attended a queen's levée, which must have involved time to prepare the correct dress, and waiting around in the palace, but still had time to attend the House of Lords, then dine with Mrs Slaney. Then two days later: 'Busy day – at 11.00 meeting of governors of Wellington College till 1.30, luncheon at St Stephens club at 2.30, office till 4.00. 4 till 6 committee of institute of naval architects – appointed committee to consider report on merchant shipping bill'. The following day he took Eleanor to see Othello with Henry Irving. His somewhat contradictory verdict was 'fine performance, but much marred by mouthing and eccentric pronunciation'. The Times was even more critical: 'Irving's violence is such as to render him almost ludicrous and altogether unintelligible'. Possibly as an antidote, a little later Lord Hampton took Eleanor to see the popular comedy by Tom Taylor and Charles Reade 'Masks and Faces'.

At that time it seems that the general hours of work in the civil service encompassed a six hour day, but some offices worked seven hours, with a consequent upgrading of pay and conditions. In March the spat with the treasury was renewed when Lord Hampton received an unpleasant letter from Lingen declining to recognise his office as one of seven hours. Although his initial reaction was to try and get the decision reversed, the next week the commissioners decided to acquiesce in the decision, which apparently gave them freedom to regulate their own hours and holidays, although presumably with lower rates of pay.

In addition to his attendance in the House of Lords, Lord Hampton still took an interest in the the House of Commons, and on 16th March was in the gallery when a 'great debate' was held on the royal titles bill. Probably at the suggestion of Disraeli, the queen had agreed to add the title 'Empress of India' to her other styles, and a bill was presented to parliament to confirm this. It was opposed by the Liberal opposition, and in the debate the Marquess of Hartington, the future 8th Duke of Devonshire and at that time leader of the Liberal party, spoke at length against it, initially on the grounds that since the proposal had been made known, public opinion had turned against it. He concluded his speech "I trust the time will never come when the people of this country will call their constitutional sovereign by any other name than that which they have so long known and loved so well". But the government won the day by 305 votes to 200. Lord Hampton was present again a week later when the bill came up for its third reading, and listened to the two great gladiators, Disraeli and Gladstone. Again the government won by a majority of 75. At the end of the month the bill was given its second reading in the House of Lords: there was an 'impressive debate', and two peers, Earls Grey and Granville spoke strongly against it, but it was not thought appropriate to express this opposition in a division.

Nevertheless, when the bill was in committee in the Lords, Lord Shaftesbury, always one to speak his mind without fear, proposed that a loyal address be sent to her majesty advising against adopting the new title. Lord Hampton thought his speech 'striking'; Shaftesbury thought the new title was not wanted either by the public here, or by those in India, who would link the title 'Emperor' (which would ultimately come) with the despotism to which India had not long before been subjected by the Moguls. Shaftesbury's motion was carried to a division, and was defeated by a majority of 46, Lord Hampton voting with the majority.

The conference of the Institute of Naval Architects was held at the beginning of April, and Lord Hampton, still the president, delivered the opening address, and attended most of the meetings over the next three days. He noted in his diary that there was an interesting paper on the Russian circular ships. These had been designed as gun platforms for use in coastal waters, but proved unsuccessful, being difficult to manoeuvre, prone to pitch and roll even in moderate seas, and, which one might have thought would have been foreseen, given to rotating through the recoil of the guns when fired off-axis. The final day of the conference kept him in meetings until 4.00 p.m., but he still had time to pick up his wife and call on his relations the Hanbury Williams, attend a music party before dinner, and after dinner take Eleanor and the Hanbury Williams girls to the Albert Hall for an amateur charity concert given by the Duke of Edinburgh.

The first half of April saw some very cold and snowy weather. On 15th Lord Hampton recorded that 'he was out in snow, thunder & lightning at the same time, with a cutting east wind', and for this reason had to delay his departure for the Easter break at Westwood till Monday 17th, passing Easter Sunday in London. Back at Westwood he met Herby, who had been working as a marshal with Judge Amphlett on circuit, and on Thursday he was due to attend a meeting of the Worcestershire Diocesan Education Society, but at Worcester railway station he heard of Lord Lyttelton's death the day before, and, after consulting the bishop, they decided to postpone the meeting.

Lord Lyttelton, 59, had been a prominent figure in Worcestershire society for many years. He was something of a liberal in many matters, but a high churchman, and a strong upholder of the rights of the Church of England. He had been involved in many other matters including the Saltley Diocesan Training College, and had been Lord Lieutenant of Worcestershire for 37 years. But he had suffered from periods of depression for a long time, so severe that the family had been warned of the possibility of suicide. Earlier in 1876 he had suffered from a particularly bad episode. He had gone abroad in a failed attempt to shake it off, and back in his London home at 18 Park Crescent, Regents Park, he spoke of suicide. On Tuesday morning as he was being shaved he asked for the barber's razor, and when this was refused he rushed out of the room and threw himself over the handrail of the staircase, sustaining serious injuries. He died early the following morning.

Lord Hampton had worked with Lyttelton on many projects, and he was 'greatly shocked' at the news. He returned to London on Saturday and he missed the funeral at Hagley – 'Poor Lord Lyttelton's funeral took place at Hagley this day, and I am much vexed that I did not attend. I would have gone any distance to do so, & as it happens I could have attended easily, but I was not aware of a wish having been expressed by the family that friends should come'.

The Earl of Dudley thought there should be a meeting to express the county's condolences and recognition of Lyttelton's works, but Earl Beauchamp objected, probably on account of the manner of Lyttelton's death. But after Lord Hampton had further discussions with Lyttelton's son-in-law, John Talbot, who with his wife Meriel was present when Lyttelton died and who was sure the family would approve and be gratified, a meeting was fixed for 13th May in the Guildhall. Nearly all county society were present or had sent letters of apology, and after the sheriff had introduced the meeting the Earl of Coventry proposed the first resolution, which paid tribute to Lord Lyttelton, both for his long period as lord lieutenant, and to 'express their admiration of his pure and exalted character, and of the unfailing energy with which, throughout his life, he devoted his great and cultivated powers to the best interests of all classes of the community'.

In seconding the motion Lord Hampton referred to a eulogy of Lyttelton written by Gladstone for The Guardian, and read out parts of it – their respective wives were sisters. But he made no mention of their differences over the Three Choirs Festival! Later Lord Hampton presided over a committee formed to consider a permanent memorial, which eventually led, as we shall see, to the fine marble monument now in Worcester cathedral.

Meanwhile his active social life continued in London as usual, and on 29th April he took Augusta Pratt to a private view at the Royal Academy, Lady Hampton not being well. Lord Hampton attended the grand dinner the following evening, which was accompanied by 'beautiful music, both in dining room and afterwards'. Always a lover of music, in early May he attended the opera on consecutive nights: on 8th to hear the first London performance of Tannhäuser (he calls this a new German opera, but in fact its German premier had been over 30 years before), and the following night Rossini's Semiramide. The next day, in what was to be a busy week, after dining in Goldsmith's Hall he went to Lady Salisbury's assembly where he was presented to the Empress of Germany. A meeting of the Spanish bondholders followed the next day, and on Friday he joined a party witnessing the return of the Prince of Wales from his visit to India, and in addition to all these events he spent time in the civil service commission office every day.

LORD HAMPTON

After the brief visit to Worcester to attend the meeting about Lord Lyttelton, the following week was just as busy, with the Prince of Wales' levée on Monday, in which he 'expressed to HRH my pleasure at seeing him home safe again', and two days later, after dining in the Middle Temple where he was 'much struck by ancient customs' attended a concert in the Albert Hall in honour of the Prince and Princess. Again there were meetings about the Spanish debt, and he attended the office every day. On Wednesday the following week 'Attended Pat. Fund committee and arranged letter to office of works. Then attended at National Society rooms convened by Archbishop of Canterbury to consider education bill. I moved and carried motion of regret that bill did not include religious instruction. Office – I dined with Lord Winmarleigh – Madre unwell'. Saturday was the queen's birthday, when traditionally dinners were held in celebration, and Lord Hampton joined Lord Beauchamp at his 'grand dinner'. Afterwards he still had time to attend a function with Lord Northcote and Lady Salisbury. And there was no let up the following week – he hosted two large dinner parties at home, one of which was followed by attendance at the Buckingham Palace Ball, and meetings about the Spanish bonds continued. Two weeks later on 16th June he chaired a meeting of the bond holders to accept the rather unfavourable terms which had now been negotiated. He wrote 'many hundreds in hall at Canon St Hotel, much clamour & complaint, but I was successful both in speech and reply and carried our plan by a large majority'.

After another brief visit to Westwood over the weekend, he returned to London on Monday to celebrate his silver wedding. His relatives the Mordaunts, Pratts and Domviles, came, as well as Johnny, and afterwards he went to Dudley House where he was presented to Leopold II, the King of the Belgians, who 'talked to me and greeted me very graciously'. Two days later was Lady Hampton's birthday, which was recorded in his diary without comment, but the following day she was so poorly that he cancelled a proposed stay at the Royal Yacht Club in Cowes. Nevertheless, he spent the weekend at Godinton Park in Kent, the seat of the Toke family, and, returning to London on Monday, after dining at the Merchant Taylor's Hall to mark the speech day of the school, he met the King of Hanover at Lady Denbigh's party. The first five Hanoverian kings had been kings of Britain and of Hanover, but Victoria was not able to inherit the throne due to the operation of salic law, and the Hanoverian crown passed instead to the Duke of Cumberland, and after his death in 1851 to his son George, who was therefore a cousin of the queen. George was blind, and by 1875 really only a pretender in exile, Hanover having become part of Prussia, but he remained a member of the British royal family.

Lord Hampton had been chairman and president of the Statistical Society in the 1860s, and remained a member of its council. In those days the society

1876 – First Civil Service Commissioner

was more interested in social statistics than with mathematics, and was closely associated with the Social Science Association. The two societies held their joint annual dinner on Tuesday, and, in the absence of the ex-home secretary Lord Aberdare, Lord Hampton took the chair.

The following day was also busy: 'Rode to office, at 12 home for luncheon and dressed for family gathering at Chislehurst [Rev. Francis Murray, the brother of Sir John's second wife Augusta, was rector there]. But found I had too many letters to write, and weather being also bad, sent excuses by Herby. Drove out with Madre and Charl'te Davies… After dinner went with Herby to Lady Northcote party – des Rosceaux with comic songs, and Mlle Krebs'. M. des Rosceaux advertised himself as available as a 'chanteur et acteur de scènes et chasonnettes comique' at private parties, and Mlle Marie Krebs was a pianist.

His engagements the following week began on Tuesday when he attended the annual meeting of the National Society, chaired by the Archbishop of Canterbury. The meeting passed resolutions affirming the importance of religious education, and Lord Hampton spoke, but, possibly because the archbishop had to leave early, he altered the order of speakers, and 'fiasco was the result – I was much annoyed' he recorded. As usual, he attended the House of Lords on the four days that it sat (it did not sit on Wednesdays), and on Friday was there to listen to the Merchant Shipping Bill being brought forward for its second reading by the Duke of Richmond. The act passed hastily the previous year was only intended to be temporary, and this bill covered the same ground, giving the Board of Trade more powers to stop unseaworthy ships going to sea and strengthening the penalties on owners. It also made the marking of a load line and deck line mandatory, but their position was left to the discretion of owners. Lord Hampton spoke briefly expressing his "great satisfaction" that the government had introduced the bill, and hoped to see it speedily enacted. On Saturday evening Disraeli entertained the Prince and Princess of Wales to a grand dinner at the foreign office, and after the dinner at 10.00 p.m. there was a reception for the diplomatic corps and other VIPs including Lord Hampton, who thought it a 'splendid reception'.

A meeting of the governors of Wellington College was held at Westminster the following week, and Lord Hampton was impressed with those attending. The Prince of Wales was the president, there were two royal dukes (Connaught and Cambridge), three other dukes including the Duke of Wellington, the Archbishop of Canterbury, and four other peers as well as five others. The new headmaster, Rev. Wickham, was 'in attendance', but the practice was for the headmaster to pace the corridor outside the room while the governors met, only to be admitted at the end. Certainly the previous headmaster, Rev. Edward Benson, objected to the practice, saying that if the governors insisted on his coming to London, at least they could provide somewhere for him to sit while waiting!

LORD HAMPTON

On 30th June Lord Hampton noted the death that day at the age of 32 of Lady Beauchamp at their London home in Belgrave Square. She was the wife of Frederick, 6th Earl Beauchamp, and had only been married for eight years, during which she had given birth to five children. On 11th June she had a premature confinement, from which she never recovered. 'A very sad case in its first aspect, but possibly a providential deliverance for her' he noted.

He next day, after his stint in the office in the morning, he took his relatives Mary and Elizabeth Pratt and Ferdy Hanbury Williams, as well as his son Herby, to see the grand volunteer review in Hyde Park by the Prince of Wales. Some 40,000 volunteers from 74 regiments were on parade, and The Times considered that the present volunteers were very improved on the rather undisciplined force of a few years before. Some men, it wrote, had done a morning's work in Nottingham, taken the train to London, and then gone on parade. Its only criticism was that a number of men did not join their units until they were assembled in Hyde Park, which may have been the cause of some ranks looking 'unsized', i.e. tall and short men mixed together.

During the first week of July Lord Hampton remained as busy as always – the office every day, the House of Lords whenever it sat, two dinner parties at home, and on three occasions parties or balls after dinner. It has been noted before that Lady Hampton was frequently absent when her husband attended a function, but in the second week of July this seems to have changed, as on 11th he noted that 'we dined with Lord and Lady Tollemache', and the following day Lady Hampton presented the prizes at the Wandsworth Asylum. On Saturday they drove out together, and although he noted that she had a bad cold on 17th, the next day they attended the large garden party given by the Prince and Princess of Wales at Chiswick. Here Lord Hampton was pleased to be presented to Sir Salar Jung, the prime minister of the Nazir of Hyderabad, and he also saw the Moorish embassy: 'picturesque group' he commented.

In 1825 Lord Hampton's sister Elizabeth Russell had married Ferdinand Hanbury-Williams of Coldbrook Park, Abergavenny. She had died in 1850, and Ferdinand married a second time in 1853. For some reason the couple then spent the next thirty years living in Boulogne, where they had four more children. If this was for financial reasons, then perhaps the unfortunate marriage of Annette, Hanbury-Williams' daughter by his first marriage, had something to do with it. She married Capt. Henry Gratton Bushe, who seems to have mistreated her, leaving her destitute, and they lived apart. They did not divorce, but after Bushe's death in 1888 Annette married again, aged 57. Hanbury-Williams' only son and heir by his first marriage was Ferdinand Capel born in 1834, and unlike his parents he seems to have lived the life of a country gentleman at Nantoer, near Coldbrook Park which had been let. Ferdinand Capel married in 1857, and

1876 – First Civil Service Commissioner

his eldest son was Ferdinand Pakington John Hanbury-Williams, then aged 18. Lord Hampton noted on the day of the Chiswick garden party that 'Ferdy H W came up for study with Mr Sharp', and again on 27th, but in between he was taken ill with a feverish attack causing the doctor to be called, but a week later he recovered.

The day after the Chiswick garden party the Lord Mayor held the traditional dinner in the Egyptian Hall of the Mansion House for the bishops. The weather had become exceedingly hot making the 280 guests feel uncomfortable, but Lord Hampton was pleased to be presented to the new American ambassador Edward Pierrepont, 'who gave a good speech'.

Wednesday 2nd August was the day Lord Hampton had chosen to leave London. Lady Hampton went directly to Westwood, but her husband travelled to Garnstone Castle near Weobley in Herefordshire, the seat of Daniel Peploe. Lord Hampton was to attend the archery match between the Worcestershire Archery Society and the Herefordshire Bowmen. 'Worcestershire sadly beaten. Otherwise charming meeting in beautiful place and nice weather'. The next day Mrs Peploe led Lord Hampton and Sir H Wilmot to the top of Burton Hill – at nearly 1,000 feet, this must have been quite a climb. On Saturday Lord Hampton went home for luncheon, where Herby, having finished his tour of duty as marshal, had also arrived, but Lord Hampton was disappointed to find his wife 'less recovered than I had hoped'.

The parliamentary session had not quite ended, so on Monday Lord Hampton was back in town, where he also had to attend the civil service commission office before it closed for the vacation. On Tuesday the Duke of Richmond proposed the second reading of the Elementary Education Bill 1876, and Lord Hampton was anxious to hear the debate. It will be recalled that the 1870 Elementary Education Act did not make attendance at school compulsory, although it gave powers to the new school boards to make it so. In his speech the Duke said that in 1870 a little less than half the number of children who could have attended school did so, and although there had been a large increase in school accommodation the number attending had risen less quickly, and in 1875 it was estimated that, of the 3 million children who could have attended school, only about 1.8 million did so.

There was still a strong feeling that making school attendance compulsory was too great an infringement on individual freedoms, but the 1876 bill went a step further in that direction. It prohibited the employment of children under the age of 10, and older children could be employed only if they had the necessary certificate showing a certain level of educational attainment. This, said the Duke of Richmond, would surely force parents to use their good judgement and, if the child could not be employed, then he or she would be sent to school. The bill would give powers to boroughs or boards of guardians, in districts where there was no school board, to pass bye-laws making attendance at school compulsory, and furthermore, where the authority considered that the parents were wilfully neglecting the education of their child, or where the child was found to be wandering the streets in bad company, then they could make application to the magistrates to enforce attendance. Various excuses could be accepted for non-attendance, but not poverty, as the bill provided for the payment of school fees by the local authority in cases of pauperism. Thus the bill took further steps to make children attend school without actually making it compulsory.

The Archbishop of Canterbury generally welcomed measures to make school attendance compulsory, but he looked forward to a time when education would be seen to be so desirable that compulsory powers would not be needed. He regretted that religion did not play as prominent a part as he would have liked in board schools, but spoke of the ever increasing number of national schools, which showed that parents still valued religion being central to a child's education.

Lord Hampton also welcomed the bill, which he thought a desirable sequel to the 1870 act, but he much regretted the fact that it had come before the House of Lords so late in the session, preventing a full debate, which he blamed on the prolonged debate on some controversial points in the other House. He also welcomed the provision in the bill to allow boards of guardians and borough councils to act in place of boards, which had proved expensive and, in some cases, very political. However, he regretted that the bill did not contain any provisions to encourage religious education of a strictly non-denominational character, which he had always favoured. In Ireland Catholics had religious instruction, and in Scotland presbyterianism was widely taught, so why could we not have a provision here that board schools should teach religion? He pointed out that many boards had already provided for an element of religious instruction. The London school board had passed a resolution that in their schools 'the bible shall be read, and there shall be given such explanations and instructions in the principles of morality and religion as are suited to the capacity of the children'. But the Birmingham school board had resolved that the bible should not be read, and the name of God never mentioned. Overall, he believed that of the 284 school boards, 167 had, in various ways, laid down by various rules that religion should be taught. He concluded:

> Here is clear proof that the country is in favour of religious teaching, and any government that made a change in this respect would receive the general support of the country... I believe that if the government had introduced clauses of a moderate nature providing that religion should be taught in all board schools, that decision would have been in general harmony with the opinion of the nation.

1876 – First Civil Service Commissioner

The bill duly received the royal assent at the end of the session. The day after the debate Lord Hampton, always interested in naval matters since his time as first lord, went down to Portsmouth, where he was met by Admiral Elliot, who showed him round HMS Inflexible. Launched in April, she had been built to maintain British superiority in the Mediterranean, and was armed with four 16 inch Armstrong muzzle loading guns in two centrally placed turrets. She had been designed to have a wide beam to aid stability but a short length to reduce her size as a target, and she incorporated several innovations, too numerous to describe here, that would have interested Lord Hampton. She still carried a full sailing rig, in contrast to HMS Thunderer, a mastless ironclad battleship with guns in turrets. On 14th July, while still undergoing trials, Thunderer had suffered a disastrous boiler explosion killing 45 crew including the captain, and Lord Hampton was shown the wreck. The boiler was a box boiler with straight sides, thus only suitable for low pressures, and the safety valve had corroded shut and the pressure gauge was not working. Henceforth cylindrical boilers only were used.

Lord Hampton had one more duty at the House of Lords – to continue his campaign in favour of British colonial sugar growers and present a petition from the Jamaica Association, asking that 'some action be taken with a view to the abolition of slavery in Cuba'.

Although Lord Hampton had noted that the army commission had 'finished' the previous December (the last evidence had been taken on 23rd July), there was still work to be done on the report. The commissioners met again on 15th and 16th March, then adjourned to await actuaries' reports, and the report was eventually published in August. The commissioners had worked long and hard over what was a very complicated subject, and the report considered the consequences of the abolition of purchase, including its impact on promotions. It started with a careful analysis of the present situation, quoting figures for the average length of time new officers spent before being promoted – 2 years 8 months to a lieutenant, 9 years to captain, nearly 19 years to major, and 23½ years before reaching the rank of lieutenant colonel. It also noted that in a typical battalion there would be one lieutenant colonel, two majors, eleven captains and eighteen subalterns. It was therefore clear that the 'bottleneck' in promotion was from captain to major, and that any system of promotion would have to ensure that sufficient numbers in the lower ranks retired to allow their more ambitious fellows a reasonable chance of promotion before they got too old. The only way to ensure a flow of retirement from the lower ranks would be to limit the length of time that could be served as a lieutenant or captain. An order in council had already limited the length of time that could be served as a major or lieutenant colonel to 5 years, and the report now recommended that lieutenants' and captains' commissions be limited to 20 years. A pension or equivalent lump sum would be given on retirement, and the commissioners recommended that this would be £200 a year for those who had completed 20 years, and a proportionally lower amount for those wishing to retire with shorter service at that rank.

This was the main recommendation, but there were many other aspects of the scheme that the report discussed in detail, too complicated to discuss here. The Times ran an editorial on the report, and considered that it 'bears witness to the very great care in its preparation, and will need to be maturely considered'. The government adopted most of its recommendations, which were incorporated in a royal charter in July the following year.

On Friday 11th August Lord Hampton returned to Westwood for the weekend. On Saturday he attended a large garden party at the Worcester deanery, though there is no reason to suppose that his relations with Dean Yorke had improved. On Monday he presided at a meeting of the Severn Commissioners, of which he had long been the president. The engineer presented a report on the navigation between Diglis in Worcester and Gloucester, which had long been problematical. When the scheme was first constructed it had been proposed to rely on dredging this stretch to maintain the depth, but it soon became clear that this would not work, and a further weir and lock were constructed at Tewkesbury to raise the water level between there and Worcester. Then in 1869 work on two new weirs at Gloucester in the eastern and western channels began. The engineer, Edward Leader Williams, reported that now this work was complete the depth of water between Gloucester and Worcester, when measured last July, was, despite the drought, at least 7 feet 6 inches – he compared this with the situation before the scheme was started in 1836, when it was mostly less than 3 feet.

The weather in early August was extremely hot, which deterred Lady Hampton from going to a garden parties on the 16th and 17th, then on the next day the rain that broke the heat-wave stopped her from going to the garden party at Hadzor Hall. However, on 22nd she was able to go to The Rhydd, the home of Sir Edmund Lechmere, for a stay which included a meeting of the Worcestershire Archery Society, always an important social event.

August and September was the season of music festivals, and in the last week of August Lord Hampton and his house guests attended the Birmingham Music Festival. As always, this opened with 'Elijah', a 'splendid performance'. The next day, he was charmed by Mlle Albani's singing of Mendelssohn's 'Hear my Prayer', but thought that George MacFarren's new oratorio 'The Resurrection' 'not very successful'. MacFarren, not so well known today, was a prolific composer throughout his long life (he was then 63), and had already composed a successful oratorio 'St John the Baptist'. The Times, however, gave 'The Resurrection' a verdict of 'entire approval… the applause, magnificent and prolonged, was redoubled in heartiness when Prof. MacFarren – led on by Sir Michael Costa himself – appeared to acknowledge it'. On Thursday the party returned for a third day, for a 'very grand' performance of Messiah.

The next day was the opening of the shooting season, and Lord Hampton, Col Aldworth and the game keeper Henry Simons accounted for twenty five brace. After entertaining more house guests the following week, on Monday 11th September Lord and Lady Hampton went to Hereford, where they had taken lodgings for the Three Choirs Festival. Feeling was still running strongly in favour of maintaining the festivals, and the full corporations of Hereford, Worcester and Gloucester had decided to attend the first day as a demonstration of their feelings. All were in their full ceremonial dress, and the colourful procession went from the Free Library down Broad Street to the cathedral, where they occupied prominent seating under the tower. Lord Hampton thought this was an 'effective demonstration'. As further signs of support, the dean and all the Hereford canons had added their names to the list of stewards, the bishop preached the sermon at the opening service, and the lord lieutenants of both Herefordshire and Worcestershire were also stewards.

After the morning service, Lord Hampton attended 'Elijah' in the afternoon, and in the evening Handel's 'Samson', and the first part of Haydn's 'Creation'. The next day saw performances of Spohr's 'Last Judgement' and Mendelssohn's 'Hymn of Praise'. In the evening they dined at the deanery, and attended the miscellaneous concert in the Shire Hall. On the last day they listened to John Francis Barnett's recently composed oratorio 'The Raising of Lazarus', which Lord Hampton found 'in parts good, but rather an imitation of Mendelssohn, and too long'. Gounod's 'Mass for St Cecilia' followed, and the concert was rounded off by 'Hallelujah' from Beethoven's 'Mount of Olives'. The Times noted that attendance at this concert was poor – perhaps the lack of a popular favourite put off concert goers. On the last day Messiah was sure to fill the cathedral, but it appears from his diary that Lord and Lady Hampton did not stay for this. He noted that they had enjoyed attending the festival from their own lodgings in the city – they had received invitations to stay at country houses, but this would have meant constant travelling back and forth, and Lord Hampton wished his wife to enjoy the music 'without fatigue'.

The following Wednesday he joined a party of Severn Commissioners to see the new docks at Sharpness. The Gloucester and Sharpness Canal had been opened in 1827 to take sea-going ships from the Severn at Sharpness to the Gloucester docks, avoiding the lengthy and dangerous tidal meanders of the river. Although originally intended just to take ships up to Gloucester, docks were also built at Sharpness, and, as these became increasingly used, new and improved docks had been opened in 1875. Lord Hampton commented that he saw an 'ingenious American invention called elevator to send grain from ship into warehouse' so we can assume that it had become an important agricultural port, as it still is to a lesser extent today.

The next day he went to inspect a cottage at Huntingdrop in Hanbury, where he had some property rights, that had been condemned – he found 'a man and his wife, two sons and three daughters sleeping in one room about 10 feet square!!!'. A new one was being built.

Lord Hampton's diary for the remainder of 1876 names many visitors to Westwood, and calls he made. In October Lord and Lady Hampton paid a visit to Elmley Park, which had been the seat of Lady Hampton's late husband Col Thomas Davies, but Lord Hampton had to leave after two nights to attend a meeting concerning Lord Lyttelton's memorial – an altar tomb in the cathedral designed by Sir Gilbert Scott was decided on.

On 16th October, after attending quarter sessions, he took the train to Mangotsfield. Here he was met by Sir Stephen Cave, MP for Shoreham and paymaster general, and joined a party at Cave's seat at Cleeve Hill which had assembled to attend the Bristol Music Festival. The next morning they went to the Colston Hall to hear 'Elijah', with many of the same soloists that had sung the oratorio in Hereford shortly before. Lord Hampton thought the Colston Hall was large and handsomer than Birmingham's town hall, but the acoustics were inferior. The oratorio the next morning was Handel's 'Israel in Egypt', but Lord Hampton did not stay to hear Messiah, and, after inspecting St Mary Redcliffe church, went home.

He probably left Bristol early as he wanted to attend a meeting of the Worcester Diocesan Board of Education on Thursday. In particular he wished to support a motion by Canon Melville aimed at encouraging the teaching of religion in board schools. It proposed that diocesan inspectors should, when desired by a school board, examine the school's teaching of the scriptures, the Lord's prayer, the ten commandments and the apostles' creed. This provoked a lively discussion at the meeting, and although it met some opposition, presumably from those who felt that an Anglican board should not favour the teaching of religion in a non-denominational way, the motion was passed by three votes. At the same meeting, Lord Hampton renewed an attempt to allow reporters into the quarterly board meetings, but this was vetoed by the reactionary Dean Yorke on the grounds that reporters would be 'out of place' in the chapter house. Berrow's was scathing in its criticism of this wholly inadequate reason: 'The dean has a perfect horror of publicity. The clear, piercing light which reporters cast on men and things is distasteful to him, and his prejudice resists all the assaults of reason and expediency. Influential mediocrity is usually endowed with a larger share of

1876 – First Civil Service Commissioner

self-complacency, but the dean shrinks from any situation in which his judgement and ability would be exposed to criticism'.

Lord Hampton had been invited to attend the following week the inauguration of a drinking fountain erected in Kidderminster by the carpet manufacturer John Brinton. The fountain was elaborate and so was the ceremony – the bishop was there and the opening was performed by his wife. The ceremony was followed by a lunch at which Lord Hampton spoke. He said an earlier speaker had suggested that public dairies should be established, but Lord Hampton wished to congratulate them, through the kind act of Mr Brinton, upon having established in that town the most valuable dairy that they could have – the dairy from which flowed the milk of human kindness! He continued:

> Mr Brinton afforded a bright example of an Englishman, who has risen to wealth and prosperity by his success in manufacturing industry, devoted a portion of his wealth so acquired to promoting the best interests of those by whose aid he has been so successful... It has been my fortune on various public occasions to visit very many of the great manufacturing centres in this country, and I am proud to say I have never visited any of them without seeing traces of that noble spirit in which Mr Brinton has been acting.

On Tuesday 31st October Lord Hampton went to London to resume attendance at the civil service commission office after an absence of nearly three months. He returned to Westwood for the next weekend, but went back to town on Monday, going to the office daily and forming a party to watch the lord mayor's show. At the end of the week he also saw Sir Francis Grant, who had painted the portrait of Lord Derby hanging at Knowsley, about the copy he was making that would be used for the statue of Derby to be erected in Parliament Square.

Carpet manufacturers Brintons were established in 1783. Under John Brinton (1827-1914), the founder's grandson, it became one of the largest in Kidderminster. John Brinton took an active part in local affairs, donating Brinton Park to the town as well as the drinking fountain, and from 1880 to 1886 represented the borough in parliament as a Liberal.

He then returned to Westwood, and the following week remained at home, and spent three days shooting, before travelling to Ragley Hall on Saturday, preparatory to a great Conservative meeting in Birmingham on Monday. The home secretary, Richard Assheton Cross, had been invited, and at 5.00 p.m. about 600 sat down to dinner in the Town Hall. Lord Hampton presided, and in his opening remarks referred to the unrest in the Ottoman empire that was in danger of leading to war, and some voices had been raised in this country that we should become involved. But, said Lord Hampton, "England is anxious for peace; England hopes that our government will make every effort for peace that is consistent with the national honour".

Finally, the home secretary spoke. He regretted the fact that all three MPs for Birmingham (Joseph Chamberlain, Philip Muntz and John Bright) were still Liberals. The purpose of instigating three-member constituencies were to represent all shades of opinion, which was not happening in Birmingham. This was a pity, as in fact Conservatives represented reform as much as Liberals, although he was still against the recently introduced secret ballot. He reiterated what Lord Hampton had said about the European conflict: "Her Majesty's Government had but one desire – which was to maintain the peace of Europe". He then spoke about the government's financial policy, which was of retrenchment – at that time the government was paying off the national debt at the rate of £1.5 million a year, and he hoped that this could be increased.

As to reform, social reform was necessary for the well-being of the community. No man who went through our large towns could avoid seeing the depth of degradation to which many of our fellow creatures were reduced. Although the

Richard Assheton Cross (1823-1914), later 1st Viscount Cross, was born to a middle class family, and built up a successful legal practice in Lancashire. He was heavily involved in local politics, and represented Preston in parliament as a Tory from 1857 to 1862. He had to leave parliament due to his position in his wife's family bank, Parrs Bank, but returned in 1868 for SW Lancs, sensationally defeating Gladstone. In 1874 he was surprisingly made home secretary, and guided a number of social reforms, including the Artisans Dwelling Act, through parliament. Later he was secretary of state for India.

government had a role to play (Cross's Artisans' Dwellings Act had given powers for the first time to local councils to buy slums for redevelopment) "they could not further the happiness of the people more than by giving them the greatest possible freedom of self-government by local institutions".

The party returned to Birmingham again the next day, and they attended a meeting of Conservative working men in the Town Hall, attended by over 5,000. 'A wonderful and striking sight, Conservative enthusiasm immense', Lord Hampton wrote. The Earl of Warwick presided, and Cross spoke again, this time largely on social topics, including the need to reduce the incidence of men serving prison sentences for petty offences. Afterwards there was a non-political dinner given by the mayor, George Baker, at which the other mainly Liberal councillors could meet the home secretary. Joseph Chamberlain, who had been mayor until he resigned on being elected to parliament earlier that year, proposed the health of Mr Cross, and thanked him for the improvements made possible by the Artisans' Dwelling Act.

The next day Lord Hampton had to return to Westwood for the annual tenants' dinner, and at the beginning of the following week the household moved to London where he attended the office after a two week absence, but only after he had attended a meeting of the Egyptian bondholders to approve the acceptance of the reduction of interest– it seems that this investment had also met problems. At the office a new project was under consideration concerned with improvements in the examinations required to enter the army, which was to occupy Lord Hampton's attention for some time. He returned again to Worcester on Friday, where he had an engagement at the School of Art, presiding at the annual soirée and making a carefully prepared speech. The following morning, after inspecting work on his new tea and dinner services at the china works, he presided at a meeting of the Association of Managers and Teachers of Church Schools. Here the vice chairman, George Hastings, who had been chairman of the Worcester School Board since its inception, said how pleased he was that the interests of the church schools of Worcestershire "had been well cared for by the school board". Another speaker remarked that this was in great contrast to the attitude of the Birmingham School Board, and in winding up Lord Hampton said he much regretted that in some districts there were conflicts between the voluntary sector and the board, and said he was "deeply convinced there was ample room for both".

On Monday, before returning to London, he went to the Midland Institute in Birmingham, where he distributed the prizes and certificates for those who had been successful in the Oxford Local Examinations. The number of candidates had increased to 117 last year, of which over three quarters of both the juniors and seniors were successful, rather above the national average, and Lord

LORD HAMPTON

Joseph Chamberlain, 1836-1914, was born to a family of shoe makers in London. In 1851 his uncle J S Nettlefold and his father purchased the patent of an American automatic screw making machine, and Joseph was sent to Birmingham to manage the enterprise. With a near monopoly of the domestic market and expanding sales overseas the business was very successful, with Joseph taking control of the costing and marketing. But he also saw the down-sides of the new large factories such as his, and, among other initiatives, in 1869 joined the National Educational League to campaign for universal elementary education. Disappointed that the 1870 Elementary Education Act still left much education in the hands of the Church of England, Chamberlain, a Unitarian, campaigned against the Liberal leadership, dividing the party, which contributed towards Gladstone's defeat in 1874. In 1873 he had been elected mayor of Birmingham, and put his radical ideas into effect by taking control of the gas and water utilities and clearing the slums from the town centre. First elected to parliament in June 1876, he cut a distinctive figure, clean shaven with his trade-mark orchid button hole and monocle.

Hampton said he was particularly pleased to see eleven girls amongst the successful candidates.

The previous spring a naval expedition under Capt. Nares had set out in two ships in an attempt to reach the north pole. When the men returned late in 1876 there was much praise for their bravery under very adverse conditions, although scurvy had hit the expedition, and four men had died. Back in London on 5th December Lord Hampton was invited to dine at the United Services Club to meet the officers, and he proposed the toast to the club chairman and veteran explorer Sir George Back. Two nights later he dined at Trinity House to meet the officers again, and proposed the toast to the master, the Duke of Edinburgh.

At the same time Lord Hampton chaired a meeting of the Patriotic Fund executive committee to consider more problems at the Royal Patriotic Asylum at Wandsworth. On several occasions during the year the visiting committee had noted that some of the asylum rules were not being adhered to, and at this meeting the committee felt the time had come to revert to having a single lady superintendent rather than the present arrangement of a male superintendent, Mr Larcombe, and his wife as matron. Accordingly the Larcombes would be invited to resign to avoid being discharged.

In the office on Saturday 9th December Lord Hampton faced the problem that not enough candidates for the Woolwich arsenal were reaching the required standards in mathematics. In the short term he could see no alternative but to artificially raising the marks of all the candidates, although 'he had a strong dislike of such a course, and only consented to act *pro hac vice*'. In the evening he took his son Herby to see the popular conjurers John Maskelyne and George Cooke perform in the Egyptian Hall in Piccadilly, who also exposed the tricks used by spiritualists in their shows.

On Monday he attended another reception for the Arctic expedition officers, this time at the Geographical Society, where Capt. Nares read his account of the expedition. The Prince of Wales was president, and Lord Hampton felt the Prince was rather 'flat' to him. Then the following week he met the officers for the fourth time, this time in the Merchant Taylor's Hall at the traditional end of term dinner, and in proposing the toast to the master he spoke about the bravery of members of the expedition. At the same time Lady Hampton had one of her spells of illness and remained in bed for three days, leading to the cancellation of their dinner party.

Sir George Nares, 1831-1915, like his father, joined the Royal Navy, and had a long and varied career, including joining the expedition to find Franklin in 1853. In 1872 he commanded an expedition that would circumnavigate the world, conducting scientific and surveying work. Proving to be a successful leader, he was recalled before it had finished to command the 1875-76 British Arctic expedition, the aim of which was to reach the north pole. Valuable surveying work was done and discoveries made, but the rough pack-ice proved too much for the sledging party, and the north pole was not reached.

LORD HAMPTON

The weekend before Christmas saw Lord Hampton at a wedding in Surrey, and on Christmas day he had a family dinner party at home. On Thursday 28th he was back in the office, and later held a 'singularly agreeable dinner party with unusual amount of agreeable conversation in which [Sir George] Dasent took an able lead'. On Saturday he travelled to Worcester for the day, mainly to attend a meeting of the Lyttelton memorial committee, at which Sir Gilbert Scott's designs were accepted, and it was decided to apply to six well known sculptors for estimates.

New Year's Eve, a Sunday, began as usual, with a visit to the Temple Church with Herby, and the Chapel Royal in the evening. But then a tragedy occurred:

> Attended chapel royal and walked home by Chapel Street to call on Johnnies – and then heard from Mr P of alarming attack of illness Diana had suffered just as she was preparing for church in morning. She had for a time lost both sight and senses, it was in fact a death stroke. She became better and quite herself during evening, but, alas!, soon after the clock had struck the termination of 1876, she breathed her last! A truly good right-minded woman, I felt for her uninterrupted affection and respect.

Lady Diana had been at her father-in-law's for the Christmas day dinner, and Lord Hampton had underlined her name in his diary, presumably because this was the last time he saw her alive and well. Chapel Street leads from Belgrave Square to Grosvenor Place, and is not far from Lord Hampton's residence at the further end of Eaton Square. We can presume that Lady Diana died of a stroke, but there is no indication that she had been in poor health except a note in Berrow's, accompanying the report of her death, that she had been passing the autumn and winter in London 'in view of the state of her health'. She was in her forty ninth year.

Lady Diana Pakington, 1828-77.

Chapter 12
The years 1877 and 1878

The beginning of 1877 was dominated by the death of Lord Hampton's daughter-in-law, and on Saturday 6th January her remains were brought from London and proceeded with the mourners to Powick Church, in which parish was Kings End, their Worcestershire residence. Berrow's reported that, as they approached the church door:

> There was a furious storm of rain and wind, and the chief mourner, in his enfeebled condition, was the object of the deepest sympathy and anxiety. The storm was so violent that he was obliged to avail himself of the assistance of those around him and even the bearers of the coffin immediately before him reeled through the strength of the wind.

She was buried in a grave just outside and north of the west church door. It is still visible, although in a much neglected state.

No diary survives for 1877, but from newspaper reports it seems that Lord Hampton attended many of the same functions that he had attended the year before, so we need not repeat those here.

Lord Hampton had been elected president of the Worcestershire Agricultural Society for the year, and he attended the show held that year in Kidderminster from 24th to 26th July. At the annual dinner on Wednesday he spoke, noting that it was the first show for two years as last year the Royal Society held their show in Birmingham. The Worcestershire Society show was not large, but the quality was good, and in particular he was pleased to see pigs that had not been over-fed to the extent that they could neither stand nor see.

The following week he distributed the prizes at Malvern College, and attended the annual meeting of the Royal Archaeological Society in Hereford. Lord Hampton used the occasion to speak about the Three Choirs Festival, and said "I cling earnestly to the hope that, however conscientious might have been the scruples on which the Worcester dean and chapter had lately acted, they would come to feel that no principle was at stake which could require the giving of offence to a great body of their neighbours, and creating ill-feeling and discord, where all was previously harmony and peace". A few days later Lord Hampton presided at the annual meeting of the Severn Commissioners, at which there was a discussion on a proposal for the commissioners to acquire the towing paths along the river banks, which were then in a different ownership.

However, the great event of August was the marriage of Lord Hampton's second son Herby to Miss Evelyn Nind Frances Baker on 23rd. Evelyn was the youngest of three daughters of Sir George Baker, 3rd baronet, of Loventor, Devon and Fillongley, Warwicks, and it was at this latter place that the ceremony took place. Sir George's grandfather, another Sir George, had been the noted physician to King George III and Queen Charlotte, treating the king during his periods of madness. He was also noted for conducting a series of experiments showing the existence of lead poisoning.

According to Berrow's report, 'the picturesque village presented quite a gay appearance, flags, banners and evergreens being displayed in all directions. The village bells rang merrily, and from the tower of the old church a flag was waving in the breeze'. Lord and Lady Hampton were, of course, among the thirty guests who sat down to the wedding breakfast in Fillongley Hall, after which the newly married couple left for a honeymoon in Dovedale in the Peak District.

The following week Lord Hampton travelled to Glasgow to preside at a meeting of the Institute of Naval Architects, following a resolution they had passed to hold an annual autumn meeting outside London in places associated with the merchant marine. In his introduction, Lord Hampton said that one quarter of the whole mercantile marine was connected with Glasgow, and in 1876 153 ships, a total of 174,000 tons, were launched at Glasgow, although this was less than it had been earlier in the decade. He was pleased to note that nearly one half of the new ships were sailing ships; "while greatly admiring", he said, "what was effected by steam machinery in carrying on the commerce of the world, for the sake of keeping up the seamanship of the British sailor I would be glad to see the use of sailing ships continued, while in our men-of-war I would rather see auxiliary screws than solely screws". While in Glasgow he was shown some of the shipyards there, including Messrs Elders, which he referred to later as perhaps the most magnificent ship building establishment in the world, and Messrs Denny lower down the Clyde.

In the first week of September the Three Choirs Festival took place in Gloucester. Once again the three city councils formed a procession through the city to show their support for the festival. After the opening service in the cathedral, when the bishop gave a sermon expressing support for the festival's continuation, the mayor gave a luncheon in the Corn Exchange. Unfortunately, Lord Hampton was prevented from attending through indisposition, but the high sheriff proposed a toast to his health, remarking on his efforts over many years in support of the continuation of the festival.

On 12th September Lord Hampton presided at a lecture given in the Natural History Society rooms in Worcester by William Bainbrigge FRCS about the beneficial effects of the Droitwich brine baths, of which he was now the proprietor. He recounted the history of the baths, and referred to the opening the year before of the large swimming bath, where, to make it more effective, the water was kept between 80° and 90°F.

Bainbrigge amplified the views he had expressed in a speech he gave at the opening of the baths in December 1873, and it was clear that he had not lost any enthusiasm for their beneficial effects. He gave an analysis of the cases he had treated in the previous six months, of which a little over one third involved rheumatism, and a further one sixth gout. The rest were made up of a wide variety of complaints, mostly categorised as 'disease arising from general derangement from various causes'. Some of his remarks would not find much favour with medical practitioners today. Rheumatism, he said, "arose out of an ill-conditioned or morbid state of the blood. A remarkable feature of the disease was its ever changing character and locality". He considered the drugs often prescribed had 'mischievous' effects, and had always found that the waters had relieved pain, obviating the need for the use of 'powerful and objectionable drugs'. Referring to gout, he said the cause was "too much animal food and an over-rich diet, together with liberal potations of every kind of alcoholic beverages, which produced this most wretched of all suffering". It was wrong, Bainbrigge said, to think that the waters were only effective in certain types of disease.

> All known disorders are dependent on an abnormal condition of the digestive functions. It was to the solvent properties of the alkalis contained in the Droitwich waters that they could alone attribute the rapidity of their effects, such as so frequently presented where patients, after a course of baths, were seen to throw away their sticks and crutches... Morbid materials in the blood became deposited in the tissues of joints and in other parts of the frame, and before these fixed deposits could be absorbed they must be reduced to almost a fluid state, so as to render them fit to be held in solution in the blood vessels.

Bainbrigge cautioned against the danger of indiscriminate use of the baths – only by following his own carefully worked out programme would cures be successful.

Modern practitioners have found that the baths can relieve the pain caused by rheumatism, and in some cases allow patients who could not walk to walk again, but such relief is generally not long-lived. And they would not agree, for example, with Bainbrigge's claim that they gave relief to diabetes sufferers.

Bainbrigge ended his talk with a plea for the facilities to be made more available to the poorer classes, who, after much manual work in adverse conditions, often tended to fall victim to rheumatism, and he felt that the poor rates would be well spent on helping these cases, rather than supporting the family while they endured long-term suffering.

Once the Gloucester Three Choirs Festival was over, thoughts turned to the 1878 festival which was due to be held in Worcester. On 11th September, the Lord Lieutenant, Earl Beauchamp, acting as an unofficial mediator, wrote to the dean in conciliatory tones expressing 'the great pleasure I shall experience if means can be found to terminate the existing unhappy state of things'. Dean Yorke replied that he had read the letter 'with the attention it deserves, as coming from a person of your high position and character'. He would be very grateful if Beauchamp could discover 'the way of reconciliation in the matter', but at the same time he wanted to make it clear that he saw no grounds for going back on the principles laid down by the capitular body in 1874, which the stewards did not wish to adopt.

Beauchamp's reply regretted the rather unilateral tones of the dean's letter, but hoped he could read in it a suggestion that the capitular body might at least reconsider these principles in the light of later experience. In his reply the dean wished to counter rumours, which he felt Beauchamp might have been referring to, that the dean and chapter had already decided to change their stance on the festival. He wrote:

> There is no absolute bar to devising a festival of the three choirs, such as shall accomplish the chief objects which were contemplated in the original foundation, viz: the cultivation of church music of the highest character, and the efficient support of the clergy widows and orphans charity. This I say, may be done, if all parties will agree to get rid of the objectionable sale of tickets of admission to the cathedral, and of the other things that appear to me inconsistent with the sanctity of the chief house of prayer in the diocese.

The correspondence, which was later published in full in Berrow's, became increasingly wordy, and one gets the impression that both parties, and particularly the dean, were now anxious to come to an arrangement, but at the same time to safeguard their principles. Beauchamp's next letter expressed the hope that he had interpreted something the dean had written as offering to consider carefully any proposal put forward by the stewards, but if not 'I have duties to discharge more important than framing proposals between parties, one of which is deliberately resolved not to reconsider, in the light of subsequent experience, the position taken up in 1874', and he would be much disappointed if they rejected his desire to terminate a state of things 'injurious to the popularity and usefulness of the whole capitular body and prejudicial to the interest of the established church. And he added that considerable doubt was thrown upon the inflexible nature of the 1874 principles, when a meeting of the parochial choirs had taken place earlier in the year and an admission charge made.

In his reply the dean made it as clear as he dare that he wished for a compromise:

> I beg to assure you that any proposals or suggestions of yours will receive respectful consideration… you must feel sure that we should gladly adopt such a means of terminating the painful state of things at present existing. You can hardly suppose that I personally enjoy the luxury of unpopularity; or that I take any pleasure in opposing the wishes and gratifications of a great number of persons with whom it would naturally be my desire to be on the most friendly terms… only a deep sense of duty would be likely to force a man like myself into such an uncomfortable position.

The dean said he would be happy to put any proposals before the chapter if Lord Beauchamp could be more specific in what was proposed for the 1878 festival. As to the meeting of the parochial choirs when there was an entrance charge, this was done entirely without the sanction of any member of the dean and chapter. A few days later the dean sent Lord Beauchamp a copy of a resolution passed on 29th September at a chapter meeting, when it was agreed that they would be prepared to give their best consideration to any proposals put to them by the festival standing committee.

A meeting of the standing committee of the Worcester festival was duly held on 6th October, presided over by Lord Beauchamp, with Lord Hampton, Sir Edmund Lechmere, the mayor of Worcester (Mr Jones), George Hastings, Harry Vernon, the banker J Swinton Isaac, past mayor and festival enthusiast Henry Goldingham, and the honorary secretary Thomas Wheeler. It was decided that 'a request be made to the dean and chapter for the use of the cathedral next year, and a minute was drawn up expressing the desire of the committee to meet the dean and chapter upon every practicable point, and especially with respect to preserving the character of the cathedral as a house of God'.

The meeting also adopted seventeen points in which they attempted to go as far as possible to meet the dean and chapters' objections. They agreed to dispense with the orchestral platform which took a long time to erect and interfered with the services. The committee just wanted to have the use of the cathedral from 1.00 p.m. till 4.30 p.m. on the first day, leaving the dean and chapter to make arrangements for a 'more solemn service than ordinary' in the morning, and on the three other days the use of the cathedral from 11.00 a.m. till 4.00 p.m., when no divine service was held.

To meet the desire of the dean and chapter for the oratorios to be made part of a religious service, they suggested that the performances be preceded by a collect from the book of common prayer, spoken by a clergyman appointed by the dean and chapter. The committee also affirmed that, as had always been the case, they left to the dean and chapter the right to veto the performance of any particular piece of music that they did not consider suitable. Finally, the committee would agree to abandon the ball which, despite intermittent objections had traditionally been held on the final evening, although it had not been held since the 1869 festival. They suggested that a service be held in the cathedral, as it had been in the recent Gloucester festival, instead.

The one remaining important point of difference was how to pay for the performances, which, the committee stressed, needed orchestral accompaniment and soloists of the highest calibre to be successful. They did not consider the raising of a public subscription to pay for the performances would be successful, so there was no alternative but to charge for admission, as in the past. The committee considered they had gone out of their way to meet all other objections of the dean and chapter, and hoped that on this one remaining issue an agreement could be reached. To achieve this, they suggested that the bishop, as the spiritual head of the diocese, could be asked to adjudicate on this question – the committee knew, of course, that the bishop would be on their side.

In its lengthy reply the dean and chapter welcomed the attempt by the festival committee to go as far as possible to meet their 1874 principles, but the suggestion about making the performances part of a service did not go nearly far enough. However, under the new Act of Uniformity the bishop had considerable powers in this field, and they hoped he would be able to reach a satisfactory compromise. They suggested that on each of the first three days a 'grand

Rt Rev. Henry Philpott DD, 1807-92. He had a distinguished career at Cambridge, culminating in him being elected master of St Catherine's College in 1845, and he served three terms as vice-chancellor. Appointed Bishop of Worcester in 1860, his 30 years as bishop (he resigned in 1890) were generally uneventful, and it seems from the minutes of the cathedral restoration committee that he left most of the decisions to them. He disliked public life, rarely attending the House of Lords, and he must have regarded the controversy over the Festival, putting him in opposition to the dean and chapter, with distaste.

morning service' should be held, in addition to the service in which the oratorio was to be performed, which would be in the afternoon. But the dean and chapter still could not accept he committee's proposal that admission should be by paid ticket only. They thought the overall expense of the festival could be reduced, and that a public subscription could be raised, to which the dean and chapter would contribute £500. But, if a large portion of the cathedral were freely open to the public, they would agree to the remaining space being at the disposal of the committee, to be occupied, one assumes, by a paying audience, although the dean and chapter could not bring themselves to actually write this in their submission. But on this matter the dean and chapter would agree to consult with the bishop, 'should he be willing to act as a mediator between the conflicting opinions'.

In its final reply the festival committee gave these proposals a guarded welcome, excepting the public subscription to meet the festival's expenses. They gladly accepted the proposal to refer the matter to the bishop to make the final decision.

This whole correspondence occupied one and a half pages in Berrow's, and reading it now gives the impression of two dancers slowly circling each other, determined eventually to come together, but wary of getting too close too fast. The festival committee's letters do seem to bear the hallmark of Lord Hampton, who in such matters was always keen to keep the temperature of debate low, and must therefore take some of the credit for the eventual reinstatement of the Worcester festivals. He must have regretted it when, after the dean caused the correspondence to be published in the Worcester papers without informing Lord Beauchamp, who was in London, Beauchamp rather abruptly demanded that the dean apologise.

The festival committee and the dean and chapter met the bishop on 22nd December, and a week later the bishop's ruling was published. He decided that the oratorios should be preceded and followed by prayers, but circumstances dictated that these should not be too long. The public would be admitted freely to the special services on the first morning, the early morning ones on the next two days, and the grand final service on Friday evening, as both the dean and chapter and committee had wished. He continued 'in regard to the remaining part of the question which respects the mode of admission to the oratorios, I am satisfied to find that there is, in my opinion, no real difference in principle in the proposals made by the two bodies'. Paying for the expenses by public subscription or paid admission ticket were, the bishop considered two sides of the same coin. So he determined that all seats in the nave, nave aisles and transepts should be reserved for subscribers with every seat numbered. The bishop avoided the use of the words 'ticket' and 'pay', but this is what it really amounted to. He also specified that the whole of the cathedral east of the tower would be placed at the disposal of the dean and chapter to admit persons at their discretion – presumably this would be the free seating.

As soon as this judgement was published both sides were quick to accept it, so plans could be made for the festival. The only fly in the ointment was the continuing opposition of the Earl of Dudley, who wrote to The Guardian newspaper (which had supported the dean and chapter) strongly opposing the bishop's award. His letter was published in Berrow's. He attacked the dean and chapter for, as he saw it, changing their mind on what they had regarded three years ago as a matter of principle. He stuck to his view that it was against the law to charge for entry to the cathedral, and if oratorios were performed 'the building would be desecrated, because it has been consecrated and dedicated to divine worship only, and oratorios, even the grandest in subject and conception, are not a part of such service; nor, I venture to say, will they become so now, by the addition of a third collect to the proposed meagre list of opening prayers'. In any case, were oratorios really sacred music? In reality, Lord Dudley thought, they were no more than a descriptive musical rendering of a subject taken from scripture. The festival should return to its roots, Lord Dudley thought, and promote services with some of the best church music, with organ accompaniment only. This form had been used in 1875 and was eminently successful in attracting large congregations, and larger than usual gifts to the charity.

But the tide of opinion was too strong for Lord Dudley to attract much support, and the stage was set for a return, at least as far as the music was concerned, to the festivals of former times.

On 2nd November 1877 Lord Hampton attended the annual meeting of Saltley College, as he had done most years since its foundation in 1852. He said he was particularly pleased that Lord Lyttelton was present, as his late father had been a long time supporter of the college, and although he and Lord Hampton had been on opposite sides of the political divide, "I do not remember a single work of importance connected with the welfare of their county in which it was not my happy lot always to act in the most cordial manner with Lord Lyttelton". He was also pleased that Sir Charles Adderley, who had given generously when the college was founded, had been appointed to succeed the late Lord Lyttelton as president.

Parliament opened early in 1878 due to the Russian-Turkish war, and Lord Hampton was in the House of Lords on 17th January when the Earl of Beaconsfield, as Benjamin Disraeli now was, addressed the House in the debate on the queen's speech: 'Lord B very effective & successful', he wrote. A few days later Lord Hampton was again present when the Earl of Carnarvon, the colonial secretary, explained in the House of Lords why he had resigned. Lord

The Years 1877 and 1878

Charles, 5th baron Lyttelton, 1842-1922. He was elected to represent East Worcestershire in the Liberal interest in 1868, but lost his seat in the Conservative landslide in 1874. He succeeded to the Lyttelton barony in 1876, and in 1888 he also succeeded to the viscountcy of Cobham on the death of a distant relative. Like his father and other members of his family he was a keen cricketer, and played a number of first class matches for Cambridge University. From a portrait at Hagley Hall.

Beaconsfield was concerned about the possible advance of the Russian army to Constantinople and had ordered the British fleet to the Dardanelles, although the order was later countermanded. Lord Carnarvon felt this went against our policy of neutrality in the war. Lord Hampton was not impressed by his speech – 'he entirely failed to justify his resignation', he wrote.

There are several references to Lord Hampton's finances about this time – a new family settlement was made in 1877, no doubt in preparation for Herby's marriage, but there are indications that all was not well. A rental drawn up at this time shows a rent roll of about £5,400 from the Westwood estate, and mortgages totalling over £34,000, the interest on which would have accounted for at least one quarter of his rental income. And although he had been reminded in 1877 that a mortgage from Owen Davies on his Welsh estate was due to be repaid, he must have omitted to do so, as on 19th January 'rec'd embarrassing letter from M[artin] C[urtler]' about Davies' mortgage (Curtler was Lord Hampton's Droitwich solicitor). At the same time he went to the Worcester Old Bank to see his friend John Whitmore Isaac about arranging an overdraft. But only his son, John Swinton Isaac was available, and Lord Hampton had a 'short and not satisfactory talk' with him. Lord Hampton managed to see Mr Isaac senior in February, when he had a 'long private talk', and an overdraft was arranged, secured on 322 acres of property including the Welsh estate, some of which was already charged.

On Saturday 26th January 1878 Lord Hampton travelled to Worcester with Lord Beauchamp for a meeting of the festival stewards' committee. Now agreement had been reached everyone was doing their upmost to ensure a successful

LORD HAMPTON

festival, and Berrow's reported that the list of stewards this year 'will be even more influential and numerous than in the past'.

While in Worcester, Lord Hampton had a long talk with Martin Curtler about 'Mr P.'s affairs' – this was a reference to Johnny. After his wife had died Johnny was reported as staying in Folkestone with his late wife's brother Lord Glasgow and his wife, and intended to stay until the summer. But at the beginning of May he was back at Kings End, still with the Glasgows, and made a few public appearances during that month. But soon after that his descent into mental illness became more apparent, and he does not seem to have been at his brother's wedding in August, and he was absent from a function on 19th December 1877 through illness. In the same month a letter from the Kent Co-operative art studios shows that he had failed to pay for some work he had commissioned for Kings End, and his father had to settle the account. Lord Hampton discussed a new will with Curtler, which was to exclude Johnny from being an executor. After leaving Worcester Lord Hampton did not travel to London, but instead went to Bath, where Johnny was under medical care.

His late wife's niece Eleanor Pratt had come to stay again, and she soon became Lord Hampton's companion at church on Sundays, special occasions in the House of Lords, or evening social events.

The civil service commission was not only responsible for admissions to the civil service, but also the army, and on 7th February there is the first mention in his diary of a scheme to assess a young man's physical qualities in addition to sitting a written exam. The following day Lord Hampton was in the House of Lords, where Lord Derby made a statement about our fleet being ordered to Constantinople. While there he engaged the Duke of Cambridge, still the army commander-in-chief, in conversation, telling him about the new army entry proposals, and, Lord Hampton wrote, 'HRH much pleased'. There was a further conference about this a few days later, and Lord Hampton examined the head of gymnastics at Aldershot as well as the Woolwich riding superintendent so as to incorporate these subjects into the new tests.

Lord Hampton's birthday was on 20th February, and he wrote, as he had in the past, 'Birthday 79! Very thankful for being so well and active now I'm entering my 80th year'. On Saturday he travelled to Worcester for a meeting of the festival stewards. So far 132 had been appointed stewards, and about seventy were present. The meeting was addressed by Lord Beauchamp, who said the finances of the festival needed careful consideration. The grand services would be free, and some parts of the cathedral reserved for the dean and chapter, so careful budgeting would be required. Each steward had guaranteed five guineas towards any loss, and as far as he could see the festival would be solvent as long as this guarantee could be called on. He also noted the much increased cost of the prestigious soloists. William Done was confirmed as the conductor – he had been cathedral organist since 1844, and would continue in that post until 1895 when he died aged 80. The bishop had accepted the presidency, and the patronage of the Queen and Prince of Wales was being sought.

A good executive committee was needed, and this was elected, to include Lord Hampton.

After dealing with some estate business and having another talk with Martin Curtler about his own and his son's affairs, he returned to London on Tuesday evening, and in the office the following day had another conference about the new tests for army recruits – 'gave up putting shot', he noted. On Sunday, out walking by Hyde Park with Eleanor, they 'saw crowd assembled for political meeting'. This was a demonstration against the possibility of war with Russia, led by Auberon Herbert, the brother of Lord Carnarvon. He had begun life as a Conservative, but had become increasingly radicalised, opposing state activity in many fields, and was, according to the Dictionary of National Biography, a neo-anarchist and bohemian. In fact the 'peace party', according to a report in The Times, were very greatly outnumbered by the 'war party', and its leaders were forcibly removed from the Park, and a certain amount of fighting took place.

Despite now being in his 80th year, Lord Hampton kept up his constant activity in London – for example on 13th March: 'Governors of Wellington College meet at Marlborough House. Office afterwards, then council of I[nstitute of] N[aval] A[rchitects] at 4 to arrange programme for annual meeting. I dined with Eustace Cecils – took Eleanor to Lady Porchester'. Lt Col Eustace Gascoyne-Cecil was Surveyor General of Ordnance, and brother of the future prime minister the 3rd Marquis of Salisbury.

At the end of that week he travelled to Worcester for a meeting of the festival executive committee. They wished to book Madame Emma Albani, but her agent's terms were 'outrageous'. However, only wanting the best, a large majority voted in favour of engaging her. On Sunday he had some estate matters to deal with – from his diary entry it seems that he was thinking of giving up his 250 acre home farm and letting it out. When he told the present farm manager, James Nisbet, he was keen to take it.

On Monday, before leaving for London, he had another talk with Martin Curtler about his Johnny's affairs, and followed this by writing a 'strong' second letter to him about 'F T'. Whatever or whoever 'F T' may have stood for, it is clear that relations between Lord Hampton and his sick son were not good at this time.

On Tuesday he attended the annual dinner at Willis's Rooms of the Princess Mary's Cottage Homes, attended by the Prince of Wales and Duke of Cambridge. Princess Mary, Duchess of Teck, was a granddaughter of George III, and mother

Marie-Louise-Emma-Cécile Lajeunesse (1847?-1930) was born to a musical family in Canada. After the death of her mother the family moved to New York, where she continued her musical studies. She then went to Paris, and finally Messina, where she adopted the name Emma Albani. She made her successful opera debut as a soprano there, and first came to London in 1872, where she sang Amina in La Sonambula at Covent Garden. She soon became an international celebrity, performing regularly in London, the USA and elsewhere until she retired in 1911. The 1878 festival was her first of many appearances in Worcester, and excited much interest.

of Queen Mary, wife of George V. The homes had been established in 1871 to look after daughters of persons convicted of crime and for 'the class of children found in the criminal haunts of the metropolis'. After the usual toasts the Prince of Wales, who seems to have been well briefed, explained that the homes were conducted on the group system, with separate houses holding ten to twelve girls, each managed by a widow, the 'mother' of the family. The institution provided general and 'industrial' education and seems to have been successful, and he said that recently Princess Mary had been unable to induce a lady who took a girl out of the laundry six months ago to part with her, so great a treasure was she. The homes held about 180 girls at that time, but had room for more, and it was hoped that those present that evening would be able to the furnish additional funds necessary to provide for these. On Saturday Lord Hampton was again at Willis's Rooms, at a grand dinner hosted by James McGarel Hogg, chairman of the metropolitan board of works. Hogg had been chairman since 1870, and would remain until its abolition in 1889, but his final years there were touched by scandal with corruption in the board's lower ranks. It was claimed that the board was 'divided between clever knaves who jobbed, and virtuous nobodies who winked'! Hogg was in the latter category. Lord Hampton still had time to take Eleanor to Lady Stanhope's party after the dinner.

The Years 1877 and 1878

A few days later Lt Col Charles Pratt, Eleanor's brother, came to stay for a few days – his elder brother John, 3rd Marquess Camden, had died young, leaving his young son John, Eleanor's nephew, as his heir.

The nation had been shocked by a maritime tragedy that had occurred on 24th March, and as usual a fund was rapidly established for the dependents of those lost. HMS Eurydice was a thirty year old frigate that, after seeing active service, had served for several years as a stationary training ship. Then in 1877 she had been refitted for sea-going service as a training ship, and on returning from a three months' tour of the West Indies had run into a severe snow storm off the Isle of Wight, and foundered with the loss of all but two of the 319 hands aboard. On 1st April the Eurydice Fund Committee met at the House of Lords, and Lord Hampton served as chairman until the arrival of the Duke of Cambridge. At the annual meeting of the Institute of Naval Architects the following week Lord Hampton, in his presidential address, referred to the 'dreadful loss' but refrained from making any comment about the cause. Some blamed the Eurydice's shallow draft, as she had been built for service in shallow waters, reducing her stability.

An illustration in the Illustrated London News showing divers on the wreck of HMS Eurydice.

LORD HAMPTON

Lord Hampton's attendance at dinners and parties left only a few evenings free for theatre or opera going, but on 6th April he was able to see the new play 'Diplomacy' by the prolific French author Victorien Sardou, adapted for the English stage from his original 'Dora'. Although The Times' critic thought the play was rather prolix, he concluded his review by calling it 'one of the cleverest, most agreeable and finished performances on our stage for many a day'.

On Good Friday Lord Hampton travelled back to Worcestershire, finding the holy day train service 'tiresome', and the next day had yet another long conference with Martin Curtler about his son's situation. He wanted to put his house in Powick, Kings End, up for sale, but there were 'doubts' about the sale – possibly legal problems. Later that day he attended another festival committee meeting – again there were problems: 'aspect of affairs unpleasant, and suggested difficulties would be interposed by chapter' he noted in his diary. But there is no record of any further difficulties coming from the dean and chapter.

Back in London on Easter Monday, he visited the office on Tuesday, then spent two nights at Ickwell Bury in Bedfordshire, the seat of the Harvey family. Returning to London on Thursday, he hosted a small dinner party at home, and the following Monday finalised his report on the new physical tests to enter the army. He had written to Lord Stanley, younger brother of the 15th Earl of Derby and war secretary, about these new tests, and Stanley's reply stated that he entirely shared Lord Hampton's views on the matter.

The next day he went to Her Majesty's Theatre to hear the American soprano Minnie Mauk in The Barber of Seville. Lord Hampton described her as 'good soprano and fair singer'. Later in the week he went to Guildford to spend some time with his niece Annette Bush (see above, page 219) and her two daughters, then in their 20s. The following day he took the train to Bath to dine with Johnny and the doctor who was caring for him, Dr John Wilson. On Sunday he does not seem to have seen Johnny, going to the service at Bath Abbey, and on Monday returned home to Westwood. There he had yet another long talk with his solicitor Martin Curtler about Johnny, and in the afternoon discussed the festival plans with Canon Wood and J Whitmore Isaac. As the House of Lords was still in the Easter recess Lord Hampton took his wife to stay in Brighton for two nights – one objective was to look for rooms for Johnny in Cliftonville. In the afternoon they went to the aquarium. 'Much amused – sea lions, king crabs, Japanese salamander and diving ducks very interesting'.

The House of Commons had resumed its sittings on 6th May, and on 9th the Civil Service estimates were under discussion. Richard O'Shaunessy, MP for Limerick, used the occasion to mount another attack on the appointment of Lord Hampton as first civil service commissioner. The commission's expenditure had increased by twenty five per cent in the last three years, which he put down

The Years 1877 and 1878

to the need to appoint a third commissioner to strengthen the department after the appointment of 76 year old Lord Hampton, who had no experience in the department. Lewis Dillwyn, MP for Swansea, seconded the motion, saying that Lord Hampton's appointment 'was one of the worst political jobs perpetrated of late' – 'jobbing' meant something corrupt.

Sir Henry Selwin-Ibbetson, a treasury under-secretary, defended Lord Hampton's appointment, pointing out that the system of open competition to enter the civil service, because of which the department had needed to be strengthened, had been agreed by the whole House. He continued:

> With regard to the attack which has been made upon the first commissioner, I feel bound to say that Lord Hampton occupies an exceptional position, and that there is hardly any public servant who devotes more time and attention to the duties of his office. True, his Lordship is advanced in years; but a good many right hon. gentlemen who have done service to the state were in the same position, and I am convinced that there are few public servants who bring so much power to bear upon the performance of the duties of his office as the noble Lord.

But the criticisms continued, and were concluded by a cutting remark from Alexander MacDonald, MP for Stafford, who called it a 'form of out-door relief to aged statesmen by giving them a living out of the public funds'. Nevertheless the government made sure they won the division, having a majority of ten.

The Brighton Aquarium was designed by the engineer Eugenius Birch (1818-84), who was mainly famous for the fourteen piers he constructed around Britain's coasts. The sea-front aquarium was entered through a clock tower, and the sea water tanks were arranged either side of a long corridor.

(Right) the opening on 10th August 1872 – the columns are of marble and granite. (Below) The distinctive clock tower was demolished in the 1920s, when extensive alterations were made.

LORD HAMPTON

Lord Hampton was still much taken up with his report on admission to the army, and on 21st May the subject was raised in the House of Lords by Earl Fortescue. In reply, Lord Hampton said he had concluded that the present system laid too much emphasis on mental attributes, and thought that physical ones should also be included. On 7th June he moved for the publication of the report, as he said that various incorrect versions were circulating. In reply, Viscount Bury, the under secretary for war, said the government had no objection to its publication, as long as it was understood that this did not imply acceptance of its recommendations by the government. He thought the standards set were very high, and a young man he had recently discussed it with had said "If that is to be the standard, I would rather take Greek!". The Duke of Cambridge also spoke, and wondered whether the plan would not put at a disadvantage young men from poor backgrounds who might not have had the chance to practice the various physical skills that were demanded. No decision would be made without the most careful consideration, and even then the Duke was not sure an unobjectionable plan could be arranged.

Lord Hampton wrote in his diary: 'I spoke well, and well supported by Lords Grey, Fortescue, & others, and motion granted, but I do not think government will carry out report'. No doubt he had recognised a lack of enthusiasm from Viscount Bury and the Duke of Cambridge. In fact the report recommended that the candidates be examined on three of six exercises: riding, walking, running, leaping, swimming and gymnastics. The report did not specify the exact level of achievement to be expected in these, but did quote a recommendation from a

Prince George, Duke of Cambridge, (1819-1904) was the only son of Adolphus Frederick, youngest son of George III, and therefore cousin to Queen Victoria. Born and brought up in Hanover, at the age of 18 he started a long career in the British army. During the early part of the Crimean war he saw action, but deteriorating health led to his returning home. In 1856 he succeeded Lord Hardinge as commander-in-chief, and so remained until he was persuaded to retire in 1895. He acted as military adviser to Sir John Pakington and other secretaries of state for war.

Colonel Hammersley and a Mr Bowen, and these standards seem quite high for a young man not specifically in training. A mile, for example, should be walked in a maximum of 10 minutes, and in only 8½ to gain maximum marks, and the same distance run in a maximum of 5½ minutes, and in 5 minutes for maximum marks.

For the Whitsun weekend Lord Hampton went to a country house party given by Sir Henry Ibbetson, at his newly rebuilt seat Down Hall in Essex. The highlight seems to have been a 14 mile trip on the 'drag', a type of private stage coach, sitting part of the way on the roof, with the grooms inside. The music provided in the evening, with a young lady violinist must have been a relaxing contrast. Lord Hampton returned to London on Tuesday, and in the evening attended the annual dinner of the Merchant Taylors School, where he replied to the toast to her majesty's ministers; 'no ministers being there, I was called upon to return thanks for government – I spoke well and much complimented'.

The next weekend Lord Hampton returned to Westwood, and yet again discussed his son's affairs and the problems with the sale of Kings End. The next week in London he hosted two dinner parties at home, and on Friday 21st June: 'Herby & Evelyn's first baby born at 5 a.m. All right in every respect except that I should have preferred a boy. But I am too thankful for a good time and a healthy child & I think of this. All in good time.'

The next Monday a matter came up in the House of Lords that Lord Hampton felt strongly about, causing him to vote against the government. An act of 1876 had given powers to poor law guardians to reclaim from Friendly Societies money due to the dependants of a pauper, but this was now felt to have been a mistake, and a short bill was introduced to repeal this part of the act. But some speakers felt this went against the principle of the Poor Law, which was that relief should only be given in cases of destitution, and if the pauper had relief owing his family, why should these not be used first? On that occasion the amendment was defeated by a single vote, but when the bill came up for its third reading a few days later, another attempt was made to restrict the guardians' access to friendly society funds to those of pauper lunatics only. On this occasions 'amendment against it carried by majority of 19 against government. I voted and spoke against it. 20 Conservative peers voted against it, and others stayed away'. But the change was later reversed in the House of Commons, and peers chose not to attempt to change it again.

On the same day Lord Hampton's niece Florence Bushe came to stay, and he took her to the Royal Academy soirée in the evening. On Saturday they went together to the aquarium, where they saw a whale, a mermaid and a gazelle, and in the evening to Beethoven's Fidelio. Florence left on Monday 'having made a very favourable impression during her visit'.

LORD HAMPTON

There is no sign from his diary that Lord Hampton's pace of life was getting any slower, although even he recognised that he crammed much into a day. He recorded Saturday 13th July thus:

> Interesting but hard day. At 12 attended meeting at Marlborough House by invitation by P of W to consider college of music. At request of HRH I opened the discussion, after memo'm had been read. Lasted 1 1/2 hours, home to luncheon. At 5 Madre and I attended garden party at Marlborough House, to meet queen. H M very gracious to me. Brilliant party, perfect weather, beautiful sight. Lord Granville brought me message from P of W that he hoped that I would take leading part about college of music – HRH afterwards spoke to me to same effect. After dinner at home I went to Bath by 9.00 train. Sat with Johnny before going to hotel to bed.

On Sunday, as with his earlier visit to Bath, Lord Hampton seemed more interested in the Abbey and a later visit with Dr Wilson to Claverton Down to see the militia, than talking to Johnny. The proposed college of music dated back to a proposal by the late Prince Consort to establish a national free college. After a long delay a National Training School for Music was established in fairly modest premises in 1876. But this did not flourish, and a merger with the Royal Academy of Music was muted. Despite his limited involvement in music (in a purely amateur capacity) Lord Hampton was appointed a director of the Royal Academy of Music in 1878. He had also been present at an earlier meeting in June 1875 at Marlborough House under the chairmanship of the Prince of Wales about a possible new music college. Following the meeting on 13th July, Lord Hampton attended another meeting the following Tuesday at Spencer House with Prince Christian, the Prince of Wales' brother-in-law, in the chair, and the new committee drafted a letter to the Royal Academy about a possible merger.

A week later Lord Hampton presided at a meeting of the Royal Academy to consider the matter. 'Rather anxious affair, but I was well satisfied with result. I moved resolution in conciliatory and successful speech – their resolution after strong and able opposition by principal MacFarren was carried by 10 to 4 – so was second for amalgamation – third for committee nem con'. However, MacFarren was determined not to surrender the Academy's independence, and on December 13th Lord Hampton noted: 'Attended meeting of directors of Royal Academy of Music & presided to consider surrender of charter – Duke of Edinburgh moved surrender – we were beaten by 12 to 8'.

Earlier in the week Lord Hampton was among those who welcomed the prime minister back to London: 'At 4 joined party at Charing X station to welcome Lord Beaconsfield & Lord Salisbury on return from Berlin. Extraordinary scene – Lord B looked ill and fatigued but much gratified'. Beaconsfield and his foreign secretary Salisbury were thought to have successfully defended and even

The Years 1877 and 1878

Very well known in his day, Sir George Alexander Macfarren (1813-87) wrote his first compositions while still a teenager studying at the Royal Academy of Music. After filling various teaching posts, he was appointed music director at Covent Garden in 1844. He was a prolific composer, working in all genres including several operas, of which Robin Hood (1860) was the most successful. While composing Robin Hood his eye-sight, never good, failed completely, but he continued composing with the aid of an amanuensis. Lord Hampton was present at the first performance of his oratorio 'Resurrection' in Birmingham in 1876, the year after he had been elected principal of the Royal Academy of Music, and professor of music at Cambridge University.

increased British interests at the Congress held after the end of the Russian-Ottoman war, at which the map of the Balkans was redrawn. Beaconsfield was increasingly suffering periods of ill health, but still found his personal involvement with European statesmen gratifying.

Two days later the prime minister reported his achievements in the House of Lords. Lord Hampton noted: 'Most interesting night in H of Lords. Lord Beaconsfield made promised statement, House crowded in every part – admirable speech'. On 27th July Beaconsfield and Salisbury's return was marked by a magnificent banquet for them given in the Duke of Wellington's riding school in Knightsbridge. This was the largest suitable venue to be found in London, but even so The Times reported that many more than the 500 who attended would have come, had their been more places. The Duke of Buccleuch presided, and as the guests took their seats at 7.30 p.m. the band played 'See the Conquering Hero Comes'. Lord Hampton, of course, was there – in the afternoon he had driven out with his wife to see the preparations.

But the grandest tribute to Lords Beaconsfield and Salisbury was on Saturday 3rd August, when they were presented with the freedom of the City of London. Large crowds lined the route from Downing Street and from Charing Cross where Salisbury's landau joined the prime minister's, and they then proceeded to the Guildhall, looking splendid in their dark blue levée dress braided with gold. Flags and banners, some bearing the motto 'Peace with Honour', lined the

LORD HAMPTON

route, and an immense crowd, swollen by excursion trains, had already seen the other notables, including Lord Hampton, arrive. There was then a tremendous cheer when Beaconsfield and Salisbury arrived. Inside over one thousand were assembled, and the various London Corporation officials, all in their full dress robes, went through the ancient ceremony, which The Times wrote went back to Anglo-Saxon times, of bestowing the freedom of the city. Lord Hampton noted:

> At 4 p.m. drove to Guildhall and attended interesting and exciting scene of presentation of freedom of city to Lord Beaconsfield and Lord Salisbury. Immense attendance in the noble old hall and great enthusiasm – after ceremony went to aldermen's rooms, with platform party for tea &c – then proceeded to Mansion House and attended dinner given by Lord Mayor to ministers.

On 24th July Lord Hampton attended the first opera he had seen that year, Bellini's 'Sonnambula'. He wanted to hear the Hungarian soprano Etelka Gerster, then making a name for herself in London; he was 'much pleased'. He

Lord Beaconsfield (in lighter costume) and Salisbury (with darker jacket behind) being greeted at Charing Cross when they arrived from Dover on 16th July 1878. The lord mayor can be seen with his chain of office. The station was decorated with flags and flowers, and large crowds lined the route thence to Downing Street, where the prime minister said he had brought "peace, but, I hope, peace with honour".

The Years 1877 and 1878

Lord Beaconsfield receiving the freedom of the City of London on 3rd August 1878 in the Guildhall.

was still a regular attender at the House of Lords, and twice at this time wrote that there was a 'shindig' (in the sense of a lively exchange). On 23rd July Lord Camperdown raised a question to do with the acquisition of Cyprus, and what the financial arrangements were. The prime minister admitted that the negotiations had been kept secret, and said everything would be revealed in due course, but Viscount Cardwell accused him of answering a different question to the one that had been put, and this led to a lively exchange. A short while later on 26th Lords Carnarvon and Bath made 'spiteful' speeches about a secret memorandum alleged to have been made between the foreign secretary and Count Schouvalov, the Russian statesman.

Having chaired the executive and finance committee of the Patriotic Fund for three years, Lord Hampton decided it was time to hand over to someone else, and at a meeting of the commissioners on 25th July announced his resignation as chairman. He was to remain on the committee, but did not attend their next meeting on 31st July, when the new chairman, Admiral Hamilton, proposed the following resolution:

> The committee desire to express their sincere regret on losing Lord Hampton as their chairman. They desire to record their sense of the valuable aid they have derived from his presidency, and at the same time to express their satisfaction

in knowing that he will continue as a member of the committee, and that his careful counsel and sound judgement will still be available to them.

Lord Hampton's involvement with the committee did not end, and later in the year he went to Wandsworth to inform the matron of the girls school, Miss Holland, of her dismissal. The committee had had doubts about her ability for many months, but kept postponing a decision. One matter that seems to have sealed her fate was an unaccountable shortage of summer stockings for the girls. Miss Holland thought they might have been disposed of accidentally as rags, but in November the secretary had a cupboard in the clothes store opened, for which the key had been lost. Inside were found 533½ pairs of stockings! The £30 that had been spent on buying replacements had therefore been wasted. Lord Hampton was present when candidates for her position were interviewed on 4th December, and he proposed the appointment of Mrs Annie Puckett.

Early August marked the end of the London season, and the day before the Guildhall and Mansion House ceremonies Lady Hampton and the servants went to Westwood. Lord Hampton, however, stayed first for these ceremonies, then also to attend to a crisis in the office, when it came to light that a secretary, Woolley, had been guilty of misconduct. A committee, headed by Sir Spencer Robinson, was appointed to look into charges of crim[inal] con[versation] – (adultery), the improper dismissal of an assistant, and the use of the office for improper purposes.

Lord Hampton stayed in London for Lord Redesdale's traditional House of Lords dinner at The Trafalgar Tavern at Greenwich on 7th August, having a 'beautiful passage home in steamboat', then the next day met his nieces Eleanor and Mary Pratt at Paddington, and took them back to Westwood. There he found his wife 'very poorly'. In July she seems to have been better than usual, having driven out to see the preparations at the Duke of Wellington Riding School, and

The riverside Trafalgar Tavern was built in 1837. The first political meeting was held in July 1846 by the protectionist Conservatives shortly after the party split over repeal of the corn laws, but Lord Hampton was not present, busy in a select committee before joining his wife on holiday at Dover. The cabinet hold 'whitebait dinners' there to this day.

on 20th she accompanied her husband to see the newly erected monument to the Duke of Wellington in St Paul's cathedral. The following day she made what seems to have been a fairly rare visit to church with him. But by 15th August she was well enough to accompany her husband and the Pratt girls to a flower show at Hanbury Hall.

Lord Hampton's late summer sojourn in Worcestershire was busy, and on his first day back he drove to Cutnall Green for a 'school feast'; after dinner back home he drove with the Pratts in an open carriage to Hanbury Hall to a party of Free Foresters where they enjoyed cricket and 'beautiful glees'. The week was rounded off by a meeting of the festival committee on Saturday. The following Monday Lord Hampton presided at a meeting of the Severn Navigation Commissioners, which had been called to consider the effect on the Severn of the proposed new lake at Vyrnwy to supply Liverpool with water. The Vyrnwy was a tributary of the Severn, therefore any water diverted to Liverpool would reduce the flow lower down. The engineer, Leader Williams, did not however think this would interfere with the navigation over the forty miles from Stourport to Gloucester controlled by the commission. It was suggested that the Vyrnwy scheme would lessen the flooding, as flood water could be used to raise the level of the new reservoir. However, some people thought the reduced flow in the estuary, which was controlled by the Gloucester and Sharpness Canal Company, might cause more silting. It was hoped that this company would co-operate with the Severn Commissioners to jointly study the effects, and Lord Hampton expressed the view that, whether or not they agreed to co-operate, the possible effects of the scheme were so serious that an investigation should take place in any case.

The next day, Tuesday, Lord Hampton had planned to travel to Portsmouth to see the grand naval review, but bad weather prevented this. At the end of the week Johnny came up to Westwood for the day accompanied by Dr Wilson. 'Mr P seemed much the same, but increased in size', his father noted. No doubt prompted by this visit, the next day Lord Hampton had another long talk with Martin Curtler about his son's situation.

On 27th August Lord Hampton attended the festivities at Hewell Grange to mark the coming of age of Robert George Lord Windsor. He was the grandson of Harriet Clive, Baroness Windsor, the daughter of Other Hickman Windsor, 5th Earl of Plymouth of the second creation. In 1905 he would become 1st Earl of Plymouth of the third creation. The family had large estates around Bromsgrove, and also at Oakley Park near Ludlow in Shropshire, and St Fagan's Castle near Cardiff, and celebrations were held at those places as well. Two hundred and fifty guests sat down to the dinner in a marquee, and Lord Hampton proposed a toast to the family. On returning to Westwood, he found Herby, Evelyn and their baby had arrived, as well as Col and Mrs Davies, the daughter and son-in-law of his sister Elizabeth, and they all sat down to a late dinner.

The next day most of the party visited Bell Hall in Belbroughton, the home of the Noel family, for a meeting of the archery society, and then returned to Hewell for a garden party attended by many tenants as well as family friends. Lord Hampton stayed the night, and the following evening saw the firework display that marked the end of the week's celebrations from an upstairs window of the house. The week ended by Lord Hampton chairing another festival committee meeting, at which it was reported that the bass singer Signor Foli (actually born in Ireland as Alan Foley, but he later Italianised his name) had dropped out of the festival through indisposition. He was replaced by Sir Charles Santley, a regular festival performer.

As usual, Lord Hampton had assembled a house party to join him in attending the Three Choirs Festival, which took place on 10th to 13th, Tuesday to Friday, September. The party consisted of Lady Ducie, wife of the Lord Lieutenant of Gloucestershire, the Dean of Hereford, George Herbert, and his wife, Sir George and Lady Baker and their daughter Alice, and Herby and Evelyn (Alice's sister), as well as the two Pratt girls.

Lord Hampton had carefully prepared for the festival, taking lodgings in Worcester to supplement Westwood, and he and his party attended the opening

Robert Windsor-Clive, 1857-1923. He was the son of Hon. Robert Windsor-Clive, MP for Ludlow, then South Shropshire, who had died in 1859 aged only 35, and Lady Mary Bridgeman, daughter of the Earl of Bradford. He inherited an estate of 37,000 acres in Glamorgan, Shropshire, and Worcestershire, and was proprietor of three stately homes: St Fagan's Castle, Cardiff, Oakly Park, Ludlow, and Hewell Grange in Tardebigge, Worcestershire. Succeeding as 14th Baron Windsor in 1869, he was an active Tory in the House of Lords, and served as first commissioner of works in 1902-05, helping to transform the Mall with the new Victoria Monument. An amateur artist and fine art expert, he served on many museum and gallery committees.

service on Tuesday morning. As had happened before, the corporations of the three cities together with many other guests attended a breakfast in the Shire Hall at the invitation of the mayor, then, wearing their robes of office, formed a procession down the High Street to the cathedral. The opening service, following the agreement between the festival committee and the dean and chapter, was open to all without charge, although the seats in the nave and aisles were reserved in advance, and the cathedral was full to over-flowing. Unlike the 'mock festival' of three years previously, a full orchestra was engaged, and, again in deference to the dean and chapters' wishes, instead of performing, with the choir, on a large raised platform at the west end, they occupied a much lower platform just to bring it up to the level of the choir, in the crossing.

A full cathedral service, which included Handel's Dettingen Te Deum, with an orchestra was somewhat novel, and the Berrow's' reporter spotted details where there was some confusion about the arrangements, perhaps not surprising in view of the large numbers who had to be rehearsed in the limited time. He also thought the new position of the orchestra and chorus was not so good acoustically as the previous one. All Lord Hampton's party attended except for his wife. He must have been proud that his efforts to complete the cathedral restoration, followed by the battles of 1874 and 1877 to save the festival, had now led to this festival in the magnificent restored cathedral. Despite the imperfections of the opening service he seemed pleased: 'very fine service and good sermon from bishop' he noted. In the evening a more traditional festival concert was given in the cathedral: part of Haydn's Creation, Mozart's Requiem Mass, and Mendelssohn's Hymn of Praise.

Wednesday morning was devoted to a performance of Mendelssohn's Elijah. Lord Hampton noted the new position of the orchestra, and the addition of prayers before and after the performances, without comment. The following morning there was a performance of Dr Philip Armes' new oratorio Hezekiah, which was given a mostly favourable review by Berrow's, although noted without comment by Lord Hampton. Mendelssohn's Hear my Prayer, and Spohr's The Last Judgement completed the performances.

Friday was Messiah day, but Lord Hampton's only comment concerns an old lady, Mrs Alison Hartshorne. He had gone to see her with Canon Wood in August: 'wonderful sight – she completed 100 years last July. Her sight is defective and she is rather deaf, but healthy, active and intelligent'. It was the custom for leading figures to hold the collection plates at the cathedral doors at the end of the performances, and on Friday he saw Mrs Hartshorne again – she 'attended the performance, as she did on Tuesday, and put a sovereign on my plate at the door (I had held a plate each day), saying "I have kept a piece for you"'. She died in June 1879, just short of her 101st birthday.

LORD HAMPTON

Lord Hampton made no mention of the event on Friday evening, a grand orchestral service to conclude the festival. The next morning he noted that he was 'rather tired by week's work and excitement', but still managed to call on the canons, presumably to thank them for the festival, but only found the dean and Mrs Yorke in residence. It is interesting to note that Lord Lyttelton, who had succeeded his father in 1876, was prominent at festival events, but there is no sign that the Earl of Dudley visited Worcester during festival week.

On Monday the following week Lord Hampton presented the prizes at the Royal Worcester Grammar School. This would normally have been done at the end of the summer term, but his engagements in London led to it being postponed till the beginning of the autumn term. The headmaster was Rev. Francis Eld, and after lunching with the Elds he gave a short speech, in which he said how glad he was to see such an ancient foundation still in existence. The school had recently started charging fees, but Lord Hampton said he was pleased to find that this had not affected numbers. He praised the fact that the school had recently opened a chemistry laboratory, and also said how much he admired the new building along the Tything that had been erected ten years before. This is now called the Eld Hall.

The monument to Lord Lyttelton, designed by Sir Gilbert Scott and sculpted by James Forsyth, who had also carved the new pulpit, was now complete. On Saturday 21st September Lord Hampton presided at a ceremony in the north transept at which the monument was handed over to the dean and chapter. In his address Lord Hampton referred to the nearby monument to Bishop Hough by Roubilliac, but the monument was later moved to the lady chapel, probably to be a partner for the similar monument to the Earl of Dudley.

A week later, as well as two more of his Pratt nieces, Lord Hampton had a visit from George Murray, a nephew of his second wife Augusta. One of the local attractions was John Corbett's new house just north of Droitwich, then called Impney Manor (see page 197). Lord Hampton made no comment about the house after he had 'lionized' it with Murray – it could not have been pleasant for him to see such a prominent sign so close to Droitwich of a man who had now surpassed him both in wealth and as an MP.

The Years 1877 and 1878

Rev. Francis Eld MA, headmaster of the Royal Worcester Grammar School from 1860 to 1893. In 1860 the school occupied poor premises near St Swithin's church, but under Eld's direction it moved to its present site on the Tything in 1868. The buildings were designed by Abraham Perkins, the cathedral restoration architect. It had been given a charter by Queen Elizabeth, but it had long been over-shadowed by the Worcester Cathedral King's School, founded in 1541. Various new schemes for the schools were put forward by the charity commissioners in the second half of the C19th, including a merger, but Eld fought to remain independent and to raise the level of its teaching, introducing more modern and scientific subjects into the curriculum. Uncertainty as to its future kept pupil numbers low (around 50) during Eld's time, but once its future was settled in 1893 there were soon over 100 boys at the school.

(Below) The monument to Lord Lyttelton, 1817-76, now in the lady chapel in Worcester cathedral.

Chapter 13
His Last Year

On Wednesday 9th October 1878, Lord Hampton, having had two months' vacation in Worcestershire, travelled to London, and after dealing with some office matters travelled to Brighton on Friday to see Johnny at his lodgings at Dr and Mrs Wilson's house at 21 Lansdowne Place, which his father found to be a 'fashionable part of west Brighton', though now just in Hove. He only stayed till Saturday lunchtime, then travelled back to London, made some calls, and took the evening train back to Droitwich. In 'The Pakingtons of Westwood' by Humphrey and Richard Pakington there is only a brief mention of Johnny's troubles: 'after his wife's death, Johnny went completely to pieces. By the end of the year he was spending quite irresponsibly, and under threat of a law suit his father had to settle some substantial outstanding debts'. That would explain why, on 19th October, Lord Hampton went again to Martin Curtler to talk about Johnny's 'money matters' – when in London before going to Brighton, his father went to see 'Mr P's proposed new house', perhaps indicating that he was engaging in an irresponsible financial commitment. But there is no evidence that Johnny ever lived in London again.

A few days earlier Lord Hampton had attended the Michaelmas quarter sessions, and two matters came up that he spoke about. One was the new Highways Act, which transferred more power to quarter sessions to create highways boards. This had been a controversial matter for some time, as some Worcestershire parishes did not want to incur what they regarded as unnecessary expense, and continued to manage the highways themselves. One feature of the Act was that roads that had been turnpike roads were to be called 'main roads', and half their maintenance costs would be paid for out of the general county rates, rather than the local poor rate. Lord Hampton spoke in favour of the Act and the proposal to appoint a committee (to include himself) to examine the consequences for Worcestershire. He regretted the present state of affairs when half the county highways were managed by local parishes, and half by highway boards.

The other matter was a report to the court about drunkenness. Convictions for drunkenness in the county had nearly doubled between 1874 and 1877, and the report's authors considered that lax implementation of the licensing laws by the magistrates and police was at least partly to blame. They recommended that the authorities should be much stricter in granting licences. Applications for new licences should be resisted, and existing licences should only be renewed if the magistrates felt there was a need, and the licensee was of good character. Another recommendation was that the police should enquire of drunks where they had been drinking, in order to identify landlords who were too lax in serving alcohol. Lord Hampton had long been an advocate of stricter laws in this area, and, after a long-running campaign, had successfully steered a bill through parliament in 1840 tightening up the regulations regarding the establishment of beer houses, which then did not need a licence, only a permit that was automatically issued as long as certain conditions were met. He spoke in favour of adopting the report, and "was sorry to say that there could be no doubt that drunkenness was one of the great evils from which the country suffered".

A week later Lord Hampton went to Birmingham to attend a lunch given by the Birmingham Conservatives for Sir Stafford Northcote, the chancellor of the exchequer. He had arrived on Saturday and attended the annual meeting of the Saltley reformatory with the president Lord Norton, formerly Sir Charles Adderley. On Saturday evening Northcote had addressed an audience estimated at 6,000 in the Birmingham Town Hall, but Lord Hampton had not been present. At the Monday luncheon, however, he was prominent, and replied to the toast to the army and navy and reserve forces. 'I spoke well', he noted.

Two days later, on 23rd October, the annual congress of the National Association for the Promotion of Social Science opened in Cheltenham, and Lord Hampton was on the platform as the president for the year. Lord Norton gave the opening address, and spoke of the evils and expense of keeping men in prison and their families in the workhouse – there were 18,000 prisoners and 10,000 convicts at that time. He also deprecated the recent occurrence of strikes and industrial unrest – how much better it would be if arbitration was a condition of employment. The numerous 'To Let' signs visible in London were a symptom of the error of thinking that reducing production would lead to higher prices and wages; this idea was in error as the men not working were also not consuming.

The next day Lord Hampton attended the session on education, presided over by George Brodrick, the essayist and future head of Merton College, Oxford. A paper was given by Jesse Collings, the mayor of Birmingham and secretary to the National Education League, which campaigned for free secular education. He explained why he believed elementary education should be free for all, but the next speaker, Rev. W R Kennedy, described Collings' scheme as 'extravagant and unnecessary', and regarded it as a plan to get rid of all voluntary schools, thereby undermining the Church of England's still dominant role in education. Kennedy even went so far as to describe Collings' plans as 'socialistic', which provoked an angry exchange which the president had to quell. Lord Hampton did not contribute to the debate, but would have sided strongly with Rev. Kennedy. That evening he dined with the mayor, the philanthropist Baron de Ferrières, and the next morning Brodrick gave a lengthy address on education to the whole association, then addressed the education section in which he disagreed with some statistics quoted by Lord Norton. Lord Hampton attended both these sessions, indeed was on the platform for the first, held in the Ladies College. He had difficulty ascending the lengthy steps to the platform, causing him to joke that the College evidently intended to give a 'high' education to women!

He spent the weekend at Westwood, then returned to London and on to Chelmsford, from where he went to Langleys in Great Waltham, the home of John Joliffe Tufnell. Tufnell had married Eleanor Margaret Murray who was the sister of Lord Hampton's late second wife Augusta, and the occasion was the wedding of their daughter Maria Louisa to Edward Gerald Strutt.

Back in London there was time for Lord Hampton to attend the office before going to Berlioz's Damnation of Faust in the evening at Her Majesty's Theatre, and two days later visited the same theatre early to get tickets for himself and Herby for Carmen, and managed to get the last seats available. He travelled back to Westwood for the weekend, but, although his diary is blank for the next week the next weekend he was still in Westwood. He had missed the prime minister's speech on the Lord Mayor's day in the Guildhall, but having read an account in

Jesse Collings (1831-1920) was born into an artisan family in Devon, and became a partner in an ironmongery firm. He early developed an interest in education, and studied the system in the USA. He moved to Birmingham, and in 1868 he published his Outline of the American School System which led to the formation of the National Educational League. He befriended Joseph Chamberlain, and was mayor from 1878-80. He was an advocate of land reform and was associated with Joseph Arch (see p. 84), and later served as a Liberal MP.

Monday's papers he was 'delighted with Lord B's speech'. On Tuesday he travelled back to London, and on Wednesday he had a busy day, travelling down to the Wandsworth boys' asylum, then attending a meeting of the Institute of Naval Architects' council to appoint a new secretary, and finally dining with Herby and Evelyn at their house at Norfolk Crescent near Paddington Station. The next day, after lunching with Herby and Evelyn, he returned to Westwood.

During the weekend he called on his old friend Thomas Gale Curtler, now 78 and going blind. Curtler lived in Bevere House north of Worcester, and had served in many positions, notably as vice-chairman to Lord Hampton of quarter sessions for 21 years. Curtler's second wife Mary, widow of Rev. Thomas Oldham, rector of Doverdale, had died two years before, and two of his three sons from his first marriage were clergymen: Thomas Gale Curtler jun. was rector of the new church of St Stephens just north of Worcester, and William Henry had been vicar of Lympstone, Devon. His third son was Martin Curtler, the solicitor that Lord Hampton had consulted about Johnny.

On Monday the following week Lord Hampton went to Elmley Castle, previously the home of his wife and her first husband, Col Thomas Davies, but as she was indisposed Lady Hampton was unable to accompany her husband. On Tuesday there were three services in the presence of the bishop, and the harvest home dinner in a marquee at which Lord Hampton proposed the toast to the clergy and bishop of the diocese. At the end of the week he spent two nights at a house party at Eastnor Castle, then on Monday he paid a similar visit to Madresfield, and was back on Wednesday in time for the annual tenants' dinner at Westwood. Agriculture was entering the depression that was to last for the rest of the century, and Lord Hampton had decided to allow a ten per cent reduction of rent in order to try and stop tenants leaving – 'most proprietors have farms in hand', he noted.

On Saturday 30th November the household left Droitwich for London, and Lord Hampton became a regular attender at his office, which he had somewhat neglected of late. After the Congress of Berlin, Russia had been pushing forward in Afghanistan, and when Britain tried to gain similar rights, the Amir refused, in contradiction of his treaty obligations. The British government felt it had no alternative but to send in troops from India, and, partly because the use of Indian revenues needed parliamentary approval, parliament was recalled on 5th December. The Liberals opposed government policy in both houses, and Lord Hampton attended the debates in the Lords. After the debate on the queen's speech, on Monday and Tuesday there was a debate on a pro-government motion, which was opened by the secretary of state for India, the Earl of Cranbrook, in what Lord Hampton wrote was 'a very admirable speech'. Lord Halifax moved an amendment of censure in what Lord Hampton called a 'sleepy and dull' speech.

The next night the debate was wound up by the prime minister, who defended the need to 'rectify' the border between India and Afghanistan and make it more rational and easy to defend. The presence of Russians in Afghanistan, and the refusal to allow our own representation there, had made the war necessary. Lord Hampton did not contribute to the debate, but his vote helped the government achieve a 'wonderful majority' of 201 to 65. At the end of the week the House of Commons also supported the government by a large majority.

On Tuesday the following week Lord Hampton had a bad fall walking home to dinner: 'violent fall, stunned and much shaken. [Dr] Leggatt forbade my dining with small dinner party'. Lady Hampton was upset by his accident and the next day was 'faint and ill'. This 'general prostration' lasted several days, and although by the end of the year Lord Hampton had recovered well, his last entry for the year on 27th still records his wife as 'still very ill and low'. On Christmas day they gave up the usual large family dinner party, and only Herby and Evelyn came.

Lord Hampton had further medical problems after Christmas. Although the last few days of his 1878 diary are blank, it is clear from his entry on 1st January 1879 that he had been suffering from gout, and was in great pain all day. But he still managed to host a family party to welcome the New Year, and on 2nd Dr Leggatt came and commenced treatment, and agreed with Lord Hampton's theory that his bad fall had brought on the attack of gout. It soon spread to both feet, and he was confined to his bedroom for some time. He slowly recovered, and was able to attend the office on 22nd January, where 'slack attendance of the examiners' was the current problem. Very cold weather during late December and January, and some bad smogs, had not helped his recovery.

On 5th February he heard what he seems to have regarded as bad news. Florence, the daughter of his niece Annette Bushe, was engaged to a naval surgeon, Dr Wilson, who had no fortune but his pay. Wishing to get further information, Lord Hampton consulted Sir Alexander Armstrong, director general of the medical department of the navy, the next day, and was told that, although Wilson was a man of good character, his prospects were not so good, which caused Lord Hampton to conclude that the marriage was 'very imprudent'. They married in June.

The following week Lord Hampton went down to Brighton, and stayed with Dr Wilson and Johnny at Lansdowne Place. Lord Hampton was 'much pleased with house' – it is less than one hundred yards from the sea front, and is an elegant semi-detached villa. The next day was fine, and Lord Hampton sat on the pier with Dr Wilson, enjoying the sea air, and went to the aquarium. Back in London the next day, Lord Hampton heard of the 'dreadful defeat and slaughter of 24th regiment in S Africa by Zulus'. Sir Henry Bartle Freer had been appointed High

21 Lansdowne Place, Brighton, where Johnny spent some time under the care of Dr Wilson.

Commissioner of South Africa, and had been encouraged to pursue a policy of bringing our own colonies, the Boer republics, and the Zulu kingdom into a South African confederation. He wasted no time, and soon delivered an ultimatum, unauthorised by London, to the Zulu king Cetshawo, designed to provoke a war. When the king did not comply Freer instructed Lord Chelmsford to lead an invasion of Zululand, and this quickly led to the battle of Isandlwana. This was a camp set up by the army, and was left poorly defended, being intended as only a temporary base. After Chelmsford had advanced on 22nd January it was attacked by a force of 20,000 Zulus, and not only were 1,357 of the 1,768 defenders killed, but much of the stores, transport and ammunition destroyed, delaying British plans by several weeks. The next day the small British fort at Rorkes Drift was attacked, but this was heroically and famously defended.

Soon afterwards Lord Hampton passed his 80th birthday, and as usual expressed gratitude for retaining all his faculties and 'almost unbroken health'. The next day he had a birthday dinner to which 'Mr P' and Dr Wilson came from Brighton, Herby and his family, and some other relatives.

Lord Chelmsford, 1827-1905. After joining the army at 17, he rose in the ranks and served in Ireland, the Crimea, and the Indian mutiny. He remained in India till 1874, and in 1878 was appointed GOC in South Africa. After the disaster at Isandlwana the government stood by him, sending reinforcements that led later in 1879 to the defeat of the Zulus. However, Chelmsford took exception to the appointment of a superior officer, Sir Garnet Wolseley, over all southern Africa, and ended his career back home.

Sir Bartle Frere, 1815-84. Both his grandparents were MPs, and his uncle founded the Royal Geographical Society. At 19, appointed to a writership in Bombay, he had an adventurous overland journey to India. In 1851 he was appointed commissioner in the newly acquired territory of Sind, and during the Indian mutiny showed himself to be courageous and competent, saving the British government in the west. After a successful spell as governor of Bombay he returned to London in 1867 to take up a seat on the Indian Council. In 1876 Lord Carnarvon, the colonial secretary, appointed him governor of Cape Colony, to carry out his aim of uniting southern Africa in a confederation. But after Carnarvon's resignation and the disaster at Isandlwana (below) Frere's control over the whole province was reduced, and after continued criticism at home he was recalled by Gladstone in 1880.

His Last Year

The following week, on 28th February, Lord Hampton must have been disappointed to receive a letter from the war secretary Lord Stanley, ruling out the proposed new physical tests for army recruits as impractical. Later that day in the House of Lords Earl Fortescue supported the proposed scheme, but the under secretary for war, Viscount Bury, explained the reasons for the government's decision. He did not see any evidence that the young men entering the army were physically lacking, and it was his belief that intellectual superiority often went with good physical fitness.

No less a person than the Duke of Cambridge also spoke against it, which left Lord Hampton little to say, saying:

> I must acknowledge that the difficulty had been met in a fair, courteous and conciliatory spirit by the authorities and the War Office. My own conviction is that the adoption of the plan recommended by the committee would have brought about a very great practical improvement upon the present system of training those young men; and therefore I deeply regretted that the authorities at the War Office should have deemed the difficulties insuperable.

During the first week of March Lord Hampton went twice to the theatre and saw contrasting entertainments. First he took Lucy Pratt to Wagner's early opera Rienzi at Her Majesty's Theatre ('a splendid performance'), and then to Gilbert and Sullivan's HMS Pinafore with Herby. It is pleasing that he was 'much amused' by this, as the first lord, Sir Joseph Porter, is made much fun of. Indeed he is almost a caricature of Lord Hampton, as part of their careers coincide:

> I grew so rich that I was sent
> By a pocket borough into Parliament.
> I always voted at my party's call,
> And I never thought of thinking for myself at all.
> I thought so little, they rewarded me,
> By making me the ruler of the queen's navee
> Now, landsmen all, whoever you may be,
> If you want to rise to the top of the tree,
> If your soul isn't fettered to an office stool,
> Be careful to be guided by this golden rule:
> Stick close to your desks, and never go to sea
> And you all may be rulers of the queen's navee!

To be fair to Lord Hampton, although there is no record of his indulging in any maritime pursuits after his election to parliament in 1837, in his younger days he was a keen sailor and member of the Royal Yacht Club, which seems to have engendered a life-long interest in matters nautical. HMS Pinafore was Gilbert and Sullivan's first big success, and had opened in May 1878. It ran for 571 performances, and Lord Hampton saw it not long after the theatre was re-opened after redecoration in the winter of 1878/79.

In the middle of March he went to Brighton again for two nights, and on his return went to a reception at Lady Beauchamp's where he met the King and Queen of the Belgians. 'King cordial and affable in his recognition of me' Lord Hampton wrote – they had met two years previously. Leopold II later acquired some notoriety by making the Congo Basin his personal fief, but this was a few years in the future. The following week there was a debate in the House of Lords on a motion critical of the government over the Zulu war and calling for the replacement of Sir Bartle Freer as high commissioner. The government had criticised Freer for giving the Zulu king an ultimatum and then declaring war without consulting it, but the prime minister, in winding up the debate, said they still regarded Freer as the best man for the job, and no man should be condemned for making a single mistake. Lord Hampton was present, and wrote that the 'D of Richmond and Lord Skelmersdale asked me to speak, but I declined on account of my views about Freer'. One presumes from this that he did not approve of Freer, but his disapproval was not strong enough for him to side with the opposition, and his vote was one of 156 that led to the defeat of the motion with only 61 in favour.

The annual conference of the Institute of Naval Architects took place on 3rd to 5th April, and as usual Lord Hampton gave the presidential address. After noting that many of the papers to be read concerned naval armament, and giving his view that breech loading guns would eventually prove to be the most successful for naval use, he came to a personal matter. He said this was the twentieth occasion he had addressed them as president, and felt the time had come for his place to be taken by a younger man. He had seen the Institute rise from infancy to maturity, and was pleased to see it in its present very prosperous condition. However, before the conference closed Lord Hampton was persuaded to remain president for one more year.

The following week he went again to Brighton, taking the Pullman service. He stayed two nights and made no mention of Johnny in his diary, although we must presume he saw his son, but remarked on 'wonderful increase of West Brighton'. The day after he returned was Good Friday, and he took his niece Eleanor to church, and on Easter Sunday Lady Hampton joined them in church. He had intended to travel to Westwood on Easter Tuesday, but unseasonable cold weather prevented this, so he missed the opening of Salters Hall in Droitwich. Instead, he went with Eleanor to see Thomas Robertson's comedy drama 'Caste' at the Prince of Wales Theatre, and two days later with Eleanor, Ellen and Lucy Pratt to see Oliver Goldsmith's classic comedy 'She Stoops to Conquer' at the Aquarium Theatre. The following week he went with Eleanor and Sophia Amphlett to 'Ladies Battle', an adaption from the French by Thomas Robertson.

His Last Year

On 21st April Anthony Mundella again led criticism of Lord Hampton's appointment as first civil service commissioner when the civil service estimates came up in the Commons. It was the most flagrant 'job' that he had witnessed during his eleven years in the House, and he repeated the points about Lord Hampton's age, and the lack of work for the department that he had made when the estimates had come up before. Peter Rylands, MP for Burnley, joined in the attack. On this occasion, Lord Hampton was defended by Henry Selwin-Ibbetson, a treasury minister. But most of the other speakers, while all paying tribute to Lord Hampton personally, and admitting that he was 'a very young old man', did not think that it had been necessary to appoint a third commissioner, and there were also comments that the use of examinations even for junior posts was unnecessary. The House divided, and this time Lord Hampton's salary was only saved by 110 votes to 94.

To be fair to Lord Hampton, since he had recovered from his attack of gout at the end of January he had attended the office almost every day when he was in London, but he must have taken some notice of these attacks, as he noted that 'I wrote to Northcote on attack on me and offered to do whatever he and Lord Beaconsfield felt right'. But the next day he received a 'kind and satisfactory answer from Lord Northcote', and no change was made in his position.

At the end of the week Lord Hampton again attended the great annual dinner given by the chairman of the Metropolitan Board of Works, Sir James Hogg at Willis's Rooms, where the Duke of Teck headed a distinguished guest list. As well

Anthony Mundella (1825-97) had an Italian father, and the family endured poverty when his mother died young, and the Leicester hosiery trade, in which young Mundella was apprenticed, suffered a down-turn. Although he later made his fortune in the trade, he retained radical ideas all his life, embracing Chartism, but always sought to join these new ideas to the existing political set-up. Making use of new steam technology, his successful business provided good wages and conditions for its employees, and he was a firm believer in trade unionism tempered by arbitration. He also worked for educational reform, and in 1868 was elected MP for Sheffield, a seat he retained for the rest of his life.

as attending his office regularly, he went to the House of Lords most evenings, and on 29th April listened to Lord Bateman propose a motion on free trade. His motion began: 'That this House, fully recognizing the benefits which would result to the community if a system of real free trade were universally adopted, is of opinion that it is expedient in all future commercial negotiations with other countries to advocate a policy of reciprocity between all inter-trading nations'. The second part called for a parliamentary enquiry into the present depression of trade, and the part that high tariffs imposed by other countries contributed to it.

Lord Bateman said he had long been a supporter of free trade, but this country had rushed into it in the middle years of the century, whereas many of our trading partners had retained high adverse tariffs. Even our Australian and Canadian colonies had put up trading barriers against us. Lord Bateman had been in favour of the repeal of the corn laws in 1846, and he still recognised the benefits which it had brought, but in other areas he thought we should adopt a principle of 'reciprocity' in our trading relations with other countries.

The speech was long and rather rambling – Lord Bateman had made a study of the subject for some years and introduced many figures showing that our imports now exceeded our exports. Lord Hampton's comment was that he 'made a sad mess of it' – he would probably have supported the motion, but the prime minister's speech ended any hope of a division. He said that the opinion of the country and the composition of the House of Commons meant that no return to protection was conceivable, and for that reason 'reciprocity' was impossible as we had no negotiating position. As to a parliamentary enquiry, the prime minister was also against that. The current depression of trade was felt throughout the industrial world, and as there was no simple solution an enquiry would only initially raise hopes, only to see them dashed later.

Lord Hampton attended another major debate on 16th May, when the Duke of Argyll moved for the latest reports from our representatives in the Porte (as the government in Istanbul was called). The Duke had been a noted critic of the government's foreign policy, and the news that he was to launch a major attack on the government caused the House to be well-attended. The Prince of Wales and two other royal dukes were seated on the cross benches, and the galleries were full. In an impassioned speech of two hours the Duke analysed the Treaty of Berlin, saying the government had given a misleading account of it, and in fact it benefitted the Russians far more than had been admitted. He went on to make many other criticisms of the government's policy, but the Earl of Beaconsfield immediately replied and carefully countered the duke's points. In The Times the next day the leader writer thought the prime minister had got the better of the argument, but Lord Hampton seems to have thought the Duke's speech effective – he wrote 'Duke of Argyll severely attacked foreign policy of government'

His Last Year

The next day Lord Hampton, always keen to keep up with new developments, went to the Royal Society, where the first telephone to be seen in Britain was demonstrated by C P Edison, nephew of the inventor. Lord Hampton called the invention 'wonderful'. The invention of the telephone is usually credited to Alexander Graham Bell, whose first patent was awarded in 1876, but Edison patented certain improvements, principally the carbon transmitter.

During this week Lord Hampton made a probably deliberately mysterious entry in his diary: 'Heard this week of F T's reported marriage and confinement. Fully confirmed by letter Saturday from J, giving particulars from Mrs H J' and 'wrote fully to Johnny about F T marriage, confinement &c'. This is the second reference in his diary to 'F T', the previous having been the previous year, but what her relationship to Johnny was is probably best left obscure. The following week Lord Hampton made this entry: 'Wrote strong and plain letter to J about state of his health, and undeceiving him. Told him real seats of his ailments'.

On Saturday, after attending a committee on the proposed statue of Lord Russell in the central lobby in the houses of parliament, he attended the opening of a coffee bar promoted by Rev. James Fleming (see above page 177) as an alternative to the public house for the working man. This was considered sufficiently important to be opened by the lord chancellor, Lord Cairns.

The following Saturday, 17th May, Lord Hampton left for Worcestershire, where he spent four nights. His time was mainly spent on tenants' business and with his game keeper Henry Simons, but he also inspected Salters Hall in Droitwich, and lunched at the Raven Hotel. His note is followed by an exclamation mark – perhaps he thought it rather strange that he should be patronising the facilities newly provided by his political opponent John Corbett. On the day of his return to London, which would not have been before about 5.00 p.m., he still managed to go to two evening parties with Eleanor. One was at the Admiralty hosted by the first lord, William Henry Smith, the other at the chancellor of the exchequer's residence in Downing Street, following a dinner that Sir Stafford and Lady Northcote had given to an aristocratic company, led by the Duke of Cambridge. The following day Lord Hampton hosted a dinner party in Eaton Square.

On the Saturday of that week the Prince and Princess of Wales presided at a ceremony marking the freeing of the bridges at Lambeth, Vauxhall, Chelsea (the Albert Bridge) and Battersea from tolls, after the Metropolitan Board of Works had purchased the interests of the toll owners. In the evening Lord Hampton took his wife to see the river-side decorations, and this still left time for him to attend a full dress dinner to celebrate the queen's birthday given by Sir Stafford Northcote in Downing Street; 'sat between Lord J Manners [postmaster general] and Lord Sandon [president of the Board of Trade] – a most pleasant dinner', he noted. In those days it was common to throw the doors of a great house open after a formal dinner party, and have a large reception, as had been done in Downing Street earlier in the week, and after dinner Lord Hampton went to an 'immense reception' at the Foreign Office.

On 29th May, accompanied this time by Lady Hampton and Eleanor, he again visited Brighton, staying at the sea-front Norfolk Hotel for three nights. He marvelled at the new development taking place in Cliftonville, a little west along the coast from Johnny's Lansdowne Place, and on the next day, having had a 'contretemps' with his wife, he took Eleanor to see Kemptown. Both evenings he dined with Johnny and Dr and Mrs Wilson.

The following week Lord Hampton made one of his periodic visits to the north, travelling to stay with industrialist George Wilton Chambers of Clough House, Rotherham. The next day he attended the annual meeting of the Yorkshire Union of Mechanics Institutes. Edward Baines, 79, was still its president, and presided at the morning meeting, at which Lord Hampton's role was confined to giving a vote of thanks. However, he presided at the evening dinner and, before awarding the prizes, spoke of his admiration of Edward Baines, MP for Leeds from 1859 to 1874, who was one of those who, like Lord Hampton, had campaigned for a national system of elementary education, and, despite its deficiencies, had supported the 1870 Act. But of course elementary education was not enough. He had no doubt that the flourishing of adult education, in which field the Yorkshire Union had been so prominent with 46,000 members in 240 institutes, had led to the improvement of our industry, which had been so clear between the Great Exhibition of 1851 and the Paris Exhibition of 1876. Mr

Sir Edward Baines (1800-90) started his working life as a journalist working for his father's newspaper the Leeds Mercury. A confirmed dissenter, he was a moderate reformer. He advocated free trade and economic freedom, and believed that poverty would be relieved through economic progress. A strong believer in education, he founded many mechanics' institutes in the 1820s, and brought them together as the Yorkshire Union of Mechanics' Institutes in 1837. He was chairman of the council of the Yorkshire College of Science from 1880 to 1887.

Leeds Museum & Art Galleries/Bridgeman Images

His Last Year

Baines, at that time staying in Europe, had written to the Union that 'I find in the Paris journals distinct and generous acknowledgement of the progress made by English industries... owing to the great educational efforts which England has put forth during the last quarter of a century'.

Lord Hampton returned the following day, breaking his journey at Peterborough to see the cathedral. The same day he noted that it was his 28th wedding anniversary, but he makes no mention of a celebration. Two days later Lady Hampton had her 80th birthday, which was celebrated with a small dinner party.

Rev. James Fleming seems to have developed a friendship with Lord Hampton through being the vicar of his local church, St Michael's, Chester Square. In 1877 he was made a canon of York Minster, a crown appointment. However, the archbishop did not grant him a prebendal stall, which had hitherto been customary, and someone else was appointed. On 16th June Lord Hampton raised the matter in the House of Lords, stating that Fleming was now in a 'most painful position' and was contemplating resignation. The fact that he was not a prebendary meant that he did not enjoy the full rights of his canonry, including the right to vote in the chapter, and the right to preach. Lord Hampton requested the prime minister to refer the matter to the royal commission which was then examining the statutes of the ancient (i.e. pre-reformation) cathedrals.

In reply, the prime minister, who had evidently gone carefully into the matter and all the complex attaching legalities, explained what had happened, and went into the different legal opinions given by the government law officers, and by the archbishop. Unfortunately, the dean and chapter did not wish to bring the case to court. They were "willing to wound but not to strike", and had in fact allowed Fleming to vote and to preach. Unless it came to court, the true legal position would remain obscure. The Archbishop of York also explained his view, after which the matter was dropped, and it was to be three years before Rev. Fleming finally obtained his stall.

June was the height of the London season, and Lord Hampton's diary entries show he still went out in the evening regularly, usually taking Eleanor as his companion. There is at this time an increase in the number of days with no entry, but this does not necessarily mean he was inactive. One invitation, from Trinity House, that he did turn down was an excursion to the Eddystone lighthouse in connection with the new tower planned to replace Smeaton's tower, which had become unsafe. In the event a heavy gale made the trip impossible, so Lord Hampton was saved a wasted day. But he did attend a Trinity House dinner a week later, at which the Duke of Edinburgh was in the chair, and Prince Leopold, fourth son of the queen, was sworn in as an elder brother. Here, models of the three lighthouses which had been built at Eddystone as well as the new one were displayed. There was a further Trinity House function at the end of the following week on July 4th, when the mayor of London entertained the Duke of Edinburgh and the elder bretheren of Trinity House for a dinner in the Egyptian Hall in the Mansion House.

The next day Lord Hampton travelled to Westwood, and he seems to have spent much of the weekend with Martin Curter talking over his affairs, before returning to London on Monday. He immediately took Eleanor to a concert given by Henry Leslie's Choir at the special request of the Prince and Princess of Wales. Leslie's Choir had become well known for singing madrigals and other unaccompanied works – The Times wrote that 'it held the palm among London societies for finished singing of unaccompanied music, both ancient and modern'. Lord Hampton had intended to go to several more parties that week, but bad weather kept him at home, although he still regularly attended his office.

Lord Hampton also attended the House of Lords whenever something important or interesting came up, and on 15th July there was a debate on vivisection, which he found 'interesting'. Lord Truro spoke on the second reading of his bill to totally outlaw vivisection. This procedure was controlled by an act of 1876, which required that anyone operating on animals needed a licence. Lord Hampton's Worcestershire neighbour, Earl Beauchamp, opposed the bill. He said that Lord Truro had attempted to belittle the importance of vivisection to medicine by saying that it was claimed that in 50 years it might produce a cure for snake bites. In fact 20,000 people died from snake bites a year in India alone, so surely if controlled vivisection led to a cure for all this human misery it would be worth while. Lord Beauchamp thought the bill would drive vivisection underground, and might have unintended consequences – even shooting a rabbit might become illegal. Their lordships obviously took fright at being told that field sports might be covered by the bill, and it was defeated by a large majority, although Lord Hampton did not stay for the division, as the bill stood no chance of becoming law anyway.

At the end of the week he noted sadly that Eleanor Pratt had left after a visit of four months. She had regularly accompanied him to evening events when appropriate, but the end of the season was now approaching, and he would be going to Worcestershire. The next day he went to Haywards Heath and passed the day with Johnny and Dr and Mrs Wilson – perhaps they had journeyed there from Brighton to save Lord Hampton the journey.

Lord Hampton's household did not leave London until 14th August, and he continued to attend the office daily, but, as Eleanor had left, on many days this is the only event recorded. Twice he travelled downstream to dine at Greenwich – on 23rd July for a 'large colonial party' at the Ship Inn, and on 5th August to attend Lord Redesdale's traditional end of session dinner for peers and officials of the House of Lords at the Trafalgar Tavern. The following day the Lord

Mayor and Lady Mayoress gave a similar dinner to the prime minister and her majesty's ministers, where Lord Hampton was amongst the two hundred guests. The same day that the Hampton household left London, the second of Herby's nine children was born, christened Edith Frances.

Lord Hampton's first task in Worcestershire was to assemble a house party to attend the Archery Society meeting at Hindlip Hall the next Wednesday. The weather that summer had been very bad, and over the weekend they had had continuous rain and thunder. Mrs Nisbet, living at Lord Hampton's home farm, had a 'wonderful escape' from lightning. All this turned the lawns at Hindlip Hall into a 'morass' according to Berrow's, and in proposing the toast to the lady paramount, Mrs Allsopp, Lord Hampton said she had reason to complain of Col Norbury, at whose residence at Leigh the first archery society meeting had been held in July, and for which he had taken possession of the only fine day that summer, "leaving our friend Mr Allsopp to receive us kindly and struggle with cloudy skies and spongy grass and all the discomforts incidental to this extraordinary state of things".

The following day there was another storm, but the next day was better, and Lord and Lady Lyttelton came for lunch and to look round Westwood. The Birmingham Triennial Music Festival took place the following week, and Lord Hampton made daily visits, beginning with Elijah on Tuesday, when he lunched with Birmingham friends, and sat with Lord

Hindlip Hall is situated near Worcester, and in the C16th and C17th centuries was inhabited by recusants, leading to its involvement in both the Babington and Gunpowder Plots. The old hall was destroyed by fire in 1820, and a new hall was built by Viscount Southwell, an Irish peer, who had married Jane, a member of the local Berkeley family. Both families were Catholic. After he died in 1860 it was bought by Henry Allsopp, and members of his family lived there until 1946, when it became the headquarters of the West Mercian police. Agatha Allsopp, widow of the 3rd baron and a descendent of the Marquess of Bath, then moved out and lived locally until she died in 1962.

Norton's party. He returned the next day to hear an arrangement of Rossini's 'Moses in Egypt', the first time it had been performed in Birmingham. 'Great success. The famous prayer most beautiful', he wrote.

Lord Hampton missed the Thursday concert as he attended a meeting in Droitwich to promote the formation of a company to take over the brine baths. The proprietor, Dr Bainbrigge, was now 73 years old, and company would provide more hotel accommodation. But he was back in Birmingham for the last, Friday, concert, which began with Cherubini's Requiem, the first orchestral performance in Birmingham. The Birmingham Daily Post was most enthusiastic, writing that 'the performance of the work was in all respects admirable. It would be impossible to convey in words any adequate idea of the solemn, awe-inspiring effect of the successive choral numbers of this masterly dirge'. But Lord Hampton found it 'heavy – not equal to Mozart'. However he enjoyed a later work, Mendelssohn's Hymn of Praise: 'very fine'.

During August and September Lord Hampton was engaged on a constant social round, and on a few occasions Lady Hampton is mentioned as accompanying him, so her health must have improved. One highlight was the visit of Rt Rev. Francis Kelly, Bishop of Derry, who was staying with Sir Edmund Lechmere at The Rhydd. Lord Hampton joined them, and on 26th September joined a party going to inspect the restoration of Tewkesbury Abbey. A series of services was being held to mark the re-opening, and the Bishop of Derry preached at the service the following week when a festival of neighbouring choirs was held, and the Abbey was particularly full. The weather, however, was stormy, and Lord Hampton did not go.

The next day he joined a party dining with John Brinton (see page 225), and afterwards they went to Kidderminster to the opening of the new school of art. The school had been established for many years, but had lacked its own

The Kidderminster School of Art, opened in 1879. Later a matching wing was added to the left housing the free library and school of science. It was demolished in the 1990s, and the new library occupies the site. Reproduced by kind permission of the Carpet Museum Trust

premises. Lord Hampton was one of the speakers, and thanked flour mill owner Daniel Goodwin who had given the land for the new building. He said that, as at Worcester where a school of art benefitted the decoration of china, so there should also be one at Kidderminster "with its beautiful manufacture of carpets".

The Bishop of Derry came to Westwood the next day and stayed the night, and the next morning the party were all shocked to hear of the sudden death of Very Rev. Dr Grantham Yorke, Dean of Worcester. He had suffered from poor health for some time and had become very deaf, so the event was not unexpected. Lord Hampton cannot have been very sorry in view of the dean's opposition to the Worcester festival, and not surprisingly did not attend the funeral.

Quarter sessions were held on Monday 13th October where Lord Hampton supported the appointment of a county surveyor. Two days later he travelled to London. He was chairman of the board of visitors to Sandhurst and Woolwich, and led the inspection of Sandhurst on Thursday and Woolwich on Friday. He found the arrangements at both places in good order, and his only comment was that the table at Woolwich was 'rather too good'. He returned to Worcestershire on Saturday, taking Eleanor Pratt, and later in the week was on the top table at the mayor of Worcester's banquet. It was a grand affair – Berrow's wrote that 'it was on a scale of completeness and splendour which has been unknown at any mayoral luncheon or banquet in this city for some years'. Lord Hampton proposed the toast to the high sheriff, an office whose functions were currently under review, and in reply the sheriff, Mr Bickerton Evans, expressed his delight at the toast being proposed 'by one whose name was reverenced in the county… it might be that he should become like the dodo, and they would never look upon his like again!'

The next day Lord Hampton had to go to Ragley Hall, the seat of the Marquess of Hertford, to prepare for a 'great Conservative demonstration' in Birmingham the next day. Lord Hertford's party included Lord and Lady Jersey, Sir Michael and Lady Hicks-Beach (secretary of state for the colonies), Capt. and Mrs Frederick Burnaby (the prospective Conservative candidate for Birmingham), Sir Henry Chaplin, MP for mid-Lincs, and Lady Chaplin, Hugh de Grey Seymour, MP for south Warwicks and son and heir to the Marquess of Hertford, and Sir Henry Drummond Wolff, MP for Christchurch and a diplomat.

The next day the party travelled to Birmingham, where the annual meeting of the National Union of Conservative and Constitutional Associations was held, presided over by the Marquis of Hertford. Afterwards there was a great demonstration attended by 30,000 in the Aston Lower Grounds, today the site of Villa Park, and at the same time a banquet attended by about 800 was held in the great hall. Sir Michael Hicks-Beach gave what Lord Hampton described as 'a great ministerial speech'. The banquet was followed by a public meeting attended by 'fully 10,000', where Lord Hampton spoke in support of the government. Birmingham at that time returned three members to parliament, all Liberal, and Lord Hampton ended his contribution by hoping that "when the moment of trial came, they would find a representative of Birmingham in the Conservative ranks on the House of Commons". Unfortunately that was not to be as in the general election the following year Birmingham still returned three Liberals.

The party returned to Ragley that night, and after attending the local church the next morning Lord Hampton went back to Westwood. Among the many visitors who called at Westwood was Admiral Sir George Sartorius and his wife and daughter. Sartorius, then aged 89 and admiral of the fleet, had had a long and adventurous naval career beginning at Trafalgar. Among many pamphlets and letters he wrote on naval affairs was one in which he described the Warrior, our first iron-clad, commissioned by Lord Hampton when first lord of the Admiralty in 1858, as 'a beautiful ship, but for the purposes of war an utter failure'. He was referring to the fact that, although Warrior's central section was armour clad, her bows and stern were more lightly constructed and vulnerable. Sartorius's daughter Rose was to wed Major Herbert Domvile, the grandson of Lord Hampton's half sister Mary Russell in September 1880 – perhaps this was when their acquaintance was made.

Lord Hampton seems to have had a fascination for elderly people. One he had remarked on was 100 year old Mrs Hartshorne (see page 255 above), and shortly after Admiral Sartorius left he called on Mrs Frances Morgan of Ladywood, who was 90. 'She having been some time confined to her room, I sat by her bedside for 1/2 hour – lively as ever', he wrote.

An election was due in 1880, and Lord Hampton was still much involved in county politics. In line with the national swing, two Conservatives had been elected to represent East Worcestershire in 1874, Henry Allsopp of Hindlip Hall and Thomas Eades Walker of Studley Castle, Warwicks. At the end of October 1879 Walker decided to retire. Lord Hampton, Lord Coventry, Charles Noel of Bell Hall, Belbroughton, and Herbert Goldingham, one-time mayor of Worcester, deliberated, and decided to telegraph Sir Richard Temple, who had expressed an interest in standing for the Conservatives. Sir Richard had spent some time in India, and had been appointed governor of Bombay in 1877, but decided to resign this post prematurely to contest East Worcestershire with Henry Allsopp, the sitting MP.

Lord Hampton spent two days marking trees for felling in the park, and then the household moved to London on 12th November, when he resumed his attendance at the office. Unusually, there are almost no diary entries for the next three weeks while he was in London, and only when he returned to Westwood for

His Last Year

the weekend in early December did they resume. He had a long interview with his new agent, Thomas Henry Davies of Orleton on Friday, and on Saturday attended a meeting to confirm the appointment of Sir Richard Temple as the prospective Conservative candidate for East Worcestershire.

London must have been quiet at this season, as parliament was not in session and most of 'society' were in their country houses, but Lord Hampton did manage to find companions to go to see Weber's opera Oberon ('much pleased'), and a double bill in St James' Theatre on new year's eve: G W Godfrey's 'The Queen's Shilling' and Alfred Tennyson's 'Falcon'. Lord Hampton wrote that he was 'disappointed'; The Times called Tennyson's attempt at a stage play 'a failure… a dramatist must be a poet, but a poet is not necessarily a dramatist!'. He also attended the annual 'Doctor's Day' banquet marking the end of the Merchant Taylors School year on 16th December, at which Lord Chelmsford, newly returned from South Africa, was the guest of honour. Replying to the toast to the Houses of Parliament, Lord Hampton praised Chelmsford for his victory over the Zulus at Ulundi in July. Lessons had been learned from the catastrophe earlier in the year, with the army reinforced and fortified camps being built as they advanced.

Christmas seems to have passed quietly, with the wedding of Lord Hampton's second wife's Augusta's niece Mary Mordaunt on 23rd, and on Christmas day a family dinner with Herby and his family and 'the Davies girls' (the daughters of his niece Mary Davies and possibly Mary Davies herself, who had divorced in 1866, as well). There must have been a traditional London smog that day – he noted 'Extraordinary day of darkness – no daylight – fine in country!'. At the end of his diary Lord Hampton wrote 'I feel glad that this year has passed away

Sir Richard Temple (1826-1902) came from a family which had been seated at The Nash, a large timber framed house near Kempsey, since 1738. After leaving Haileybury he went to India when 21, and rose rapidly to become finance minister to the government of India, then lieutenant governor of Bengal, and finally in 1877 governor of Bombay. After his unsuccessful election attempt in 1880 in 1885 and again in 1892 he was elected for south Worcestershire, and later represented Kingston upon Thames. He was a prolific writer about his time in India and other subjects.

– except my first fit of gout at its commencement, I have to be thankful for good health almost unbroken although in Feb'y I completed my 80th year'. Why he was glad to see the year end is not clear, but there is no doubt that his energy continued unabated, as is shown by the entries for the new year. The only sacrifice to age may have been his absence from Worcester for the epiphany quarter sessions and other local functions, and he remained in London, going regularly to the office, seeing Henry Irving and Ellen Terry in the Merchant of Venice ('a great treat') and the French composer Ambroise Thomas's opera Mignon, and dining out regularly.

In the office he had to deal with a problem when the examiners attended late, in violation of rules made last year when the same thing happened – standing no nonsense 'we saw and lectured Mr Post on irregularity of examiners' attendance'. There were problems in selecting a new president of the Institute of Naval Architects, as Lord Hampton would be resigning at the next annual meeting. From his diary entries it seems that a member, John Scott Russell, had approached the Duke of Edinburgh late in 1879 to take on this role, but Lord Hampton thought this was quite out of order, and wrote to the Duke telling him so. After further behind-the-scenes discussions, Henry George Liddell, since 1878 Earl of Ravensworth, and President of the North of England ship owners association, was chosen as Lord Hampton's successor at the annual meeting in March. On 18th March Lord Hampton noted 'Evening sitting was close of my long presidency of 21 years and much good feeling was shown, and a beautiful illuminated address was presented to me'.

The other matter to take up Lord Hampton's time in early 1880 was his son Johnny's condition. It seems that Johnny was reluctant or unable to realise the severity of his condition, so his father engaged Sir John Bucknill, the leading psychiatrist of his day, to see Johnny in Brighton. He saw him twice, and immediately after the second meeting on 25th January sent a report to Lord Hampton that 'Johnny is of unsound mind and unfit to manage his own affairs'. Presumably this was necessary before he could transfer management of Johnny's affairs to another party. Shortly afterwards Lord Hampton 'heard from Dr Wilson with insane letter from Mr P to Florence Wilson – also his insane conversations with Mrs Wilson. Also rec'd long and very weak letter from J in reference to Dr B's visit'. In response to this, his father decided to go to Brighton to explain to Johnny in person what was being done. He wanted to go on 2nd February, but the fog was so bad 'I could not see either body or horse of a passing cab', but the next day was better. He made a day trip to Brighton and had a long talk with Johnny.

The next step was to apply to make him a ward of chancery, and notice was served on him on 17th February. 'He much hurt by form of papers', his father

His Last Year

noted, and the next day 'received a letter from Johnny with much vexation & offence of forms of notice. I wrote him a conciliatory and explanatory letter'. On 19th March an enquiry was held in Brighton by a Mr Graham, a master in lunacy, into Johnny's mental state. Graham was satisfied by the evidence of Johnny's 'unsoundness', and he then became a ward of chancery. Lord Hampton attended and remained in Brighton nearly a week, staying with Dr Wilson. The final stage was to appoint a 'committee', which in that sense is similar to someone who is given power of attorney. Johnny's brother-in-law, the George Frederick Boyle, 6th Earl of Glasgow, was appointed to this important position, as many legalities would have to be dealt with once Johnny inherited his father's barony.

The queen opened parliament in person on 5th February – since the death of Albert she had been a very irregular attender on these occasions, and never read the speech herself, as she used to do before. Lord Hampton got tickets for his daughter-in-law Evelyn to attend. In the ensuing debate the Duke of Argyll again attacked government foreign policy, but, wrote Lord Hampton, Lord Cranbrook answered him well. Lord Beaconsfield also spoke in defence of the government, but Lord Hampton found his speech 'rather feeble – unwell'. The next day Lord Hampton met the prime minister who looked 'ill and aged', and who told him he was 'very shaky'. Beaconsfield would have little more than a year to live. But on the same day there was good news for the Conservatives. A by-election at Liverpool had created great interest and efforts by both sides to win, and the Conservative won by over 2,000 votes. When Lord Hampton visited the

Lord Beaconsfield towards the end of his life. The late 1870s saw an economic depression both in agriculture and commerce, and this was the main factor leading to the defeat of the Conservatives in spring 1880. He remained leader of the opposition in the Lords, and last spoke in March 1881. The following month he developed bronchitis, and died on 19th April. He declined a final visit from the queen – he said she would only want him to take a message to Albert! His favourite flower was said to be the primrose, and after his death the Primrose League was founded to preserve his Conservative values.

Carlton Club he found 'great excitement', as there was again a few days later when the Conservatives won another by-election at Southwark. However, the Conservatives' success was not repeated at the general election in the spring.

Lord Hampton still took an interest in the Severn Navigation. Controversy was continuing about the effect of the proposed Vyrnwy dam, which would allow a large volume of water to be diverted to Liverpool, lessening the amount going downstream to join the Severn. On 10th February Lord Hampton led a delegation representing many interests to see the president of the Local Government Board, George Sclater-Booth, opposing the scheme. However the health of Liverpudlians took precedence over the various bodies to do with the Severn, and the dam was started the following year. It took seven years to build.

The 20th February marked Lord Hampton's 81st birthday, and as usual in his diary he wrote 'How thankful I ought to be, and I hope I am, for my health and almost youthful activity and appearance, at this advanced age!' He had a small family luncheon party, but was absent at dinner as he wished to hear the Duke of Argyll make yet another attack on the government's policy over Afghanistan. The Earl of Beaconsfield wound up the debate, and on this occasion Lord Hampton thought he spoke well. On 27th February he had a dinner party at home, and the next day attended a grand dinner party given by Sir Stafford and Lady Northcote. Lord Hampton noted that forty sat down to dinner in 11 Downing Street, and that he took Mme de Montebello, the English widow of the 2nd Duc de Montebello, into dinner.

Lord Hampton's diary for the next two weeks is blank, and he resumed his diary by describing the Institute of Naval Architects' annual conference, immediately after which he went to Brighton for the enquiry, as mentioned above. He returned on 24th March, attended the office, and dined with Mrs Greville.

This is the last entry in Lord Hampton's diary, and he died, after a short illness, on Thursday 9th April at his London home. His death certificate says that the cause was 'catarrh of bladder 13 days'. This would indicate that he had an inflammation of the bladder, and, in the days before antibiotics, this might have worsened quickly and caused fatal septicaemia.

There are only slight indications that his pace of life was slowing down in his last year or two, and it is hard to resist the conclusion that the stress and unhappiness of his stay in Brighton, when Johnny became a ward of chancery, may have contributed to his illness. His remains were sent by rail to Droitwich on 15th April and remained in Westwood over night. The funeral took place the next day. He was buried in the old family vault under the chancel of Hampton Lovett church, where there were already fifteen coffins. The last burial there had been of his second wife Augusta in 1848, to whom there is also a monumental cross in the churchyard. His son Herby was present of course, but Johnny also managed to come up from Brighton. A stained glass window was erected by way of a monument at the east end of the Pakington chapel.

Epilogue

There are a large number of papers to do with the winding up of Lord Hampton's estate in the family archives, and they indicate that his financial affairs were not in a good state when he died. There were two reasons – firstly, like all landed proprietors, he was suffering from the agricultural depression that was starting to have an effect on rents and in particular was leading to tenants getting into arrears, and secondly the estate was heavily mortgaged. A summary of the settled estate of just under 3,000 acres drawn up later that year shows that the rental income was about £6,000, and the mortgage interest and other fixed costs totalled £2,366. This included a £473 rent charge for the Coventry Charity, which dated back to 1677, when the 3rd baronet had lost a wager on a horse

The stained glass window in the Pakington chapel in Hampton Lovett church. The simple inscription reads: 'To the glory of God and in memory of John Somerset PAKINGTON 1st Baron Hampton of Hampton Lovett PC and GCB baronet born 20th February 1799 died 9th April 1880'.

race to Henry Coventry, and had to found a charity in Droitwich, which still exists. There were also large loans from both his wife's and his son's trustees. In addition, there was a large loan for drainage which Lord Hampton had taken out under a government scheme, with interest running at £425 a year.

In addition to these fixed costs there were also expenses including repairs and insurance coming to an estimated £2,150. This included a large allowance against future rental payments due to the depression, and a rather optimistic provision of 'repairs to the mansion' of £100 a year. Lord Hampton had also taken out an overdraft with Worcester bankers Berwick & Co which amounted to £4,200 on his death, and was secured by an equitable charge over the whole of his estates.

Lord Hampton still owned the Freystrop property in Carmarthenshire, but this was also mortgaged and produced little net income, the Robin Hood public house in Dodderhill, and the remains of the Powick Court estate of about 120 acres, which he had inherited from his father (some land had been sold to establish the Powick lunatic asylum). This was let, but according to the financial summary, produced a net income of only £17 9s 6d after mortgage interest.

The financial summary concludes that the estate's net disposable income was only about £1,500 a year, although this could be increased by letting the mansion and sporting rights. And there was also some timber that could be felled.

Lady Hampton's position was secured by a settlement, and she was probably still benefiting from the estate of her first husband, and Lord Hampton had left her all the contents of their London home at 9 Eaton Square. She continued to live there in some style until her death in 1892, just past her 93rd birthday, so it seems that her indifferent health of earlier years had improved.

Johnny's position was again secured by his settlement, and he spent the rest of his life under medical care, dying in Kingston, Surrey, in 1893 aged 66, living with a Dr Edward Clapham.

Herby was left to deal with his father's affairs after his death, and it soon became clear that he could not afford to live in Westwood even if he had wanted to. The estate had immediate debts to pay off, and Lady Hampton agreed to give the executors £2,000, in return for which they would make no claim on any of the items in the London house. By the end of the year there was still £6,450 to pay off, including the Berwick & Co overdraft. By selling Fresytrop, the Robin Hood pub, other small parcels of land, and collecting arrears of rent, the executors reckoned they could settle most of this, and they would also need to sell Lord Hampton's collection of books. This existence of this collection was a surprise after his death, as it was never remarked on during his lifetime. In fact Lord Hampton had accumulated a collection of antiquarian books, including prayer books and bibles, and these were auctioned over three days in February 1881.

The most valuable item was a Coverdale bible of 1565 which sold for £285, and there were several other bibles and prayer books from the same century. The proceeds totalled over £3,500, rather more than the executors had estimated.

Caretakers were installed at Westwood, and in 1885 it was let to a Mr J Spiller of Tyberton Court, Herefordshire, who stayed for five years and paid a rent of £402 a year to include the sporting rights of the whole estate, but there was a long list of improvements to be made to the mansion first. Later it was let to Sir Augustus Godson, MP for Kidderminster, and later his brother Major Robert Godson. After Major Godson died in 1899 it was sold and occupied by the Ward family, estate agents. Between the wars it was the home of the Partington family, Lords Doverdale, who were related to the Wards. After the war it was converted into flats, which it is now.

Herbert Pakington became the 3rd Lord Hampton on the death of his brother in 1893, and he does not seem to have pursued his legal career, as in the 1881 census he was described as a 'barrister (not practising) living chiefly on own means; artist and painter'. By 1901 had moved his family to Worcestershire where they lived in Waresley Court, Hartlebury, where he died in 1906. Herby and Evelyn had a large family, and, remarkably, seven of their nine children lived to be over 70. Two of their sons were successively 4th and 5th barons Hampton, the latter being Humphrey Arthur Pakington, who died in 1974. His son Richard was the 6th baron, and together Humphrey and Richard wrote 'The Pakingtons of Westwood', a privately published account of the whole history of the family.

John Slaney Pakington, or Johnny as his father called him, seems to have led a fairly normal life in his younger years, being educated at Eton and Christ Church, Oxford. Only 23 when he married in 1849, he played a full part in local affairs, becoming a magistrate and deputy lieutenant, and was particularly interested in supporting local adult educational institutes. He also served in both the Worcestershire Yeomanry Cavalry and the Rifle Volunteers. However he seems to have had no interest in field sports, and his only appointment of importance was in 1855 as a director of the Oxford, Worcester and Wolverhampton Railway in its independent days. He had one attempt to get into national politics when he stood as the Tory candidate for East Worcestershire at a by-election in 1859. However he was widely seen as the son of his father rather than an independent man, and was no match for his Liberal opponent, Frederick Gough-Calthorpe, who had strong support from the populous northern part of the constituency. His campaign was not helped by the fact that he was indisposed for most of the time, and only appeared in public on nomination day.

That was not the first time that Johnny had been ill – at Easter 1854 his 'serious indisposition' prevented his father from attending quarter sessions, and in July 1856 he went to the spa at Marienbad to regain his health, where he remained for a month. Although he returned in better shape, the following April he went to a German spa for further treatment. In a letter to Disraeli at this time his father said he was 'very ill'.

Then followed a period when he seems to have regained his health, and in 1860 undertook a tour of the USA and Canada with his relative Henry Domvile. But in 1869 he was prevented from taking part in cavalry drill due to indisposition, and in July 1873 Martin Curtler wrote in a letter to his father that he was sorry to hear that Johnny was unwell again, as he thought he had recovered. Thereafter his health seems to have steadily declined, and in January 1875 his father wrote of 'poor Johnny', and later that year Johnny had to postpone a visit to his wife's family in Scotland because he had a 'slight relapse'. His wife died suddenly on 1st January the following year, and after this, as already noted, he gradually descended into mental illness, his last public appearance having been in May 1877. His death certificate (1893) states that he died from a brain haemorrhage.

Without knowing the symptoms of his earlier bouts of illness it is impossible to give any certain diagnosis, and it is possible, of course, that each of his illnesses was unrelated. But one possible diagnosis that would fit what we know of his ill-health was that he had syphilis. In the earlier stages the disease is usually marked by skin lesions and rashes, which might account for his visits to the continental spas (when he might have gone to Droitwich), then there is a period of remission, which would have been in the 1860s. Untreated patients then often go on to develop tertiary syphilis, sometime 20 years or more after the initial infection, which can affect the brain and lead to problems of mental health.

Johnny and his wife never had any children, and his father developed a particular interest in venereal disease. As noted in chapter 5, Sir John, as he was then, became a leading campaigner in favour of the Contagious Diseases Acts, and in the early 1870s he led the campaign to kill the bill to repeal them. Personal knowledge of the horrible effects of advancing syphilis might explain his high level of interest and commitment to this issue.

Chapter 14
Lord Hampton in Retrospect

Born the younger son of Elizabeth and William Russell, a lawyer of gentry status, John Somerset Russell displayed characteristics from the outset that marked him apart from his elder brother William Herbert. William seems to have suffered from indifferent health and had to be withdrawn from Eton, whereas John was boisterous and energetic from the start. After both his parents had died by the time he was 14, and his elder brother when he was 20, John assumed the position of head of the family, although by then his only sibling was Elizabeth. His maiden aunt Dorothy was still alive, as was his uncle Sir John Pakington, unmarried and eccentric, living in Westwood. John seems to have enjoyed a good relationship with his aunt, but his uncle regarded him as irresponsible and they had several arguments, as recorded in John's diary. However, when his uncle died in 1830 John took the lead in challenging his will, and when it was successfully overturned he and his aunt inherited the Pakington estates. John assumed the name Pakington, and was very conscious of his being the latest in the long line of the family that had occupied Westwood since Elizabethan times.

That he enjoyed all the pastimes of a healthy young man is clear from his diary: a regular huntsman, he was often out shooting, and, as shown by his tour of Scotland when he was 21 and when he later visited his uncle's shooting lodge near Braemar, thought nothing of going for long hikes. Throughout his life he was also an inveterate traveller, frequently taking the stage coach from Worcester to London when the journey would have taken all day, and in the later railway age he regularly travelled between Droitwich and London, when, in the early days at least, the journey would still have taken five hours or so. We also know that he undertook a long continental tour for his first honeymoon in 1823, and ten years later, with his wife and seven year old son, he toured the USA and Canada, when crossing the Atlantic in a sailing ship was still quite an adventure, but unfortunately his accounts of these have been lost. He was also a keen yachtsman before entering parliament.

Being appointed a magistrate at the young age of 25 would not have been very unusual, but his appointment as chairman of the quarter sessions in 1834 when he was only 35 shows that he was well regarded by his fellow magistrates and keen on advancement. But this was not the first sign of his ambition. In 1831 he had acted as agent for Col Henry Lygon who was candidate for the county at the general election caused by the difficult passage of the Reform Bill. Lygon was a Tory, and Pakington probably never had to think very deeply about which party to support. Although his father's family does not seem to had been involved in politics, his Pakington uncle's family had produced several MPs, all staunch Conservatives, and it would have been unusual to have changed sides.

How far Pakington's beliefs were genuinely Tory is more difficult to say. He expressed opposition to the Reform Bill in 1831, but later, like most Tories, accepted it as necessary, but he tended to oppose later reform bills, and expressed horror at the potential results of widening the franchise too far. However, when Disraeli introduced the radical reform bill of 1867 when Sir John was a minister, he did not oppose it, even though he had come up with some suggestions of his own about different ways to widen the franchise. Similarly, he had always expressed opposition to the secret ballot, even though he could clearly see some of the evils of the open poll, and he seems to have tried to have the best of both worlds when he expressed opposition in principle but the value of it in practice.

Lord Hampton's career in parliament from his first election in 1837 shows some curious contradictions. His involvement with the labouring and criminal classes through his chairmanship of quarter sessions and his work as a magistrate made him genuinely anxious to delve into the causes of crime and ways to eliminate them. His first campaign in parliament in 1839 and 1840 was to tighten up the issue of licences to beer shops, as these were regarded by many as hot-beds of crime. It was evidently something he felt strongly about, and had even referred to it in his first election campaign. His campaign only achieved moderate success, but later in the century the government increasingly came round to his view that the sale of alcohol should be more controlled, and everything was eventually brought under the control of the magistracy.

His experience as a magistrate had shown him that the great majority of criminals were uneducated, not only in the 3R's, but in morals and religion. He also showed his unprejudiced mind when he campaigned in the 1840s for juvenile offenders not to be incarcerated with adult criminals awaiting trial at quarter sessions nor to be imprisoned in the county jail with them after conviction. This resulted in his Juvenile Offenders Act of 1842 allowing young offenders to be tried speedily by summary justice, and later he took great interest in and supported the movement to put convicted youngsters in reformatories rather than prison, where they could be educated and set on the path of righteousness.

Lord Hampton in Retrospect

From his observation that offenders were usually uneducated he formed the opinion that furthering education would reduce crime, and this led to his long campaign to have a national scheme for elementary education. Although his bills of 1855 and 1858 were unsuccessful in parliament, they did raise the level of debate on education taking place at this time, and, much to Lord Hampton's frustration, only failed to become law due to the strong religious and secular prejudices of the various camps. It would not be correct to say that his campaign led directly to the 1870 Act, as by that time our educational deficiencies were widely recognised, but he did succeed to keeping the subject constantly to the fore. One result of the debate was that it slowly became recognised that attendance at schools would have to be compulsory for the benefits of education to extend to all children. In the 1850s such an idea ran contrary to traditional ideas of freedom still held by many people, and even the 1870 Elementary Education Act only provided for compulsion if so decided by an education board, and it was to be another ten years before attendance at school was at last made compulsory. Lord Hampton himself held mixed views on this in the 1850s, and in any case realised that compulsion at that time stood no chance of passing the House of Commons.

The importance he attached to the teaching of religion and therefore Christian morals in schools is shown by the fact that he continued to raise this subject, which had not been fully provided for in the 1870 Act, until the end of his life.

His 1850s bills were introduced as private member's bills, for which he was criticised by Disraeli, as he did not feel that a front bench spokesman should promote private bills on important matters of national policy. Disraeli knew that some senior members of the party would oppose the measures, and, at a time when the Conservative party was in a constant minority in the House, he was against anything that disturbed party unity. So it says much for Lord Hampton's courage and strength of feeling that he risked losing his front bench position through this measure, and it was probably through the moderating influence of the party leader Lord Derby that Disraeli pulled back from sacking him.

Lord Hampton's interest in education extended beyond elementary education to actively encouraging the various adult education institutes that were a feature of Victoria's reign. Towards the end of his life he often referred to his belief that Britain was falling behind in the international industrial competitive race, and blamed this on the lack of education, both elementary and later. Not only did he (and his son Johnny) encourage the local Worcestershire Mechanics and Literary Institutes, but during the parliamentary autumn recess he undertook a number of journeys to the north where he spoke at the opening or annual meeting of one. Allied to this was his enthusiastic support for a school of naval architecture in the early days of the Institute of Naval Architects, for similar reasons.

Lord Hampton's relationship with Disraeli was certainly put under stress when he introduced his private member's education bill, but there were others times too. Disraeli told Lord Hampton to forget his proposals for extra expenditure on various occasions when first lord of the Admiralty, and on Lord Hampton's part he was highly critical of Disraeli's poor communication with the rest of his front bench, his tendency to make policy 'on the hoof', and his over-use of patronage. Although Lord Hampton's surviving letters to Disraeli are deferential, they display a firmness of intention and reluctance to be cowed that probably stems from the fact that he always regarded Disraeli as a social inferior and more 'political' in his judgements. Nevertheless he recognised that Disraeli was his boss, and, through his debating skills, a great asset to the party. The few letters that survive from Disraeli to Lord Hampton, on the other hand, are somewhat curt. Disraeli was probably relieved when in 1874 Lord Hampton lost his seat. He would have had to find a post for his long standing loyal colleague, but at the age of 75 and with a tendency to over-spend government money this might have been difficult. His relationship with the party leader Lord Derby, on the other hand, seems to have been business-like, and although they were never close, there is no indication of any problems.

Whether one can categorise his long standing support for the Patriotic Fund, and his chairmanship of the executive committee, as further evidence of his liberal tendencies is not so clear, but he did take a great interest in the Wandsworth Asylum, and was keen to see it well run, and had to deal with a number of crises.

Lord Hampton was in opposition for the long period from 1859 till he lost his seat in 1874, and his activity in parliament became less, probably because he knew the limits of the ability of an opposition to change government policy, and, by now an experienced parliamentary campaigner, he restricted his interventions to occasions when it would have been expected of him, or when an issue arose that he felt strongly about. In 1870, for example, although he felt strongly about some aspects of the Elementary Education Bill, he only took small parts in the debates as he recognised the greater importance of the bill passing.

As recounted earlier in this book, in the summer of 1871 he embarked on a brief association with the 'new social movement' – an alliance of working-class leaders and aristocratic Conservatives led by John Scott Russell to find common ground on social issues. It seems strange that Lord Hampton, normally a very practical person who knew the limits of what could be achieved, should associate himself with these rather vague and socialist ideas. Lord Derby, in his diary, wrote that Lord Hampton came to see him about it in July, and that he was 'hot for it', and that Disraeli, always the politician, 'saw it as a way of out-bidding the Whigs, or at least Gladstone'. Lord Derby thought the ideas, or at least those that he understood, vague and impractical, and perhaps we should draw a veil over this brief period of Lord Hampton's career as a rare one when he did not keep his feet on the ground.

Lord Hampton's main characteristics, for which he was well known, were his administrative ability and his continued energy. The fact that he became chairman of most organisations he joined speaks for itself. He must have been a fair and impartial chairman with an ability to sense the best way forward and be conciliatory, even though on some occasions he felt strongly enough about something to persist in opposing the majority. As to his energy, his remaining diaries speak for themselves, right up to when he suffered a collapse in his health two weeks before his death, and indicated that he must have led a sober life, despite the innumerable dinners he attended, whether his own dinner parties, dining at other peoples' parties, or attending a public function.

Throughout his life Lord Hampton was a regular church goer, usually twice on Sundays and other religious festivals. He always counted himself a middle of the road Church of England man, although there was a time when his son Johnny was accused of being high church. On many occasions he expressed his gratitude for his continuing excellent health, yet never referred to the sadnesses of his life: the early deaths of two wives, the death of a baby child, and the continuing illness of his eldest son, which eventually descended into insanity. Such events, of course, were not unusual in earlier times, yet they might still serve to make one question the central beliefs in religion. But Lord Hampton was a great supporter of all the traditional institutions of his country, in which Anglicanism played a central part and was supported by the establishment as much as for its central part in the structure and order of society, as for purely religious reasons.

Perhaps one can sum up Lord Hampton as calling him a man of his time. He was well aware of the momentous changes that were taking place throughout his life, and on the whole supported them. He could see society changing and was no doubt able to look forward to the day when the lowest classes would have a much higher standard of living, and which he encouraged. Yet he believed in the maintenance of the existing structures – the two houses of parliament, the established church, and the aristocracy, and as long as society evolved within that structure, he was content.

His best kept secret was his collection of antiquarian books, never mentioned in his diaries. His worst legacy was an impoverished estate caused (like many others) by his living the style which his position as a senior MP and minister demanded, without the means to support it. His most charming aspect was his love of music, even as a singer when a young man, leading to constant visits to the opera and concerts, and his vigorous and ultimately successful defence of the Three Choirs Festival. And one has to count his leading role in raising funds for the restoration of Worcester cathedral as one of his main achievements.

LORD HAMPTON

Why is Lord Hampton so relatively little remembered today? His status as a leading Conservative was surely as high as many other leading Tory ministers of the time, yet, until now, his life has not been remembered in a biography. One reason must be that, for the period after the fall of Peel in 1846 until Lord Hampton lost his seat in 1874, the Conservatives were only in office for three short periods, so inevitably the leading Whigs of the period had a much bigger impact on history than their Tory coounterparts. Even the 14th Earl of Derby, prime minister three times, is not so well remembered as Palmerston and Gladstone, and, of course, all Tories of the period pale against the fame of Disraeli, who eclipsed them all.

A large silver salver was presented to Lord Hampton at a public dinner on 28th December 1859 in the Worcester Guildhall. The inscription reads:
PRESENTED TO THE RT HON SIR JOHN PAKINGTON BART GCB MP BY THE COUNTY AND CITY OF WORCESTER IN GRATEFUL RECOGNITION OF HIS SERVICES FOR 24 YEARS AS CHAIRMAN OF THE COUNTY QUARTER SESSIONS THIS SHIELD ALSO ILLUSTRATES HIS PUBLIC AND & OFFICIAL CAREER AS FIR[S]T LORD OF THE ADMIRALTY SECRETARY OF STATE FOR THE COLONIES AND AN ABLE ADVOCATE OF GENERAL EDUCATION.

A portrait of Sir John Pakington (as he was then) holding a copy of his 1855 private members' bill to establish a national education scheme. He was best known for his campaign to provide sufficient schools for poor children, particularly in the new large industrial towns, many of which never went to school.

INDEX

Abbott, Rev. Edwin 41
Abyssinian expedition 20
Acland, H D 8
Afghanistan 261
Albani, Emma 241
Albert Hall 188, 202
Albright, Arthur 117
Allcroft, John 27
Allsopp, Henry 101, 117, 118, 276
Ames, Frederick 102
Amphlett, Richard 200
Arch, Joseph 83, 85
Argyll, George Campbell 8th Duke of 268, 279, 280
Arkwright, John of Hampton Court 164
Army Exchanges Bill 188
Army Promotion & Retirement, Royal Commission on 175, 201, 202, 213, 221
Army Regulation Bill 65, 69
Aumale, Duc d' 26
Bainbrigge, William 108 et seq, 187, 209, 233, 274
Baines, Edward 270
Baker, Evelyn Nind Frances 232
Baker, George 227
Baker, Sir George 232
Baring, Thomas 74
Barry, Canon Alfred 155 et seq, 196
Bateman-Hanbury, William 2nd Lord Bateman 268
Bates, Sir Edward 184
Baxter, William 211
Beaconsfield, Earl of – see Disraeli, Benjamin
Bearcroft, Edward 23
Bearcroft, Henry 10, 16
Beauchamp, Catherine Lady, widow of 3rd Earl Beauchamp 201
Beauchamp, Frederick 6th Earl 79, 131, 163, 172, 201, 216, 235, 240, 272

Beauchamp, Lady Mary, w. of 6th Earl 218
Bell Hall, Belbroughton 254
Benson, Rev. Edward White 34
Bentinck, William 80
Berlin, Congress of 249
Berwick & Co. 281
Birkbeck Literary & Scientific Association 80
Birmingham Education League 43
Birmingham Triennial Music Festival 222, 273
Bishop of Worcester – see Philpott, Rt Rev Henry
Bishops Cleeve, Pakington's estates in 76
Blair, Rev. Robert 39
Blind College, Worcester 201
Blind, charities for the 39
Boxer, Col Edward 52
Bozward, John 168
Bradford Mechanics Institute 76
Bradley, John 113
Bright, Jacob 96
Brighton Aquarium 219, 244
Brinton, John 225, 274
Bristol Music Festival 224
British Archeological Society 193
Brodrick, George 259
Bromsgrove Literary & Mechanics Institute 44
Brougham, Lord Henry 77
Bruce, Herbert Austin 96
Bucknill, Sir John 278
Burghley House 177
Burma, King of 83
Bury, George Thomas, 6th Viscount 245
Bury, William Keppel Viscount 265
Bushe, Annette 219, 244
Bushe, Capt. Henry Gratton 219
Bushe, Florence 262
Butler, Josephine 91, 95

Page 292

Cambridge, Duke of 184, 240, 246, 265
Canham, Rev. Henry 99
Captain, HMS 73
Cardwell, Edward 52, 60, 65
Carnarvon, Henry Herbert 4th Earl of 239
Cattley, Rev. Richard 132, 139
Cave, Sir Stephen 224
Central Chamber of Agriculture 119, 177, 182, 184, 201
Chadwick, Edwin 63
Chamberlain, Joseph 227
Chapel Royal, St James' Palace 176
Chateau Impney 197, 256
Chelmsford, Frederick Thesiger 2nd Baron 277
Childers, Hugh 73
Christian, Prince & Princess 60
Civil Service Commission 203 et seq
Coles, Capt Cowper Phipps 73
Collings, Jesse 259
Commissions, abolition of purchase 66
Committee of Council, Education 121
Contagious Diseases Acts Chapter 5
Contagious Diseases (Animals) Act 120
Corbett, John 9 et seq, 112 et seq, 197
Coventry Charity 281
Coventry, George William 9th Earl of 102, 215
Cowper-Temple, William 54
Cranbrook Gathorne Hardy, 1st Earl of 261
Craven, Joseph 199
Cross, Richard Assheton 226
Crystal Palace 184
Curtler, Martin 239, 244, 261, 272
Curtler, Thomas Gale 261
Dalton Mill 199
Dartmouth, William Legge, 5th Earl of 118
Dasent, George Webbe 208
Derby, Edward Stanley 14th Earl of 34, 38

Devonshire, William Cavendish 7th Duke of 198
Dilke, Sir Charles 103
Dillwyn, Lewis 245
Disraeli, Benjamin 38, 55, 80, 115, 120, 203, 248 et seq, 262, 268, 271, 279, 280
Dixon, George 49, 50, 81
Domvile, Herbert 203, 276
Done, William 241
Douglas, Rev. Henry 16
Droitwich Benefit Building Society 44, 106
Droitwich Brine Baths 107, 177, 187, 233
Droitwich, borough of 7, 20, 109
Drunkenness in Worcestershire 259
Dudley, William Ward 1st Earl of 111, 132, 136, 140, 143, 145 et seq, 238
Edinburgh, Alfred Duke of 121, 248
Edison, C P 269
Egyptian bonds 227
Eld, Rev. Francis 256
Elementary Education Act 1870 44 et seq
Elementary Education Act 1876 219
Eley Bros 52
Elmley Castle 37, 193, 261
Endowed Schools Act 30, 41
Essays & Reviews 42
Eurydice, HMS 243
Fawkes, Ayscough 198
Ferrand, William 199
Fielden, Joshua 51
Filey, harbour of refuge in 67, 102
Fleming, Rev. James 176, 269, 271
Foot & Mouth Disease 200, 201
Forster, William 29, 30, 44 et seq, 76
Fortescue, Hugh 3rd Earl 265
Fowler, William 97
Franco-Prussian War 60, 61
Freer, Sir Henry Bartle 262, 266
Freystrop, Carmarthenshire 282
Friends of the Clergy Corporation 103
Gabb, William 107

Galton, Theodore 12
Gascoyne-Cecil, Eustace 241
Gedge, Sydney 118
General election 1874 112 et seq
Gerster, Etelka 251
Gladstone, William 26, 68, 103
Glasgow, James Carr-Boyle 5th Earl of 240, 278
Glasgow, merchant marine 232
Gloucester & Sharpness Canal 223
Godson, Sir Augustus 283
Goldingham, Herbert 152
Goschen, George 71
Gough-Calthorpe, Frederick 283
Goulburn, Rev. Dr Edward 42
Gurney stoves 133
Halifax, Charles Wood Viscount 261
Hamilton, Lord Claud 67
Hampton, Lady Augusta 176, 181, 186, 194, 218, 219, 222, 229, 253, 261, 262, 270, 274, 282
Hampton, Lady Diana 230, 231
Hanbury-Williams, Annette 219
Hanbury-Williams, Ferdinand 218
Hardman & Co 137
Hartington, Spencer Cavendish Marquess of 213
Hartshorne, Mrs Alison 255
Hastings, George Woodyatt 77, 101, 106, 108, 166, 227
Hastings, Sir Charles 107
Hay, Sir John 71
Henry Leslie's Choir 272
Herbert, Auberon 241
Hereford Journal 163
Hertford, Francis Seymour 5th Marquess of 193, 275
Hicks-Beach, Sir Michael 275
Highways Act 1878 258
Hill, Thomas Rowley 144
Hill, Thomas, organ builder 136
Hindlip Hall 273
Hogg, James McGarel 242

Holden, Hyla 144
Home for Little Boys, Farningham 190
Inflexible, HMS 221
Institute of Naval Architects 63, 101, 182, 213, 214, 232, 241, 260, 266, 278, 280
Irish Church 19, 26, 32, 103
Isaac, John Swinton 239
Isandlwana, Battle of 263
Jenkins, George 23
Johnson, Hon. Reverdy 21
Justice of the Peace Qualification Bill 187
Keighley School of Science & Art 198
Kell, Edwin 99
Kelly, Rev. Francis, Bishop of Derry 274
Kennedy, Rev. W R 260
Kidderminster School of Art 274
King George V of Hanover 216
King Leopold II of the Belgians 216, 266
Kings End, Powick 35, 193, 231, 240, 244, 247
Knight, James 99
Kynoch 53
Landlord & Tenant Act 182, 203
Laslett, William 88
Lechmere, Edmund 61, 133, 159, 274
Leeds 77
Lefevre, John Shaw 207
Leggatt, Dr 262
Leigh, William Henry 2nd Baron of Stoneleigh 131, 138
Lingen, Ralph 209
Local Taxation 62, 119
London, HMS 63
Lopez, Sir Massey 64, 106
Lowe, Robert 69
Lysons, Rev. Samuel 163
Lyttelton, Charles 5th Baron 117, 238, 273
Lyttelton, George William 4th Baron Chapters 8 & 9, 194, 201, 214, 256
MacDonald, Alexander 211, 245
MacFarren, George 223, 248
Magaera, HMS 71

Malvern College 32, 104
Manchester Education Union 43
Massey, William Nathaniel 92
Mauk, Minnie 244
Maynooth College 27
Melly, George 28
Merchant Shipping Act 1876 217
Merchant Shipping Bill 1875 184
Merchant Shipping Survey Bill 63
Merchant Taylors School 247, 277
Merrifield, Charles 100
Miall, Edward 58, 76
Midland Institute 227
Milner, Mrs Sarah Georgina 176
Mitchell, John Harper 198
Montagu, Lord Robert 48, 211
Moody & Sankey 185
Mordaunt, Sir John & Caroline 123
Mordaunt, Sir Charles & Harriet 124
Morley, Samuel 100
Mundella, Anthony 211, 267
Muntz, George Frederick 120
Murray, George Herbert 203
Murray, Herbert 38, 203
Murray, Herbert Francis 74
Murray, Lady Sarah 179
Murray, Rev. Francis Henry 74
Napier of Magdala, Lord 20
Nares, Sir George 228
Nasser al-Din, Shah of Persia 104
National Association for the Promotion of Social Science – see Social Science Association
National Education League 100
National Education Union 100
National Society 217
National Union of Conservative & Constitutional Associations 275
New Social Movement 78
Nisbet, James 241
Northcote-Trevelyan Report 204
Northcote, Sir Stafford 203 et seq, 259, 269, 280

Northfleet, SS 101
Norton, Charles Adderley 1st Baron 259
O'Shaunessy, Richard 219, 244
Oxford, Worcester & Wolverhampton Railway 283
Pakington, Herbert Murray 35, 36, 179, 214, 232, 247, 260, 273, 282, 283
Pakington, John Slaney 35, 38, 44, 133, 175, 240, 244, 253, 258, 262, 263, 266, 270, 278, 282, 283
Pakington, Lady Augusta 37
Parkinson-Fortescue, Chichester 64
Peel, Very Rev. John, Dean of Worcester Chapter 8, 154, 181
Penzance, James Wilde 1st Baron 175
Peploe, Daniel 219
Perkins, Abraham Edward Chapter 8
Philpott, Rt Rev. Henry, Bishop of Worcester 37, 39, 40, 119, 141, 159, 178, 236
Physical tests for army 240, 244, 246
Pierrepont, Edward 219
Pinafore, HMS 265
Plimsoll, Samuel 63, 101, 184
Poor Law 188
Powick Lunatic Asylum 79
Pratt, Eleanor 272
Prince Albert 34
Prince of Wales, Edward 81, 124, 216, 242
Princess Mary's Cottage Homes 241
Queen Victoria 213, 278
Ragley Hall 193
Raven Hotel 269
Ravensworth, Henry Liddell 2nd Earl of 278
Rayson, Rev. William 144
Reed, Edward 71
Richard, Henry 55
Richmond, Charles Gordon-Lennox 6th Duke of 73, 120, 122, 123, 182, 219
Robin Hood public house, Dodderhill 282
Rochdale Conservative Association 79
Roden, Dr Sergeant 110

Romilly, Edward 207
Rorkes Drift 263
Royal Academy 188, 215
Royal Academy of Music 248
Royal Archeological Society 231
Royal College of Music 248
Royal Patriotic Fund 34, 70, 178, 191, 251
Royal Victoria Patriotic Asylum for Boys 190
Royal Victoria Patriotic Asylum for Girls 70, 179, 190, 202, 229, 252
Royal Worcester Grammar School 256
Russell, John Scott 78, 181, 288
Ryan, Sir Edward 207
Salisbury, Robert Gascoyne-Cecil 3rd Marquess 248 et seq
Saltley Diocesan Training College 201, 238
Sartorius, Admiral Sir George 276
School of Art, Worcester 227
Scott, George Gilbert 130, 133, 147, 149, 154, 215
Scully, Vincent 208
Selwin-Ibbetson, Sir Henry 245, 247, 267
Severn Navigation 36, 222, 232, 253, 279
Shaftesbury, Anthony Ashley-Cooper 7th Earl of 214
Sharpness docks 223
Simons, Henry 269
Smith, Gustavus 176
Smith, Rev. Isaac 104
Smith, Thomas Grove 113
Smith, William Henry 57, 209
Social Science Association 43, 76, 259
Society of Arts 44, 62, 202
Spanish bonds 125, 175, 193, 216
St George, Gen. Sir John 53
St Michael's, Chester Square 176
St Nicholas, Droitwich 40
Stanhope, Edward 178
Stanley, Frederick Arthur Lord 244, 265
Statistical Society 217

Sugar, tariffs on 192, 221
Talbot, John 41, 215
Taylor, Col Thomas 38
Taylor, Rev. William 39
Telephone 269
Temple, Rt Rev. Frederick 41
Temple, Sir Richard 276, 277
Tewkesbury Abbey 274
Three Choirs Festival 1869 37
Three Choirs Festival 1871 76
Three Choirs Festival 1872 87
Three Choirs Festival 1875 'Mock Festival' 159 et seq, 195
Three Choirs Festival 1876 223
Three Choirs Festival 1877 232
Three Choirs Festival 1878 233 et seq, 244, 254
Thunderer, HMS 221
Town, Joseph & Sons 197, 199
Trafalgar Tavern, The 252, 272
Trevelyan, George 66, 67
Trevelyan, Sir Charles 204
Trinity House Corporation 70, 271
Truro, Charles Wilde 2nd Baron 272
Tufnell, John Joliffe 260
Turkey Mill, Keighley 199
Union of Agricultural Labourers 83
Unseaworthy Ships Bill 192
Unseaworthy Ships, Royal Commission on 183
Vernon, Harry 8 et seq, 139, 195
Vyrnwy, Lake & River 253
Walker, Thomas Eades 117, 118, 276
Wall, Mayor Edward 87
Walrond, Theodore 208
War Office Act 1870 51
Warrior, HMS 276
Webb, Ald. William 116, 141
Wellington College 33, 189, 191, 213, 217, 241
Westwood House 282, 283
Wickham, Rev. Edward 35, 191
Williams, Edward Leader 36, 61, 222, 253

Wilson, Dr John 244, 258, 262, 278
Windsor, Lord Robert George 253
Wood, Canon Ryle 153
Woodward, Robert 86
Worcester Cathedral Chapter 8
Worcester Chamber of Agriculture 80
Worcester Diocesan Board of Education 80, 101, 119, 209, 224
Worcester Education Board 106
Worcester to be centre of military district 82
Worcestershire Agricultural Society 75, 83, 85, 176, 193, 231
Worcestershire Archery Society 194
Worcestershire Society for the Sick and Wounded in War 61
Worcestershire Union of Literary & Mechanics Institutes 44
Yorke, Very Rev. Grantham Munton 154 et seq, 224, 235 et seq, 275
Yorkshire College of Science 198
Yorkshire Union of Mechanics Institutes 270

INDEX OF ILLUSTRATIONS

Albani, Emma 242
Allsopp, Henry 102
Arch, Joseph 84
Baines, Sir Edward 270
Barry, Rev. Canon Alfred 156
Beaconsfield, Earl of – see Disraeli, Benjamin
Beauchamp, Frederick 6th Earl 173
Boxer, Col Edward 52
Bradford Mechanics Institute 76
Brighton Aquarium 245
Brighton, 21 Landsowne Place 263
Brine Baths, Droitwich 111
Brinton, John 225
Butler, Josephine 91
Cambridge, George Duke of 246
Captain, HMS 74
Cardwell, Edward 65
Chamberlain, Joseph 228
Chapel Royal, St James Palace 178
Chateau Impney 197
Chelmsford, Frederick 2nd Baron 263
Coles, Capt. Cowper 73
Collings, Jesse 260
Corbett, John 9
Coventry, George William 9th Earl of
Cowper-Temple, William 56
Cross, Richard Assheton 226
Crystal Palace 185
Disraeli, Benjamin 81, 250, 251, 279
Dixon, George 49
Dudley, William Ward 1st Earl of 132
Eld, Rev. Francis 257
Election poster 1868 15
Electors Look Out poster 12
Eurydice, HMS 243
Fleming, Rev. James 177
Forster, William 45
Fowler, William 98
Freer, Sir Bartle 264

George & Royal Hotel, Droitwich 107
Gladstone, William 69
Gurney stove 134
Hampton Lovett church, window in 281
Hampton, Lord 6, 291
Hanbury Hall 8
Hindlip Hall 273
Home for little boys, Farningham 191
Irving, Henry 200
Isandlwana, Battle of 264
Keighley Mechanics Institute 199
Kidderminster School of Art 274
Kings End, Powick 194
Laslett, William 88
Lechmere, Sir Edmund 160
Leigh, William 2nd Baron 138
Lyttelton, Charles 5th Baron 239
Lyttelton, George 4th Baron 130, 257
Macfarren, George 249
Malvern College 33
Massey, William 92
Megaera, HMS 72
Melly, George 28
Miall, Edward 59
Moody & Sankey 186
Mordaunt, Georgina 124
Mordaunt, Harriet 124
Mundella, Anthony 267
Nares, Capt. George 229
Netherlands, Queen Sophie of 190
Northcote, Sir Stafford 205
Norton Barracks, Worcester 83
Pakington, Lady Diana 230
Pakington, Sir John – see Lord Hampton
Peel, Very Rev. John 129
Penzance, James Wilde Lord 176
Philpott, Rt Rev. Henry, Bishop of Worcester 236
Plimsoll, Samuel 64
Pusey, Edward 42

Richmond, 6th Duke of 122
Royal Brine Baths, Droitwich 109
Royal Victoria Patriotic Asylum for Girls 179
Said of Zanzibar, Sultan Bargesh bin 190
Salisbury, Robert 3rd Marquess of 250, 251
Scott, George Gilbert 129
Shaftesbury, 7th Earl of 42
Shah of Persia 105
Smith, William Henry 210
Stoke Works school 115
Temple, Rt Rev. Frederick 42
Temple, Sir Richard 277
Trafalgar Tavern 252
Trevelyan, Sir Charles 204
Vernon, Harry 9
Ward, Georgina Countess of Dudley 124
Wellington College 34
Westwood House 7
Windsor-Clive, Robert 254
Worcester Cathedral 1673 128
Worcester Cathedral choir 151
Worcester Cathedral choir vault 150
Worcester Cathedral freemasons window 153
Worcester Cathedral great west window 174
Worcester Cathedral nave 1823 135
Worcester Cathedral screen 148
Yorke, Very Rev. Grantham 155